Printed in the United States of America
by Lightning Source Inc.
Cover design by Dennis Davidson
Cover artwork by Marcos Souza

Unless otherwise indicated
all Scriptures taken from the Holy Bible
NEW AMERICAN STANDARD BIBLE
1962, 1963, 1968, 1971, 1972, 1973, 1975, 1977
by The Lockman Foundation. Used by permission.

Library of Congress Control Number: 2010933943
ISBN 978-1-934749-90-6

Hannibal Books
PO Box 461592
Garland, TX 75046
1-800-747-0738

www.hannibalbooks.com

Dedication

Throughout this book God is exalted as the Supreme Being that directs our lives in the United States of America as well as Brazil. Leona and I dedicate this book to God because of His Power, Knowledge, and constant Presence in our parents before we were born. God is the reason for this book!

However, we also dedicate this book to our God-fearing parents, Tony and Irma Kincanon Isbell and Joe Thomas and Hazel Cox Tarry, for getting us started in the right spiritual direction. We dedicate this book to our siblings as having an important part in our lives. Leona acknowledges that her siblings Doris, Wayne, Alton, and Connie have blessed her life in special ways. Many thanks to Wayne for his expertise of putting the pictures in the right format! Joe wants everyone to know that his siblings Bill, Helen, Margaret, and Thomas (Skeeter) all have enriched his life immensely. Our nieces and nephews also bless our lives. This book expresses our gratitude to our children—Carl, Jonathan, and Charlotte—for during the time they were home, they were a great part of our ministry. They continue to bless us. We also want to include our two Christian, God-given daughters-in-law, Kathy Doyle Tarry and Kellie Hopper Tarry, as well as a missionary son-in-law, Jim Whitley. Jim and Charlotte served the Lord in Romania and now are with their family in Brazil. God has given us six grandchildren—Michelle, Andrew, and Jennifer Tarry, and Janis, Charis, and James Whitley. These all have a part in The Marvel of it All.

We also include several pastors, Sunday-school teachers, and youth leaders in First Baptist Church of Portales and First Baptist Church of Lovington as instruments that helped shape our lives. They are many; therefore, not wanting to leave out anyone, we leave this anonymous list in the heavenly reference files. Most of them already are enjoying their heavenly home.

Special gratitude goes to Tommy and Martha Donham of Albuquerque, NM; since 1953 they closely have followed our lives. Their many acts of kindness exemplify the depth of Christian love.

5

While Charlotte studied at the University of New Mexico, Tommy and Martha were her Albuquerque dad and mom. By the time Martha had suffered a stroke that has impaired her speaking and writing, she had read most of the manuscript of *The Marvel of It All*. God is blessing her with a slow recovery. We love Tommy and Martha as brother and sister!

What people are saying about this book . . .

I highly recommend this book as required reading for anyone that believes he or she has a calling from God to work or witness to people of another country or culture. Joe and Leona have described correctly the ups and downs of being away from extended family and friends. *The Marvel of It All* reminds me that we just have to face life one day at a time and depend on God to take care of us as He would.

Leo Weatherman, emeritus missionary to Minas Gerais and all Brazil
International Mission Board, Southern Baptist Convention

These experiences of career missionaries in Brazil show how God responds to the faith and obedience of His servants. Also, the Scripture emphases and stories of growing up in southeastern New Mexico illustrate how these qualities of faith and obedience were developed.

Thoma Mauldin
Joe Tarry's seventh-grade English teacher and lifetime friend

You have the opportunity before you to share some intimate stories that will allow you the privilege of walking alongside Joe and Leona Tarry and their family through a few years of their service as your missionaries in Brazil. How do "ordinary people" become servants that God can use in such extraordinary ways? Impossible, yes, but through God all things are possible.

Judith Edwards, emeritus North American missionary to Navajo Nation 1969-1992
Baptist Convention of New Mexico Mission Department 1996-2007

This book never is boring. Well-documented and told with courage, the story of the Tarry family is sublime. Their lives, their children, and their labor have been blessings to countless souls that only eternity can measure. They were *always abounding in the work of the Lord* (1 Cor. 15:58). *The Marvel of It All* is a "marvel" indeed.

Jesse and Wilma Kidd, emeritus missionaries to Rio de Janeiro, Santa Catarina, and Minas Gerais, Brazil, International Mission Board, SBC

7

Contents

Foreword

For our 27 years in Brazil, Joe and Leona Tarry were our missionary colleagues. Along with another Southern Baptist missionary couple, Billy and Noreta Morgan, we traveled together on a ship and set out to serve in South Brazil. With total missionary fervor and naiveté we three couples took our young children—10 in all—into a land that just a year before had experienced a military coup to keep the country from going communist.

Largely unaware of unsettled conditions throughout the country we set our focus on learning the language and customs of Brazilians as we studied at language school in Campinas, São Paulo. There our circle of missionary colleagues expanded as we met other Baptist couples. Some of them were planning to go to other parts of Brazil such as North Brazil or Equatorial Brazil.

After our year in language school we moved to Belo Horizonte, the capital of the state; the Tarrys moved to Governador Valadares, one of the larger interior cities in Minas Gerais, a state about the size of Texas. So our relationship in missionary service and activities grew into a long and deepening friendship and our separate lives in an ever-increasing volume of missionary experiences.

The experiences Joe and Leona Tarry relate in these next pages represent their own unique story, yet many of them are common to missionary service. What one cannot miss in reading this book with all its panorama of varied missionary endeavors and challenges is the underlying commitment of an ordinary couple with deep passion to lead Brazilians to faith in Jesus Christ and to obtain property and establish church buildings in which Brazilians could grow in Christ and share His love with others.

Passion for souls and new churches is at the heart of missionary service. Certainly it was at the heart of Joe and Leona's 36 years of service in Brazil. As you will see in the unfolding story of how they sought to be Christ's servants and to fulfill the passion Christ planted in them, they endured and overcame much. With Brazilian Baptist and

11

missionary colleagues by their side, they transplanted that passion into many others.

The book ends, but the Holy Spirit who worked through the Tarrys continues "writing" the rest of the story in the lives they touched and in the churches they planted.

Bill and Kathryn Richardson
Emeritus missionaries to Brazil
International Mission Board, Southern Baptist Convention

The Reason for Writing
The Marvel of it All

1. To give praise, thanks, and glory to Almighty God, the author and finisher of our faith.

2. To share with others our amazing experiences in serving people in two cultures.

3. To demonstrate that in unimaginable circumstances God provides a positive solution.

4. To give a stewardship account to a multitude of Southern Baptist people that for more than 36 years supported us as missionaries to Brazilians.

5. To show how the Holy Spirit always is working before we meet a challenge.

6. Leona and I are amazed that God chose to take us on a journey packed with experiences that only He could have orchestrated—far beyond what we could have imagined!

7. Therefore we want to share our victorious lives of spiritual growth and victory over Satan through decades of spiritual warfare.

8. All who consider themselves to be "nobodies" under the leadership of the Holy Spirit are "somebodies". Praise God!!

9. The apostle Paul defends himself before *false apostles* (2 Cor. 11:13) in the Corinthian church who chide him into giving the amazing account of his life (2 Cor. 11:23-28). Then he says: *And He has said to me, "My grace is sufficient for you, for power is perfected in weakness." Most gladly, therefore, I will rather boast about my weaknesses, that the power of Christ may dwell in me* (2 Cor. 12:9). Leona's and my accomplishments are small compared to those of the Apostle Paul, yet Paul himself encourages every believer, by total submission to Christ, to become all that is humanly possible. But like Paul, if in any way we seem to be boasting in ourselves, we are striving to show God's working in our weaknesses to bring about fruit pleasing to God. We truly want God to get the credit for the victories you will read about in this book!

Chapter 1

Our Journey to a Foreign Land

*For whosoever will call upon the name of the Lord will be
saved. How then shall they call upon Him in whom they have not
believed? And how shall they believe in Him whom they have not
heard? And how shall they hear without a preacher?*
(Rom. 10:13-15).

THE MARVEL OF IT ALL
*Have you been impressed in such a way spiritually
That you have stopped, lingered in meditation recently
Long enough to be enamored, thrilled, or stricken in awe
About the Heavenly Father, the Lord Jesus,
and the marvel of it all?*

*Many occasions are in the entire Holy Bible—
In fact so many that it is factually undeniable—
In which individuals or peoples were amazed
and overwhelmed
When they felt God's mysterious presence all around.*

*They reflected on their experiences with God and pondered
About life, God's grace, His power and glory, and wondered
As to their purpose of life and management of resources
in their hands,
Also of the mysterious and spectacular things
they did in the land.*

We finally were standing on the deck of the cargo/passenger ship *Del Norte*. Each passenger held thin, colorful paper streamers that flapped in the breeze as the ship began to move. The captain seemed to enjoy blowing the deep bass foghorn to announce the ship's leaving the New Orleans harbor. The multicolored streamers began to flow instead of flap in the breeze as the throbbing engines gained momentum. We finally were participating in the *Del Norte*'s departing ritual from the North American continent. Figures on the dock grew dimmer until they were unrecognizable. We were saying goodbye to our country, our lifestyle, and our friends and loved ones that we did not expect to see again for five years. At the same time we felt a mixture of joy and loneliness. Most of the passengers would return in a month, so for them this was not as great an event as this journey was for us. Time had arrived to turn our minds to the future.

Three new missionary couples and 10 young children finally were on their way to Brazil, the land they would adopt for their new home. Three-month-old Charlotte Tarry and 11-month-old Jonathan Richardson seemed to be excited about whatever was going on and all the attention they were getting from everyone on the ship. Bill and Kathy Richardson from Oklahoma and Missouri had four boys; Billy and Noreta Morgan from Memphis, TN, had two boys and one girl; and we—Joe and Leona Tarry from New Mexico—had two boys and one girl. God had joined together these three families to add to the South Brazil mission, the largest of all Southern Baptist mission groups in the world, with more than 300 missionaries including their children. Our mission goal was to help bring more Brazilians to Jesus Christ as soon as possible in a country that was ripe for the harvest.

Traveling by ship posed some concern for safety for those of us with small children. One danger was found in the heavy, thick doors to our rooms. A disaster could happen if a door closed on a finger or a child. The second danger was the deck. The parents were warned not to allow the children on deck without supervision. Our son Jonathan loved to look over the side to see the water. We held his hand whenever we walked on deck. Then the third danger was found in the stairwells because of the swaying of the ship.

Although the ship principally was for cargo, the 150 passengers were treated royally; the trip was great. One other American couple, which hailed from Vanderbilt University, was on board with a boy and a girl. The husband was traveling to teach for a couple of years in a Brazilian university. On the cruise children were the main attraction, because most of the other passengers were older; many were grandparents. Some were appalled that we would take our precious children to live in a third-world country.

Many of the tourists enjoyed the drinking, dancing, movies, and parties. We missionaries spent the two weeks getting to know each other and playing games after the children were in bed. We found that we all were different in some ways. The Morgans believed that breakfast was not complete without grits. Since they were told that Brazil didn't have grits, the Morgans had packed some with their household goods. One night Billy expressed amazement that peanut butter was on the breakfast trays. "Who would ever eat peanut butter for breakfast?" I replied that my kids and I use peanut butter with toast and jelly as well as with pancakes. After that Bill Richardson and one or two of his boys learned to eat peanut butter for breakfast. Bill's favorite expression was "Great day!" That expression rubbed off on us.

We missionaries tried to get acquainted with others on the ship so we could witness to them. We played shuffleboard, swam in the small swimming pool, and participated in a few other activities.

The ship's captain granted permission for us to have worship services on the two Sundays at sea. One of those Sundays was Easter. Billy or Bill preached, I led the singing, and Noreta played the piano. We had good attendance. A Jewish lawyer gave each of us men $10 to buy a flower vase for the first mission that we started in Brazil. On Easter each child received a big, beautiful basket filled with goodies. That afternoon the children had a special party.

The biggest event on a South American cruise is a special party planned by the social director when the ship crossed the Equator. At the initiation as *pollywogs* all participants were to wear costumes or to do something silly for the crowd. Leona had an Indian dress (which at the time was popular in New Mexico). My sons, Carl and Jonathan, and I took off our shirts and I painted our bodies and faces as Indian warriors, even though the boys' hair was blond. We prepared Charlotte's carrier as a cradle board; I carried her on my back.

17

Crossing the Equator makes one a *pollywog*.

The meals on the ship were fabulous. The noon meal was a buffet on deck; we ate as a family. At night babies were not allowed in the main dining room, so an attendant took care of Charlotte. The evening meals were planned around a theme of a different country, with decorations and the food that corresponded to the country chosen. Even the waiters' costumes followed the theme. Birthdays and wedding anniversaries were commemorated with a special decorated cake presented to the honored guests. Everyone but me enjoyed the food. Most of the two weeks aboard I was sick. The ship's doctor, a retired military man, thought what I had might be appendicitis; however, I did not have a fever. This was so unreal—the one time I had the opportunity to dine on delicious, fancy food, most of the time I could only eat soup and ice cream. While we were on board the ship, Leona and I celebrated our eighth wedding anniversary, but the servers mistakenly took the cake to another couple.

The ship stopped for one day in San Juan, Puerto Rico. I went to a doctor for a second opinion to make sure my problem was not appendicitis; then each of the three families rented a Volkswagen. Billy had the map and planned our trip. All the street signs were in Spanish. At one point Billy turned onto a one-way street but did not know we were traveling the wrong way. At the end of the street we had to turn right; a police officer jumped into the street. He waved his hands and blew his shrill whistle. The officer was shaking his fist at Billy as Billy zoomed around the corner. When the officer saw that the car wasn't going to stop, he jumped back up onto the sidewalk. Suddenly the officer realized another car was traveling down the street the wrong way. Bill could not let the Morgans get out of his sight, so he buzzed past as the officer in disbelief waved his hands frantically. We had no idea where we were in the city and couldn't risk getting separated from the others. Leona and I also didn't want to miss the ship, so we, too, blared past the officer, who at that moment may have swallowed his whistle in amazement. In seconds three Volkswagens had defied him and left him dazed. Our tour was cut short; we returned to the ship. We all were thankful to be back on the ship and sailing out of the harbor without having to answer for our actions.

The ship stopped for a short visit on the gorgeous island of Barbados. Some of us took taxis to a very beautiful beach to swim for about three hours.

The Stress Test Before We Sailed

I tried to understand why I was unable to eat the delicious food. I remembered the stress we had in getting everything ready. The months after our appointment on June 17, 1964, had been hectic. The Foreign Mission Board (now International Mission Board) wanted us to sail for Brazil in September, but we had girls' and boys' camp to supervise and unfinished plans to be completed for the church. First Southern Baptist Church in Porterville, CA, was to celebrate its 25th anniversary. Leona was expecting our third child in January, so the next sailing in December was too close to the due date of our baby. The next sailing date after that was the first part of April, so we made plans for that departure date. We made our plans to leave Porterville the third week of December so we could visit with our families for Christmas. Staying until December 1964 enabled us to complete three-and-a-half years at the church.

Packing our things to ship to New Orleans, LA, was hectic. Not that we possessed so much, but the FMB had given us an allowance to buy necessities such as a refrigerator, mattresses, a washing machine, a dryer, and a few other things. Based on projections for the next five years we bought clothes for the children. We stuffed most of the clothes into the box-spring mattresses. Getting these things crated and getting paperwork done for our visas was pressing, since we also had activities to finish our ministry in Porterville.

We celebrated Christmas in New Mexico with family. We visited my father in Lovington, 90 miles south of Portales. A widower since my mother died in 1942, he had reared his five children and now was alone; we needed to spend time with him. As we waited for our daughter's birth, we visited relatives in the area and got documents together for our trip. The paperwork done in California for our visas was not valid, because with our move to New Mexico we now needed to go to the Brazilian consulate in Houston. We had a frustrating snag in getting police clearance from Roosevelt County in New Mexico. Since Leona's dad, Mr. Isbell, had lived in the county for more than 25 years and was a well-known farmer, we thought the proper law-enforcement agency would be the county sheriff. The recently elected sheriff did not know us and was not sympathetic with our problem. Leona grew up in the county, but we had been out of the state for 6 1/2 years. The clearance from the California police department did not mean anything to him. He refused to give us a clearance because we had not been in New Mexico long enough to establish a record. The fact that we had been in California for seminary and that I had served as pastor of a church there did not matter. His attitude was obnoxious. When she arrived home, Leona shed tears of dismay and frustration. Since the sheriff rejected us, Mr. Isbell suggested that he go with Leona to the city police department. The chief had known the whole Isbell family for years and knew of Joe because he had been to the university in Portales. The police chief had no problem in giving us the police clearance.

Charlotte was born on January 25, 1965, in Portales. Five weeks later she became sick with a cold. We took her to our doctor on Monday. Dr. Coleman examined her and told us she had a virus and that antibiotics would not affect it. The only thing to do was let the virus run its course. We watched her and often used a syringe to clean her nose of the thick mucus. On Wednesday she was not better, so we took her back to the doctor. He told us we could put her in the hospital but said the people there couldn't do more for her than we could. We just needed to watch and keep her nose clear with a syringe. The thick mucus made breathing or nursing difficult.

Dr. Coleman was the Isbell family doctor; he knew that Mr. Isbell was a farmer and had welding equipment for repairing broken farm machinery. The doctor told us that in the worse-case scenario we were to use Mr. Isbell's oxygen tank. Later the doctor said that if he had realized how seriously ill Charlotte was, he never would have allowed us to return to the farm 10 miles in the country. We know that even at that point God was directing. This was the first of March; the nights still were cold. The house didn't have central heating, so we slept on a hide-a-bed in the living room in which the gas stove was situated.

All day Leona had been taking care of Charlotte. At about 11 p.m. she asked me to watch Charlotte while she got a little sleep. With every intention of staying awake I laid Charlotte on my chest.

20

Somewhere around 1 a.m. I realized I had nodded off; Charlotte was not breathing. In her face she had no color of life. My commotion awoke Leona; her first thought was the oxygen tank. She ran to her parents' bedroom door, knocked, and asked her dad for the oxygen tank. He immediately dressed to go get it. I gave Charlotte to Leona and ran to the telephone. I was so frustrated that I could not find the doctor's number. I knew Leona could find it faster, so I took Charlotte. God guided me to give Charlotte rescue breathing. I put my mouth to her tiny mouth and blew, but the air would not go in. Her lungs were blocked. I blew more firmly but still saw no results. I blew still a little more firmly. Suddenly the obstruction moved; air went into her lungs. The Lord oriented me not to blow too firmly because of her tiny lungs.

By now Leona had Dr. Coleman on the phone; he gave us three options. He could travel to the farm, 10 miles out of town; we could take her to the hospital and meet him; or he could send an ambulance and he would meet us at the hospital. Leona thought the last suggestion was best. Mr. Isbell arrived with the oxygen tank; Dr. Coleman gave instructions on how to use it by giving a phrase of instruction at a time. Leona repeated each phrase for me to hear. He advised me to hold Charlotte up close to the oxygen tank. Mr. Isbell was holding the tank; Mrs. Isbell was praying and watching. I was to gulp the oxygen and blow it into her mouth.

Meanwhile Leona was at the door waiting for the ambulance. She could do nothing but pray and wait. She poured her heart out to God as she presented our case. We gladly had answered the call to go to Brazil. We were on our way to be missionaries. Why was this happening to us? Our prayers had been answered when God gave us a girl— our family was complete! Charlotte was such a beautiful little baby! *"Why, oh why, God is this happening to us?"* Leona prayed urgently. *"Besides these things, oh Heavenly Father, you know what a difficult time I had in my pregnancy and delivery! God, you know my pregnancy with Charlotte was more difficult than with the boys. Then I had thrombophlebitis. You cannot take our baby!"* The Lord gently guided Leona to a calmer understanding of the situation. What if Charlotte lived but as a vegetable without the mental capacity to ever do anything for herself? Leona finally was able to surrender Charlotte to

God. She concluded her prayer by saying, "*Lord, she is Yours more than ours. Your will be done.*" At that moment a great peace swept through Leona's entire body. I think this might have been the moment that Charlotte began giving the first signs of life.

After I started giving Charlotte rescue breathing, I thought she would recover quickly. Five minutes passed without a sign of life except her body accepting the air. Ten minutes passed; still nothing happened. Fifteen minutes passed; she was still and silent. I remember that my back and arms began to ache because the oxygen tank was only about four-feet tall at the air spout, so I had to elevate my arms a little to get her body near the spout. I am amazed that I did not stop trying. God gave me the calmness and determination to continue blowing oxygen into her mouth. Twenty minutes passed, then 25. Finally Charlotte gave a tiny moan or groan, so I stopped and looked at her face. Her eyes fluttered but then closed again. I put my mouth to hers and started blowing oxygen again. About that time the ambulance zoomed past the house even though the porch light was on. Leona could not believe it! Who else at 1 in the morning would have on house lights? Soon the ambulance driver realized he had passed the house and returned. Charlotte was getting stronger, but if I stopped, she could not breathe alone.

Moments later the paramedics rushed into the house. Suddenly one paramedic saw we were standing near the stove; he immediately was horrified. He screamed, "Get that fire out! Get that fire out! What do you want to do, blow up the whole house?" He partially was right. In our confusion about Charlotte's condition we were standing right in front of the big propane gas stove while the oxygen tank spewed out oxygen. Even though one could see the fire, the flame was enclosed. That did not matter; the paramedics were frightened. If the flame had been open, none of us would have been around to tell this story. The Lord had protected us. The paramedics placed a tiny mask connected to a small oxygen tank over Charlotte's nose. As she received the pure oxygen, Charlotte's color began to improve. We rushed to the hospital.

Charlotte's hospital room was next to the nurses' station. They put our daughter in a tent that had oxygen blowing in. The next day at noon she stopped breathing again. Leona pressed the panic button; the nurses ran in alongside Dr. Coleman. At that moment of our crisis Dr. Coleman had just walked into the hospital. He was prepared to do a tracheotomy on Charlotte but worked on her first and got her past the danger again. He remembered a new medicine that in that hospital had been used only two times. This medicine was named "mucomist" and worked to loosen and dissolve the mucus. As this new medication dripped, the oxygen blew it into the incubator. It formed a mist for Charlotte to breathe. Three days later we were able to take Charlotte home. She had a hoarse cough that Dr. Coleman said probably would continue until warm weather arrived, but as far as he could tell, she would be normal. Because of her weak situation the doctor wanted her protected from germs as much as possible.

Later Dr. Coleman told a close friend of ours that the night we called, he didn't think Charlotte would survive; he said he wouldn't have given a dime for her life. I personally think that she died and that God gave her back to us. I do not tell this for any reason other than to praise God for His special blessing to us. Our confidence in God's ability to do anything He desires became a reality. We were not special people just because we were willing to go to Brazil. We are no better than others that have suffered the death of a child and for whom God did not answer their prayers. God is a just God; unworthy as we were, God chose to give Charlotte back to us. Our daughter graduated from University of New Mexico and from Southwestern Baptist Theological Seminary in Fort Worth. For seven years she and her husband, Jim Whitley, served as missionaries in Romania with the Roma (Gypsies) before the Whitleys transferred to Brazil to work with the Gypsy people. They have twin daughters and a son. Praise the Lord!

The day after Charlotte was put in the hospital, we were supposed to be in Houston with our documents so we could visit the Brazilian consulate to get our visas. I called the consulate, which graciously gave us more time. A week after Charlotte left the hospital, by train we took her from Clovis, NM, to Houston. She enjoyed the rocking train. The Brazilian consulate officials were kind and sympathetic about the cause of our delay, but the situation rushed them to get the visas ready for our departure date.

One week before the date for our departure from New Mexico, I called the Brazilian consulate; it could not confirm whether it could get the documents to us. We began to be concerned. The passages had already been bought for the voyage on the *Del Norte* ship. We did not want to miss it. Our train tickets from Clovis to New Orleans went through Houston. On Friday morning I called the consulate to see whether the passports had been mailed. The passports were ready but had not been mailed. Another miracle! The consulate agreed to allow Kenneth Wise, a Houstonian who had been Leona's classmate in Portales, to pick up the documents. We called to ask him to pick up our passports from the consulate and to meet us at the train station on Sunday. Again, in this development, we saw the hand of God working.

On Saturday afternoon we left Clovis, NM. When we arrived in Houston about 10 on Sunday morning, Kenneth Wise was on the platform and waited for us with our passports. Trusting that this plan would work we had gone by faith. We didn't know we would have to go to a different train station to continue our journey to New Orleans. Kenneth and a taxi took us and all our luggage to the other train station. We arrived in New Orleans and found two taxis to get us and the luggage to our hotel. We were making our way up the sidewalk to the hotel just as the Morgans and Richardsons were leaving for a stroll. With these two missionary families we were to journey to Brazil. This was not just a journey to Brazil but a life journey of Christian love, fellowship, and experiences.

Yes, God was present with us all along the way, to the most minute detail. Now more than 45 years later I still have my appendix. I began to understand that I have a very sensitive nervous system and that emotional stress can show up in various parts of my body, especially my stomach, even though I think I am calm. One thing I really enjoy is eating, but under stress my digestive system does not accept food. Despite all that wonderful food on the voyage to Brazil I could eat only ice cream and soup.

Arrival in Brazil
Late in the afternoon of April 21, 1965, we were advised that the ship was entering the famous Rio de Janeiro harbor. We were eager to set our feet on Brazilian soil. As the passengers stood on the deck, one could hear exclamations of *ooh's* and *ahh's*. We had a clear view of

the spectacular panorama of the world-famous Rio de Janeiro Bay. Corcovado, the great statue of Christ the Redeemer, towered over the area. To the right and below was Sugar Loaf Mountain, also a famous landmark of the bay. The famous Copacabana beach also became visible as we neared the dock. The background of towering rugged mountains, bluish and green in color, made a spectacular panorama for the gleaming maze of skyscrapers that crowded right to the docks. The ship was to be at this port only until midnight. Our destination as missionaries was further down the coast, about 200 miles south to the Port of Santos. The missionaries in Rio had planned a welcome and get-acquainted meal at the South Brazil Seminary dining room. At that time about 20 missionary couples were stationed in Rio de Janeiro, because the all-Brazil mission headquarters, the largest of three seminaries, the Baptist publishing house, the women's training school, and other Brazilian Baptist organizations were situated here. The Morgans, Richardsons, and Tarrys—all except for me—were taken to the seminary. Missionary colleague Dr. Lester Bell took me to see a doctor at the Evangelical Hospital. That was some ride! By the time we left the ship, darkness was setting in. As he drove, Dr. Bell zoomed in and out of the crowded lanes just as the Brazilians do. Motorists don't use their headlights at night unless they want to warn the approaching car of some maneuver. Dim streetlights represented all the light they needed. Anyway, I had never seen such a ride—nor was I prepared for it. Dr. Bell didn't try to scare me, for he was a very kind and considerate man. I later learned how to drive in the Brazilian traffic, too; doing so simply became natural. But that ride did not lower my blood pressure any. The doctor assured me that I did not have appendicitis. Whatever the problem was, I would just have to live with it.

By the time Dr. Bell and I returned to the seminary, the meal and most of the welcoming celebrations were over. The mission treasurer gave each of us three new couples a package of money. We all became instant millionaires. Inflation was so bad in Brazil that our monthly salary in their currency was worth more than a million *cruzeiros*. We were taken back to the ship. By the time the kids were in bed, the tugboat had pulled the *Del Norte* far enough into the bay that the powerful engines could be turned up into a dull, throbbing noise. Forward progress began; the loud bass foghorn began its ritual of warning the ships and fish that we were picking up speed and leaving Rio de Janeiro Bay.

"Last call for breakfast; last call for breakfast," the steward called as he rang a little bell in his hand. As the steward's voice faded down the corridor, I remembered that this was the last day aboard the ship. Because of our small children we missionaries received our breakfast in our rooms. Joy and anxiety raced through my body and mind as I thought of reaching our destination. The other missionary families on board seemed to experience the same feeling. Not that we were complaining about our ship, because Southern Baptists provided us with an opportunity that we might never have again. With high-class food, excellent service, and time for leisure, why the anxiety? Well, appointment service, two weeks of orientation, getting physicals, getting proper shots and documents for passports and visas, buying clothes and even Christmas presents for a five-year term in Brazil all were exhausting. Add to that the crating process to ship all these things while we were busy completing the plans on the church calendar. We packed and moved to New Mexico things that we didn't want to take to Brazil. We had three months with our parents as we waited for Charlotte to be born and for time for our ship to leave. We had two weeks on the ship, which should have been restful, but I began to feel my nerve fibers pulling. We were ready to settle into our new location. We were not accustomed to being unsettled so long. And of course we were eager to be in the land God had laid on our hearts to serve Him.

On this last morning a birthday party was planned for Carl. Carl's 5th birthday really was the next day, April 23, but the ship's social director had planned a party for him before we reached Santos. Carl had a birthday cake and several presents the ship's social department provided. The attendant that cared for Charlotte each evening during the dinnertime was very good to us. She gave us a box of baby bottles and a box of baby food that had been bought for Charlotte.

As we descended the gangplank on Friday, about 30 language-school missionaries, including their children, met us. We three men would return to Santos on Monday with a veteran missionary to begin the paper work to get our things out of customs. We ate our first Brazilian meal at a restaurant. The first thing the waiters brought was a drink unfamiliar to us. Everyone was drinking the same thing: *Guarana*. I examined the label on the bottle and read *champagne*. My heart sank! I could not believe that my Baptist colleagues could sink so low as to drink champagne. When they poured their drinks into their glasses, white foam rose to the top. I put mine down with the resolution not to drink it. Soon some of them started laughing. They explained that it had no alcoholic content. *Guarana* is made from the *Guarana* berry and is perfectly harmless. Well, that became a favorite joke the Tarrys later played on visiting guests from the States.

The language students took us to a beautiful beach and made a full day out of the trip to meet us. We had a great time on the beach, but the fun ended when jellyfish stung two of us. Darkness was setting in as we left Santos for Campinas. As we left the coast, we started climbing a curvy, mountainous road. We discovered a new custom: when a car wanted to pass, the bus driver turned off his lights. Our driver could see a little from the lights behind us and from the moon. By the glow of lights about to top the hill in front of us, the car behind could see whether another vehicle was approaching. According to the custom the driver felt safe to pass if he didn't see any approaching lights. After the car passed, our driver turned his lights on again.

We arrived in Campinas about 10 p.m. Arrangements had been made for us to stay with Gene and Aleene Wise (brother of Kenneth Wise, who had helped us in Houston) when we arrived in Campinas. The Wises had not gone to Santos to meet us because Aleene was sick. They graciously welcomed us. Our assignment in Brazil officially had begun.

Chapter 2

Strange Feelings, Impressions, Customs, and Language

I can do all things through Christ who strengthens me
(Philippians 4:13).

Many acts of God's glory have been written down on pages
In poems, songs, and historic events through the ages.
But God's mysterious ways in our day we must also feel,
In our individual lives He wants to be very real.

God moves in mysterious ways to perform His wonders,
The rainbow, skies, beautiful valleys, and in the thunder.
And in our age, in our time, God is just as gloriously real.
He desires to do great things through us according to His will.

The Amazing First Week

When we arrived in Campinas, São Paulo, we were taken to Gene and Aleene Wise's home to stay until we moved into our new home. Gene was the older brother of Kenneth Wise that met us with our visas at the Houston train station. On Sunday we went with the Wises to the small church at which Gene served as pastor. On Monday morning Dr. Thurman Bryant, a missionary/pastor and teacher at the state seminary in São Paulo, picked up Bill, Billy, and me to do the paperwork in Santos to get our household things out of customs. We had to pass through the great city of São Paulo, capital of the State of São Paulo, with about eight-million people at that time. Dr. Bryant picked up a

Catholic priest, Anibal Pereira Reis. On our way from Campinas to São Paulo, Thurman had told us about Anibal. Here is a condensed story about this remarkable man.

The story of Anibal begins several years earlier in the State of São Paulo. He had been reared a faithful Catholic. When Anibal was a child, one of his buddies drowned; that made Anibal fearful about what happened after death. He became a priest in hopes of obtaining salvation. Still he had not found peace in all that he had done for catholicism. Years passed; he was asked to serve as director of social projects in the city of Recife in the northern part of Brazil. He served in that area for several years but became disenchanted with having to raise so much money for Rome when the poverty was so great in Recife. He also became disenchanted with the politics among the various orders of charity. Yet the greatest discouragement was that he still had no assurance that when he died, he would go to heaven. This fear increased when he was called to hear the confessions of the archbishop of that area. The archbishop was seriously ill; he, too, was terrified of death. He kept repeating the same confessions. Anibal reminded the archbishop that he already had prayed for the forgiveness of those sins and did not need to keep repenting of them. Anibal was with the archbishop when he died and saw his anguish. If the archbishop had that much fear and no assurance of salvation, what hope did Anibal as a simple priest have? Anibal was very troubled. He thought if he could just serve near the cathedral of Brazil's patron saint, Aparecida, and be pastor of a church again, he could find peace.

Anibal Pereira Reis was a brilliant man with doctorate degrees in the *Direito Canonico* (scriptural law), dogmatic theology, and judicial science. He again was transferred to São Paulo and served near the great basilica (cathedral) of Aparecida. To serve near or in the basilica would be the greatest honor for which a priest could hope. This cathedral for the patroness saint of Brazil, Maria Aparecida (Mary Appeared), is huge and is next in size to Saint Peter's Cathedral of Rome. But instead of finding peace Anibal began to see the corruption occurring and was even more disillusioned. Miserable, he thought if he could just work in a parish near where he grew up, an area which was close to the basilica, he might find peace. So he requested to move again.

Anibal worked more diligently than ever and soon was involved in building projects to expand his new parish. Even with all his labors in his diocese in São Paulo, in which he did more than was expected of him in building churches and missions, he still had no peace. Under his door Evangelicals left tracts about salvation, but he threw them away. He led a campaign for Catholics to accept all the Bibles offered to them by Evangelicals so that he could collect and burn them. Often he went up to a beautiful hillside to sort out his spiritual problems. One day he was so spiritually disturbed that he went home and prayed a long time. Here is how he explains what happened: "I had reached the top of my misfortune. All of my interior castles had been reduced to powder when I encountered the brutal reality. Nothing up to that moment had produced spiritual security. All of my enthusiasm for the 'holy church' was useless! My dedication for social works was useless! My priesthood was useless! The sacraments, masses, and devotion to the saints were useless! My penitence was useless! My subjection to the ecclesiastical authorities was useless! My consecration to Mary was useless! My parish leadership has been useless! Everything has been useless! The scandal about the patroness saint of Brazil, Mary Aparecida, has brought all of my deceptions to an end. At that moment, in my library, with my heart bleeding with bitterness, a horrible, gruesome thought passed like lightening through my mind. *Why not take my life? Why live like this? May it be that my tragic end be an evil omen to the pompous and deceptive hierarchy of Roman Catholicism!* Stoned by immense pain I raised my staring eyes, seeking in God one last encouragement for my discouraged life as a disillusioned bitter priest. By the mercy of my good God, my eyes were drawn to two words stamped on a book snuggled tightly in among others: A *Biblia Sagrada* (The Holy Bible). I had this book since 1955 without opening its pages. We had been discouraged from reading the Bible in seminary. With trembling hands, I reached for my Bible and opened it. I began reading in John, about the resurrection of Lazarus. I felt resurrected in my hope. The Holy Scripture was a balm to my soul. I arose, took the Bible to my room, and read until daylight."

At every opportunity during the day Anibal continued reading the Bible. When he reached the book of Romans, he remembered that in the seminary the professors warned: "Be careful with the Epistle of

Paul to the Romans! The book of Romans caused the downfall of Martin Luther!" He began reading and found out that *the wages of sin is death but the gift of God is eternal life in Jesus Christ our Lord* (Rom. 6:23). He became excited; as he read on, the truth became a reality in his heart and mind. He got to Romans 10:9-10: *That if you confess with your mouth Jesus as Lord, and believe in your heart that God raised Him from the dead, you shall be saved; for with the heart man believes, resulting in righteousness, and with the mouth he confesses, resulting in salvation.* As he wept Anibal dropped to his knees and confessed Jesus as his Lord and Savior.

Anibal, as the priest over the parish or district, had several projects under way; he knew he could not leave the Roman Catholic Church until these projects were finished and paid for. Carefully he began making his messages more evangelical. Some of his people alerted the bishop. He gathered evangelical tracts from different denominations and examined the Bible carefully by comparing their various doctrines. His decision was that Baptist doctrines were closest to the Bible and that he should unite with them. In disguise he began to visit pastors and occasionally First Baptist Church in Santos. As time went on, he made contact with some Baptist people closer to his parish. Sometimes he secretly attended home worship services. A Catholic woman whose husband was a Baptist alerted the bishop about Anibal's visits to the home worship services. Months beforehand the bishop already had been sending a spy to follow Anibal—even to Santos. Some pastors and Dr. Thurman Bryant were aware of his situation and his desire to leave the Catholic Church. For about three years priest Anibal Pereira Reis had been trying to leave the Catholic Church.

One day he was summoned to the bishop's mansion in the city of Ribeirao Preto, State of São Paulo. He was kept in the bishop's mansion as a prisoner. Officials did everything to persuade him to change his position, but these efforts did not succeed. Finally the bishop and some soldiers forced him to drink hard liquor until he was drunk. Then they forced Anibal to sign some documents about swindling money from construction projects for which he had been responsible in his diocese. His signature, however, was so illegible that no judge would accept his signature in court. Anibal suffered greatly at the hands of the bishop. Officials even castrated him and left him in a cold shower all night.

The bishop's mansion was near a high school. The officials became afraid he might have talked to some of the students that passed by his window. The students knew something strange was going on, because they had seen police there. The bishop decided to release him but kept him under house arrest in Anibal's own home. For fear of what the Bishop might do, Anibal had some Baptist friends secretly watching after him. Anibal, in a weakened condition but in his own home, contacted a pastor who then contacted Thurman. An arrangement was made for Thurman to pick him up. Anibal left his home "for a walk" with only his priest clothes on his back and his vast archives of written material about the Catholic Church. Thurman took him to São Paulo, where he recuperated and prepared to officially leave the Roman Catholic Church.

We three missionaries were riding in Thurman's car when he picked up Anibal to take him to Santos. The next Sunday at First Baptist Church Anibal officially would take off his Catholic robe. How privileged I was to know him! Until Anibal's death about 30 years later I had a friendship with this courageous man. As he preached hundreds of revivals and wrote more than 40 books, he became a powerful man for Evangelical Christianity. After his freedom he married a wonderful Christian woman.

After we left Anibal at a home in Santos, we went to the warehouse in which customs officials were to open our crates. Thurman hoped to get inspectors that would be friendly to Americans. He showed us a 1958 Plymouth car he had imported seven years earlier but still had not been able to get it released from customs. When they opened my crates, I had my list of everything in the crates; they had the list that we had sent with the Del Norte freight lines. Customs people examined everything carefully and closed the crate. Other inspectors had done the same with Bill and Billy. Thurman took us back to Campinas to wait until the process was finished and our crates were released. This took about two weeks.

Settling Down in Campinas

Campinas, a city of about 200,000 people, was the most

Americanized city of all Brazil. Campinas was clean, well-organized, and had an American school. For the first week we stayed with Gene and Aleene Wise and then for the second week in a house of a family. The family members had gone to Equatorial Brazil to visit the field in which they were to work when they finished language school in four more months. After two weeks from our arrival date we were able to move into our house.

The language school was established and operated by Presbyterians, but by the time we arrived, the Methodists and Southern Baptists shared in its operation. Southern Baptists by far had the most missionaries attending. A few other groups, such as Brethren and the Christian Church, also studied there. Soon after we left Campinas, Southern Baptists bought the school from the Presbyterians and Methodists and for many years ran the school.

Sons of a Presbyterian missionary owned and operated a good medical clinic next door to the language school. A house was rented for us on Clovis Bevelaqua Street, only about three blocks from the school and the Lane Clinic. This was nice, because we would be close to the school and to a doctor for Charlotte. Since missionaries who studied in language school didn't have cars, we easily could get to school by walking. The other missionaries had to walk a longer distance or take a taxi or bus.

We heard about one "supermarket" a family from South Africa owned. The supermarket was small in comparison to the supermarkets in the States, but the family spoke English and delivered for free. We bought most of our food there; however, many small items and bread and milk were bought at small stores near our home. These small stores had shelves all the way to the ceiling on the wall behind the counter that stretched across the width of the store. Since we could not tell the operators what we wanted, we had to point at the item on the shelf. If the item was higher than the clerk could reach, to get what we wanted the clerk climbed the ladder that ran along a rail. Sometimes we performed funny antics to get the clerk to understand what we desired at the store. Dried beans and rice were measured on antique scales and put into sacks for us. After the clerk had put everything we ordered on the counter, he put the pile of groceries with one item on top or beside the other until all the groceries made a uniform stack on top of a layer of spread-out newspapers. The clerk then wrapped the newspapers around the bundle of items and from a big spool began pulling the string. He wrapped the string around and around and around the package, one way and then another. At the end he made a nice handle until the package was ready to carry home. These packages were difficult to carry if you had to take a bus or the old rail streetcar (*bonde*).

Missionary Marlene Boswell, also in language school, got on a streetcar one day with one of these packages. Brazilian men did not get up to offer women a place to sit. When all the benches were taken, people stood and held on to high handrails. A person had trouble holding a package with one hand and simultaneously gripping the handrail with the other hand. The streetcar lurched, as streetcars seemed always to do when they started to move. Marlene fell backward onto a man's lap. She hastily exclaimed "*com licenca*", which means "with your permission", instead of "*perdao*", which means "pardon me".

Once a week we bought fresh vegetables at the street market that set up for business on Thursday mornings near our house. Each day of the week this street market would be in a different location in the city. Small trucks, Volkswagen vans, and horse-drawn carts could be heard arriving before daybreak. For this mobile market the street of a whole block was blocked off before sunrise until about noon. At sunrise people started gathering to get the pick of the best vegetables and also meat. Live chickens, pigs, and a variety of fresh fish were available. Mops, brooms, and just about anything one needed could be bought at the street markets. Many of the shoppers were maids. Maids and gardeners were cheap labor for the upper class and even the small group of middle-class people. Most shoppers pulled a two-wheel wire handcart or else carried strong cloth or bamboo-woven baskets to take their purchases home.

All missionaries have made blunders learning the language. One day for our noon meal Leona wanted our maid to cook some carrots, so Leona showed her a carrot. When we gathered around the table for the meal, Antonia had cooked that one carrot for our whole family to eat. If Leona had put out the proper amount of carrots, Antonia would have understood. Even the word for *carrot* was tricky, because *cenora* means *carrot* and *senhora* (*c* sounds like an *s*) means *woman*. The two words sound nearly the same. A missionary went to a stand at which the vegetables were behind the counter. He asked for a kilo of *senhoras*. The clerk told the missionary they did not have any *senhoras* (ladies) for sale. The missionary mystified, argued back: "Yes, you do; they are right over there." "Oh, *cenoras*," replied the clerk. "*Sim, senhor!* We have *cenoras* but not *senhoras*."

The word for *old* also was confusing. *Velha* means *old woman* and *velho, old man*. All things are masculine or feminine; they usually end with "a" or "o". A missionary needed some candles because electricity frequently failed. *Velas* means *candles*. He told the clerk he wanted some *velhas*. The clerk replied that he did not have *velhas*. The missionary protested, "Yes, you do, *senhor*." The clerk shook his head and replied, "We do not!" The missionary pointed at candles; the clerk's puzzled face turned into a wide grin. "Oh! You mean *velas*, right?" The missionary laughed at himself and made his purchase.

Oh! Learning the Portuguese Language!

Bill Richardson and I were in the same beginner's class. The classes had three to five students. The men met in the morning and the women in the afternoon. That usually allowed Leona to be with the children in the mornings. The Spanish I had in high school helped me a little, for some Spanish and Portuguese words were spelled alike. However, sometimes the words had different meanings. We used a mimeographed syllabus that the Brazilian teachers had developed. These classes had to be very stressful for the teachers as well as for the students. The teacher would speak the word; we would try to repeat it just as she had. Each of us had our time to read sentences or to pronounce the words we were learning. Portuguese has accents that give the letters a different sound. The "a" in the word *não* or *são* has an accent showing it has a nasal sound. When a "c" has an apostrophe under it, the "c" has an "s" sound. The accent also denotes which syllable receives the emphasis. Over and over and over we would repeat after the teacher; all the while we thought we were saying the word just as she was. She still would say, "No, this is the way." That was the most frustrating part, for we just could not seem to grasp the difference in our pronunciation and hers.

35

Below the Equator the seasons are reversed, but seasons are not all that seems to be different. In the South water draining from the sink or commode swirls the opposite direction than it does north of the Equator. I checked that out. Dogs seem to chase their tails in the opposite direction also. Anyway, some things were different for us. I knew the temperature rarely would freeze and snow never would fall in the place in which we lived. Campinas is a little south of central Brazil, North and South-wise. Brazil is a country about the size of the continental United States. The United States is wide east and west, while Brazil is long north and south. I was glad I had brought my overcoat, for that first winter in Campinas was the coldest recorded there in a long time. Brazilians have a custom of opening the windows or shutters—even in winter. Brazilians said opening the windows lets pure, fresh air in. The first thing the teacher did when she entered the classroom was to open the windows all the way. We Americans froze. Many days that winter in class I wore my overcoat and gloves, whereas the Brazilians wore sweaters or light coats. The coffee trees and banana trees froze in parts of Brazil that year; they even froze in São Paulo.

Our maid, Antonia, was very good with Charlotte and was a good cook. She had a small daughter, but her husband had died. We were not worried about her neglecting Charlotte. Each afternoon Carl and Jonathan attended a Brazilian preschool. I walked them to school and returned to get them. Jonathan was only 3-years old; his little legs would get tired, so he begged me to carry him. One day I was very tired and decided Jonathan could stay at home if he couldn't walk. He begged me so sadly to let him go. Well, Jonathan soon got tired and begged me to carry him. I agreed but declared that the next day he would stay at home. The next day Carl said pitifully: "Daddy, I will carry Jonathan if you will let him go." Every time Leona tells this story, my heart gets a lump in it.

São Paulo state had a large population of Japanese. The first foreign missionaries appointed by the Japanese Baptist Convention to Brazilian Japanese people were in language school with us. The Togamis had two boys the ages of our boys. At home the family usually spoke Japanese. Before they went to Brazil, the Togamis had attended Southwestern Seminary in Fort Worth, so the family also learned English. Now they began learning Portuguese. Carl and Jonathan stayed with the Togamis when we took one of our field trips; their boys stayed with us one time. This was a fun time to see those two little Japanese boys and our boys just being boys together and trying to speak English and Portuguese.

Walking on Hot Coals

June is a month of several Catholic festivities, with the main ones being for St. Antonio (June 13), St. John (June 24), and St. Peter (June 29). The most important is St. John. During the month almost every day one could hear firecrackers sporadically, especially all night before St. John's day. For a few Catholics one highlight of these festivities was walking on red-hot coals. Some of the language-school students visited one of these festivities. Two of them decided they would prove that faith in St. John wasn't what made walking on red-hot coals possible without burning their feet. They, too, walked without burning their feet but with their faith in Jesus. St. Antonio is the Brazilian marriage saint as St. Valentine is for Americans. Unmarried women pray to St. Antonio for a husband. Brazilians celebrate St. John and St. Antonio with something akin to our Sadie Hawkins Day festivities (*Festa Junina*). For the *festa* they dress in hillbilly clothes; a man and woman dressed as bride and groom have a fake wedding. The popular food served is *canjica*, which is hominy cooked with milk, sugar, coconut, and peanuts.

Each saint has a banner with symbols representing him or her. Catholic believers choose their favorite saint and put that saint's banner on a pole at the front of the house. This is supposed to bring good luck to the family.

Another unique part of the celebrations during this month is the use of paper balloons. These balloons have a wick soaked in oil; when the wick is lit, the hot air causes the balloon to rise into the air. These are released at night; the flame makes the paper balloon glow until it is out of sight. The rainy season usually ended by March, so by June the fields are dry. These paper balloons occasionally caused fires. Years later they were prohibited, but some violators still made them.

A Spiritual Dryness

We attended the church at which Gene Wise served as pastor. Gene's official responsibility with the South Brazil mission was developing visual aids—mostly making filmstrips and slides—for evangelism and Bible teaching. On the side he—like many other missionaries—worked as a pastor. The church he served was about 10 blocks from our home. This church was very simple, as most of the churches were and still are. The benches were hard and uncomfortable. The church had no nursery. The teachers had to make all the aids they used for children. The men's and women's Sunday-school classes met in small groups in the auditorium. The only learning aid was the Sunday-school quarterly. The men that had suits wore them on Sundays. Many men shaved only once a week—on Sundays. I was shocked at the bathroom—the commode didn't have a seat. I told Gene that I would be glad to buy seats for the commodes. He sort of laughed and told me that seats would not be used, because the members were not accustomed to commode seats. Even in restrooms at restaurants I found that to be true.

The most difficult thing about that first year in Brazil was that I understood very little of the Sunday-school lesson or the preaching. I had to depend on many promises of God. One of these verses was *I can do all things through Christ who strengthens me* (Phil. 4:13). We sang many familiar hymns that I knew in English, but straining to pick up a few familiar words in Portuguese was a miserable task. With our busy schedules and all of us making adjustments, our family had morning devotionals; that was about all of the spiritual help I got. We studied the Sunday-school lesson, but at first we had to look up nearly every word. One of us had to hold Charlotte during Sunday school and worship service; most of the time she wanted me to hold her. I was a little embarrassed, because men just did not hold their children in church (or in public); that was considered the woman's responsibility. I enjoyed holding Charlotte, but I wondered what the men were thinking. Our boys had a tough time. Can you imagine an hour service including two little boys who didn't understand anything? We were told that Brazilians did not discipline their children in public, so we did not either. But what would the Brazilians think if our children refused to obey us during church services? Brazilians, however, are very kind and considerate of their American friends. I learned that the difference between Brazilians and Americans taking care of children in public was a difference only in customs. Before we left Brazil 36 years later, many Christian men had learned to help take care of the children in public.

Our Surroundings

Our house in Campinas was nice; it belonged to a Presbyterian pastor. The rooms had beautiful hardwood tile floors of two colors of wood. The kitchen and bathroom walls and floors were tile from bottom to top. The roof was made of red clay, cup-style tile. We had a small front yard with grass and many flowers. The house was the wall on one side. One side and back of the house had high walls made of clay bricks covered with stucco and paint. On top of these walls were many small pieces of different-colored glass to keep the thieves out. Some homes also had high front walls, but those in our neighborhood had a wrought-iron fence that made seeing everything that was going on in front of the house possible.

All houses had water boxes on the roof; water filled the box only during a certain time—usually at night. The family always had to be careful not to use all the water supply, or it would be without until the water filled the box again. One didn't drink the water directly from the facet. Every home, even the poorest, had a clay water jar with a type of sandstone filter to purify the water as it passed through. These sandstone filters (or whatever material from which the purifier was made) could be cleaned, but eventually these needed to be replaced. The word for the inner piece which filtered the water is called *vela*, the same word for candle.

The cook stove used natural gas. The ones we used were small bottles such as those on campers; under normal use these lasted about two weeks. The gas tanks we used in Belo were taller cylinders; they required two men to carry one. Most households had two or three of these bottles. We had the schedule stating when the gas truck would pass on our street, so one needed to be prepared to buy on that day or else have transportation to go to the gas deposit to buy a refilled bottle. The houses had no heating system, so during the winter we got accustomed to dressing in layers to stay warm. Of course the temperature rarely got down below 40 degrees, but that felt cold. No windows had screens to keep out mosquitoes or flies in the summer. For health reasons missionaries were provided funds to get screens made for the windows. Twice a day most people have rice and beans. Various cuts of beef, chicken, pork, or fish were served each meal for those who could afford meat. Irish potatoes, various types of fresh greens, some vegetables, and many fruit were abundant year-around.

The only complaint with the location of our house was the cookie bakery right behind our house. The bakers worked all night, except Saturday and Sunday nights. I loved the smell, but it really stimulated my "sweet tooth". The worst part was that the bakers sang, talked loudly, and banged pans all night. Many times I didn't get much sleep, but complaining about it didn't help. The streets were noisy during the day. Peddlers would shout out their wares from horse-drawn wagons or bicycles with a platform over the front wheel. These bicycles carried just about anything you could imagine. Street peddlers regularly visited the neighborhood to sharpen knives and to sell oranges, coconuts, or you name it. Noise started early in the morning with a boy shouting "*o jornaleiro*" (newspaper boy) as he walked down the street. Nevertheless, Brazil was an exciting and interesting place. We were happy, because we knew this was the place in which God wanted us to be.

Two of the most famous sights to see in San Francisco, CA, are Chinatown and the famous trolley car. While we attended Golden Gate Seminary, for three years we lived in Berkeley and the Bay Area. Even though we drove through San Francisco every weekend for two years, Leona was disappointed that we never drove through Chinatown or never took a ride on the trolley car. On a seminary project I had been to a Chinese church in Chinatown, but I never rode on the famous San Francisco trolley car either. Well, Leona got all the trolley-car riding she wanted in Campinas, because that was our major mode of transportation from language school to downtown. During the rainy season the open-sided trolley car gave little shelter from the rain. A few times we rode the city buses, but with a baby and two small boys buses were too crowded; our family members hardly could stay together.

I had to go downtown to pay our light and water bills. Our salaries were deposited directly into a bank of our choice. Every time I went to town, I saw a lot of poor children shining shoes and selling candy, shoestrings, or things their mothers had made at home. I wanted to buy from all of them, but I couldn't. I usually had my shoes shined, although I was a good shoe-shiner myself because when I was a boy, I had shined shoes in two barbershops. I sometimes brought Leona and the kids some of the homemade candy the candy vendors sold.

I felt very satisfied about one thing in Brazil: the size of the men. At 5-feet, 6 1/2-inches, I was taller than most of the Brazilian men. I could see over them while I stood in long bank lines to pay bills. Bill, Billy, and I had noticed that most of the Brazilian men had mustaches. To blend in with the culture we decided we would grow mustaches. Our wives soon noticed this strange development. When they were sure they had been betrayed (not consulted), they confronted each of us and made issues out of our struggling mustaches. I will tell only my story. Leona informed me that I could grow a mustache but not to expect a kiss from her. She did not like my mustache at all. I was hurt because I was just trying, as the other two, to fit in. Leona didn't believe I had to grow that gross extra hair above my upper lip. Therefore I was forced to put an end to my new style. However, first I went downtown to have a mug shot made before I shaved my mustache off.

Many customs were different! When they wanted to visit or talk, instead of knocking on the door Brazilians stood on the sidewalk in front of the house and clapped their hands. They didn't enter the yard until they were invited. Another custom very different from North Americans is the way Brazilians pick their teeth; they cover their mouth with one hand and pick their teeth with the other hand. Toothpicks always were available on tables in homes and restaurants, but salt or pepper shakers never were there. We found the people to be very polite.

Strange Religions
Park Renshaw, our Methodist language-school director, thought we students should get acquainted with religions that are shocking to Evangelical Christianity. He made arrangements for us to see some firsthand bits of spiritism, "a system of professed communication

with departed spirits, especially through mediums." The four different categories of this type of worship are Kardecism, Umbanda, Macumba, and Condomble. I can best explain these spiritist groups by paraphrasing an article I wrote in 1966 for *Commission* magazine, the missionary magazine for the Southern Baptist Convention. Contrary to what most people think, the largest growth among religious groups in Brazil is neither among Catholics nor Evangelicals. By far the most rapid growth statistics show is spiritism.

On a visit to a session of the Umbanda branch of spiritism I caught a glimpse of the activities and appeal of this religion, which features communication with spirits of the dead. Arriving at the building at which meetings were held every Monday and Friday nights, I at once was aware I should have followed advice to arrive at least 30-minutes early. The building that seated about 250 already was full; some people were standing at the back. A rail and a curtain divided about a third of the dimly lit room. As the service began, the curtain was opened to reveal about 30 men and women dressed in white robes and seated. Some wore beads. Against the wall, center stage, sat an elderly, gray-haired woman. Above her head hung a picture of a black slave woman. Colored lights in each corner splashed the scene with varied hues.

The white-clad participants are mediums who call themselves *cavalos* (horses), because, in their trances, spirits ride them. A *combono* is a helper that sits beside each medium to assist, if by nothing more than lighting the pipe or cigar that the medium smokes.

Chant-singing opened the ceremony. These chants, with words taken mainly from Catholic worship, address Mary and other designated saints that are from an African line of gods, but many have biblical names. Gradually the *cavalos* or mediums began to walk about and swayed side to side as their emotional fervor accelerated. A drummer started beating out a strange rhythm while the men and women in white continued to move about. They twisted and writhed as though they were in agony.

Suddenly a woman began to jerk violently, as if she were unable to control herself. Other mediums gathered about to help her stand or let her writhe on the floor until the spasm ceased. Regaining control, one of the mediums walked toward the old woman—the most powerful of the mediums—and knelt there. Leaning forward, the elderly women blew smoke on the other medium and whispered to her. At this point the kneeling, recovering woman was handed a pipe; she began to smoke slowly.

Rapidly, the remaining mediums also started to shake and jerk; some had more animation than others did. One by one each would receive the spirit of the person through which he or she would commune that night; he or she began to smoke a long cigar or pipe. Each medium had been given a spirit by name, such as Papa Jeremiah or Mama Maria. These spirit-endowed mediums were now ready to give counsel from the spirit world to anyone in the crowd that had a problem.

Each person desiring counsel was given a number when he or she entered the room. As a participant's number was called, the person removed his or her shoes, arrived at the front of the room, knelt before the medium that held his or her number, and related the person's problem, whether these concerned one's profession, family, love, getting revenge, or sickness. Patiently the mediums listened; the one "guided by a spirit" proclaimed an answer. Purportedly the medium drew on what is believed to be the wider knowledge of the spirit world. Having received help, the inquirer returned to his or her seat and waited until all who wished had received counseling. In these sessions crossing legs or arms is taboo!

Occasionally, while listening to an inquirer's request, a medium would reel with severe spasms and then collapse onto the floor. Another of the white-clad mediums would help make the prostrate form comfortable. According to their belief the exhausted medium had exorcised an evil spirit from the inquirer and took the evil spirit into herself, since the medium is considered strong enough to dominate the evil spirit.

Such is the activity at an Umbanda session. However, this is but one of the four groups of spiritualists in Brazil. Catholic priests that accompanied the early Portuguese settlers to Brazil sought to put the spiritists' beliefs into their Catholic doctrine. Also arriving in those colonization days were slaves that brought with them their African *orishas*. Catholic landowners forced their religion on their slaves, but the African chiefs and witch doctors usually were able to continue their traditional rites and passed their secrets on to their sons and daughters. Much of this was done secretly.

Some of the slaves, however, became more devoted Catholics and added to the Catholic saints their own deities—in a sense "baptizing" their gods in the name of Christianity. For instance, Ogum, an African powerful god of war, today is St. George, the favored saint in spiritism. Yemanja, queen of waters, with flowing hair and siren beauty, has become the Virgin Mary. This syncretism saw the Catholic saint-cult merge with fetishism and rituals of the African gods.

Until 1968, at the time I wrote the article, Macumba and Umbanda stayed, for the most part, on the *fazendas*. *Fazendas* are coffee or sugar-cane plantations and ranches. But now multitudes of the descendants of the slaves have moved into the cities and have taken their mixed religion with them. The attraction of Macumba and Umbanda, however, by no means is limited to the inhabitants of the city slums. Many well-to-do and respectable citizens attend the Spirits sessions. Most of the adherents generally cling to their membership in the Catholic Church, but to them the Spirit session is more important than worship in church. The coastal city Salvador (first National capital), in the State of Bahia, has a church which is strictly for the Umbanda Catholics.

To spiritists living near the beaches New Year's Eve is considered an important day of worship. Leona and I watched the ceremonies at the beach in Rio de Janeiro. On our first New Year's Day in Brazil we were visiting missionary Dorotha (Dot) Lott. Thousands of small holes had been dug in the sand of Copacabana beach. The beach was covered with thousands of white-robed men and women—so many on this long, wide beach that to walk through them was difficult. Worshipers, some seemingly in a trance, joined the white clad people as they crowded around the holes with candles and flowers. The holes sheltered the candle from the breeze, but hardly any breeze could have reached a candle for the multitude of people. In the gathering we were observing, a teen-age girl began acting as if she was having an epileptic seizure. She fell on the ground; in the light of the candles her face portrayed a person in desperate anguish. She was ministered to by some of the other mediums and finally recovered.

I felt very weird in this crowd, just as I had felt in other spiritualist sessions I had attended. Mediums in their white tunics and many beads conducted the rituals. As drums mournfully set a frenetic rhythm and chants reached a feverish pitch, some of the mediums began to twist convulsively. After such a seizure, each received a cigar and, seemingly in a daze, milled about the group. Just before midnight each group put flowers, food, and other offerings in small boats (about a yard long). These items were things to be offered to the spirit of Yemanja, goddess of the sea. At midnight the principal medium and the hundreds of groups picked up the little boats laden with food and flowers and walked into the water to about knee-deep. Each group watched its leader medium release its boat into the water; they stood watching the boats disappear into the dark ocean. They believe the boats with the offerings that do not return to shore are accepted by the goddess Yemanja.

The Macumba branch of spiritism attracts the more uneducated followers and incorporates black magic. The Umbanda branch is somewhat more refined but still includes the saints of the gods of the black-slave era.

A higher educated system of spiritism also was developed in France. In past centuries France greatly influenced Brazilian culture because wealthy plantation owners frequently sent their sons to France to study. From the later 19th century some Brazilians made contact with Leon Denizarth Hippolyte Rivail, better known as Allan Kardec. This late 19th-century Frenchman became intrigued with the phenomenon of table-tapping, in which spirits were believed to communicate with the living. This phenomenon was a spin off from the Fox sisters, Margaret and Katherine Fox of Hidesville, NY, in 1848. Allen Kardec of France took the early beginnings of the Fox sisters and went far beyond the study of rapping sounds to make a worldwide religion. Kardecism is an intellectually upper-class type of spiritism. These followers do not believe in black magic of lower African spiritism. In this category of spiritism mediums exist among almost all walks of life.

When Kardec began to study this phenomenon, a medium told him he had been chosen by the spirits to develop the religion of "higher spiritism". Kardec became the father of the spiritist movement principally among "whites"; he wrote several books on the subject. Today bookstores have hundreds of books along the Kardec line of belief. This cult believes in contacting and communing with the spirits, but the procedure is carried on in a quieter and more intellectual manner. These people claim they communicate only with good spirits—great and good men or women who are waiting for their "reincarnation" into another body. While one waits, these spirits are available to give advice they had learned in a past life. Their doctrine is one of "good works"; Kardec spiritists give much to charity.

The Kardec followers use a few Bible verses. For example, to support their doctrine of reincarnation they refer to the third chapter of John in which Jesus tells Nicodemus "*You must be born again*", so they say Jesus believed in reincarnation. They also point out the prophecy of Malachi 4:5. Elijah will return as John the Baptist; therefore, this confirms reincarnation. This confirmation occurs when the 12 disciples asks Jesus about this prophecy and Jesus tells them Elijah has already returned, which they say had to mean "in form of John the Baptist". Later on in this book I will go further into this.

Kardec's *Spirits Book*, which has been translated in English, sets forth the groups' beliefs. One interesting view explains a dream as occurring when the spirit leaves the body and travels through the spirit world while a person sleeps. Thus a dream actually is a vision to the mind of what a person's spirit does while the body sleeps.

One spiritist, a former banker by profession but now a Baptist pastor, reported that undeniable, amazing things have happened in many of the spiritist sessions and to many participants. He added that since Jesus talks about demons in a realistic way, no doubt these events are the work of demons.

Park Renshaw, language-school director, furnished some of this information. He commented, "Protestantism has done well in Brazil. For years, the Brazilian evangelical churches have been among the most rapidly growing churches in the world. But spiritism, in its three major forms, is growing much faster."

Field Trips to Discover the Place in Which God Was Calling

The Foreign Mission Board had divided Brazil into three areas: Equatorial, North, and South. All missionaries going to any region of

Brazil went to language school in Campinas in the South Brazil area. Once the missionaries left language school, we rarely saw those of the other regions.

Before we arrived in Brazil, we had chosen the South Brazil region but not the state. While in language school the missionaries were allowed to visit three states to help them decide the place in which God wanted them to serve. All the southern state conventions issued requests according to their needs and sent them to the South Brazil mission. For our first trip we chose to visit the State of Rio de Janeiro to fill the request to take the place of missionaries Dr. John and Prudence Riffey, as they were to retire. Dr. Riffey's work had been with Bible institutes in the northern part of Rio de Janeiro state. We took Charlotte with us since she had not been weaned; the boys stayed with the Togamis. Most of the airplanes were two-motored propeller D.C. 3's that carried about 40 people. These planes had a small tail wheel. Before we arrived at the Santos Dumont airport, lightening flashed around us closer than we ever had seen before; the thunder was deafening. The plane pitched up and down. We were right in the midst of God's atmospheric mystery that causes thunder and lighting. Needless to say, we prayed, but we weren't panicking as some of the passengers were. As we plowed through the clouds, I don't know how the pilot could see where he was going. I remembered that the statue of Christ and Sugar Loaf stuck up pretty high into the sky. To miss these the pilot went out over the ocean, so we descended from the bay. The airport is situated on a finger of land in the Rio de Janeiro Bay, so we flew in skimming the water.

The Riffeys took us to their home in the mountain town of Teresopolis. A range of beautiful rugged mountains, covered with thick forest, parallels the coastal beaches throughout the States of Rio de Janeiro and Espirito Santo. We visited two Bible institutes further north. These institutes also offered correspondence courses. We had an enjoyable time, but I did not feel called to lead institute work. John and Prudence Riffey really liked us and begged us to move to the State of Rio de Janeiro to take their places. As far as the beauty was concerned, we would not have had difficulty adapting to this beautiful state with its beaches nearby, but we did not believe God was leading us there. We didn't want to disappoint this elderly couple, but we had to tell them that this wasn't what we were trained to do.

We also visited the State of Espirito Santo, the coastal state north of Rio State. *Espirito Santo* means *Holy Spirit*. This small state had had two missionary couples and two mission houses in Victoria, but one couple recently had moved. Victoria, the capital, was a beautiful city built on an island in the ocean. The Baptist work was strong because pioneer missionary Loren Reno and his wife had laid a firm foundation. Loren Reno and his wife are buried in Victoria. We were taken to Cachoeiro de Itapimirim to the south and to the city of Colatina in central/western part of the state. We did not go on a Sunday or visit a church, so we did not feel excited about the work.

James Lunsford, missionary in Brasilia, visited us in Campinas and shared of the need for a missionary couple there. He marked a date for our visit. We really were excited about the trip, but the following week Brother Lunsford called and told us the Brasilia field was closed. An older missionary had decided to fill that spot. We were disappointed and questioned, "Lord, what has happened? How could we have misunderstood?" Since our trip to Brasilia already was planned, Jack Young, executive director of Minas Gerais, insisted we stop in Minas Gerais and visit. Since our Brasilia trip was canceled, our plans changed. Jack Young met us in the western city of Uberaba. Uberaba is a city of more than 100,000 people but has only one Baptist church. This city was a clean and beautiful interior city built on rolling hills. We didn't see any beggars in the city. A Brazilian pastor met us and showed us around. He made a special drink for us—an avocado vitamin drink called *Smoothie* in English. This city was strong in spiritism.

We flew from Uberaba to the northeastern city of Governador Valadares, also called the Princess of the Sweet River Valley. This city of 140,000 people was a dirty city. Because it was in a valley only 300 feet above sea level, humidity was high; the heat was extreme. The few cobblestone streets were very bumpy. Most of the people were poor. This city was situated on the only paved highway that linked North Brazil to South Brazil. The Sweet River ran through the city. A railroad connected the heart of the state to the coastal city of Victoria. The high rock mountain peak on the East was very impressive with its statue of Mary on top. The city claimed to have 40,000 bicycles.

Bill Davenport, Ronny Boswell, and Bill Gilmore were in the city for a weekend conference. First Baptist Church was on a wonderful piece of property in the center of the city. Pastor Hilton Carneiro de Souza scheduled a special Monday-night evangelistic service at First Baptist Church. The church was packed; many people crowded around the windows outside. I preached; 20 decisions were made that night. Our welcome was so great that we believed God was leading us to Governador Valadares. The original Baptists had four Baptist churches and about three missions in the city. A total of 48 churches and 70 missions made up the Sweet River Valley Baptist Association, but only 135 churches existed in Minas Gerais, a state of about 12-million people. Governador Valadares and the eastern part of the Sweet River Valley Association had been the most promising region for winning souls in the whole state. I was asked to work as the associational missionary. What an opportunity! We accepted.

Receiving Our Rural Willys

After nine months in language school we were eligible for an automobile. We were interested in the best automobile for family and travel on dirt, country roads. We had two choices: a Willys Rural (station wagon) or a Volkswagen van called a *Kombi*. We chose the Rural Willys because the motor was in front of the driver. The driver of the Volkswagen sat above the left front wheel; therefore, the driver had no protection from anything he struck. We were excited to have our car. With an automobile I was able to accept several preaching invitations. I had some good experiences. I even once preached over the radio. Well, I should say I *read* my sermons. I prepared seven sermons that a language-school teacher corrected before we left language school.

Summary Thoughts

We lived in a nice, middle-class neighborhood in Campinas. The middle class was small in comparison to the total population. Although Campinas was a very nice city and São Paulo was the most advanced state, enough poverty was noticeable to make me feel blessed to have been born in the United States. We were learning that we were the ones to be blessed because of the warm acceptance of the Brazilians. We didn't feel completely at ease in our new culture, but

49

we had enough contact with Brazilians to know they were people just as we were.

Chapter 3

The Call to Governador Valadares

And a vision appeared to Paul in the night: a certain man of
Macedonia was standing and appealing to him, and saying, "Come
over to Macedonia and help us" (Acts 16:9).

Jesus told Nicodemus that he would have to be born again.
He described the experience by using the mystery of the wind.
Nicodemus, do you know where the wind begins?
Or can you tell me where the wind diminishes to an end?

Puzzled and disturbed Nicodemus looked into Jesus' face:
Enter my mother's womb and be born again into the human race?
A mystery is something we experience but cannot logically explain.
Like the wind, Nicodemus, you feel it and accept it in faith.

So as with the experience to be spiritually born again.
It is something you feel, unexplainable, that surges from within—
So great that you wonder about it throughout your years;
So mysterious, but fresh, that it takes away your fears.

Introduction

Finally we knew we were going to Governador Valadares, Minas
Gerais. God knew where He wanted us. Having settled this, we were
excited to be on our way to the State of Minas Gerais, which means
General Mines. This is the place in which we would plant our lives to

51

tell the wonderful "love of Jesus Christ and His Glory" to hundreds. Furniture still was pretty cheap; our $480 monthly salary went further than we ever could have dreamed. We bought (or had made) furniture for the dining room, living room, two bedrooms, and a few extra pieces. We needed two medium-sized trucks to move our furniture. The moving crew arrived late to start loading, so the crew members didn't finish until about 10 p.m. We were exhausted! The next morning we had to pay some bills and close out our bank account before we could start our trip to Governador Valadares by way of Belo Horizonte.

We had our first experience driving on one of the busiest roads in Brazil. It connected the largest city in Brazil, São Paulo, to the third-largest, Belo Horizonte, capital of Minas Gerais. This highway was about 450 miles of only two lanes on mostly a winding, mountainous road. Since trucks transported most of the freight, we passed truck after truck after truck. Brazil had only a few railroads. Buses were the main mode of transportation. Brazilians have the courtesy passing system to aid those wanting to pass by giving a signal with the left blinker light when the road is clear or the right blinker as a warning not to pass. After two or three near-accidents following their safe passing system, I decided the safest thing was to wait until I could see for myself. Even when a truck driver gave the signal to pass, this did not mean he would wait on you to pass. When they go down a hill, the truckers don't want to miss out on picking up speed. So if you cannot pass when you are going up a hill, you are better off waiting for another chance while you go up another hill. The speed limit was 50-miles an hour (80 kilometers), but to pass sometimes we had to get up to about 80-miles per hour. Needless to say any trip was always very stressful.

The five missionary families in Belo Horizonte had planned a "welcome" dinner for us. A few days earlier the Bill Richardsons had moved to Belo Horizonte. Arnol and Edna Harrington, who had arrived in Minas Gerais in 1932, were the senior missionaries. The Jack Young family had been on the field four years. Jack was the executive secretary for the Minas Gerais Baptist Convention. The Bill Davenport family had been on the field about three years; the Ronald Boswell family had been in Belo eight months. We didn't arrive in

Belo until about 10 p.m., but the group still was waiting for us. About midnight we fell into bed exhausted.

Bill Davenport had agreed to go with us as our guide; by 9 the next morning we were on the road to Governador Valadares. This was the first time that we had traveled that road; we didn't know what to expect. The car was loaded; the kids were cramped. On a narrow two-lane highway with potholes and scarcely a place to get off the road if necessary we headed toward higher mountains with hundreds of curves. At times tree branches were on the pavement to warn motorists that a vehicle was blocking the right lane of the road ahead. The terrain was beautiful! Coffee, banana, corn, and coconut trees covered the hillsides that had been cleared of native trees and vines. However, large areas of original native jungle changed the landscape now and then. We were about 2,000 miles from the Equatorial jungles, but before this land was settled, all the terrain was jungle in a semitropical region.

Occasionally we met or pulled up behind trucks that were heavily laden with blackened sacks of something. These sacks were carefully stacked so high that the truck looked as though it easily could tip over because the sacks were stacked wider at the top than at the bottom. We later learned that these were sacks of charcoal used to heat furnaces at the steel mills. We saw several large forests of eucalyptus trees that were planted principally to make charcoal. These trees weren't native to Brazil but were popular because they grow quickly and will re-sprout three times before having to be replanted. The big mud ovens, much larger than Navajo ovens, near the highway burned the eucalyptus into charcoal.

After about four hours of traveling on the paved highway we arrived in Ipatinga, about two-thirds the distance to Governador Valadares. We had entered the Sweet River Valley area. At the edge of town for three miles was a huge steel mill with its towering smoke stacks spouting black smoke into the sky. The next 60 miles on to Governador Valadares was a dirt road. This was April, the beginning of dry season, so the road was dusty except for a few large and small mud holes. Occasionally to our right we could see the Sweet River. As we traveled we had to stop once in a while for cattle that were blocking the road. They were huge Zebu with humps on their shoulders and were similar to the Brahman cattle. In both directions on the road people were traveling on horseback, bicycles, ox carts, buggies, or cars or were walking. Finally in the far distance we saw the mountain peak Ibituruna; we told the kids that the peak was our destination. We all were so tired; the kids were irritable. We thought we never would get to Governador Valadares. On subsequent trips we made a game out of who could be first to catch a glimpse of the mountain peak. Late Friday afternoon we finally arrived at our house. The trucks were waiting for us; the drivers were eager to unload. We were hungry. so Bill Davenport bought some pizzas and soft drinks for the truck drivers and us. As soon as the beds were unloaded, Bill Davenport helped me put them up so we could have a decent night's sleep. About 10 p.m. the moving people finished unloading everything and left. Early the next morning Bill and I bought two gas bottles for our cook stove. Then I took him to the bus station so he could return to Belo Horizonte. We were thankful for the help he gave us.

My First Trip into the Interior

Before we left Campinas, Pastor Waldemar Pereira Vaz and I had made the plan to go to the annual associational meeting together. Early Monday morning Pastor Waldemar arrived at our gate and was ready to go. He had invited a lay preacher that served some country churches to meet us on the side of the highway about 30 miles south of Governador Valadares. When Pastor Gabriel got into the car, I didn't think to ask whether he got carsick, but I soon found out. We hadn't driven more than 30 more miles when Gabriel threw up all over the back seat. I guess he didn't know how to get the window open and didn't want to disturb us. I hadn't brought any cleaning materials; the situation was horrible! Gabriel had a "sort of green" color to his face. Of course he was embarrassed but so sick that he just moaned and groaned. We were traveling south on the Rio-Bahia Highway, the only paved highway that linked South Brazil to North Brazil. This was the only paved road in the area. This major asphalt artery ran from Rio de Janeiro through the States of Minas Gerais and Bahia and far beyond. We finally left the paved road and started on the dirt one to the city of Manhuacu, in which we stopped at a pastor's home. We cleaned the car; Pastor Gabriel drank some herb tea to settle his stomach.

Our destiny was Mutum, Minas Gerais. I was coping with the different accent spoken by the Mineiros, people of Minas. I became very tired trying to participate in the conversation with Waldemar and Gabriel. I did understand that Mutum was known to be a wild town that was famous for shootouts between cowboys and politicians. Such a town was called *bange-bange*, or *bang-bang town* (expression picked up from U.S. Western movies). The further we went, the narrower the road became until finally we were going through cornfields, with corn stalks brushing each side of the car. Waldemar entertained me by telling about the American missionary that had opened up the town for Jesus Christ.

Steven and Pauline Jackson were the only missionaries that before us had worked in the Sweet River Valley. The priest heard that Steven was moving to Mutum. Amazingly he told the people to welcome Steven. No Evangelical work existed in Mutum. For a priest not to be very antagonistic when Evangelicals wanted to move in was highly unusual. So Steven was surprised when he was able to easily arrange a house to rent. He was told that buying necessities would be no problem. He arranged for a farmer to deliver milk for his family. Steven returned happily to Governador Valadares, where he was serving First Baptist Church. Later when Steven arrived in Mutum with his family, he was aghast to find that they weren't welcomed. The man that had promised to rent the house now refused. They couldn't buy food or milk. The family was stranded. This burdened some of the townspeople when they saw the young family. Some people soon provided the family members with everything they needed. The priest's plan failed.

I had expected Mutum to be a pretty nice town, since it was chosen to have the annual associational meeting. The towns and cities in São Paulo state were cleaner and more attractive than in the Sweet River Valley that I had seen, but I didn't expect what I found in Mutum. The only cobblestone pavement was around the center square. We stopped at the only boarding house (no hotels) on the square to check in. We could see into the kitchen. The first thing I noticed were the shiny pots and pans hanging on the walls; however, smoky cobwebs hung abundantly from the ceiling. The walls and ceiling were very black from the woodburning cook stove.

My room was just large enough for two narrow single beds and a tiny table and chair between the beds. The mattresses were hard; the light bulb hanging from the ceiling produced a very dim light. The room had one window with a wooden shutter; it was wide open (no windowpane). I shut the door that was made out of boards and noticed that I could see through a wide crack in the door into the lobby of the boarding house. The floor was of planks with cracks big enough for me to see the ground below. Pastor Jose Alves da Silva Bittencourt, assistant to Jack Young at the state Baptist office, was to occupy the other bed in our room. He spoke some English.

About 3 p.m. we arrived very tired, so I lay down on the bed in the sweltering heat. With the packing and moving during the past week I had had little rest. Yet I couldn't sleep, because I was having my worst culture-shock attack. For one thing I had left our house in a mess with boxes stacked everywhere and only the furniture put into place. Without a car Leona had no way to purchase anything. She had no telephone; the only way I could communicate with her was by telegraph. On Saturday some dear ladies from First Baptist Church had arrived to help unpack. I knew that Mibzar, wife of Pastor Hilton, was ready to help in any way necessary. Yes, Leona and our children were in good hands, but I still was overwrought with worry about them. I began to wonder why in the world I had agreed with God to be a missionary. Already I was very tired of hearing Portuguese. Everything around me was strange and not what I had expected. I was definitely depressed! And I would be staying three days and three nights in Mutum.

My mind drifted back into the past in a way that seemed to indicate that God was reminding me of my call as I struggled with my questions. I began remembering the saddest day of my life. We lived on a farm 12 miles from Lovington, NM. I was 7-years old. My siblings William Esteen was 10; Helen Pauline, 9; Margaret Lee, 5; and baby brother Thomas Edgar, 6 months. My mother, Hazel Pauline, had been sick for a while. Her illness had worsened until her left arm was paralyzed and her throat was very sore. One morning, before the school bus arrived, a big long black car arrived to take her to a hospital. My mother called the children to her side and talked to us. I do not remember all she said, but she encouraged us to be good children. She had been a good mother and the adult Sunday-school teacher at the neighborhood community church. This little church was basically Baptist. My mother was well-known in the farming community. She must have known that she wouldn't be returning home. She wanted us to follow Jesus and to continue to go to church. They took her to a hospital in Hobbs, NM.

After school that day we three older children did not ride the bus back to the farm. We went to our great Aunt Ginny and Uncle Dave's house, which was not far from school. Two days later, October 27, 1942, mother died. We were greatly shocked when we received the word. I didn't know much about death. Our farm was adjacent to my grandfather and grandmother Tarry's farm. My grandfather Tarry had died about a year-and-a-half earlier. I remember that we stayed up all night at their house. Esteen and I passed time under the dining table, at which much of the conversation was held while the men drank coffee. Grandpa's coffin was in the living room; I could hear some of the conversations among the women. Those thoughts returned to my mind when I heard about my mother's death. I felt very sad.

We didn't go to school the next day. I wanted to see my mother, but none of the family offered to take us to the funeral home. After school Mrs. Duke, a teacher arrived to visit and asked us whether we wanted to see our mother. We did, so she walked with us to the funeral home. I was glad she took us, but sadness overcame me even more. I could see in my mother's lifeless body and face that she really was gone forever. I could hardly bear it. The day she was buried was cold, dreary, and misty. Dismal weather was fitting for my feelings. The only thing that brought a little happiness was my first pair of waist pants my Uncle Guy LeCroy bought for me to wear to the funeral. I only had bib overalls which I wore to school, church, and everywhere else. Two or three other boys wore overalls, but the style had become waist pants for the financially abled. To me bib overalls seemed a sign of being poor.

In January my dad traded a car as part payment on three lots and a four-room house on the outskirts of Lovington, NM. Daddy loved farming, but he believed that to rear five kids on a farm would be very difficult. Later I learned that my mother had asked my dad to keep us kids together. Daddy took into town a cow, some pigs, and a big stack of feed for the cow. A few weeks passed before Daddy felt as though he could attend church services again, but Esteen and I went to church soon after we moved to town. First Baptist Church was about 10 blocks from the place in which we lived. Soon we all were going to church faithfully. About a year later I accepted Jesus as my Savior.

Years went by; during the summer between my junior and senior high-school year I surrendered to do anything God wanted me to do. Two years later, just two months before the end of my freshman year in college, I surrendered to be a preacher/missionary. Pastor Chester Watt of First Baptist Church in Lovington immediately invited me to preach on a Sunday night. After I had finished the message, Pastor Watt asked me to stand at the front of the auditorium so people could encourage me. The last two were women from the rural area in which I had lived until my mother died. They told me that my surrendering to preach was an answer to my mother's prayers. This brought back memories of my mother's last words as we gathered at her bedside. Her prayers for me are part of The Marvel of It All.

Once more, as I lay on the hard bed in the boarding house, I re-examined my life. The street was noisy outside with horses' hooves stamping the cobblestone, people greeting each other, and peddlers announcing their items for sale. I found myself wondering again why my mother had prayed so diligently for me. Helen and Esteen often had reminded me how stubborn I was. Even my Grandmother Tarry and Aunt Susie had mentioned it. Yes, I did give my mother more trouble than the other children did. When we needed punishing, she told us kids to go to the cherry orchard and choose our own switch for our thrashing. If we didn't get one that pleased her, she would get one bigger. I sometimes hid the switches or made catching me difficult. I found I could crawl under my mother and father's bed. Mama couldn't get me out, for I rolled back and forth from side to side. Even when Helen and Bill caught one of my legs or arms, they suffered a kick with the other foot or fist. Mama would remind me that I eventually would have to leave my place of refuge, for dark would fall and I would miss my supper! Furthermore, if I did not leave my place of refuge willingly, my daddy would take care of me! I would get the razor strap or his big hand. Well, I was afraid of the dark; under the bed in a dark room everything becomes spooky, so before dark I always crawled out. After Mama died, my heart ached over these things. For a year or more I begged God to let me see my mother in my dreams, but He never did. Yet, I never was angry with God. I later wrote a poem about my Mother.

A MOUND OF DIRT

Did you ever sit beside a dirt mound
When all around you the only sound
Was of rustling leaves and twittering birds?
And other than this, nothing else could be heard
Because a deathly silence hoveringly fills
The atmosphere over the moundlike hills!

Sitting beside such a mound one day,
My mind could not help but wander astray!
Old memories crept into my brain
Of a cold fall day overcast with rain!
My mournful thoughts shut out the birds
So that only my inner self could be heard!

Soon, enveloped in the recent past,
The cruelness of life had arrived too fast!
Just five years ago I did not know this mound
And in this place was level ground.
And yet, if it had only been five years
Why is the past so unforgettable and clear?

Dim memories gradually began to appear—
Memories that I want always to hold dear!—
Of my mother mending my clothes by the stove
Or doctoring my skinned and bruised nose—
To ponder anew my childhood past,
For my years already were speeding by fast.

A stranger looking at this mound
Would not be impressed by what he found.
Hardly could I expect him to see

What this mound means to me,
For she wiped my dirty face on her dress
And pressed me close to her warm breast.

Sometimes I bring a rake and a hoe,
Because upon this mound weeds like to grow!
And other times around the stone,
Assorted flowers I have sown,
But animals, wind, rain, and snow,
Would like for this mound to sink down low.

So within this mound like a lid,
Many fond memories for me are hid!
And from this fountain I withdraw,
My treasured dreams I never saw!
But it took this grave for me to see
What the loss of my mother would mean to me!

Pastor Waldemar had told me that Steven and Pauline Jackson for three-and-a-half years had lived and worked establishing the church in Mutum. Before Pastor Bittencourt arrived, I had decided that if Steven could stay three-and-a-half years, I could stay three-and-a-half days. I was glad to see Pastor Bittencourt and glad that we could converse in English. The associational meeting was very long, with reports from every organization, a lot of singing, testimonies, and preaching. This association covered an enormous area, so this was a time of fellowship. Most of the people brought their pallets and slept in a school—the men in one room and women in another. I found this was a popular practice because the fee was very cheap. A few messengers stayed in homes.

I was an attraction, especially for the young people. Pastor Bittencourt had to interpret for me to answer some of their questions. Until about midnight on Saturday and Sunday the young people kept me up asking questions about the United States and other things. One subject was about Caryl Chessman's execution at San Quentin Penitentiary in California.

Caryl Chessman was a U.S. medical doctor who murdered his

wife. While he was in prison, he wrote a book that many people liked. His story caused some people to want him pardoned. While I was studying at Golden Gate, he eventually was electrocuted. I knew San Quentin prison because this famous prison was close to Golden Gate Seminary. I went with some seminary students to familiarize ourselves with the prison system. We saw the electric chair. I was amazed that these young people in the interior of Minas Gerais knew about that event and had definite opinions about his execution. They were not for capital punishment. They put me on the spot to defend our American position.

While in seminary Leona and I also visited Alcatraz. A group of seminary students went to Alcatraz to give a party for the guards' children. That was an interesting trip as we traveled by boat to visit Alcatraz and visited the families of the guards that lived on Alcatraz Island.

Adapting to Governador Valadares

Governador Valadares, named after a governor, was first called *Figueiro do Rio Doce*. In some places near Governador Valadares the Rio Doce (Sweet River) was about a third of a mile wide. Several islands rose above the water near Governador Valadares; the largest was named Araujo Island. At the upper end of the Araujo Island a barge was connected to a cable to get it across the river. At the lower end of the island was a bridge to the center of the city. The Rio-Bahia Highway crossed the river over a two-lane bridge at the upper or west end of the city. In 1966 Governador Valadares, also called the Princess of the Sweet River Valley, was the third-largest city in Minas Gerais; it had a population of about 140,000.

To us Governador Valadares was an exotic city. The Sweet River was not navigable except for small fishing boats. The city was the first major stop for trucks and buses from Rio de Janeiro to the distant regions of north Brazil. A major railroad from Belo Horizonte to the coast city of Victoria passed through: a passenger train traveled through once a day and a train carrying iron ore many times a day. Governador Valadares was a busy city, with fishermen in their small boats going and returning on the river as well as men shoveling sand from the river bed in low places. Taking sand from the river bed could be done only in the winter in which the river was low. They put the sand into their small boats and piled it on the bank. This sand was used in concrete for the buildings.

Three little rivers from the hills and mountains to the north passed through the city and emptied into the Sweet River. Unfortunately these little rivers also were used to deposit sewage from the city slums which went into the Sweet River. Directly south from the center of the city, and just across the Sweet River, the Ibituruna mountain rises into the sky. The northern side of the peak is composed of sheer granite, almost as if it had been chipped off straight down for hundreds of feet. The eastern descent from the peak is more gradual than the one on the western side; cars can drive up. The western side slopes down near to the Rio-Bahia Highway and the southern end of Governador Valadares. Today this mountain is one of the favorite hang-glider places in all of South America.

Governador Valadares is only about 300 feet above sea level and 400 miles from the coast. For this reason Governador Valadares is miserably hot in the summer. For health reasons the mission required missionaries to put screens on the windows. Brazilians do not like screens because they think these keep the breeze or air out. During World War II a group of American army engineers were stationed in Governador Valadares to widen the narrow-gauge railroad to get iron ore from the center of Minas Gerais to the port city of Vitoria. The wooden houses built for these engineers still existed when we arrived and still had screens on the windows. Yet, to my knowledge, not one family in the city put screens on its windows even though the mosquitoes swarmed at night. A green chemical mosquito deterrent formed into a spiral could be bought to keep the mosquitoes away at night. This flat spiral was put on a little tin stand and lit on one end. It would burn for several hours and put out a smoke that kept the mosquitoes away. The ashes from the burnt spiral fell harmlessly onto a pad on the floor of the room. I could not easily adapt to the odor and smoke from this mosquito repellent, but they were better than getting mosquito bites. We had to buy the screen wire in Belo Horizonte and had the frames made to fit our windows. Even so, at night we still burnt spirals to suffocate the mosquitoes that found a way into our house.

Fifth Baptist Church

Before we left Campinas, I received a letter from Pastor Hilton Carneiro de Souza telling me that Fifth Baptist Church had been organized and that I was elected as the new pastor. The Boa Vista neighborhood was in a new development later changed to Santa Rita. Being relatively new the development had no electricity, sewer, or water system. I had not planned to serve as pastor to a church, but would I be unfriendly by refusing to accept the invitation? Friday after I returned from Mutum, we drove out to find the church. When we arrived in Governador Valadares from Belo Horizonte, we had passed near Fifth Baptist Church in the Saint Rita neighborhood. All the streets were dirt and narrow; many had almost washed away from the rains. Being a new neighborhood only a few houses had been built. The people were poor but were not in the slum category. The place in which the church met had been a house with the inside walls removed; it set about 20 yards from the street. A smaller building had been built at the back of the lot for the children. Also on the back of the lot were an outdoor toilet and hand-pumped water well. On the lot next door was a bar situated about 20 yards to the front of the place in which our church property began. The central neighborhood *praca* (or plaza) had been planned for this area. Though it had not been developed, eventually the church property would be facing the *praca*. This location was excellent for the church.

First Baptist Church, at which Pastor Hilton was pastor, had four or five other missions. Two of the other four churches in town were without a pastor. Fifth Baptist Church needed a pastor, so the next Sunday at 9 a.m. our family was there to accept this responsibility. Pastor Hilton introduced us and then left to take care of other missions and to preach at his church.

All the people arrived by foot or by bicycle. One family of six arrived on a bicycle. As I mentioned earlier, many of the bicycles had a platform over the front wheel. Joao Leite was the song leader. His wife, riding sidesaddle on the seat over the back wheel, had a baby in her arms; another girl rode on the bar between Joao and the handlebars; and two other girls rode on the platform over the front wheel. Most of the stores had boys or men to deliver merchandize on bicycles. I remember seeing one furniture store delivering a couch that was balanced on a platform over the front wheel of the bicycle.

The church had two windows (wooden shutters without glass) on both sides. Every service of the year these shutters were opened for light. The furniture consisted of 10 benches on each side of the aisle, a small table, and a pulpit. Two lanterns, one over the pulpit and the other in the middle of the room, provided light for the evening services.

Everyone made us feel very welcome. The women and teen-age girls wanted to hold Charlotte. This was disturbing for us, since we almost had lost Charlotte before and under much better hygienic conditions. Many of the children had stomachs that were bloated because of worms. A sign of this illness was the secretion oozing out of their noses; their noses and lips were red as though they were inflamed. We were not prepared for such a situation. But God took care of Charlotte; we grew to love the people.

The evening services in Brazil by far were the best-attended. That first Sunday night the building was full; people crowded around the windows and the front and back doors just to hear the gospel preached. This was true nearly every Sunday night. I had seven sermons written out and corrected by a teacher in the language school. What would I do after these had been preached, or I should say read, to the congregation?

Adapting to Home and Neighborhood

Since no missionary lived close to Governador Valadares to help us find a house, we had asked Pastor Hilton to search for us. Most homes had very small rooms, since Brazilians had very little furniture. He located a nice-sized, four-bedroom house that was very spacious—more space than we needed for our furniture, including a piano. The owner made us a good offer. This house had a partial indoor flower garden, which was nice but also was a breeding place for mosquitoes. That part of the house was cooler; this felt good in the summer but was cold in the winter, since no heating system was in the homes. We had a big room in which we put a ping-pong table and the TV (terrible reception). I bought two big mats for wrestling with Carl and Jonathan—and Charlotte, since she thought she had to be in the middle of everything with the boys.

The house was on an area of almost half a city block. We had rented only the house. Just outside the kitchen door were two smaller houses. The property owner had a caretaker living in one; our maid lived in the other. The caretaker took care of all the property, which was sort of like a jungle. Our children enjoyed playing among the various fruit trees: bananas, oranges, guava, mangos, coconuts, limes, papaya, and others. The small yard in front was full of bushes and flowers. The caretaker and his wife became very fond of our kids, especially Charlotte. This couple was very black, as were many at the church; our children were learning that black people and white people are very much alike. The area between our houses was cement, which was excellent for the boys to ride their bicycle and Charlotte her tricycle. Charlotte often visited the couple at the back of our house. Leona eventually found out that every morning the caretaker's wife was giving Charlotte coffee mixed with milk. For breakfast the coffee is very strong and sweet and served with half a cup of hot milk. Many boil water with sugar and pour this through coffee grounds. Most Brazilians love coffee and all day have a pot ready. The *cafezinho* is a small demitasse cup of very strong and very sweet coffee. It is served between meals and at the end a meal. We found that most of the people with whom we worked used small water glasses for coffee. They did this mainly because they didn't have money to buy cups.

When we moved to Governador Valadares in 1966, cars or trucks were few, so most people used horse or donkey carts or bicycles. The saying was that Governador Valadares had about 40,000 bicycles. I don't know how anyone counted all the bicycles to make this statement, but we believed the remark was correct. Even though the city was built on hills, enough flat ground along the river existed to make bicycles a very profitable way of transportation. When we arrived, the main streets for several blocks in every direction from the downtown shopping area had *paralelepipedos* (cobblestones) pavement with no asphalt. Jonathan had fun saying this word over and over carefully: *pa-ra-le-le-pi-pe-dos*, with a strong accent on "pi".

Our street, as with most, was just dirt, which meant dust in the dry season and mud in the rainy season. The street always was full of action: people selling all kinds of things, beggars almost every day, and boys playing soccer (*futebol*). The people had to contend with pigs and chickens running wild and bicycles, donkeys and cars passing through their game. *Peteca*, a feathered, leather thing similar to badminton, was played by hand instead of a racket. Girls and boys played this game together. Another game for boys was like throwing knives, but rather than using a knife they used a sharp piece of an iron rod to try to hit a target. During the 14 months we lived at that house, our boys were too small to get involved with the street activities. They did attract attention. Sometimes children would watch through the fence, for in front this house had an unusual low fence that permitted people to see through. The entire huge fruit-and-jungle-tree area behind our house, however, had a high wall around it with broken glass on a concrete ledge on top of the wall to keep thieves out. Since we were renting only the house and front yard, we had no right to any of the fruit at the back of the house.

Making Friends and Learning to Fellowship

The communists thought they were strong enough to take over the government. In fact a president had been elected that was sympathetic to communism. In 1964 a revolution took place. The army overthrew that president; he went into exile in Uruguay. The coup lasted only a few days, but we heard that many people that had grudges took the opportunity to kill those they disliked whether they were communist or not. A military general was made president; the military government also appointed state governors.

When we arrived in Governador Valadares in April 1966, some painted signs reading "Go Home, Yankees" still were visible on walls. We understood the sign to mean for America to stay out of Brazilian political life. We felt well-received among the five Baptist churches. The treatment we had in the commercial places showed that the majority of people didn't have animosity against Americans.

A Presbyterian English teacher, *Dona* (Mrs.) Ideir Silva dos Santos, heard about us and sought us out. She was studying English at the Oxford Institute in Belo Horizonte and wanted experience in conversation. This began a lasting friendship and a God-sent trade-off as she could correct messages for me. Brazilian Presbyterians were very evangelistic and didn't allow their members to smoke, drink, or dance. Presbyterians had chosen Minas Gerais and State of São Paulo as their principal missionary endeavor in Brazil. Governador Valadares had seven Presbyterian churches; some of their members weren't only wealthy but also were involved in city politics. Baptists hadn't reached that status.

Another person that sought us out was an Assembly of God man, a sergeant in the Army battalion band in our city. He very much wanted to learn English. He had bought tapes and dedicated himself to learning English. He stuttered badly in Portuguese, but we discovered that he didn't stutter when he spoke English. Leona's parents had bought her an accordion; she had taught herself how to play it. Somehow this Army musician found out that she was playing the accordion at Fifth Baptist Church. He wanted to help Leona perfect her accordion skills in exchange for English conversation. Another trade-off for help in English! The accordion also was perfect for open-air and home evangelistic services. About four-years later the sergeant was transferred to another battalion in Montes Claros, the largest city of North Minas Gerais. The last time I saw him was when I attended a state convention in that city. He had been promoted to be the Battalion band director. He took me to one of his band rehearsals. As a second occupation he also was teaching English.

We soon met a British family that were Baptists but were with a non-denominational mission board. They were assigned to work with the Presbyterians; principally they were to run the Evangelical bookstore. They had small children about the ages of our children. We discovered two Peace Corps workers that were near the end of their Peace Corps contract in Valadares. The woman agreed to help Leona teach a nutrition class at Fifth Baptist Church. She had some good materials that they used; the ladies seemed to enjoy the classes. The other Peace Corps worker was an engineer and had helped with the design of the new city hall. After they left, we were the only Americans in the city.

The Sweet River Valley Baptist Association

In 1966 Minas Gerais had 135 churches in the state, a state the size of Texas with about nine-million people. More than a third of these churches—48 churches and 70 missions—were in the Sweet River Valley. The Sweet River Valley Association covered about a fifth of the state. It was divided into four regions—North, East, Central, and Valley of Aco (Steel). Governador Valadares was centrally located east and west but not north and south. About six-and-one-half hours were necessary for me to reach the farthest church to the east, about the same distance to reach the farthest to the south, and about seven-and a-half hours to reach the associational boundary to the west. No-churches or missions were west of the Rio-Bahia Highway that cut the region about in the middle. We had more churches in the Sweet River Association than some states had in their entire state. The reason was because the Baptists in the coastal State of Espirito Santo found fertile ground for the gospel in the eastern part of the Sweet River Valley. If, when I was invited to this field, I had realized what a big area I had to cover, I might have been afraid to accept the challenge.

Pastor Waldemar Vaz was trying to be the coordinator and troubleshooter for this vast area, but he had no automobile or the funds to travel. He was a very humble man that for many years had served as an *evangelista* (lay preacher). Throughout the region he was dearly loved, even though his wife never had accepted the Lord. He began traveling with me throughout the region to acquaint me with churches, some of the missions, and preaching points in the area.

We made our trips mostly during the dry season. I was totally unprepared for the dusty roads. The dust poured into the Rural Willys Wagon even though it was new. During World War II the Willys Company made jeeps for the U.S. Army. The Rural was a modernized Jeep Wagon; it had a heater but no air-conditioner. The summer heat was too uncomfortable to keep the windows up. Traveling behind a truck or other automobile was horrible. You couldn't see anything for all the dust. Driving with the windows closed almost was unbearable, but this was healthier than inhaling the dust was. Bicyclists, pedestrians, horseback riders, or donkeys pulling buggies or carts always were on the roads. For a long time I slowed down drastically when I passed these people so I wouldn't choke them with the dust. I noticed Brazilian motorists didn't have such mercy on their fellow Brazilians. After a while I reached the point that I also covered them with dust.

One has to see to believe how dusty the roads were in the dry season. The tree leaves along the roads were covered with so much dust that you hardly could see any green. The leaves became weighted down with dust as snow does to the pine trees in the States. One time I was driving with a group of pastors on our way to visit a sick pastor friend; we hit a place in the road that had about eight inches of dust powder. The engine immediately stopped and drowned out—not with water but with dust in the carburetor. I always carried tools, although I had little mechanical knowledge. Pastor Hilton, however, was an excellent mechanic and before long had the carburetor off and cleaned out so we could continue our journey. Once when he and I arrived at the Ron Boswells' house in Belo Horizonte, we were covered with so much dust that at first the Boswells didn't recognize us.

I was amazed how nearly everybody in the whole northern, central, and eastern regions of the Sweet River Valley knew Pastor Waldemar. He likewise knew them. Often as we traveled, he recognized someone walking along the road, so we gave the person a ride. Many times the person wasn't a Christian when he or she got in but was by the time of leaving the car. One time I offered a ride to a man that didn't know Pastor Waldemar. The man asked how much he would have to pay. I said, "You don't have to pay anything!" The man couldn't believe this, so he asked again, "How much do you charge?" "Nothing, mister, nothing!" He couldn't believe us and wouldn't accept the ride. For Waldemar and me this became a sermon illustration about how salvation is a free gift from God. People have to believe that "no one has to pay anything" to be saved! That man couldn't believe that the ride offered him was really without charge.

Waldemar became such a dear friend that I always referred to him as my Brazilian father and Pastor Bittencourt as my Brazilian uncle. I admired him, for he had no jealousy with my arrival to help in the associational work. His children were also close to me. Two of the boys became pastors and the girls good Christians, but Waldemar's wife never accepted Jesus. She finally left him and married another man. Much later Waldemar, with the approval of his children, married a fine Christian woman. During the rest of his ministry he enjoyed a companion until he died in 2000.

My First Journey Alone
My first time to travel by myself was to the small town named

Independencia. The pastor had scheduled me to lead a three-day clinic on Sunday-school growth. I was to arrive on Friday in time for the night service and return to Governador Valadares on Monday. I decided to leave the car with Leona so she could take Carl and Jonathan to the Presbyterian school. New experiences were happening nearly every day for me, but my first venture outside the city by myself was special. I took the train to Resplendor, crossed the river in a small boat, and boarded an old country bus. People were carrying purchases of all kinds from Resplendor to their country home or village. What couldn't be put in the luggage compartment had to be carried in the passenger area. The pastor and his family welcomed me as I arrived in Independencia.

That night during the Sunday-school study rain began to fall. We had to finish the service before 10 because the generator that produced electricity would be turned off. The streetlights gave only enough light to see vaguely. The light in the church building and homes were all low-wattage light bulbs. So by 10 we were in bed. I shared a room with the pastor's father. The room had only two narrow cots with a little space between them for a tiny table, big enough for me to put my Bible and a glass of water. When the lights went out, the darkness was solid black. This darkness was as black as Carlsbad Caverns in New Mexico when officials turned out the lights and sang "Rock of Ages". Because of the rain the shutters were closed.

This was early September—not yet the normal time for rain—but the rain fell steadily all night. In the early morning hours I was startled by a strange, mournful sound way off in the distance. By spreading the edges of your lips together and cheeks as wide as possible and making a high "*eeeeeeeeeeeeeee*" sound, you might get an idea of what the strange, lonesome sound was like. I listened and listened as it gradually approached. I was very puzzled. What in the world could be approaching? An hour seemed to pass until I could tell the sound was almost in front of the house. I opened the shutter; to my surprise daylight flooded the room. Outside I saw two oxen were pulling a large cart with two huge wheels. The noise was made by those wheels. I didn't see how anyone could still be sleeping in that entire town. The screeching noise was LOUD! Later I was told that when the wooden axles are new, they give a perfect musical pitch to tune a violin.

Because of the rain I had no incentive to get out of the house and walk around the town. The kitchen table was very small—just large enough for four people. The general custom was that only adults ate at the table. The wife served the children's plates; to eat they sat on the floor. The wife served us and then stood up as she ate. To cut meat this family had only one knife that we passed around. The knife blade was so worn that I was afraid I would break it if I pressed hard to cut the meat. The pastor's father was sick and during the night had coughed much. I hoped I wouldn't catch his cold.

We had rice and beans, always the staple for both the noon and evening meal. Boiled okra in a sauce was served on top of cornmeal mush. Squash, seasoned with garlic and onion, was served. I was served a good piece of fried pork, beef, or chicken. Dessert, either homemade or bought, was a thick jam of bananas, papaya, or guava. One can buy these fruits in a big round, flat, tin about an inch-and-a-half high. The jam is hard enough to cut with a knife as though we were cutting a piece of pie. A slice of cheese called *Minas cheese* often was served with this. After we three men had finished our main meal, the pastor's wife took our forks to the kitchen faucet, ran water over them, dried them and brought them back to us to eat dessert. After the second meal, partially because the father was sick, I didn't see any reason to switch forks, since she wasn't washing them with soap. I decided to keep my fork, so I put my right hand over my fork and pretended to be listening to the pastor and his father's conversation (by this time I always was tired of listening to Portuguese). The wife gently pulled my fork out from under my hand, under the faucet rinsed the forks, and handed them out. No way could I know whose fork I was getting; this happened every meal.

This church was growing and was crowded. The adults met in the auditorium, the youth in another building, and the children in another room. I showed them how they, by building more space and using more teachers, could improve. Sunday morning and evening I preached evangelistic messages. Several made decisions to accept Jesus as their Savior and Lord. I had experienced a good weekend, but I was worried. *Was my faith as strong as it should be?* I was very tired of hearing Portuguese and still not understanding very well. In the thick darkness I lay in bed and listened to the old man having trouble breathing. What if one of my children was to have an accident, or get violently ill? What if one of them died? No telegraph or telephone existed in this town. In Brazil people had to be buried within 24 hours. If a family member died, he or she would be buried before I could get word and return to Governador Valadares.

The devil sure was working on me. God gave me relief by reminding me of the real pioneer missionaries. The male missionaries 50 years before me had to travel by horse, horse and buggy, or boat and were gone for weeks and sometimes months before they returned home. A few really did return home to find out that loved ones had died in their absence. Those really were difficult days. With these thoughts I found peace and assurance from the Lord. Another thing that bothered me, besides getting sick, was the rain. The rain hadn't stopped. I wondered whether the bus would be able to return to Resplendor. I was eager to get home.

On Monday morning the bus started out, but we had traveled only a few miles when it slid into the bar-ditch against the embankment. All the men had to get out and help push the bus back onto the road. We got wet and muddy, but we succeeded. I arrived home that day. How nice to be back in my own bed! About 3 a.m. I awoke with a terrible stomachache. I rolled and turned and moaned and groaned. Leona likes to tell people that I thought I was dying. I don't know why in language school we hadn't been told always to carry stomach medicine. Pastor Hilton helped sick people all the time. I tried to get Leona to call him by phone. She wouldn't because she didn't want to bother him that early. I knew that all the time despite the hour he helped sick people from the country. As I twisted and turned, I begged, but her response was: "Joe, just wait a little longer!" Finally at about 6 a.m. she called Pastor Hilton. He brought some medicine that relieved me. From that time on I always carried medicine for stomach problems.

Chapter 4

Settling into a Busy Routine

*And the Lord said to him: "Who has made man's mouth? Or
who makes him dumb or deaf, or seeing or blind? Is it not I the
Lord? Now then go, and I, even I, will be with your mouth and teach
you what you are to say"* (Ex. 4:11-12).

*Jesus has no others through which He can do His work on earth
Except the redeemed, who have been washed in His blood.
If only this responsibility all the redeemed understood!*

*Salvation is about more than most Christians want to understand.
Some don't read their Bibles, give testimonies, or do
what Jesus commands.
The mysteries and wonders of God in the world today
are not noticed because God cannot have His way.*

After a year of formal language study in Campinas Leona and I
were supposed to continue studying the language on our field of service. Only a short time passed before we were so busy, we didn't take
time to study Portuguese. Then I had an experience that emphasized
the value of continuing to learn Portuguese.

Two or three months after we arrived in Governador Valadares,
we drove into Belo Horizonte for a mission-station meeting. The station was made up of all the missionaries working in Minas Gerais.
Most of the missionaries lived in Belo, so most of the station meet-

ings were held there. We went to Belo Horizonte on Friday and returned on Monday afternoon. The next day I was supposed to return to Belo Horizonte and preach for a church in the citywide evangelistic crusade. By the time we arrived in Governador Valadares on Monday I was so tired, I knew I wouldn't be in condition to drive six hours back on Tuesday and still preach that night. Besides that Leona needed the car. As soon as we arrived in Governador Valadares. I called the airline office to get a passage on the plane the next morning for Belo Horizonte. The woman talked about some bankers and said that the flight was full. I told her that if a cancellation was made, I would appreciate her notifying me.

Early the next morning the airline ticket agent called. She went into detail about some bankers, but I just tuned her out. After all, what did bankers have to do with my plane ticket? She assured me that I would have a seat on the plane but chattered on about things I didn't see involved me. When she finished, she asked whether I still wanted the empty seat. I said *yes*! She asked whether I wanted to drive to the airport or go in the company Volkswagen mini-bus. The Valadares air strip was being paved, so passengers had to go north on the Rio-Bahia Highway for about 50 miles to the closest airstrip. I didn't want Leona to drive by herself on the Rio-Bahia Highway with its many potholes, so I told her I wanted to go in the minibus. About 7 a.m. Leona took me to the airlines office.

When I got into the old minibus van, I noticed the back seat had been removed. I sat on the far left side of the second seat. To my surprise the driver took off with just me. I was really puzzled when we went to the police station where two soldiers (policemen) got in the seat beside me. One had a submachine gun and the other had a pistol. Now I began to understand why the woman at the airlines was carefully trying to explain things, but I didn't pay enough attention. I sensed something strange about to happen.

The next stop was at the Bank of Brazil in downtown Valadares. The driver backed the Volkswagen up close to the door of the bank. Officials were ready to transfer five big square duffle bags and a half-size bag into the back of the van. That explained why the seat had been removed. Some pedestrians gathered around to observe this early morning transfer of money from the bank into the van. The police officers sat down again by me. Two bankers took the front seat with the driver. We were on our way to the airplane.

After we had left the city, I noticed many side roads entering the Rio-Bahia Highway. Some were from the dense forest. I began to get a little nervous as the van rattled along the highway. The old van didn't go very fast—not more than 50-miles an hour. I thought about how easily thieves could force this van off onto one of the side roads. Finally I said to the officers: "Do you always take money to the airplane like this?" The man next to me laughed, as if he could tell by my voice that I was perplexed and afraid. "We don't have a problem in Brazil with hijackers or bank robbers. Relax!" I thought to myself: "Why then are you two police officers going with the money?" When we arrived at the airstrip, the plane was waiting. I boarded the DC 3 plane with the bankers and police officers. When we arrived in Belo Horizonte, however, officers were everywhere to see the money transferred from the plane to the waiting vehicle.

Up to this time I hadn't seen an armored car in Brazil. But only a few months after this happened, the communist guerrillas kidnapped the American Ambassador in Rio and held him for ransom. Then the guerrillas began robbing the banks. Soon after this, guards were hired to stand at the doorways of the banks and the government started to provide armored cars. Forty-two years later this precaution still is practiced. From this experience I realized the importance to continue learning Portuguese. If I had known the language better, I would have understood more about the plane flight on which I was booked.

In my busy schedule I was neglecting my second year of language study. *Dona* Ideir, an English teacher and friend, had helped me mainly by correcting my sermons in Portuguese, but I took more advantage to study more Portuguese.

Fifth Baptist Church Experiences

Fifth Baptist Church was going well. I don't know how they put up with my heavy accented Portuguese. The people were very patient as I struggled with the language; they loved Leona and the kids. Each Sunday afternoon we had an open-air evangelistic service in a church member's yard. Neighbors were invited. I sometimes played my trumpet and Leona played the accordion. Somehow the people understood enough to make decisions for Christ.

In the winter hazy clouds covered the sky until 9 a.m.; then suddenly the sky would clear. The rest of the day would be warm, but the nights were chilly. Even in the winter the temperature normally reached about 80 degrees during the day. The rainy season was during the summer, but without the clouds or rain the sun was blazing hot and the humidity was high. Sunday afternoons during the open-air services we would just about melt in the heat. Just sitting and doing nothing the sweat would run down my legs.

The bankers and most men store clerks wore suits to work. If important people wore suits, why not the pastors? All pastors wore suits even to go to town. A few of the churches had ceiling or wall fans, but for the first year Fifth Baptist Church didn't even have electricity. During the services we just about melted.

Most of the Baptist churches had good choirs; our church was no exception. Joao Leite was the choir director. Leona played the accordion for the congregational singing, but the choir sang *a capella*. He would give the bass their tone, then the tenors, the altos, and finally the sopranos. Then he would stand before the choir and lift his hands; the choir began singing in beautiful harmony. I was amazed. I sang in our high-school choir, university choir, men's glee club, and the seminary choir. I directed the choir at East Oakland Baptist Church and also at Porterville until I trained another man to lead the music. I was trained to sing with perfection and with sophistication. Well, the Fifth Baptist Church choir didn't sing with sophistication, but the harmony was beautiful. I appreciated the choir members very much, because they sang from their hearts without any intimidation about making mistakes. They blessed my heart!

One night after I had started the message, a huge black tarantula entered the back door. Remember, we only had two oil lanterns — one in the middle and one positioned right over the pulpit. The light from the lantern glowed brighter on my sermon notes and in front of the pulpit. That tarantula, about the size of my hand, finally arrived near the pulpit and turned toward the choir to the right of the pulpit. I realized we would have panic when it reached the women on the first row of the choir, so I ended the message. One of the men killed the tarantula and things settled down again, but the service ended.

In all of the smaller churches and most homes, the rafters are visible, since these buildings don't have ceilings. White lizards commonly played around the rafters as they looked for mosquitoes or other bugs. These lizards were often entertainment for children that were not paying attention to the sermon. When I was not preaching, I even occasionally watched those little fellows hunt for their dinner. One night we even had an owl in the rafters.

John Leite, our song leader, was a bricklayer. One day he became deathly ill with a bad case of tetanus from stepping on a rusty nail. I was called to his home to take him to the hospital. We were thankful that God spared his life; I later took him back home. One of John's little daughters suffered a trauma when I took her daddy away; for a long time she would cry when she saw the car or me. Only after months passed did she let me get close to her. She identified me with the man that had taken her daddy away. Many times we were called to take church members to a doctor or to the hospital, because none of them had a car. When they became too sick to go by the city bus, they called us. This also was the case with other people in town.

Fifth Baptist Church not only was strategically located on the main *praca* of the neighborhood, but also west of the highway and railroad was an area designated for the future Industrial Park. At this point the airport was the only thing in the park area. We needed more property for the church to grow with the needs of the neighborhood. Two vacant lots were on the left of our church and extended to the street. Since a *praca* eventually would be in front of our church, this meant that the nightlife of the community would be on that *praca*. A bar already existed on the right; we didn't want one on the left. We had to have the other two lots. At a Wednesday-night prayer meeting I asked the church to start praying about buying those two lots. One of the deacons knew the rancher that owned them, so on Monday we drove out to the rancher's house. Since we arrived about noon, he invited us to eat with the family. We asked him whether he would sell the lots to us. His reply was: "In no way will I sell the lots; I have plans for those lots." He was friendly, although he was not a religious man.

On Wednesday night we prayed that the man would change his mind. The whole church was praying about the lots. Early Monday morning, one week after we had visited the man, we heard a vigorous clapping at our front gate before I even was out of bed. Clapping is the custom rather than entering a yard and knocking at the door or ringing the doorbell. In 1966 very few houses had doorbells. I dressed and went to the front gate. To my surprise the visitor was the rancher. He was ready to sell the lots.

Why should I have been surprised? We had prayed; where was my faith? Jesus said: *"Therefore I say to you, all things for which you pray and ask, believe that you have received them, and they will be granted you"* (Mark 11:24). I guess I was surprised the man had changed his mind so quickly. I did believe that only God could change the rancher's mind. We didn't even have enough money to buy the lots, but God was performing one of His wonders. Now we had to arrange some money. God was beginning to teach me that a person is blessed more through giving than receiving. Along with the other members we had to dig deeper into our pockets.

When I accepted the invitation to be pastor of the church, I had a goal to teach the members to prepare a church budget. I proposed that they put an amount in the budget for my salary. This would prepare them to have money for a pastor when I left. Wages were determined by minimum salaries. A minimum salary in *cruzeiros* was equivalent to $35 a month. Many Brazilian pastors lived on two or three minimum salaries, which was equivalent to $70 to $105. Our church could pay only one minimum salary for a pastor—the equivalent of $35 a month I put into the building fund. We put the rest of our tithe into a special fund which later was spent for church construction or for buying properties.

Around the House

Joaquin, the grounds caretaker, and Maria Carvalho lived at the back of our house. When Charlotte was only 2-years old, Maria taught Charlotte to enjoy coffee. Maria Roberta, our maid, was dating Maria Carvalho's brother, Amavel, which means "lovable". Amavel and his mother, Josefa, lived across the street from us. All were Catholics and very poor. We took Maria Roberta to church with us; Leona lead Maria Roberta to Christ.

One day Amavel told us his sister, who lived on the Morro de

Carapina, had died in childbirth. Her death probably was from improper care after the birth. Morro de Carapina was a high hill almost in downtown Valadares. The whole hill was a slum area. We took our maid Maria, Joaquin and Maria Carvalho, Amavel, and his mother Josefa to the shanty home on the Morro de Carapina. The hill was so steep that our Rural Willys had difficulty getting to the top. The dirt streets were so narrow that the car had difficulty making the turns at the corners of the blocks. Once we got to their house, we blocked the street. The black open sewage ditches gave off a horrible odor. Scrawny dogs lounged around everywhere. The flies were terrible. These shocking scenes were sad to see. Amavel's sister and *Dona* Josefa's daughter was young and had left a new baby. To add to their sadness they didn't have money to pay the priest or for a funeral mass, so the priest refused to visit them at their house. The tiny room was crowded and the casket took up most of the room. Those who couldn't get into the room stood outside. As was the custom friends brought fresh flowers to cover the space around the body. The sweet smell of the flowers in the small, low-roofed room in about 100-degree heat was so stifling that I felt sick.

I had to make an effort to comfort those people. What can one say when the soul of the person certainly wasn't prepared to die? I read a passage in the Bible and prayed for the family members. Then the casket lid was screwed tight; some strong men lifted it up to take it to our vehicle. The door of the house was too narrow for the already narrow casket to enter, so they turned it on its side. The casket was the cheapest made. I saw that it didn't have a solid board bottom, only narrow slats, so I could see the body of the deceased. Only a few friends went to the cemetery because they didn't have transportation. Our car was the hearse; I took all of the family members that I could. The fact that we did this without any pay made an impression on the family.

That night Amavel received word that his grandmother, *Dona* Josefa's mother, had died also in the town of Divinolandia about the same time as her granddaughter had in Valadares. Early the next morning I left for Divinolandia with Joaquin and Maria Carvalho, our maid, Amavel, and his mother. I hoped to arrive in time for the funeral. I had not been on that mountainous dirt road before. Probably the funeral would be before noon, because the body needed to be buried within 24 hours. I drove as fast as possible but didn't arrive until nearly noon. The family members had returned home from the cemetery. I was presented to the other family members and given the opportunity to read the Bible and pray for them. In those days they didn't have antiperspirant deodorant in Brazil. I used the regular deodorant; it didn't help me for long either. The poorer people didn't have money to buy these extras, so on hot days perspiring bodies produced a terrible odor. I was invited to remain in the house, but they really didn't have room for everyone, so I chose to sit on the front-door steps where I was cooler and the air was fresher. They served me rice covered with black beans and a type of homemade weenie. The house was right on the road on the outskirts of the village, so it got covered with dust by an occasional passing vehicle. I prayed for the family members as they visited and mourned in desperation. Frequently I heard interruptions of wailing. Double sorrow had stricken the family. Some of the relatives around the village hadn't heard about the death in Valadares. The family had decided to have the priest perform the High Mass for the grandmother's funeral, the most expensive mass the Catholic Church administered. The saddest part was their discussion about the cost of the high mass and their dilemma of how they were going to pay for it.

During the months that followed, Maria Roberta's three sisters from the country visited in Valadares for a few days. Leona led them to Christ. Maria Roberta and Amavel made their plans for marriage. They planned to adopt the baby of Amavel's sister that had died. Before they were married, however, the baby died. Leona took some of the family to the home in the *favela* and conducted a little service. Then she took the family and casket with the baby to the cemetery. This act of love touched the heart of the husband/father. The next day he called and said that he wanted to go to church with us the next Sunday.

About this time I talked to Joaquin Carvalho, who lived at the back of our house; he accepted Christ. We knew that his wife Maria Carvalho would be the toughest to win, because she was the most devout Catholic of all of them. Every day at noon and every evening at 6 she turned the radio up loud so everyone could hear the *Ave Maria*. A few nights later Amavel arrived to talk to me; he too accepted Christ. Two Sundays later, Amavel and Santos, who had lost his wife and baby, both made their decisions public in our church. Both men were exceedingly happy.

Maria Carvalho, however, became very bitter toward all those who had trusted the Lord. She wouldn't speak to them or to us. You remember she was the one that loved Charlotte and gave her milk/coffee each morning. *Dona* Josefa, Amavel's mother, was a little bitter also. But seven souls had been won to the Lord Jesus Christ. The family insisted that Maria Roberta and Amavel's wedding be at the Catholic Church to please both families. Maria Roberta rented a pretty wedding gown. Our family went to the wedding and arrived a little early. Couples getting married were lined up outside the church waiting, as the weddings were scheduled one after the other. The two couples getting married before Maria and Amavel had flowers, music, and several minutes of words from the priest. But all of the flowers were removed before Amavel and Maria, without music, were allowed to enter the church. The priest took about two minutes and their wedding was over. I don't know how much they paid, but I learned that in the Catholic Church one pays for everything he or she gets.

Organizing Work in the City

After a few months four of the churches in the city had pastors. These churches didn't seem to do anything together. One reason was the ill feeling toward Pastor Hilton of First Baptist Church. Pastor Hilton had been the organizer and head of a shirt-factory board. Several Christians bought stocks to form a company for the purpose of furnishing jobs for Evangelicals. This company had built a large building and bought many old machines for making material. Things never went well; only a few sacks were made for rice and other cereals. A lot of disappointment over the failure of the company existed, for it never fulfilled the purpose for which the shareholders had dreamed; they distrusted Pastor Hilton.

Pastor Hilton was a very talented and unusual person. When he was young, he had been a spiritist medium. After he was converted, he felt called to the ministry and went to the seminary. He was a musician and a superb preacher and knew a lot about construction and medicine. Sick people, mostly Baptists, from all around the area sought his medical help because he didn't charge. He was not a faith-healer but was able to prescribe medicine correctly for many illnesses. Many of the pharmacists would accept his prescriptions for the poor people. This got him into trouble with females over some of his medical help. This was another reason some people in the churches weren't very eager to do things together with First Baptist Church. But Pastor Hilton, his wife Mibzar, and children were very good to us and we loved them.

In a different Baptist church each month I organized citywide monthly youth rallies; these were as well-attended by adults as they were by youth. We had music, devotionals, sermons, and fellowship. Through these meetings during the following years I was able to get the churches together for other things. We had yearly speaker tournaments for the youth. The winners were given spiritual books. We also promoted a youth banquet every year on Sweetheart's Day in June with special speakers; many adults attended, too.

A year after we had been in Valadares, another Baptist church, the sixth, was ready to organize. The people named the church Esperanca (Hope) Baptist and called me to be their pastor. I finally agreed to give them one Sunday a month for a year, since Fifth Baptist Church was doing pretty well. Esperanca Baptist Church was organized from a group of 80 members that left Central Baptist Church. They bought two strategic lots on the north end of the main street. They had capable leadership and were well-organized to work on their own. My main responsibilities were to direct the Lord's Supper ordinance, baptize converts, visit their preaching point on one Sunday afternoon, perform weddings, and conduct funerals.

The last day we served this church was in December just before leaving on our first furlough. Esperanca Baptist Church gave each of us, including our children, a present in thanks for our work. The custom is to open the presents when they are given. My present was black cloth material. I'm sure I had a puzzled look on my face, because I couldn't understand why black cloth material; if this gift were for Leona, I could understand, but what would I need with black cloth? I thanked them, but I was puzzled and confused. After the service I was told that the material was to have a tailored suit made. Yes! I knew tailors were abundant in Valadares, but I never dreamed of having a suit made. I remembered I hadn't seen any ready-made suits anywhere. Seeing me so puzzled over the gift, the deacons brought me a nice travel clock with an engraving on it from Esperanca Baptist Church. I have apologized to them several times over the years for my embarrassing mistake. This incident became our joke. When we left Brazil, some 35 years later, one of the men from that church (a youth when I was his pastor) helped present me with a gift from the Minas Gerais Baptist Men. This time a ready-made suit was given to me. The men from Esperanca Baptist Church explained to the crowd why a suit was chosen for me as my "leaving Brazil gift". We had another good laugh about my embarrassing mistake years earlier.

Understanding Brazilian Culture

While I was pastor of Fifth Baptist Church, I believed the church ought to start a new mission work. The church chose to open a preaching point in the village of Baguari, about five miles from our church on the Belo Horizonte highway and also by the edge of the Sweet River. For several months we had rented the largest room of a house from a family. This room served as our preaching point. The family members decided to move to the State of Parana and were willing to sell us their old house. Many field workers and villagers from the North and also from our state were moving to find work in São Paulo, Rio de Janeiro, Brasilia, and Parana. Parana, south of São Paulo, was clearing millions of acres of land for coffee.

The largest room was used only for their shrine and storage of liquor bottles. Their stash of liquor and bottles covered with dust and cobwebs were on shelves on one side of the room. The shrine covered one end of the room; it was made up of images of various saints, pictures, and holy day fetishes. They took the bottles and religious fetishes; from the shelves we made benches without backs. I asked the mission for $1,000 from the Strategic Mission Fund to buy the house and lot. The money soon was in the bank; the man of the house made arrangements for a truck to move them to Parana. We set a date to meet at the county abstract and recording office to close the deal. At the county office an official explained that I was to get a deed for the house but not a deed for the land. I hadn't understood that I wouldn't get a deed for the lot. I don't think the owner had mentioned that. Counties in that area just didn't give deeds for the land in the villages; I guess the people understood that. Under that situation I couldn't buy the property, because the Foreign Mission Board required a deed to the land. I had to back out of the deal; the man was furious. He had the right to be furious because he already had made arrangements for the truck to move his family members and his furniture to Parana on Monday; he needed the money. I really felt deeply for the man. This misunderstanding happened on Friday. Early Saturday morning Joao Venancio rode his bicycle from Santa Rita to our house to warn me to be careful because the man said he was going to kill me. The beginning of the first mission was exciting, but the consequence was a wake-up experience to a different culture. I had heard that people often were shot for similar misunderstandings. I certainly didn't go out to Baguari but turned the matter over to the Lord. This happened just before we left Brazil on our first furlough.

Exciting Experiences

We didn't have a baptistery in Fifth Baptist Church, so I baptized in the Sweet River. The Sweet River was muddy all but about two months out of the year. I had never baptized in a river before but thought this opportunity would be neat. I knew we had to be careful about getting in rivers in which water didn't continually flow because of the problem of Schistosomiases, a severe endemic disease for people in much of Asia, Africa, and South America. The disease was common and caused blood loss and tissue damage.

When he was only 6, Carl asked us about accepting the Lord, but we were afraid he didn't understand. The Holy Spirit was dealing with him. We talked and prayed with him; he prayed to receive Jesus. In a revival at Fifth Baptist Church, led by Samuel de Souza Leite from Aimores, Carl, along with 46 others, made public his decision for Christ. Before they were baptized, converts had to go through a doctrinal class that lasted about three months. When Carl was 7, I was thrilled to be able to baptize him in the muddy Sweet River!

One day we were driving along the Sweet River on the outskirts of Governador Valadares when our observant Jonathan asked this question: "Mom, Dad, where is the sugar that makes the river sweet?

Is it at the bottom?' I don't know why the river was named *Rio Doce* (*Sweet River*), but that is the name and the muddy water wasn't sweet.

The Richardsons visited us soon after we had settled into our home in Valadares. Their son, Tim, was older, but sons Curtis and Phillip were close to Carl and Jonathan's ages. Their Jonathan (Jon Jon) was 5-months older than Charlotte. They had a Rural Willys Jeep just like the one we had. We decided we would go to the top of Ibituruna mountain. This mountain is 3,429-feet high, more than 3,000-feet higher than Governador Valadares. We didn't get very far up the mountain, because neither car had four-wheel drive or the power to climb any further. The sharp turns were treacherous; the road was narrow. On one side was a gully made by the rain. Once an automobile reaches the steepest part, turning around is impossible! We hadn't arrived at the "no-turning-back" area when we realized the cars couldn't make it. Bill was maneuvering his vehicle backward carefully to turn around but accidently backed into the gully. With Bill inside and everyone pushing, we got the car out and turned around. Some years later we tried that climb by way of a different road and made it to the top in the Volkswagen bug.

Governador Valadares was in the center of the precious and semi-precious gem industry. In Teofoli Otoni, 80-miles north on the Rio-Bahia Highway, a visitor, especially Americans, would be surrounded by gemstone street dealers as soon as he got out of his car. Once cornered, the visitor had difficulty getting away, for the street peddlers believed that Americans were loaded with money. Street peddlers in Governador Valadares were not as much of a nuisance. In both cities lapidaries were abundant. Watching the lapidary process from a rough gemstone to a polished jewel is interesting. While we were living in Campinas, I bought Leona an amethyst stone and had it set in a ring. When I saw the better amethysts in Valadares, I was ashamed of what I had given Leona. Before we moved to Valadares, we never had been exposed to gemstones, so we knew very little about them. We met a few men that owned or worked in lapidaries in Valadares. I soon bought Leona a beautiful amethyst stone and had it mounted into a gold ring.

Occasionally a missionary family from North Brazil would go to Rio de Janeiro or vice versa and stop to stay with us. We always enjoyed these visits. The tourists usually were interested in looking at some stones, so we would take them to some of the people we knew. These people would show them the whole process of cutting and polishing stones and also would sell stones at a good price. We made friends with an Egyptian Jew that had fled Egypt after the Suez Canal exchanged hands from the British to the Egyptians. He had been a pharmacist, but soon after arriving in Brazil he got into the stone business. His lapidary was in Valadares, but his main sales point was in Rio de Janeiro. I have seen piles of stones on his tables: garnets, amethysts, aquamarines, yellow topaz, blue topaz, green and rose tourmalines, and others. We were always amazed at the beautiful things God had hidden in the ground! Some lapidaries had enormous, ugly black rocks that hid a beautiful wonder of God inside. When split open the rocks were partially hollow but the inside walls had gorgeous facets of amethysts, as if the facets had been shaped by tools of God. Living in Governador Valadares gave me the opportunity to see another part of God's marvels to which I might never have been exposed so clearly anywhere else in the world.

The poverty still bothered me greatly. Seeing the sickness, disease, and hunger made me feel so blessed that I had been born in America. Baptists were reaching mostly the poorer people; this was very good, but we didn't have members with means to help the poor and dying. For instance in all of the 48 churches in the whole Sweet River Valley, only four or five Baptist churches could afford a used Rural Willys or Volkswagen Kombi for their pastors and less than a dozen laypeople had a vehicle. But God was doing marvels; He was at work!

Moving to a Mission-Owned House

When our year contract on the rented house was up, we found a house on the Island do Araujo for the South Brazil mission to buy for us. The house was high in the front and tapered off gradually to the back. The house had three sections: a long hall in the center that ran the length of the house, three bedrooms and two baths on the right side of the hall, and a living room, breakfast room, and kitchen on the left side. These two side sections had ceilings, but the hall had no ceiling. The hall—the walls as well as the roof—was painted a barnyard red. The roof was made of long panels of fragile, asbestos-like material that was similar to tin roofing. We discovered the roof had a leaking problem.

The property was two lots—the house was situated on one and the other lot was yard except for the garage and a chicken pen. The front yard had two young coconut trees, a flamboyant tree that produced brilliant red blooms, three acacia trees that produced beautiful yellow blooms, and another large tree in the front yard. I don't know the name of the large tree, but from time to time people would request a small amount of bark to make medicine. The back yard was blessed with a guava tree, a huge *caja mango* tree, two papaya trees, and a fig bush. Our kids had a yard large enough to play. We bought a strong swing set made out of iron pipe with a double swinging chair, regular swing, and a swinging seesaw. I had the idea of building a tree house in the huge *caja mango* tree, but I got only the platform built, which was enough. Our yard was open to the neighbor kids and friends at church. All Brazilian cities and towns had neighborhood parks, but none had playground equipment, so our yard was a popular spot.

Moving into a mission-owned house made a great difference to us. Living in rented property has an unsettled effect on life. The possibility of having to move often is discouraging. Rent usually was expensive. For about $1,000 the mission bought a telephone, when one was available, for the missionary. At this point the telephone system was not good in Brazil. When we placed a call to Belo Horizonte, our capital city, the telephone operator always said: "That will be a six-hour delay!" The problem to call overseas was greater still and was expensive, so we never called to the U.S.

The Bible Institute in Governador Valadares
At the first Sweet River Valley associational meeting I attended in Mutum, the association approved the beginning of a Bible institute in Valadares. The institute was needed to train lay preachers who never would have the opportunity to go to a seminary. Dr. Bill Richardson, heading up the state department of religious education, was the key founder of this institute. Bill had to hastily recruit writers for first year's Bible institute studies. Courses on religious education, social work, and arts and crafts for children were planned for the women.

The women also could take the courses on Bible studies. The classes ran for eight hours a day, five days a week for a month. Eleven students enrolled for the first year of the four-year program. The out-of-town students stayed at First Baptist Church and slept in the class-rooms. I taught the class on general Sunday-school organization and another on church organizations. For the women Leona taught a class on religious education for younger preschool. Bill asked each of us to prepare the syllabus for the class we taught. This was a real chore with our limited use of the language. In the following years we both helped prepare other syllabi that we used in teaching.

My Trumpet and a Clown
One Sunday morning I visited the Baptist church in Lajinha. That afternoon a group of us went to a church in a small town about an hour's drive away. This church was celebrating its anniversary. We had planned an open-air service and a special night service. We set up our loudspeaker; a woman was ready to play the accordion and a youth the guitar for singing the hymns. We were surprised that so few were at this normally popular gathering place in the village. We could see a circus tent in the distance, but no one was milling around the place in which open-air services were usually held. Then on the street to our left we heard screaming and yelling in the distance. As the noise drew nearer, we could see a clown walking on stilts. A mob of children, youth, and adults were poking fun at him; he interacted to their remarks by his own funny personality.

How could an open-air evangelistic service be held that afternoon with that clown in the area? As he passed us, someone in the group said: "Joe, play your trumpet". I began playing my trumpet. Behold, many in the group stopped to listen to me and left the clown wandering down the street. If this wasn't the work of the Holy Spirit, how else could one explain this abrupt change in the crowd? We had a good service; two men accepted Christ as their Savior.

About dark everyone gathered for the church's anniversary cele-bration. During the song service a drunk man interrupted the singing by yelling, "*Quero ouvir o alemao*" (I want to hear the German)! He repeated this loudly over and over again and caused an atmosphere of agitation among the congregation. After a while he changed his phrase to: "I'm here to hear the German", which he uttered in a garbled drunken state. He was talking about me! This surprised me, because this was the first time anyone had thought I was German. Several thought I was Japanese, because I was short and my eyes a little squinted. The visiting pastors, including Pastor Waldemar Vaz, finally ushered the man outside because he was disrupting the service.

Annual Mission Meeting

For several years the South Brazil annual mission meeting was in Caxambu, in our own state. The trip took 11 hours of travel time, so we drove to Belo Horizonte and spent a night with the Richardsons and then went on to Caxambu. The South Brazil mission was composed of about 300 missionaries, including the kids. New missionaries had the responsibility of leading Vacation Bible School, so we didn't participate in the morning deliberations. The deliberations of the annual meeting (morning and afternoon) were about opening up new work, approving places in which new missionaries would serve, studying financial allocations for housing, transportation, seminaries, women's educational institution, and the publishing house, and allotments for conventions and properties. The South Brazil mission was made of nine states and the Federal District. Financial requests from these states and their requests for new missionaries were treated. The evenings were worship time, with testimonies, music, and preaching by our own missionaries. We never lacked for special music because we had several talented musicians. One night would be "fun night", in which each state would present something funny. One year for fun night we wore costumes; we had Raggedy Ann and Andy, the Pink Panther, Minnie Pearl, and many more "funny characters".

Everyone, including missionaries, had the problem of picking up parasites and amoebas. One missionary at mission meeting heard two 4-year-old girls talking. One said: "My daddy has amoebas". The other replied: "So does my daddy". Then the first girl said: "I have worms", and the second girl replied, "I think I do, too". The missionaries were required to have medical exams every year. We were glad the FMB insisted on annual exams and provided the funds. We lived in an area in which tuberculosis was common, so we were tested for that disease as well.

Winding Down for Furlough

I probably should have titled this section "winding up for furlough", because the title gives the idea we were slowing down. That was not the case. Our emotions and eagerness to see relatives and friends in the States were in high gear, but the opportunities to do things for the Lord didn't slow down.

As we returned from a Minas mission-station meeting in Belo Horizonte, we had a strange incident. We had left the paved highway at Ipatinga and gone a short distance on the dirt road to Valadares. We neared a side-road intersection at the same time as did a horse and buggy with three people. The man tried to get the horse to stop, but the horse panicked. I suddenly saw the frightened horse but too late to stop. I swerved to the left instantly. The man was pulling back on the reins with all his might. The horse finally stopped with the tongue of the buggy against the door. The people were as frightened as Leona was. The horse had blinds on, but I could see his frightened eyes almost against the right door window where Leona sat. We learned to be cautious on the country roads.

I had requested $2,000 from the strategic property fund to help start the first stage of a two-story building for Fifth Baptist Church. I had an architect draw plans for future building on those three small lots. In the future the first floor would be used for the sanctuary and the second floor for classrooms, but this first small unit at the back of the lot would serve for classrooms below and the top for the worship area. I wanted to start construction on this building when we returned from our first four-month furlough.

One day a member of Fifth Baptist Church wanted me to take a sick woman to a doctor. The sick woman lived in a village a few miles from town. She was very frail. The doctor prescribed glucose intravenously for her. She had no money, so none of the hospitals would take her. She needed help badly and quickly. The pharmacists could sell glucose and administer its procedure in a home, so I took her to our house on the island. For two days she stayed there and received glucose. When she was better, I took her back to the Santa Rita, where her relative lived. I hoped we could win her to Christ and through her win others in her family. We rejoiced that another church member led her to Christ. She was happy and smiling again. However, she was afraid of what the priest might do and that her Catholic friends might cause problems. This poor, uneducated woman died a few days later. The wonderful thing is that a few days before she died, she had a place prepared for her in heaven.

When we were appointed for South Brazil, the furlough schedule was every five years. The FMB changed that policy and in fact put the North and South Brazil missions on the same four-year plan. A year after we were on the field, the "mini-furloughs" were allowed for all missionaries after two years and eight months on the field. The Bill Morgans, Bill Richardsons, and we decided to take a mini-furlough. Having arrived in Brazil together we were eligible for furloughs on the same day. Our plan was to leave Brazil on the same plane and return to Brazil on the same plane.

In those days a lot of paperwork was required to leave Brazil. We had to spend at least three days in Rio de Janeiro for the paperwork to be done. But leaving Valadares wasn't so easy either—not because of paperwork but to leave everything in order, including finding someone to stay in our house. We couldn't leave the house vacant or vandals would strip it of everything of any value. I arranged for the man to continue taking care of the yard while we were gone. Money had to be left for the house bills. I worked out for someone to care for the Fifth and Esperanca Baptist Churches. Documents, medical records of each of us, and a police clearance had to be taken to Rio de Janeiro. We couldn't forget anything.

Preparing for this first furlough we experienced something that turned out to be a pattern for every furlough. Many people arrived on the last day to say goodbye, to bring something, or just to be helpful in some way. Therefore leaving for furlough always was hectic, but we always appreciated our Brazilian brothers' and sisters' concern for us. One cannot wait until the last day to pack! On the last day we received a phone call from the nephew of the gemstone friend. The nephew said his uncle wanted me to drop by the lapidary. I couldn't imagine why, but I hurried to the lapidary. The nephew said, "My uncle wanted to give you some stones in appreciation of you and your family." He handed me a large orange Mexican opal and a beautifully multifaceted pale pink kunzite stone for Leona, two small garnets for Charlotte, and two medium-sized square tourmalines for me. I looked at the nephew and said, "These stones are valuable and we thank you very much. Something exists that is more valuable, however, that God has to give to you as a gift. Through Jesus, eternal salvation is also a gift. You only have to believe with all your heart and mind in Him for eternal salvation and forgiveness. As you give me these as gifts, so God has a precious gift for you, too." Tears welled up in his eyes. Our friendship had been to the point that he called me once for counseling. He, a Jewish boy, was dating a Catholic girl; she was very interested in marrying him. His question was whether to marry her or not. I encouraged him to compare his beliefs with those of Catholicism. This last-minute call to go to the lapidary on a very busy day surprised me, as God often does, and gave me the best chance I had had to witness to the nephew. The uncle was not in town but thought enough of us to remember our departure date and gave some unexpected gifts.

A Sunburn and Snow

We three missionary families had some leisure time while a Brazilian agent (*despachante*) took care of getting our papers ready to leave the country, so we all went to Copacabana beach. Because of an overcast sky the weather was unusually cool for December. The water was so cold that it chilled us to the bone, so we just lay around on the beach. This was the middle of summer in Brazil and normally was very hot. I wasn't on the beach more than an hour, but I got the worst sunburn of my life. I didn't realize a hazy sky was so dangerous. Leona seems to have fairer skin than I do, but I always burn worse than she does. By nighttime I was miserable—so miserable I couldn't sleep. The next night we left for the U.S. All the way home I felt as though I still was cooking from the sunburn. When we arrived at Clovis, NM, airport late the next day, snow was on the ground, but I was red as a beet from my sunburn. On Christmas Day I was peeling!

Chapter 5

A Missionary Wife's View

Life with Jesus is wonderful and everything but a disaster,
When dedicated willfully to Him our beloved Master
For spreading over this world His redemptive Plan
And glorify Jesus as best as you can.

I'm amazed how God has a place for every child, woman,
and man—
How important it is for everyone in his or her place to stand.
The local church is a mystery of the fellowship of the Redeemed,
But when only a third are active, churches accomplish less than
Jesus dreamed.

"I give you all power in heaven and on earth,"
Jesus said to the believers of his beloved Church.
Just one dedicated person has often caused me to wonder,
And this is amazing: what God has done with a larger
dedicated number!

When we arrived in Campinas, Brazil, we stayed for two weeks in the homes of two different missionaries. If you add those two weeks to the two weeks on the ship, needless to say we were so excited to get into our own house. We were tired of living out of suitcases. We had a nice house that was owned by a Presbyterian pastor. Even so, the differences in Brazilian customs were challenges to which we needed to become accustomed. The kitchen had almost no cabinets or counter space. The space under the sink was open and had no shelves. The house was chosen for us because it was only two blocks from language school and three blocks from the medical clinic.

Antonia had been hired to work for us. She was a very jolly lady and had experience working for Americans. With our having three small children (Carl was 5, Jonathan was 3, and Charlotte was 3-months old), having a helper that loved children was wonderful. When we left the ship, we were given about a month's supply of bottled baby food that had been bought for Charlotte. That was very helpful to get us started, for I soon found that the bottled baby food wasn't fresh because of the price. Most Brazilians made their own baby food, so I learned from Antonia how to make Charlotte's food in the blender. I had many new customs to learn.

One thing I learned to appreciate about Brazilian houses was the washing tank in the service area. This tank had a rub board front of porcelain or cement, so one could rub dirty spots before the clothes went into the washing machine. The area next to the tank was large enough for the washing machine, even though at the time very few Brazilians had washing machines. Without a washing machine they washed everything by hand in the tank in cold water, as most houses didn't have a hot-water tank. Only a cold-water faucet existed for the washing machine. Antonia was very good about spot-washing the shirt collars, cuffs, and other extra dirty spots before she placed them into the washing machine. The soap was proper for washing in cold water; the clothes were amazingly clean. At the last minute we bought a clothes dryer to be put in our crate before we left the United States. Since dryers weren't sold in Brazil yet, the houses weren't wired for 220 volts, nor was space provided for a dryer. We set the dryer in the garage and ran it with 110 volts during that year only to dry the diapers. The sun helps kill germs in diapers, so I used the dryer only on rainy days. In 1965 disposable diapers were unheard of in Brazil. Antonia ironed all the washing except the towels. I was so surprised at her ironing the diapers. I told our doctor and he explained that since we washed everything in cold water, the heat of the iron would kill any germs that still remained. We were blessed to have doctors that could speak English. Earlier we mentioned that the medical clinic was started by two brothers who were sons of Presbyterian missionaries.

94

For me to accept the lizards crawling on the ceilings took a while. I wasn't afraid of them, but I was afraid they would fall on me. One night one was on the ceiling over our bed. I told Joe I couldn't lie down with the lizard over my head. The poor thing didn't have a chance when Joe got after him with a broom. In time I realized they weren't going to fall, as God had given them the ability to stick to the ceiling. They were great to eat the mosquitoes and other small flying things. I learned to appreciate them.

The men studied at the language school in the mornings and the women studied in the afternoons. That gave me an opportunity to be with the children in the mornings. In the afternoons Antonia kept Charlotte and Joe would walk the boys to a nursery school where several other young MK's (missionary kids) attended.

Brazilians purchase bread fresh every morning to go with a cup of hot milk with coffee. For many, that is all they have for breakfast. Even children received enough coffee in the milk to make the drink turn a light brown. Some have a slice of cheese and some fruit.

Antonia was a good cook. All food had to be prepared from scratch, as canned foods were almost unknown. Buying groceries was a real challenge. We bought meat at the meat market, bread from the bakery, and fresh vegetables and eggs at the street market that was in our area every Friday. That meant that if you wanted green beans for dinner, you bought them fresh, washed, snapped, and then cooked them, which is true there even until today. Even today very few canned vegetables are on the market. Meals were more time-consuming to prepare but were more delicious and nourishing.

We discovered a grocery store in which the owners were from South Africa and spoke English. They also delivered our groceries in their car, which was an added help. If we bought at other stores, we had to carry the groceries in a shopping bag on the streetcar, bus, or taxi. Needless to say, since we had to carry them, we didn't buy many things at a time. The aisles in the stories were narrow; even though the carts were small, we had to be very careful. One day Carl was pushing my cart; as he made the curve at the end of the row of shelves, the cart hit the fancy arrangement of liquor bottles. Some fell; one was broken. We were so embarrassed, but to make matters worse, the store wanted us to pay for the broken bottle. I used my limited Portuguese to explain that the accident was the store's fault because it had made a pyramid of bottles on the end of the row.

The first year was difficult in some aspects, but on the other hand we enjoyed the fellowship with other missionary colleagues. Telling Antonia goodbye was difficult. She had been very dear to us. She was a widow and had one small child. We explained the plan of salvation and she accepted the Lord. That was a joy to us. We visited her once when we returned to Campinas for a visit.

Living in Governador Valadares

Getting into our new home in Governador Valadares was exciting for all of us. The house was very big, so we had space for everything and then some. Our maid, Maria Roberta, lived in a small house beside us, so she was always available to help. Most maids were expected to work on Sunday to at least prepare the noon meal. She was Catholic, but on Sundays she sometimes would go to church with us because I didn't want her working on Sunday. She did help prepare lunch on Sunday since she always ate with us. She was very good with Charlotte and also a very good cook.

When we wanted chicken, we had to buy a live one. The maid killed and cleaned the chicken. She was very good at this; we enjoyed fried chicken and the new ways she knew to fix it. When she killed the chicken, she would put a bowl under the throat to catch the blood. As the blood cooled, it would gel and was considered a delicacy to fry. The dish looked like fried liver. I had told her that if she wanted the blood, that was OK but not to serve it to us. I also told her she could have the feet and head. One day when we had a missionary colleague with us, this "new delicacy" was on the platter. I inquired about the strange dish; Maria said it was blood. This liberty she had taken upset me, but then I had to remember that she considered this a delicacy. I am sure they at times thought our ways were strange.

Joe soon began his duties as pastor of Fifth Baptist Church, which was situated in a new neighborhood on the outskirts of town. Since the neighborhood was new, no water or sewer system existed, so no running water was in the church or in the homes. Also only a few electric lines existed. Every home and church had a private well. Fifth Baptist Church had a hand pump over the well to draw water. I was careful to boil our drinking water at home, especially for Charlotte since she was less than 2-years old. To give Charlotte boiled water at home and then allow her to drink filtered water in the homes seemed foolish, so I quit boiling it. We loved the people and were loved by them.

The front yard of our home had a sidewalk between the bushes and flowers; it was wide enough for Charlotte to ride her tricycle. One particular bush had beautiful, tiny red peppers. These red peppers attracted Charlotte's attention, so she picked one to eat. Suddenly Maria and I heard a shrill cry of woe and torment. Wondering what could have caused such a terrible cry, we ran out the front door. Maria smelled the pepper and knew at once that Charlotte had picked one of the hot peppers from the bush. The maid knew a solution—fresh orange juice—to diminish the pain. That did the job.

Across the street from our house was a lot with several one-room houses. These people were very poor and most were young couples with small children. Small boys did not wear any clothes, not even a diaper in the summertime, but little girls always had to be dressed. This was a custom we had to accept. I was worried that someday I would find a baby abandoned on our front porch.

Difficulties with the Language

The house we rented in Governador Valadares had three bath-rooms—one in each bedroom. One had a bathtub in place of a shower. The tub was good to give Charlotte a bath, except it didn't have a stopper for the drain; neither did any of the drains have stoppers. So about two weeks after we arrived, I resolved to buy some rubber stoppers for the bathroom sinks and tub. I went to the stores that sold kitchen and bathroom supplies and in my best Portuguese asked a salesperson, "*Quero um pneu para a pia.*" I thought I was asking for a rubber stopper for a sink. The salesperson politely replied that this store didn't have them, but I could find them at a certain store on another street. I went to the store he indicated and asked the same question. That salesperson said, "We don't carry them, but you can find them at another certain store." This went on at several stores until I was very frustrated and tired. Finally one store had all the bathroom fixtures displayed together; the sink had a stopper in it. I tried to buy the stopper, but the man said, "No, that goes with the sink." He did tell me the correct location and name of the store to find what I wanted, but by this hour the stores were closing. I had spent about three hours and went home empty-handed. Almost in tears, I told the maid what had happened. The maid laughed and said, "Leona, you were asking for a *tire* for a sink instead of stopper. You find stoppers for sinks at the rubber store." The word *pneu* means tire and not *rubber*. I had seen billboard signs advertising tires and confused the word *pneu* (a rubber tire) for anything made of rubber. Cities have stores that specialize only in certain products. I could find the rubber stopper in one that sold only rubber products. The next day I went to the rubber store and bought several rubber sink and tub stoppers. One thing for sure, I gave several a good laugh for the day. I never forgot the name for a tire or a sink stopper.

The Potter

Down the street from our house was the potter's house and workshop. We met the potter's family members in Fourth Baptist Church; they invited us to visit in their home. This gave us an opportunity to actually see him working with a potter's wheel. As he turned the wheel with his feet, he explained about the preparation of the clay and showed us the making of a jar. We were amazed at the ease with which he took the block of clay and began gently shaping the sides upward until the shape was what he wanted. The most common water jugs in the homes for holding filtered water were made of this type of clay. What a striking lesson to me as I compared myself to the clay! I must allow God to prepare my life so He can mold me into the type of vessel He wants me to be. The potter shaped the clay as the wheel turned. If a lump or object was in the clay, the result would be a defect in the vessel. The potter will discard the vessel if it is not perfect, because he wants a perfect vessel. Joe wrote a book, *The Foolishness of Fighting Against God*, that tells how God called various men for a given job, but each wanted to obey God in his own way—not God's way. I didn't want to be like Jonah or Samson that fought against God's will.

Brazilian Schools

The Brazilian schools have two or three sessions a day; this allows for more students to use the same buildings. The morning session starts at 7 a.m. and ends at noon. The afternoon students are at school from 1 to 5 p.m. Then many schools also have an evening session from 7 to 10:30 p.m.; these mainly are for young people and adults. The schools have different ways to decide which session the children study. Some have the third and fourth grades in the mornings and the first and second grades in the afternoon, but that depends on the school. Their first years our three children went to the Presbyterian school. This was a large school that covered from pre-school through high school (11th grade).

We arrived in Valadares in April; the school year started in February, so Carl was late entering the kindergarten at the Presbyterian school. A British family, the Greenings, lived in Governador Valadares; their daughter, Nancy, was the same age as Carl. The teacher was very considerate—even put him at the same desk as Nancy so she could help him if he didn't understand something. The only problem with this arrangement was that Nancy was embarrassed to speak to him in English.

The Greenings also had two boys, Paul and John. John was in Charlotte's class. The children became friends with our children and enjoyed playing together at our homes, but they always spoke in Portuguese. Before too long our children also were speaking Portuguese. Charlotte learned both languages; she would speak English with us at home but Portuguese with the maid and at church. She mixed the two languages by saying things such as, "A *lua* (the moon) is pretty." When she got hurt, she always said, "*Doi, doi*" (hurt).

In their first years of school the teacher would write the lessons and homework on the chalkboard; the students would copy this information into their notebooks. Each subject required two notebooks, one for homework and one for the lessons, because they didn't have textbooks. At least 35 students were in each classroom. The first years were more intense, because many students didn't go beyond the first four years of schooling. The students were never taught printing but went directly into cursive writing. We were amazed that in spite of the lack of resources and large classes the children learned.

All schools required uniforms, including black shoes. Once Carl's black shoes needed to be resoled, so Joe put them in the shop and Carl wore his flip-flops (*chinelos*). When Carl arrived at the school gate, the keeper wouldn't let him in because he wasn't in his complete uniform. Joe tried to explain the situation, but this didn't help; Carl missed school that day. The gatekeeper always locked the gates at 10 minutes after the hour for school to begin; anyone that arrived later just missed school that day.

September 7 is Independence Day, the day Brazil was liberated from Portugal. Schools in Governador Valadares, as well as all towns and cities, went all-out to celebrate with a parade. The military band and fire trucks led the way for the many school groups. The children marched in their school uniforms. For several days they had practiced to keep their lines straight. One year the Presbyterian school led the parade; Carl was chosen to be the lead student of his fourth-grade class. This was an honor for an American to be the class leader at a Brazilian Independence celebration. The teachers had requested the students to buy ribbon that was half yellow and the other half green to decorate the uniform. To get the ribbon I went to the store that sold sewing notions. One young sales clerk in the store had been to the States. Each time I bought something at the store, we spoke English. Those that know a little English always want to practice speaking. I explained that I needed a centimeter of the yellow/green ribbon. He knew which ribbon I wanted but was puzzled that I requested only one centimeter. He questioned me two times: "ONE centimeter?" I replied, "Yes, I believe that would be enough." The third time he questioned me, he held up his fingers to show and said: "ONE centimeter?" Then I realized my mistake. "Oh, no, not centimeter; I mean one meter," I said in correction. We both had a good laugh and did so many other times after that day.

Then in 1972 the meningitis epidemic caused a change in customs. September is the beginning of the hot season; many in the hospitals were sick. The state health department had a campaign for free meningitis shots. To get a shot several hundred people lined up for blocks. The fear of meningitis made the sacrifice of aching feet and legs and tired kids worth the wait in line. That year the parade was canceled; I don't recall the schools marching the last two or three years we were in Valadares.

One morning about 6:30 I was taking the boys to school. I was in a line of traffic from the bridge into the city when a man on a bicycle descended the hill on the left and ran into the driver's side of our car. This accident frightened us both. As he was picking up himself and his bicycle, I jumped out to see whether he was injured. The front tire was folded almost in half, but thank God he wasn't hurt. I said, "Sir, didn't you see me? Why didn't you stop?" He replied that his brakes didn't work. I told him that he better get them fixed, or his faulty brakes could cost him his life the next time instead of just the bent wheel. He picked up the bicycle and parked it in front of a barber shop and the boys and I continued on to school. Several people witnessed the incident. Later the man at the barber shop told Joe that the man looked for us to charge us for the repair of his bicycle. The man at the barber shop told him we lived on the opposite side of town.

Carl graduated from primary school (fourth grade) with excellent grades and transferred to a new school called *Polivalente*. Two years after Carl, Jonathan graduated from fourth grade and also entered Polivalente School. This school was a mixture of American and Russian school systems. The basic courses were taught, but they added professional training courses as electives, with a different one added each semester. The elective courses were gardening, wood-work, simple electrical knowledge, bookkeeping, and bookmaking. This was only middle school—fifth through eighth grade. The elec-tives would give them a taste of some profession they could follow. This system was good because only about half of the students would go on to high school. Most high schools weren't free; the books had to be bought, so many couldn't go further in education for lack of funds.

By the time Jonathan entered Polivalente, we had bought another bicycle. One of the teachers at Polivalente was a member of our church on the island. She told us she went to school on the barge. Carl and Jonathan started riding their bicycles to the upper end of the island. They would ride a barge across the river and then ride their bicycles on to the Polivalente school. We felt this was safe for them. That was a much shorter route; we didn't have to take them by car and pick them up from school every day. We never had allowed them to ride their bicycles off the island, because the heavy city traffic was too dangerous, especially on the bridge.

When Charlotte was in the third grade, we transferred her from the Presbyterian school to a small school, the Grupo Escolar Nacle Miguel Habib about two blocks from our house. This adjustment was much easier for us, as we had been taking her and picking her up each day by car—about two miles. Josefa, a boy of our church, lived with his grandparents, Sr. Sebastiao and Etionilia, on a tiny island above the large Araujo Island in the Sweet River. They couldn't help him with his school work, because they didn't read or write. He was in the same class as Charlotte, so each day I invited him to have lunch with us and do their homework together. I was present to help if needed. I found I learned more Portuguese by helping the children with their homework.

All three of our children had light-colored hair, which made them stand out from the others, as most Brazilians have beautiful black hair. Charlotte had long, blonde hair. One day she complained about an itch on her neck. I looked but did not recognize the symptoms of the red rash. Fortunately almost on a daily basis Brazilians were in and out of our house for various reasons. That day a young woman who was helping me said, "Oh, *Dona* Leona, that is lice." Once we knew the problem was lice, we treated it. But to keep Charlotte from putting her head on the desk or walking with her friends with their heads together was not so easy to correct.

Even though the children went to Brazilian schools, I also taught them English at home. I used the Calvert Course. Our general rule was that we would speak only English in the home unless we had guests, because they spoke only Portuguese at other times. We knew if they didn't learn English in the home, they wouldn't learn it. Reading and writing were the main things we addressed. As we traveled to Belo Horizonte or other places, we would make spelling a game. Trips were always several hours—enough to get in a lot of English reading and spelling.

We tried to have family worship time faithfully. As each child progressed, during the devotional periods he or she took turns reading lengthier Bible passages. We read the Bible through as a family and had some interesting discussions. During our early morning breakfast devotionals the children also learned geography of the world. We had a large world map on the wall of the breakfast room; our kids took turns pointing out the countries of the missionaries on the prayer calendar each day. Not only did they learn geography, but they also were made aware of Christian work in other parts of the world.

Women's Missionary Work

At our church I was involved in the women's missionary organization, which met weekly. The week we didn't have a program or prayer meeting at church, we did home visitation. We always had visitors' cards from the worship services. We mostly visited non-Christians or family or lost friends. Even though the life of a Brazilian woman was difficult, several found time to visit and attend the meetings. A Brazilian woman didn't have a paid helper or a washing machine; many times her cookstove was fueled with wood. She would leave clothes to soak in the tank if by the time of our meeting she hadn't finished washing. These women's dedication to the Lord's work made me realize how important the church was to them. Most were from a Catholic background.

After a time the pastors' wives helped organize and plan programs for the women of all the Baptist churches to meet together every three months in one of the churches. This gave a wonderful opportunity for the women to meet other Christian women and have fellowship with new friends. We used these meetings to promote all the mission organizations, including the girls' and boys' organizations. None of the women drove cars or even had cars to drive, so they walked or took the city bus to get to the various churches. The women enjoyed these meetings, which have continued until this day. I picked up our women and took them to the meetings or for the weekly visitation. For several years I was the only woman driver in Governador Valadares. In fact hardly any Baptist families had cars, but after four years we noticed that gradually more families were able to buy at least a clunker Volkswagen.

The popular sport in Governador Valadares was to climb Ibituruna peak at 3,429 feet. The city was only 300 feet in altitude. In about 1972 we planned a mission study for our island church—G.A.

and R.A. mission organizations on top of Ibituruna. The kids hiked up the mountain, but I drove my Volks bug. I knew if I walked, I never would reach the top—at least not in time to have the study with the kids. Their enthusiasm to climb reminded me of trips each summer to the mountains in New Mexico. When I was a teen-ager, more than once our youth group climbed Wheeler Peak (more than 13,000 feet). Our Sword Drill leaders, Taylor and Ola McCasland, had a cabin near Taos. They rewarded all the youth that memorized all the Sword Drill Scriptures and attended all of the practices by allowing us to spend a week at their cabin. Each year about 15 youth had a wonderful week hiking all over the mountains. More than 100 verses had to be memorized; we had practice two afternoons a week. We had contests to see who could say the books of the Bible the fastest and of course who could find the Scriptures the fastest, too. The average for finding the Scriptures was down to three seconds to win. The reward paid off, because for at least nine years Portales First Baptist Church had a state winner in the youth sword drill. Doris and Wayne (my older siblings) and I were some of those. The state winner received a trip to Ridgecrest, NC, to participate in the southwide contest during Training Union Week. The year I won was the first year to have the contest at Glorieta. I was disappointed because Doris and Wayne got to go to Ridgecrest but I got to go to Glorieta. Looking back I see the value of having dedicated youth workers; without their patience and work we wouldn't have learned the Scriptures. The Scriptures I memorized back then still are with me today and have helped form my Christian life. I pray that I, too, have touched lives and helped them to follow God's calling. Climbing Ibituruna with the girls and boys for a picnic and mission study reminded me of my early years.

About 1974 the Valadares daily newspaper had an article about the "first woman" to drive a car up Ibituruna. The editor wasn't aware that several times I had driven up the mountain before the other woman did.

A Seed Planted in VBS Bears Fruit

Vacation Bible School is an evangelistic outreach for children. VBS is a helpful way to get the neighborhood kids to attend Bible teaching in a church. This method does not prove to be an easy way to keep them once the summer Bible school is over. A few Catholic parents don't think Evangelical VBS will "harm" their children but wouldn't think of allowing them to attend on Sundays. This was the case of Fernando. He and Carl were about the same age. He was about 11-years old when he attended VBS. On the last day we had a time for decisions; Fernando made his decision for Christ. Joe and I visited in his home. His father and mother, devout Catholics, were polite but firm in telling us he couldn't return to an Evangelical church. They asked us to respect their desire for their children to remain Catholics. Years went by and he didn't return to our church. When his grandfather died, he went to live with his grandmother in Vila Isa so she wouldn't be alone. She was a Catholic but was open to other churches. Fernando was attending the university and was attracted to a pretty girl in his class. His friends ridiculed him for wanting to date her because she was a believer—a Presbyterian. He remembered his boyhood experience at Island Baptist Church. In his heart he also was a believer. His grandmother didn't oppose his dating the Christian but his parents, especially his father, did. After his first visit to her church, he didn't want to miss another Sunday. They married and he became a devout member in the Presbyterian church. We didn't know about his story until about 30 years later. We took Genilda Ribeiro, a friend, back to visit her friends in Governador Valadares while Joe had a conference. We didn't remember that the house where we left Genilda was the same house in which Fernando lived. Now only his mother was living in it. We helped Genilda with her luggage, greeted the woman (not remembering her from years ago), and left. Fernando's mother told him that we were in town. He called us and requested we visit him at his downtown regional office in the telephone company.

The next morning he told us the full story. Our hearts were thrilled as we listened. About a year earlier he decided he wanted to thank us for leading him to the Lord. He wrote a letter of gratitude to us but, not knowing our address, he had kept the letter in his Bible. Fernando now was an elder in his Presbyterian church. His eyes and facial expressions portrayed a spiritual joy that his heart was bursting to share with us. He had never forgotten our son, Carl. In that one week of VBS together Carl had made a lasting impact on him. He had longed to be free to follow Christ openly. Now God had put him as one of the major directors of the telephone company. As we sat face to face, Fernando was thrilled, because his heart had burned with a desire to thank us personally for being a part of his salvation experience. Fernando's story reminded us of the value of God's Word planted in the hearts of children. This experience was one of God's reasons He called us to serve in Valadares for nine years. We never knew how VBS would touch the children, many of whom were from non-Christian homes. Only in heaven will we know the extent of our witness. While years pass, some seeds sprout and grow; therefore God's promise is true: *So will My word be which goes forth from My mouth; It will not return to Me empty, Without accomplishing what I desire, And without succeeding in the matter for which I sent it* (Isa. 55:11).

Fernando's story humbled us with joy, for he was thanking God more than he thanked us. He is one among hundreds in the area that had benefited spiritually. If Southern Baptists hadn't supported us, we wouldn't have had that opportunity. When a Christian sees the harvest of one seed planted, he has a fulfillment that money can't buy.

Experience on the Train

A dear woman of Fifth Baptist Church became very ill. The husband, Tertuliano, decided to take her to Belo Horizonte for medical help. I picked them up and took them to the railway station. Since the woman couldn't walk, their two adult daughters and grandbaby went to carry the mother onto the train. I carried the baby and the father led the way. One daughter had given him her purse to carry. Their coach was about the last car; the conductor started calling "all-aboard" before the girls arrived at the mother's seat. Inside I felt panic, because the next stop for the train would be at a village about an hour down the track and we wouldn't have had a ride back into town. When the conductor gave the last call and the train started moving, we realized that we couldn't get to their mother and father's seats, so the girls put their mother in a vacant chair and we hurried to descend from the train. I jumped with the baby before the train got up too much speed. One sister jumped and landed upright, but by the time the second sister jumped, the train was moving too fast and she landed flat. We were all so frightened that we didn't realize their purse with their house key had remained on the train with the father. I took the girls to our house and told Joe what had happened. I remembered the box of keys that were in the house when it was bought. We took the box of keys to see if we could unlock their house. We finally found a key to unlock the door, but it wouldn't lock the door. At least they could get inside for the night. A brother, who lived in next major city, met his parents at the train station. The father gave him the purse to take back to Governador Valadares. Oh, how God takes care of His children! For many years after that we laughed about that experience—but at the time this experience wasn't funny.

Death of Sr. Sebastiao

We knew that Sr. Sebastiao and Etionilia had tuberculosis. From time to time we traveled by boat to visit them on their little island. They had both accepted Christ and attended church services when they could. These were the grandparents of Josefa, the boy that studied with Charlotte. One morning early I heard a clap at our gate. A deacon of our church was bringing news that Sr. Sebastiao, the grandfather, had died. Joe was traveling in my little Volkswagen, but I had the Chevrolet van. The deacon wanted to know whether I would be willing to go to the end of Araujo Island and meet the boat with the son and the casket and transport it to the church for the service. I agreed to do this and the deacon would take care of the rest of the paperwork for the funeral that afternoon. At the appointed time I was at the end of Araujo Island to wait for the small boat to get the casket. Some of the island church members also were waiting for the body to be brought to Araujo Island. These members were very worried about my putting the casket into the van, because they believed the germs would leave the body and enter me. I wasn't afraid; not only did I transport the casket to the church for the funeral service, I also transported it from the church to the cemetery. His widow, Etionilia, then went to Belo Horizonte for treatment for tuberculosis and was cured.

The Difference Christ Makes

Dona Domingas was in her 50's when she was converted through the witness of a nephew. While he was attending an open-air service, her nephew had found Christ as Savior. Open-air services were common each Sunday afternoon and holidays. Domingas' husband had died; she had no children, so she was very lonely. She was afraid to turn the light off at night even to sleep. But after she accepted Jesus, she no longer had fear of the dark. She didn't know how to read, but she wanted to read the Bible. Little by little she taught herself to read and used the Bible as her textbook. She started attending our church on the island; the church was only two blocks from her home. She knew many people in the neighborhood that didn't attend church, so she invited them to go with her. One young woman she invited was Enedina. After Enedina was saved, she became my Girls in Action (GA) helper. Girls in Action is a girls mission organization. Enedina was a willing helper and was ready to learn new things. Years later she married a young man won to Christ also by the influence of *Dona* Domingas. He had studied at the Catholic seminary to be a priest but dropped out. He became a Baptist preacher.

Mud Holes
On trips Joe and I always have traded off driving. The trip to Belo Horizonte was a six- or seven-hour drive and mostly was on winding mountain roads. Until about 1971, depending on the time of the year, the last 60 miles from Belo to Valadares was dirt or mud. We discovered that if we crossed the Rio Doce River north of Ipatinga, we could travel about 30 miles on a dirt road southeast and meet the Rio-Bahia Highway 50 miles south of Governador Valadares. Even though that road was further, we had half as much dirt. The scary part was a long, rickety, wooden, single-lane bridge that crossed the Rio Doce.

Because of the rains, we had chosen the longer route to avoid the slippery muddy road. I had driven about 15 miles when I arrived at a mud puddle that crossed the road. I could have left the road to go around the muddy hole, but I didn't think this was necessary. I was driving slowly when—*wham!* The front end of the car went down into a deeper hole. The Rural Willys had the speed to get out of the muddy water before the vehicle stopped. Muddy water ran out over the fenders on both sides. Joe raised the hood and saw that thick, muddy water had splashed over the motor. About the time Joe found some rags in the tool box, a Volkswagen stopped to check on us. The man was a mechanic. Wouldn't you know God was looking after us! He cleaned the carburetor and spark plugs. Our car started, so he drove around the mud hole and went on his way.

The Rural Willys did fine until we started up the first hill; then it chugged up with difficulty. We were getting hungry and thankful for the few bananas and crackers. The car was running even if only about 20-miles an hour. About 8 p.m. we reached the busy Rio-Bahia Highway. Now we faced the danger of a car approaching us in the dark and not realizing how slow we were going. We were afraid this might cause a wreck. Nevertheless, we kept chugging along and arrived safely in Governador Valadares at about 10 p.m.

Our Pets

One day Jonathan brought home a jar of tadpoles that he had taken from a puddle in the street. During the rainy season we had a choir of croaking frogs at night. Most of the streets were dirt, so the frogs had many puddles in which to lay their eggs. Jonathan wanted to raise these tadpoles and watch them develop into frogs. This was a science project; how could I say no? He was thrilled with them, but I was not. I could just see those tadpoles becoming frogs and jumping around in the house. He put them in the home's small, closed area that had open air. The poor things didn't last long; either they got too hot or starved. In a few days, much to Jonathan's dismay, they all were dead. I didn't let him know I wasn't sorry.

We had many pets besides a dog and cat. We had turtles, rabbits, a *maritaca* (small parrot), and miniature monkeys, about five-inches tall. We enjoyed Lelico, the first monkey, because he was tame enough to ride on our shoulders and liked to be petted. We had a cage for him, but at times we let Lelico out to play. While Joe worked in the office, he allowed the monkey to be free, but if Joe left for a few minutes, Lelico would play with the typewriter tape and pull the ribbon off the spool. When Joe returned, the monkey would scamper up the curtain and leave his little black footprints on the curtain. The day Lelico died, all of us felt various degrees of sadness. Later Pastor Hilton brought us another monkey, but this animal never was as tame as Lelico. The new monkey didn't like a broom and didn't like the maid; he would screech at her until she left the room.

The *maritaca* parrot, named Louro, was a mess; I was sorry I had bought him. He liked me and I could carry him on my shoulder, but if something upset him, he would bite and nearly pierce the ear but not necessarily in the correct location for an earring. Later I gave him to one of our maids to take home.

Too often our cat had a litter of kittens; we soon ran out of friends to whom we could give the kittens away. One Christmas Day Joe disguised his voice and called our dear friend Pastor Hilton. Joe told our friend that if he would go to a certain address, he would receive a surprise gift. Certainly Pastor Hilton recognized the address and knew the voice. The surprise for him was a kitten. After all, Pastor Hilton had given us both miniature monkeys. Joe wanted to return the favor and find a new home for a kitten.

Help in Time of Grief

One Wednesday night a family of six new visitors attended the prayer service at the island church. They were new in the community; no one in our church had met them before. The amazing thing was that they weren't Christians. During the prayer time, the mother asked us to pray for their oldest daughter, Lucimar, age 14. Later in private she told me that Lucimar had leukemia and had been receiving treatment in Belo Horizonte.

The next weekend in our home we had a couple of visitors from Rio de Janeiro. The man was a national Brotherhood worker and was in Governador Valadares for a men's conference. His wife, a medical doctor, had joined for the ride. I asked the wife whether she would go with me to visit Lucimar on Sunday afternoon while the men were in their conference. We had a good visit with Lucimar and her mother, Lucia. Lucia said that past Friday night, as a result of a visit from another person, she had accepted Jesus. I carefully explained the plan of salvation to Lucimar, but she was not ready to make her decision. We prayed for Lucimar's health but especially that she accept Jesus in her heart. After we left, the medical doctor told me that Lucimar didn't have long to live. The next day the parents took Lucimar back to Belo. About two weeks passed before Lucimar was back to visit. I visited with her; she assured me that she had made everything right with God. Each time she was in Valadares we held a home service because Lucimar was too weak to attend church. She had to spend more and more time in the hospital in Belo.

During this time the family moved from the island to a company-owned house of the iron ore plant where her father worked. We were happy that a family from Fifth Baptist Church had also moved to that neighborhood. This mature Christian family from Fifth Church could give Lucimar and her family daily spiritual guidance during this difficult time. One Sunday we drove by to pick up Lucia and a friend to take them to our Baptist mission in a neighborhood nearby. Lucimar was home and begged us to stay, but since we had to be at the mission, we told her we would return and have a service with her.

Monday night the kids, *Dona* Lourdes (a church member), and I loaded up my little Volks bug and went to the home for a service with Lucimar and her family. Soon after we arrived, Lucimar had a sinking spell. As her pain grew worse, we thought she was dying. Her parents became hysterical; the brothers and sisters began crying loudly. *Dona* Lourdes stayed with Lucimar and the parents while I took Lucimar's brothers and sisters out of the room to talk with them. I explained to them that death was like a move. Lucimar would be moving from her physical body to a glorified body to be with Jesus. They knew what moving was, because recently they had moved two times. After we prayed, they calmed down; I went back to be with Lucimar. I asked Lourdes to pray. She prayed, "God, if Your plan is not for Lucimar to live, please relieve the pain." The pain did cease and didn't return. Lucimar called her parents to her side and said: "Don't cry for me. God is coming to get me to take me to my real home. Don't cry for me!" Then she requested that we sing two of her favorite hymns: "Count Your Many Blessings" and "O Happy Day". We prayed and left. Those words are so real: "O happy day that fixed my choice on Thee, my Saviour and my God! Well may this glowing heart rejoice, and tell its raptures all abroad. Happy day, happy day, when Jesus washed my sins away! He taught me how to watch and pray and live rejoicing every day; happy day, happy day, when Jesus washed my sins away!" What a testimony of her short life as a Christian! I believe she had had a vision of Jesus.

The next afternoon we returned to check on Lucimar and have prayer with her and her parents. She again requested the same two songs; we had a Scripture and prayer. She again told her parents: "Don't cry for me, for God's coming to get me today to take me to my real home." About two hours after we left, God did take Lucimar. This time the family calmly accepted her death. What a testimony this 14-year-old new Christian gave to her family and neighbors! My G.A. helper, Enedina, and Domingas went back with me to the home. Why was Joe away so many times at the time of a death? That was my first (and only) experience to help prepare a body for burial. I never had touched a dead person. God gave me strength to remain calm and do what was necessary and to comfort the family. The casket was brought to the home; we put her body in it. Together we planned for the funeral service in the home the next afternoon. The next day I felt the power of many prayers from the United States and around the world strengthening me in my situation; the day was my birthday, when my name would have been on prayer calendars throughout my homeland.

Chapter 6

Beginning Our Second Term

Remember the Children of Israel in the land of the Nile—
How Joseph rose to be the second in the Kingdom for a while?
But Joseph's death terminated his fame and glory
And horrible slavery in Egypt continued Israel's story!

Have you wondered about Moses and His miraculous rod?
Yielding to God's will toward Egypt He trod.
He succeeded in doing what a great army could not.
Yes, not him, but God using him—together they did a lot.

And Gideon and his 300 faithful with horns and lamps
Rioted thousands of enemies by surrounding their camp.
No! Not by Gideon's own power or that of his 300 men.
This was God Himself really overpowering the army of sin.

For our first furlough we arrived in New Mexico to see snow on the ground—quite a change from the heat of Brazil. The day before we had gone to the beach in Rio. That was when I got the bad sunburn and was miserable. For our four-month furlough we lived in Roswell. We were near Leona's older sister, Doris; Doris' husband, Pat; and their family. Their children were about the same age as our kids were, so the cousins enjoyed being together. Roswell is exactly 90 miles southwest of Portales, in which Leona's parents lived, and 90 miles northwest of Lovington, in which my father lived. The activities in our four-month furlough kept us busy. We visited all of our siblings and their families and most importantly visited our parents. We also visited some churches. We were allowed to take back to Brazil a crate of household things. We learned to use every square inch of our allotted footage in the crate. Before we left by airplane for Brazil the crate was shipped to New Orleans.

We Face Trouble

We had left our Rural Willys wagon with Ronny Boswell in Belo Horizonte. After we rested a night, we loaded our car to return to Governador Valadares. Leaving the U.S. and especially leaving our parents was difficult. Now we were back to our adopted country, in which things still were very different. The strangeness gave me an uncanny feeling in the pit of my stomach. I was glad to be back, because I knew God had called us to Brazil, but for a few days the transition was difficult.

The road from Belo to Valadares is mostly mountainous, with steep inclines and dangerous curves. We had left Brazil just before Christmas when Brazil still was in the summer season; four months later we left the U.S. in the spring and returned to Brazil in the fall. The rainy season had just about passed and had left many potholes in the pavement. About an hour out of Belo as we neared the top of a steep mountain, we had a flat. A three- or four-foot shoulder was all that existed between the edge of the pavement and the edge of the cliff. I couldn't get the car completely off the road. I was nervous, because about 50 feet in front was a curve; cars approaching the curve wouldn't have much time to see us. I started jacking up the car, but the jack broke before the tire was off the ground completely. The jack wouldn't go up or down. Cars going up the mountain behind us had to swerve into the approaching traffic lane to get around us. Traffic approaching the curve from the downhill direction posed another danger. We both were nervous! The mountainside dropped off several-hundred feet to the right. I had put on the road our emergency triangle required by law; this way the cars traveling up the hill could see trouble ahead. I didn't have another triangle or time to gather tree branches to place along on the edge of the road ahead of us to give a danger warning to approaching cars swerving around the curve. Leona strongly suggested that I move the car forward—farther up the curve so the cars approaching the downhill curve could see us better.

114

I moved the car forward until it was off the jack and drove on the flat tire a short distance farther up the hill. I motioned for cars traveling up the hill to stop so I could borrow a jack. Finally a man stopped. As he drove up behind the car, he had noticed that gasoline was streaming from the gas tank. I had smelled gasoline but hadn't thought to look under the car. The square jack base had flipped and cut a gash in the gas tank as I drove off of it. About 15 minutes earlier we had given the kids bubble gum. I immediately requested their wads of bubble gum and made a ball out of it, crawled underneath the car far enough to reach the gash of the tank, and stuffed the bubble gum into the gash. This stopped the leak. The man loaned us a jack, so we changed the tire.

Until this day the kids claim that they didn't even have time to get the sweetness out of the gum. At least their sacrifice helped us get to a service station. The man at the station told me he had learned an old army trick that would be better than bubble gum. He took out the bubble gum and used a bar of homemade dish soap. He pressed his bar of soap hard against the open gash and rubbed it in a crisscross fashion; this closed the gash with soap. For older Americans this soap was comparable to lye soap our parents and ancestors made on the farm. This sealed the gash better until we could get back into Belo.

We returned to the Boswells' house and unloaded. I took the car to the mechanic that missionaries in Belo had been using for many years. We had to spend the night to give time for the gas tank to be drained and repaired. That did not make us sad, for that night we had more time to visit with the Boswells and Richardsons. The next day we were warmly received in Governador Valadares with no problem on the road.

In a few days all the lonesomeness we had for the U.S. passed; we again were going full-blast in our work. The big yard with trees to climb and neighborhood friends made our children happy. Their Portuguese began to return quickly. They seemed to understand their friends better than Leona and I understood our friends in conversation. Leona hired a maid and I hired a gardener. Lawnmowers were not yet used in our area of Brazil. Lawn grass was cut with huge scissors. At the Bible institute I had met a young man that had surrendered to preach. He lived across the Rio Doce River in the neighborhood at the foot of mountain. He was without a job, had two little children, and desperately needed work. I hired him to be our gardener and handyman for a minimum wage of only $35, which was what most people paid. We supplemented this salary with extra things such as clothes or food. This also was the salary we gave our maid, Odete. In language school we were told that for good relationships with the neighbors we should not pay more than the going rate. Odete was a member of an Assembly of God church and very trustworthy. She had club feet, which made walking difficult for her. She was one of the best helpers we had; until she got married, she stayed with us.

I supervised construction on Fifth Baptist Church. The little room for the children was torn down and the outdoor toilet moved so the first unit of the new building could be built at the back of the lot. The church now had electricity and city water lines were being laid, so the Santa Rita neighborhood was in a phase of important improvement. Restrooms would be put in this building. I made many trips to the city to get materials for construction; I brought what I could in the car. Most of the sand and gravel taken from the river was taken on donkey-pulled carts to construction sites. Donkey-drawn (or pulled) carts even brought the steel rebar for the concrete pillars as the rebar was moved from the city. Big, heavy hoes mixed by hand the concrete and plaster. Each Saturday I paid each worker weekly wages; most of the workers were church members. Before we finished, we used up the $2,000 from the strategic property fund given by the Southern Baptist Foreign Mission Board through our state Baptist convention (COBAM). The church borrowed $1,000 from the Brazilian Baptist lending board; we made monthly payments. This "lending board" basically is funded by Southern Baptist funds. The difference is that the COBAM funds are gifts directly from the FMB to the fields and the national lending board funds have to be returned.

COBAM—The State Strategic Property Organization

Each state had a COBAM committee, made up of missionaries and Brazilians, to distribute strategic property funds provided by the Foreign Mission Board in its state. Each year the South Brazil mission designated a certain amount of money for this fund to help churches buy properties and help build a small chapel. This fund was one of the major items of discussion at our annual mission meeting. Eight states and the Federal District of Brasilia made up the South Brazil mission. The new Federal District was being developed and was extremely needy to get properties within the pilot plan and surrounding satellite cities. By far, most of the population of Brazil was in the South Brazil mission area. At the time our state alone had more than 750 counties and Baptist work in about 100 counties. On two or three special occasions the South Brazil mission received nearly $300,000 and one time $750,000, but normally the amount was less for this fund. Can you imagine dividing this money among nine states when any one state could use that much money? Until this fund ceased to exist, I usually was on this committee in Minas and three or four times was the chairperson. This committee required a lot of paperwork.

I truthfully can say that at least two-thirds of the churches in Minas Gerais received some money this way from Southern Baptists either for buying a lot or to help build their first one-room worship place. This financial help was a great help for new churches, since poverty really was bad in Brazil.

One experience with buying property in the association was at the foot of a large slum (*favela*) in Governador Valadares. During the 10 years we were in the Sweet River Valley Association, we received some financial aid to buy the initial lot for many new churches. Two or three pastors and I made frequent trips to purchase a lot or oversee the use of the money. I always was responsible for signing the final papers for the deeds and for sending the deeds to the national convention foundation board. Years later I served on this national foundation board for one three-year term. As these new churches became independent and sound in doctrine, they could request from the foundation the deed to the property; this was the desire of the Foreign Mission Board.

Organizing the Fellowship of Baptist Pastors and Wives in Valadares

Most of the six Baptist churches now had pastors. We saw the need to have a meeting once a month for fellowship and prayer with the pastors and wives. Occasionally we invited them for a potluck meal at our house. Pastor Hilton and I were the only ones that had automobiles. My jeep wagon didn't have four-wheel drive, so at one of these early meetings I was explaining why I couldn't get to certain areas. I said my car had only two wheels. I thought I was saying that our vehicle didn't have four-wheel drive. Pastor Hilton said, "Joe, your car has four wheels." I insisted that it didn't. Everyone laughed but did so only because all the people knew me; otherwise they would have thought the laughter would have hurt my feelings. We found Brazilians to be very courteous about the many mistakes Americans made with the language. They probably laughed behind our backs but without our knowing about it.

During these meetings the pastors prayed together and planned for the evangelization of Governador Valadares. The pastors' wives also met to pray. They faced problems they could not share with members, so these meetings were also for encouragement.

As a group we participated in the frequent organization of new churches in the association. The pastors' wives started quarterly meetings with the women of the churches. Once a month I met with the youth; a sweet fellowship began to prevail in our city among the youth. This was a blessing, since Christian youth were in the minority; this gave them opportunities to meet other Christians. God was blessing!

Brazilian Baptist Missions and the Cooperative Program

First Baptist Church of Brazil was organized on October 15, 1882, in Salvador, Bahia, in northern Brazil. Salvador was the ecclesiastical capital of Brazil where the Catholic See (the highest Catholic official, usually an archbishop) was situated. Salvador was the first Brazilian capital city and always has been the most religious fanatical Catholic region of Brazil. The Baptist church was organized with five members: missionaries William Buck and Anne Luther Bagby, Z.C. and Kate Crawford Taylor, and Antonio Teixeira de Albuquerque, a converted priest. A few other Southern Baptist missionaries were working in other areas. Soon American missionaries led in the organization of mission-support groups of men and women to support Brazilian preachers and *colporteurs* (Bible distributors). From this humble beginning soon other small churches sprang up in Rio de Janeiro and other places. On October 15, 1907, the Brazilian Baptist

Convention was organized, the Brazilian Foreign Mission Board was organized, and the first missionary was sent to Portugal. The Home Mission Board also was organized with the object of reaching lost people farther into the interior. Most of the population was along the coastline and therefore merited most of the evangelistic activity.

During the early years by far the majority of funds for the three seminaries, two women's training schools, the building of educational schools particularly in state capitals, and funds to start many of the churches and the publishing house were provided by Southern Baptists. By 1962 the Brazilian Baptist Cooperative Program was begun with the purpose of expanding Brazilian home and foreign mission endeavors. Another major reason for the Cooperative Program was to get Brazil moving toward self-support. This became a major emphasis of mine in the Sweet River Association.

About 1969 Jack Young had wisely stepped down as general secretary of the Minas Gerais State Convention; Pastor Jose Alves da Silva Bittencourt, his assistant, became the first Brazilian to occupy that position. Jack took the responsibility of promoting state missions. Along with this was a state mission offering promotion by all missionaries in the state. For at least one week a year a Brazilian pastor and I visited churches, usually in the northeastern part of our state, and promoted state missions in isolated churches.

Our Little Garden

Mr. Nelson, the treasurer of Fifth Baptist Church, borrowed money from me so he could get married. He hadn't been able to pay me back, so after we returned from our first furlough he insisted on paying me by giving us a lot by the river. He had three lots and wanted to give me the one going down to the river. I didn't want to accept this piece of land, but he said he wouldn't be happy if I did not accept his offer. I accepted the land with the idea of growing fruit and vegetables. Our kids needed some education on growing food products; a little work in the garden wouldn't hurt them. Leona and I had had that experience when we were kids. The land already had bananas, oranges, limes, and papayas. I paid Nelson to take care of the fruits and things we planted. Leona and I planted cantaloupe (seeds from the States) and pineapple. The cantaloupe didn't produce, because we planted in the rainy season; too much water wasn't good for the cantaloupe. The pineapples were small but very delicious. I let Nelson plant corn, beans, blackeyed peas (seeds from the States), okra, and other things. The kids didn't enjoy the farm work, but picking the produce wasn't so bad. We enjoyed the fresh corn even though it was field corn and not sweet. The kids didn't mind shucking corn, even though a worm had made its home in the corn. As a family we sometimes went to get the okra, corn, bananas, and other things. This didn't turn out to be the most enjoyable family project as I had hoped. Carl got burned out on bananas because I brought in a stalk at a time. He says I made them eat every banana so that not one would go to waste.

Just a little ways from our lot was the place in which I baptized new converts, because the church didn't have a baptistery. Carl was baptized in that river. I enjoyed going there and listening to the river, although we lived on the island where from our bedroom I could hear the rapids in the river. I thought I could sell the property later and put the money into a college fund for the kids.

Things We Never Had Imagined

We continued to experience things *which eye has not seen and ear has not heard, and which have not entered the heart of man, all that God has prepared for those who love Him* (1 Cor. 2:9). I believe God continually reveals Himself and puts those who love Him in earthly situations that never can be imagined. The exciting life with Jesus can be full on this earth; therefore, this verse does not only speak of heaven in the future but earth in the present.

The pastors and I planned our first citywide evangelism campaign for January 1969. I was to be the director. We planned a parade involving all of our Baptist churches. We had a choir made up from the six churches. We invited an outside pastor and popular Baptist singer to be the evangelist and singer. A big, covered area near the center of the city was rented. Each church was responsible for bringing all of its benches. Leona and I recently had bought a small electric organ from a Seventh-Day Adventist missionary who lived in a neighboring city. We used the organ as our main musical instrument for the crusade. The revival went from Monday night through Sunday.

Nearly 100 decisions for salvation were recorded from this effort. The first citywide revival was worth all the effort.

This first experience was very profitable. The crusade took a lot of work, but just to have all the churches working together and to see the crowd that attended every night was a great joy. One thing disturbed us, however. We didn't have the follow-up visits on those that made decisions immediately; we waited until after the crusade. We found out that another denomination in town had already visited them and persuaded many of them to join them. Does that matter? Yes, if they weren't clear on the plan of salvation!

Our missionary career always was busy. Dr. Bill Richardson gave me the responsibility to write four study books for the Bible institute in Valadares. Leona was to write three. We had about two years to get them ready. One of mine was on Baptist history in Brazil. Our Portuguese was not good yet nor the vocabulary extensive, so we had to spend a lot of time and almost wore out the Portuguese dictionary preparing these study books. The 13 lessons had to be typed out with questions for each lesson. They were to contain the minimum information, because most of the students hadn't finished more than the fourth grade. We never would have guessed we would be doing such things.

Part of The Marvel of It All was doing many things we never had dreamed of doing. On the island we were surrounded by Presbyterians; one of these fine families became close friends. The people had two sons who became very good friends to Carl and Jonathan. *Dona* Dulce was a schoolteacher but also was a good piano player and teacher. She accepted the job of teaching piano to our kids.

Family Times

Very early in our ministry I realized that I had to make time for my family. In the backyard driveway I poured a slab of concrete for a basketball court. Even though for the first two or three years the boys had difficulty throwing the ball to the basket, the goal was to challenge them. The slab of concrete also served for skating, since our street was dirt. Monday night was family night and our time for wrestling. I put the mats out; we always had fun wrestling. Charlotte had to be added to my frolicking with the boys. For them, she was in the way, but for her, she never could get enough. When I wasn't traveling, we also used Saturday afternoons for doing things together.

Occasionally during the school vacation I took Carl on a trip with me. One day Carl and I took the train to Itueta, a town about three hours down the river. I needed to check with the pastor to see if he still needed the $25 a month that the state board was sending him. We spent about four hours in Itueta and caught the train back to Valadares. Yes, the pastor really needed to continue receiving the money. As a father of six children he received about $50 from his church. Two or three years later one of the daughters lived with us to study and also to help around the house. She was very sweet and served us well.

Much of our family time occurred during our travels, mainly to Belo Horizonte for station meetings and the yearly trip to our annual South Brazil mission meeting. On these trips we taught the children spelling, both in Portuguese and English. We made up travel games to keep the kids interested, especially when they were getting irritated with each other. They enjoyed throwing gospel tracts out the windows as we passed people on horseback, bicycle, or walking on the dirt road. Usually men or women dismounted their horses or bicycles to pick up the gospel tracts. Those walking always curiously stooped down to pick up the gospel tracts. We knew that many of those who picked up the tracts didn't know how to read, but we trusted that they would take the tract to someone they knew who could read. Perhaps that person, too, would get to know how to be saved. We whispered prayers to our Lord for those people. Rarely did anyone ever throw the track away.

During the rainy season I surmised that at least 100 inches fell during a normal season. We dreaded trips by car on the muddy roads. One time we got stuck in a mud hole. The more we tried to get out, the deeper and more slippery the hole became. After about 45 minutes we were about to give up when five adolescent boys walking on the road met us. I paid them to put their muscles to the test and help us out. They sure were muddy from that experience, but we were happy to be moving again and they were happy with their tip.

The last 60 miles on the more-direct road to Valadares was not the easiest. If we crossed the Rio Doce just out of Ipatinga, we faced only 45 miles on the dirt road that led to the Rio-Bahia Highway. But this

122

route took us about 80 miles south of Valadares; therefore, we had about an hour and a half farther to drive back north on the highway to get to Valadares. But in the rainy season traveling 45 miles in mud and then 80 more on asphalt was much better than traveling 90 miles in mud.

Our first summer vacations were in Victoria or Rio de Janeiro as we visited fellow missionaries and the beaches. One summer we went north as far as Sergipe, a state noted for its oil wells. Most of our journey was on the Rio-Bahia Highway. The highway was a narrow, two-lane road with constant curves. Trucks and buses were thicker than passenger cars because not many families had cars. About 60 miles before we reached the Bahia state border, a bus kept riding on our bumper and blinking its lights, meaning that the driver wanted to pass. We were driving the speed limit and were very close to a truck in front of us. The bus driver behind us impatiently honked his horn after we did nothing to get out of his way. The road didn't have a shoulder; trees, brushes, or deep canyons formed the edge of the pavement. We had no way to pull over and let the bus driver pass.

Finally Leona turned around and shook her hand at the bus driver. She said, "Stupid, stupid, stupid!" Of course the bus driver couldn't hear her voice, but he knew she was mad. He knew she had written down his license number. I knew the danger of making a truck or bus driver mad. Once a truck driver pulled out to pass another truck and forced Ronny Boswell with his family off the road. Ronny turned around quickly, pulled up beside the driver, and shook his fist at him. The truck driver calmly pulled out a revolver and pointed it at Marlene as they drove beside each other. Ronny immediately slowed down, turned around, and continued his journey home.

As soon as we had the opportunity, I let the bus pass. For a good ways the man drove very slowly in front of us, but I didn't dare go around him. Finally he gave up and went on. We thought we had seen the last of him. About 30 minutes later we arrived at the border of Bahia and Minas Gerais. We saw that the bus had stopped at the police checkpoint. As we drew near an officer motioned for us to stop. He told us that the bus driver had registered a complaint against us. The driver told him that we had tried to cause him to have an accident. We told the officer that he was the one that tried to run us off the road and maybe kill our family. He said that Leona had cursed him. Leona told the officer that she had called him "stupid". The officer told us that he had to stop just across the border at a restaurant for his passengers to eat and we would see him no more. The bus driver knew Leona had written down his license number and evidently was going to turn him in, so he stopped to make a false accusation against us first.

Most Brazilians are courteous drivers, but some are like Americans. We had no further problems and had a wonderful vacation. In Feira de Santana we visited with some missionaries who had been with us in language school. Then we went on to Sergipe to visit with another family we also had met in language school. The beaches in Sergipe were beautiful. We visited the state Baptist camp; this was the first time to see poles with hammock hooks instead of beds in the long dorms.

One day I returned from an executive mission meeting in Rio to find that Leona had made the down-payment on a condominium vacation plan. From that time on for many years, using that plan, we went to the beach sites nearest us. Our vacations always were a time to grow in the Lord and strengthen our bonds as a family. When the kids grew to adolescents, I let them chose a book of the Bible that we would study each day for the week in our devotional time. On Sundays we visited a Baptist church in the beach town. Carl didn't care for the beach as much as the rest of us did, because he didn't like the sticky feeling that salt water left on his skin. But all and all as a family we had wonderful vacations.

Judy Ritchie, Our Journeyperson

Leona was not a great pianist, but she knew the basics of music and believed she could pass on what she knew to students interested in playing for churches. Our Baptist churches had a shortage of someone to play the pump organs, if they had an instrument. Two students that requested lessons were daughters of a rancher. Their parents arranged a piano on which the girls could practice, so Leona accepted them as students. One Thanksgiving, as thanks for the lessons, the father gave us a turkey from his ranch, since Leona didn't charge. One of the girls later married a pastor.

About 1966 the Foreign Mission Board started the Journeyman

program for college graduates, usually still single. We requested a music teacher, because so many churches had pump organs but no one to play them. Most of the journeypersons taught Homeschool for missionary children as well as helped in some phase of evangelism. Journeymen assignments normally were for two years. A few journeyguys married and later returned as career missionaries. Leona and I decided to request a journeyperson to teach music; that would be a great help to the churches. Our request was filled by Judy Ritchie.

Judy had a very shocking arrival at the Valadares airport. Because of the problem of communicating by phone between Valadares and Belo Horizonte, we didn't receive communication that Judy would arrive a little earlier than expected. When we arrived at the airport, that now had asphalt, Judy was standing by herself in front of the tiny, wooden terminal. The airport terminal was a rundown, two-room building. Judy didn't understand one word of Portuguese; she knew the Brazilians had offered her a ride into town, but she wouldn't take the offer. She knew the best thing would be to wait for us, so with her suitcases she stood all alone in the blazing hot sun.

We had arranged for Judy to stay with *Dona* Ideir Silva dos Santos, an English teacher at the Presbyterian school. But a few days before Judy arrived, Ideir's husband suffered a stroke and needed constant care. We prepared the guest room for Judy to stay with us. We think this arrangement worked out well even though the mission board didn't recommend journeypeople staying with their sponsors. We had her working with students in Portuguese—also not recommended. Judy was great with our children; we all loved her. Judy brightened up our home life.

Dona Ideir taught Portuguese to Judy; within two months she began her pump-organ lessons—in Portuguese. To some extent Judy was handicapped but had learned enough musical terms in Portuguese that she felt comfortable. She had 40 students signed up. Twice a week she went to four churches in town that had pump organs. Soon after her arrival Seventh Baptist Church was organized; someone loaned that church a pump organ. Soon the pastor of First Baptist Church in Teofoli Otoni, about 90 miles north of Valadares, also wanted her to teach music at his church. So she began going on Saturdays. She also played the piano for our island mission, which met in our home. After the first Sunday service one of the members expressed her surprise that Judy already could play in Portuguese. She did have trouble understanding page numbers for a while.

Judy had a beautiful voice also. Judy prepared quartet music for women; we formed a young women's quintet using three sisters in our mission. Many churches had young men's quartets, but our church had the only young women's quintet of which we were aware.

At Christmas I gave Judy a special present—as a joke, of course. We had a problem with huge rats that traveled up through a drainpipe into a small enclosed area for flowers outside the breakfast room. On Christmas Eve after Judy and the kids had gone to bed, I happened to trap one in a cage. I wrapped the cage in Christmas paper and put Judy's name on it. Of course that is not the only gift she received. Her shock lasted only an instant, but her expression of surprise brought delight from the kids.

Judy played for weddings in both Baptist and Presbyterian churches. The second year she was with us, she taught music at the Bible institute. While she was with us, the mission moved from our home into its church building on the island; her home church paid for a new pump organ. She also served as the music director for the annual Sweet River Valley Association meeting. For her short time with us she made many contributions.

First School of Music

Leona and I planned a school of music principally for the Baptist churches in Valadares. Brazilians love to sing, so we thought a music festival would be successful; we were not disappointed. Clint Kimbrough was the music missionary for the State of Rio de Janeiro; he accepted the challenge of directing this clinic. At First Baptist Church each night for a week he taught music theory and other subjects. On Sunday afternoon we held a music concert for the public at the radio station's 800-seat auditorium. A choir of students of the school of music sang. Five of the seven Baptist churches participated. Clint's wife, Dolores, and Sarah Faris from Vitoria, Espirito Santo, both had professional opera voices. They arrived on Saturday to participate in the Sunday concert. Delores, Sarah, and Judy Ritchie sang spiritual numbers accompanied by Clint on the piano. Clint also played two classical piano pieces. I played a trumpet number. Scripture-reading filled the gap between the musical presentations. The school of music was a great success and a good experience to expose non-Christians to bits of the gospel.

Acquiring Land for Island Baptist Church

When we were looking for property or mission house, for a very cheap price we found lots on the upper end of the island Araujo. We made a down-payment and started making monthly payments. About two years later the real-estate man that sold that property called me and wanted to buy the property back because the government wanted to build about 50 low-income houses on that end of the island. I didn't want to sell, so he offered to trade me two lots in the center of the island for the three. I was impressed because the two lots were on a main street. The city planning commission had reserved four city blocks for the largest park in the whole city. The church would be facing that park. How amazing God is! Those two lots definitely were worth more and had a much better location for a church than did the three, so we made the deal.

This area, however, was covered with tall grass and bushes. The street in front of the lots had been graded but now was hardly recognizable as a street. Around the area I put up a five-feet-high fence made of thin prefabricated slabs of concrete. Lots in Brazil are smaller than in the U.S.—about 13-yards wide and 27-yards long. We really needed at least one more lot.

The mission had been saving money for buying another lot and for constructing a church building. We began praying for another lot. I started searching for the owner of the lot next to ours and discovered that he lived in Belo Horizonte, so I made a trip to Belo to find him. An interesting fact was that he lived on Avenue Mucuri in Belo Horizonte—the same name as the street we lived on in Valadares. He had sold the lot to a young husband and wife that were members of First Baptist Church in Valadares; we knew them. I went to see the couple; the man told me they would sell us the lot because his wife didn't want to live on the island since it had snakes and floods. This was on a Friday. He said we could sign the papers on Monday at 1 p.m. but that he would have to have the total payment so he could pay off the other man. Into the offering Leona and I put as much money as we could, but the amount was short. On Sunday I made an appeal for the rest of the money needed, but still not enough was given to make the purchase. About 12:30 Monday afternoon a young Presbyterian man who was dating a girl in our mission brought the rest of the money. He said he and his mother wanted to complete the amount necessary for buying the lot. Praise the Lord because He is faithful! We had water hooked up to the lots and cut the grass so that the youth could have a private soccer and volleyball field. Time had arrived to plan the first unit of our worship center.

Equipment for My Work

I had a rack put on top of the car and bought a portable loud-speaker to use for the open-air services. I used the speaker in many places. Nearly all Evangelical churches had loudspeakers on their roof; for 30 minutes before morning and evening services most of them played good, recorded evangelical music. Some good LP records had been produced by missionaries and Brazilian musicians. Loudspeaker systems and filmstrip projectors were standard equipment for field missionaries. These were bought through the South Brazil small equipment fund after approval by the mission. I bought an old mimeograph machine for printing out monthly newsletters to the churches in the association. It was a headache to operate. The mission also paid for stencils and ink, but I paid for the envelopes and postage for the letters. I spent a lot of time on correspondence that dealt with our mission and church work. Missionaries never had the luxury of personal secretaries as U.S. pastors and area missionaries had.

On our second furlough a dear couple, Jack and Catharine Gregory, from Lovington, NM, bought for our work a new 16-millimeter movie projector. The mission had bought a few Christian movies that could be used. For the rest of my carerer this Kodak projector was a blessing. During the last 15 years I used it to show the Jesus film.

Surprise at the Post Office

On one of our furloughs a dear Baptist man in Lovington, Claude

Porter, gave us a used electric IBM typewriter. We used it a lot; finally the automatic return broke. By manually making it return we still could use it. I wrote to Claude and asked him to send me a new part to replace the damaged one. About three months later the central post office in Belo Horizonte sent us a note about a package. Leona and I were mystified and concerned about this. *What had we done wrong?* We knew that importing anything without permission was illegal. As soon as we could, we made a trip to Belo.

We went to the customs section on the second floor of the large central post office. We presented our summons notice; the man led us into a room in which a new IBM typewriter still in the original package was sitting on a table. He very gruffly reprimanded us for trying to import a new electric typewriter without the proper documents. We were flabbergasted! I guess the shock on both of our faces was obvious; we had no acceptable explanation. We explained that we had requested that our friend send us a simple piece to the typewriter we already had. The new typewriter was from our dear friend Claude Porter. The postal man's question was, "How is this possible that you didn't know about the typewriter being sent to you?" We hadn't been told! The officials wanted more than $300 for the typewriter—more than it originally cost. We didn't have the money, so what were we going to do? About that time the manager of the customs department entered and wanted to know what the problem was. We explained to him everything. He told us that he had been a student at the Baptist school in Belo and that his education at the school had been very valuable to him. At that time his children were students there. He believed us and let us take the typewriter with us for a small customs fee. God works in wondrous ways, His wonders to perform. God put on our friend's heart to send us the typewriter; Claude did not know about the strict importation laws. God knew about the difficulty of getting the typewriter out of customs and arranged for the leader of the customs department to appear at the right minute. *Wow!*

Chapter 7

The Eyes of the Lord on Us

God is absolutely amazing. We were working in a tiny area of the world, yet God through His Holy Spirit was working in the whole world and not just with us. I am reminded of the Scripture, *For the eyes of the Lord move to and fro throughout the earth that He may strongly support those whose heart is completely His* (2 Chron. 16:9).

The people of Jericho felt secure and at ease
As Joshua and the Israelites walked around it in the breeze,
For the Children of Israel had no weapons of great might,
So a disastrous defeat could not possibly be in sight.

Illogical, impossible, and militarily absurd,
Yet the people of Jericho for seven days were very perturbed
While Israel marched around them according to God's plan
And conquered Jericho without losing a single man!

As Israel was pepped up spiritually for its conquest of Jericho, missionaries likewise strive to be pepped up for every day. We certainly didn't have the grade of faith as Israel had at that time, but as the years went by God did increase our faith. Every day was a challenge; every day had blessings.

Introduction
In our early ministry in Brazil, television reception was bad; only a few people had televisions. Good Evangelicals didn't go to the cin-

emas, so for the 10 years we lived in Governador Valadares, we didn't go until *The Ten Commandments* film was shown in Valadares. The various churches encouraged their members to go and take their families and friends. Even for the upper grades the schools had very few extracurricular activities during the year. Carl and Jonathan did participate in a chess club of the city, but between them the schools had no sports. One extra activity celebrated was Brazil's independence from Portugal on September 7. So with few attractions (or distractions) the church was the main social activity. Christians had time to do more things for our Lord Jesus. Night services were well-attended and lasted two or three hours.

God's Protection in the Car

Several of our missionary colleagues that used the Rural Willys had experiences of various car problems. I, too, had my share of troubles with my Rural Willys. I will tell a few experiences and how God always provided help. I had been invited to lead a Sunday-afternoon evangelistic service in the home of a member of Vila Isa Baptist Church, a neighborhood across the river. I was told that the road leaving Vila Isa to the home to which I wanted to travel would end and only a foot path took people to the house; however, I could drive through the grass to get to the house. They didn't tell me to watch for tree stumps. On the way back I hit a stump hidden in the tall grass and knocked the wheel alignment completely crazy. I could go straight and make right turns, but I couldn't turn the wheels left. How was I going to get home without the ability to turn left?

I was fine until I reached the Rio-Bahia Highway, on which I needed to turn left. Fortunately the street I was on crossed the highway, so I went straight across. By making three right turns I was on the highway that went across the bridge. To get off the highway onto the main street was easy, because this was a right turn, but later I needed to turn left onto my street. I traveled another block; by making three right turns, this put me in the direction of our house. On Monday I took the car to a mechanic and made the same maneuvers. This experience was not the Willys' fault, so I can't blame it.

Once on a Saturday afternoon we were traveling home from Belo Horizonte when the back axle broke. Judy Ritchie, our journeygirl, also was with us. We were about five miles from the city of Joao Monlevade. We prayed for God to help us, which we did on all occasions when we had car trouble. The first car to pass stopped to help us. God answered our prayer; the Volkswagen van had four missionaries from Bethany Press. They lived in Coronel Fabriciano, another two hours further down the highway toward Governador Valadares. We all piled into their automobile. I left Leona and the family at a little hotel on the highway at the edge of Joao Monlevade to wait until I could find out what could be done to the car. I figured we would have to catch a bus home or spend the night at Joao Monlevade.

My greatest concern about leaving the car unattended for any length of time on the highway was that we had to leave our suitcases in the car. Normally all businesses close on Saturday at 1 p.m., but a few miles ahead I found a mechanic shop still open. I thanked the Bethany missionaries as they left me at the garage. I told the mechanic my problem. He quit what he was doing; we took off in his old wrecker that sputtered all the way to our car. He pulled our car to his garage but told me that two other cars were waiting to be fixed ahead of me. The hour would be very late before he could fix our car. He called a friend who sold auto parts. Although the friend's store was closed, the friend brought a new axle to the shop. One of the men waiting for his car to be fixed also was from Governador Valadares.

At about 9 p.m the mechanic started working on our car. The new axle from the parts store was for a car one year newer than our car and wouldn't fit. In the shop the mechanic had an older Jeep wagon that he recently had bought; the axle was the size needed, so he removed it and replaced ours. I had phoned Leona from the shop to tell her that probably the car would be fixed that night, so they could stay in the lobby of the hotel until we knew for sure. If the mechanic couldn't fix the car, we would have to try catching a bus so we could be at church the next morning. God blessed; about 10 p.m. I picked up the family and continued our journey for Governador Valadares. We arrived home about 1 a.m. and thanked God for being with us again. This is a part of The Marvel of It All!

On another occasion I had been traveling for a week on rough roads. As I drove into Governador Valadares, I had a feeling that I should have the front tie-rods of the car checked. I planned to do this the next day after I arrived. However, when I arrived on Monday afternoon, I had a message that Pastor Hilton and other pastors had arranged to look on Tuesday at some property for a mission in Inhapim. Inhapim was situated about 75 miles south on the Rio-Bahia Highway. We needed the mission car for the trip, so I wouldn't be able to take the car to the shop until Wednesday. Wednesday morning I left the house to take the car to the shop. Two blocks after crossing the bridge from the island on which we lived I turned left onto the major street. Halfway into the turn I heard a loud snap; in my hands the steering wheel spun around freely. The wheels had turned enough that I could coast up beside the cars parked parallel along the sidewalk in front of the stores, so I was able to stop. Would you say that God was with me? Had this happened the day before on the winding highway, the pastors and I could have been killed!

Another time I needed to contact the pastors about a new pastor arriving to lead Central Baptist Church in Governador Valadares. Since only one pastor had a phone, I had to go to their homes to let them know the arrival date, so we could go as a group to welcome Pastor Josias Antunes and his wife. Although I felt sure Pastor Josias hadn't arrived, an inner feeling led me to drive by and check. I touched the brakes to slow down to turn left onto the street passing in front of Central Baptist Church. At that point I had brakes. The Esplanada neighborhood is a very quiet, middle-class neighborhood with little traffic and usually no children playing in the street. Arriving near the front of the church building I applied the brakes to stop, but I had no brakes. I zoomed right on past and pushed frantically on the brake pedal. If I had gone to Esperanca Church on the main street as I first planned, I surely would have mowed down a few pedestrians, bicyclists, or a donkey and its cart. How happy I was that God had directed me to go by Central Baptist Church first, even though I knew that Pastor Josias wasn't to arrive until the next day.

Another time God helped was when my car was loaded with pastors going to the opening of our Baptist state camp near Belo Horizonte. Because of the rainy season I took the longer route. This time the clutch system went out. I know I sound as though I was very rough on cars, but I truly take pride in the cars I drive. To understand you would have to see the roads. We were fortunate that a bus on the way to Belo Horizonte stopped and we all got on. I got off at the next little town of Iapu; the pastors went on to camp. I doubted the little town would have a mechanic, but I was wrong. I had the car pulled to the shop. After two days at Iapu the car was fixed; I went on to camp for two enjoyable days with the pastors. Again God resolved my problem but not as fast as in other cases.

An Unforgettable Christmas in Santa Catarina

For Christmas 1970 we went to the Billy Morgans' home in the State of Santa Catarina. On our ship to Brazil we had sailed with the Morgans and looked forward to this visit. Judy Ritchie was with us; we had a good time as we traveled through the States of Minas, São Paulo, Parana, and to the coast of the State of Santa Catarina. We spent two-and-one-half days in getting to Florianopolis. Santa Catarina is next to the furthest state south in Brazil.

Before Christmas a Women's Missionary Union retreat was held for the Baptist women of Santa Catarina. Noreta Morgan had asked Leona to prepare and lead a program with the younger children while the women's study was occurring. All of the missionary wives, Judy Ritchie, and daughters went to the camp.

For the men and boys Marshall Flournoy planned a trip in his boat. We got up at 5 a.m. and went to the docks; we left at about 8 a.m. Marshall and his son, Billy Morgan and his two sons, my two sons and I, Richard Grant, and Jesse Kidd were those that went on this trip. All were of the Santa Catarina mission team except Carl, Jonathan, and me. We went to an island on which an old Portuguese fortress rested in ruins. For about an hour and a half we climbed around the ruins. When we left home, the weather was calm, but by this time the wind was blowing pretty strong. We had some difficulty getting into the boat with it rocking. As we started into the open sea, rain began to fall. Marshall had a Brazilian motorman helping. Billy Morgan was suffering with a cold, so he and the four boys stayed in the enclosed part of the boat. Waves crashed into the boat; although the boat had a motor to pump water out, the waves brought in more water than the motor could pump out. Marshall, Jesse, Richard, and I were in the open part of the boat. Each time we met a wave, the nose of the boat rose high and then dipped sharply down as the wave rolled under us.

134

Up and down, up and down we went as the rain pounded us. The boat also rocked dangerously from one side to the other. We were trying to stand up and bail water out of the boat as we rocked right and left and up and down at the same time.

Marshall knew we couldn't get to the dock in the city, so the Brazilian driver headed the boat toward the beach near the camp. We all were praying, for we were in a predicament that we hadn't imagined. We had on life jackets, but the danger was mounting. The driver knew that because of the rocks he couldn't beach at the camp, so he landed, by God's mercy, just above the Baptist camp. The boys and I went for help at the camp. The women knew we had planned to take the trip that day but consoled themselves by rationalizing: "Surely our husbands have more sense than to be out in this weather!" Boy, were they surprised when we walked into camp and were drenched from the rain! Our wives were glad to know we were safely back to shore. They took the cars to get the men who had stayed to secure the boat safely on the beach. *Wow!* God is good!

Marshall had planned a missionaries' New Year's retreat at the camp. More than 50 missionaries were present for this retreat. The rain kept us inside the big lodge, so we played games and stayed warm by the large fireplace. One night we had an opportunity to sing for the missionaries a song that I had written about traveling in a Rural Willys wagon, the type of car that at least half the missionaries drove. We sang to the tune of *Jingle Bells:*

RURAL WILLYS DAYS
Cruising over the hills
in a white and green Rural,
Enthralled with all the thrills,
Having such a ball.
We are going on our way,
Hoping to arrive at Florianopolis,
Before Christmas Day

(Chorus)
Oh, rattle, rattle, rattle, rattle, rattle all the way,
Oh what fun it is to ride in a Rural all the day.

Sailing over the bumps,
On modern coil springs,
Your heart really thumps,
And your ears begin to ring.
There is nothing like a ride
In a Rural all the way
To Florianopolis, for the Christmas holiday.

Now to all you former owners
Of the Rural wagon class,
You remember how to be careful
Not to run out of gas.
I will tell you what to do,
I will give you a hint,
Just pray that you return
From the place you just went.

Marshall had planned fireworks for a New Year's Eve festivities. We all were standing at a safe distance, but one of the fireworks fell over and went off. Its contents ablaze shot right at the crowd. Every one scampered; Richard Pamplin collided with Leona. In a split second all missionaries in its path managed to hit the ground or knock someone out of their way. No damage was done, but some laughs went along with the moaning and groaning. We made our three-day trip back home rejoicing because we didn't have any car trouble.

One of My Great Wishes
When I was traveling by myself, I had a lot of time to reminisce about the past. Traveling through the beautiful eastern part of Minas Gerais, Espirito Santo, or the mountains of Rio de Janeiro was always enjoyable and inspiring. Oh, how I would have loved to have had relatives or friends from the States to be able to see what I was seeing. These were times of worship for me—to meditate about God's creation and how He had blessed this part of the world with exceptional beauty. But loneliness invaded my being at times, too, so my mind would wander to the past. The most difficult times were during the rainy season in which I had to stay cooped up in a home during the

daytime while I waited to preach at night. I want to take you on an imaginary trip with me to Alegria de Simonesia, a village in my area.

After we left the asphalt of the Rio-Bahia Highway, we traveled on a very narrow, twisting road, with trees almost brushing the car on both sides. In places the road was shady and more enjoyable in the dry season but not too dusty. I hadn't been to Alegria de Simonesia before. I knew the church was an old church, but I didn't know what to expect. Arriving in the village I wondered who the *colporteur* (traveling Bible salesperson) was that had taken the message to this place, or perhaps the salvation message was proclaimed first by a village citizen who had been converted elsewhere. Finding the home of the one who invited me wasn't difficult, because she was the village clerk (*escrivao*) for the county. She recorded weddings and other legal matters.

Under the dim glow of a 25-watt light bulb we sat down to eat in the kitchen/dining-room area. Pots and pans were on the wood-fueled stove that filled the room with smoke and the aroma of our supper. Rice, beans, some yellow squash mixed with onion and a strong flavor of garlic, and crisp-fried cassava root were in some of those pots. I like the fried cassava root very much. More than beef, pork or chicken are the usual meats in the villages, because a steer is a larger animal and the people have no mechanical refrigeration. However, dried beef also is found. Hogs are smaller; a village can consume a hog in one day. Fried banana was the dessert.

That night during the worship service rain began falling very loudly—so loudly that the worshipers could barely hear me speaking. With the rain and darkness the temperature dropped quickly. The lights were so dim that we hardly could find our way the short distance to the house. I walked to church; therefore, I had to walk back. I was soaked because I didn't take my umbrella to church with me. I started shaking with a chill—shaking like a leaf. I barely got my wet clothes off and into some dry ones before the gas-fueled town generator went off. The woman of the house already had lit her small oil lamps. This lamp was made out of a tin can and on top was shaped like a funnel. A wick soaked in the oil stuck out of the hole on top. The woman hung my wet clothes on chairs close to the cookstove that was still warm.

My room was very, very tiny—just big enough for a single bed and tiny table. I was given a urinal so I wouldn't have to go outside during the night. The bed had a very thin mattress, but at least I had a room to myself. The darkness was so dense that one couldn't see an outline of anything in the room. The rain poured down like you couldn't believe unless you have been to a semi-tropical region. My mind wandered back to my decision ultimately to move to Brazil as a missionary. That decision was made about a month before the end of my freshman year in college. When I made that decision, also I knew I wanted to go to Jamaica as a Baptist Student Union missionary while I was in college. How would I be able to pay for my last year of college if I didn't work during that summer? If I went to Jamaica, I would need a suitcase and a camera, I didn't have either. I stopped buying sodas and other unnecessary things and saved enough money the last month to buy a suitcase at the PX in Ft. Bliss, TX, during our two-week National Guard summer maneuvers.

Most of the summer I worked as a "jug-hustler" for Amerada Petroleum Corp. I saved that money. When university classes started again, for three hours a day I worked as a janitor at the university. On Saturdays I worked for farmers or for a man that had a concrete business. Each month I also earned a little money from the National Guard weekly training sessions. During the two-week Christmas holidays I worked for a construction company and helped build a gasoline refinery. My goal was at the end of my sophomore year to have enough money to buy a good camera. I also had a ring fund (some day to buy an engagement ring for a woman) and a little money in a fund to go to Israel.

During the summer between my sophomore and junior college years I again worked for Amerada Petroleum. At National Guard maneuvers at the army base in Ft. Sill, OK, I bought a camera. My goal for my junior year was to have enough money saved to pay my tuition for the first semester plus one month of room and board. I didn't dare use this money for anything else. I was going to trust God to supply my needs for the rest of my senior year.

I applied to go to Jamaica but received word that the missionary in Jamaica was not making any requests for the summer of 1956. Somehow I didn't worry like I usually did. Two weeks later a letter arrived saying that the career missionary in Jamaica had decided to ask for nine student missionaries; I had been one of those chosen. In my room I finally drifted off to sleep. The next day was dark and gloomy and still pouring down rain. I visited with the family and talked and joked with the children. The hours passed slowly. I tried to read my Bible some, but the darkness was almost too great for me to read. I couldn't open the shutter because of the rain. After a while my mind wandered back to the subject I left off the night before.

I went to Jamaica and had a marvelous time. I preached some, led singing some, and helped lead Vacation Bible Schools. Since missionary McCullough was disappointed that I didn't take my trumpet, I bought a harmonica, which I enjoyed playing. My calling to missions was confirmed as I saw God working His wonders. Leona and I were going steady; she was a missions volunteer. After I had been away for two months in Jamaica, you can imagine the thrill I had to see her again.

Harold and Dorothy Runnels were the leaders of the Sunday-night youth department in my home church in Lovington. After National Guard duty I visited my dad and was invited to show my slides and speak about Jamaica in the youth department. Harold asked me to visit him in his office the next day.

I couldn't imagine why Harold wanted to see me at his office. After we had talked a while, he surprised me beyond expectations. He said he was going to send me $75 a month and gave me a gift certificate of $75 to buy whatever I wanted at Tipp's men's store. I went directly to Tipp's men's store in Lovington and bought a $75 suit that I saved for our wedding. The $75 a month was exactly what I needed to make up the difference between my monthly janitorial job at the university campus, National Guard earnings, and my monthly expenses. How did Harold know that? He didn't, but I knew God was providing. The Baptist Men of New Mexico also gave me $50 a semester to help pay tuition. God provided exactly what I needed to get through my last year in college. I had prepared only to pay my first-semester tuition and one month's rent and food supplies. Yes, God was still doing great things just as He did for the Israelites at Jericho.

All day Sunday in Alegria de Simonesia rain poured down. I was happy to arrive home the next day after I slipped and slid all over the muddy road until I reached the Rio-Bahia Highway. Yet I was blessed by the simple hospitality I received in that home, for the opportunity to preach and teach God's Word, and for the quiet time with God, but also I was thankful for the precious opportunity to reminisce about The Marvel of It All!

An Unexpected Visit

Each day many opportunities occurred for us to be a blessing in and out of our home—unexpected things that made the Christian life exciting. One day our family returned home to find a Volkswagen van parked in front of our house. The vehicle windows were covered with decals of every country and maps of many places around the world. We couldn't imagine whose van this could be. This was a new Volkswagen but different because it had a sliding door—something that hadn't arrived at the Volkswagen factory in Brazil. An elderly, humpbacked, white-haired woman got out of the car and asked whether we were the Tarrys. We affirmed that we were. She was Mrs. Burton, a 74-year-old who was making a tour through South America. She had bought the car in Germany, had it equipped inside with a bed, a writing table, a stove, a little snack table, and other essentials, and then had it shipped to Belem near the mouth of the Amazon River. South America was the last continent for her to tour. She wasn't interested in eating or sleeping in our house but just wanted to park her car inside the safety of our yard. We insisted that she eat and visit with us. She requested to take a shower. She let us know that she was not accustomed to children and that they sometimes got on her nerves.

Mrs. Burton had owned a piano conservatory just off the campus of the University of Los Angeles. When she wasn't traveling, she resided in San Luis Obispo, CA. She sold the conservatory and began to travel. Mrs. Burton had been all over the world and even to Moscow and only places in Russia and China allowed for tourists.

Mrs. Burton arrived at Belem before her special automobile arrived, so she took a boat trip up the Amazon River to Manaus. The day before she arrived in Manaus, a spider bit her. Her leg turned black; she passed out on the dock. Not knowing Portuguese she asked the officials in Manaus whether any Americans were living in that city. Someone gave her SBC missionary Lonnie Doyle's name.

Lonnie and Janelle took her to a doctor and then to their home for her to recuperate. Lonnie Doyle was well-known to us because his father, Lonnie Doyle Sr., was pastor of First Baptist Church of Portales, NM, in which Leona grew up and I was a member while I studied at Eastern New Mexico University. On one of the Doyles' furloughs Leona had met him.

Mrs. Burton thought she would be traveling down the new Belem-Brasilia highway; she didn't know the highway wasn't paved. She traveled about 1,000 miles or more on a treacherous dirt road cut through the jungle. She didn't travel at night but ate and slept in her van because few towns or villages existed along the way. By the time she arrived in Anapolis, Goias, near Brasilia, the engine in her Volkswagen van was about to fall off its engine struts. The Volkswagen company in Anapolis installed a new engine for her. (After all, she was good publicity for them!)

Mrs. Burton told us some of her experiences. I asked her what her children thought about her adventures. She said, "They think I am crazy!" She wasn't able to see the coastland of North Brazil, since she had traveled south through the middle of Brazil on the Belem-Brasilia highway. She had arrived in Governador Valadares to get on the Rio-Bahia Highway to travel north to see such cities as Fortaleza, Recife, and beyond. Mrs. Burton was a Methodist, but I gave her the names of Baptist missionaries to the north and called the nearest ones to let them know when she was to arrive.

About two weeks later she was back in Valadares to continue her journey south to Rio de Janeiro and as far as she could go in Argentina, across and up through Chile on the Pan American Highway, and back to the United States sometime near the end of 1970. I called missionaries in Rio de Janeiro; she stayed in Rio several days before she went to São Paulo. The amazing thing to me was that she spoke just a few words of Portuguese and only a little Spanish, yet she made her way through Rio de Janeiro and São Paulo with their millions of people. She found the missionary residences that for me were difficult to find. The last we heard about her, she was in Peru and was getting very tired. Mrs. Burton, the courageous Methodist explorer, found Southern Baptist missionaries to be very hospitable.

Remodeling Our House

Another goal we had before we went on our second furlough was to enclose the small room I used for my study at the back of our house. We wanted to make an area for the breakfast room. Because the office door was outside, the hard rains would get into the office. The former breakfast room would be another bedroom for guests. The hallway area, with no windows, was dark and still was barnyard red—we had it painted light cream. Air-conditioners were very rare, but we bought an old one and installed it at the entrance of the house to cool just the hallway, but with no ceiling the air-conditioner didn't help much. We were approved to make these changes. For our bedroom we planned to bring from the States a smaller air-conditioner. The heat was very humid and drained us of our energy.

Leona and I had the opinion that the men were dragging their feet and wouldn't get the house finished before we had to leave on furlough. At this time in Brazil most men would take no advice whatsoever from a woman. One day when I wasn't at home, Leona saw that the man wasn't working because the other man had to go buy something. She suggested he could scrape the wall, which needed to be done. He got angry and walked off the job as he said, "If she were my wife, I'd kill her." The work was finally completed before our furlough. I enjoyed having the office open into the house, especially in rainy weather.

One mysterious but wonderful thing about our situation on the island was that at about 9 on almost every calm, summer night, a cool breeze would blow over the water from the east into our bedroom windows. Whoever built the house knew that and put the bedrooms on that side for a purpose. By that breeze you could almost set your watch if you needed to do so. But before the breeze you sweltered in the heat. Another memorable thing about the location was that we were about two blocks from the lower end (east) where the rapids in the river were. Because of these rapids the river at the east end of the island was not navigable for anything but canoes; the rapids were dangerous even for them. At night we enjoyed hearing the rhythm of the rapids; this helped me sleep, except in the rainy season when the river was rising. Several times the river invaded the lower parts of the island. Several times it was dangerously close to overflowing at the east point.

My Writings

In college I enjoyed my literature classes and did a little bit of writing—mainly poetry. In seminary I had one semester of writing under Dr. Dobbins. The first year in Brazil I wrote four major stories that were published in the Foreign Mission Board monthly magazine *The Commission*. In 1968 the FMB wanted better coverage of the global work missionaries were doing, so I was elected the first South Brazil mission reporter. This was an honor but brought a lot more responsibility. I was to report to *The Commission* important happenings going on in the South Brazil mission area and also encourage other missionaries to write about things in their local fields. I crammed this responsibility in among the other things I was already doing.

During the next three years I made several trips throughout most of the South Brazil mission area and covered various meetings. On one of the trips one thing I discovered was that the personalities of missionaries sometimes was different when they attended the annual mission meeting than it was when they were on their fields. For instance one certain strongly opinionated missionary talked on nearly every subject that was discussed in the meetings. His face got very red as he defended or presented his opinion about the things close to his heart. He was the one that picked me up at the airport in Porto Alegre, Rio Grande do Sul, when I went on a press assignment. He took me to the dedication of the state camp and also to the ceremony in which the administrative part of their Baptist school was turned over to Brazilian leadership.

I spent the first night in the home of the man and his wife; then we went to the camp. By the time he left me at the airport three days later, I had a completely different opinion about him. He really was a dear, beloved, mild, diligent-working missionary. From that point on I resolved not to judge any missionary on how the person acted at annual mission meeting. The whole problem revolves around so many needs that all of us saw on our fields; each of us wanted our work to go forward. Therefore, some of us had difficulty presenting our needs without showing emotion; this would give a misconception about our real daily spiritual dispositions.

One day I received a notice to meet with Dr. Jesse Fletcher of the Foreign Mission Board and Dr. W. C. Fields, director of Baptist Press. They requested that I attend a press-representative clinic in Rio de Janeiro. At this meeting I received the plans for the future press-representative program. I knew that I would have to make a choice, because the press representative would be a full-time job. Dr. North, editor of *The Commission*, had asked me to write three articles; I hadn't had time to write them. The idea to train for a full-time position as a reporter tugged at my heart, but I didn't believe that was God's plan for my life. After I served for three years part-time, Roberta Hampton was appointed to be press representative on a full-time basis.

Island Baptist Mission Moves

The island mission had received $1,500 from the strategic property fund supplied by Southern Baptists. This money helped us build a 24-foot-wide by 36-foot-long chapel as a beginning. On March 15, 1970, the Island Baptist Mission moved out of our house into the first small part of a large future church building. I had the plans drawn up for a three-floor building that would all be used for the educational building after building a larger worship center in the future. We had a problem getting the floor plans approved because of the same problem we had at Fifth Church. Since Brazil is a Catholic country and Catholic churches don't have Sunday-school rooms, the construction authorities couldn't understand why a church needed small rooms. Catholics have many schools; the schoolrooms have the standard size like the secular schools have. Therefore the authorities wanted us to keep the standard schoolroom size for all rooms except for the collective worship area. Most Evangelical churches never sought to get their buildings approved by the city, because most didn't plan very far ahead or want to be out that expense of paying fees to architects and city ordinances. I wanted to do things legally; that cost us extra money and some delays. You wouldn't believe how difficult our idea of Sunday-school rooms was to get approved.

When we moved to our new facility, we had only one big room and two bathrooms in a separate small building. We divided the area with curtains for Sunday-school divisions just like I remembered from the little country church I attended when I was a boy. All classes together made a lot of noise! The building was not plastered yet, so it was rather drab. Various friends from the States sent money to help: a woman that kept up with our ministry through the prayer calendar, Judy Ritchie's parents, and her aunt sent enough money to have the cement floor finished and the walls plastered. Judy Ritchie's folks also sent $400 to buy a pump organ. Our people also sacrificed to help in the construction of the building.

My heart also was with Fifth Baptist Church because it still didn't have the roof on the second floor of the building that was started two years earlier. The pastor that took my place didn't stay very long, so I became the interim pastor; I gave one Sunday a month to them. People at Fifth Baptist Church were more needy financially than people at the island church, so we continued to help them as much as we could.

A New Association Organized

I have already given you an idea of the great size of the Sweet River Valley Association. The distance and bad roads were the reasons that some churches had difficulty sending representatives to associational meetings. We had already divided the area into four regions with the idea for future smaller associations. The northeastern region with 11 strong churches, about 15 missions, and many preaching points organized itself into an association. They wanted me to continue to work with them. This meant I would be expected to be at the meetings of both associations but wouldn't be responsible for their program of activities. In some ways my responsibility with them was diminished; that was a good thing.

Architectural Advice

Earlier in life I had helped my father some in concrete work that involved some small buildings. I had visited many Stateside churches and had an imagination for helping improve the Sunday-school space in Brazilian churches. I was sought after in the area of helping plan a few churches beautify their buildings. A missionary never knows what all he or she may be sought after to do. In a way this is a part of The Marvel of It All. We surrender to God's plan; sometimes God pulls out of us so many other things that we are amazed. Besides drawing up the general plan for Fifth Baptist Church and Island Baptist Church in Valadares, Bill Richardson and I helped First Baptist Church in Mantena plan its educational building. Mantena is situated at the extreme eastern boundary of the association. I helped two other churches in Mantena with remodeling and another planning a larger worship building. I drew up the plans for a two-story educational building for the thriving church in Resplendor. I think my emphasis on Sunday school at several of the associational meetings helped the churches get a vision that all age groups are important. Almost all the churches built a big room for the young people and a tiny room for the children. Children from about 6 to 12 years of age were put together in the same class. I stressed that the young people could meet with the adults, but babies needed a room separate so the mothers wouldn't have to deal with them for two to three hours each Sunday morning. I encouraged them to divide the children into at least three classes.

I want Southern Baptists to know about the places in which a little bit of their money has gone for helping to buy properties and build chapels. By the middle of 1970 I had been responsible for distributing several thousand dollars on many projects in the Sweet River Valley Association. By the time we left the Sweet River Valley, several more thousand dollars were used in helping buy properties and help build buildings. Dollars went a long way, because during those 10 years the value of Brazilian money was inflated from 30 percent to more than 100 percent. Labor and construction materials were very cheap; this helped the dollars go further.

Other Doors of Opportunity

In April 1970 the daily Baptist radio program was initiated. The main preacher for this 25-minute program was Pastor Hilton, but when he was traveling, other pastors preached. The new Radio and Television Commission of Brazilian Baptists had taped programs we could use when needed. Occasionally, when my time arrived for me to lead the radio program, I used those taped programs, because my Portuguese still was not good enough for me to preach on the radio.

A former pastor of First Baptist Church left the domination for a while, but after he saw his mistake, he returned. He opened a private school on the other side of the city. Every day he planned a devotional time at school. Every Baptist pastor that could arrange to do so was scheduled for these services. I went once a month. In one of our programs Leona, Judy, and I sang while Leona played the accordion. I also played a special trumpet number.

Leona and I had added Bible drills and speakers tournaments for the teens and young peoples' monthly activities for the churches in Valadares. We prepared and mimeographed the materials to send out to the churches. The judges for the events had to be trained. We felt as though this extra effort would be worthwhile. We gave good religious books to the winners—books by Billy Graham and a few other well-known spiritual leaders whose books had been translated into Portuguese.

Troubleshooting for the Lord

Trying to help messed-up lives was part of our daily work, but sometimes special or more difficult cases took a lot of time. A missionary colleague in Volta Redonda, Rio de Janeiro, called us to help a beautiful young Baptist woman who had run away from her husband. They suggested she and her two small boys go to Valadares to hide. This woman had been offered a scholarship to study piano in France to prepare to be a concert pianist. Instead she had married a man who had no ambition, but even worse he became abusive to her. Leona and I met her and saw that the woman was in a desperate situation. Leona tried to arrange a few piano students for her but wasn't successful. We offered our piano and living room for her studio.

She hired a maid from off the street to take care of her boys while she worked. The maid turned out to be wicked. This maid gave the woman misery; after a while she fired her and hired another. The first maid refused to leave. The pianist was afraid of the first maid because she told stories of how the maid fought with knives. Twice I moved the pianist in an effort to stop the woman from stalking her. When for the third time she appeared at the pianist's house, I told the wicked maid very emphatically that if she didn't disappear immediately, I was going to call the police. The pianist was afraid for me to talk to the maid that way, because she was afraid that the woman would harm

147

me. The pianist finally took her two boys to relatives in Salvador so she could concentrate on paying off her debts in Valadares. This situation was one of the saddest we had encountered; she was a beautiful, talented woman who had a messed-up life.

Our Little Missionaries

As much as possible we involved our children in our work. Brazilians adore children, so our children were assets in visitation. When they weren't in school, they went visiting with Leona and me. Our kids also participated in most of the home and Sunday-afternoon outdoor evangelistic services.

When the island mission had the first revival in the new building, I had 1,000 invitations made to hand out on the island. After the volunteers had covered the whole island, Carl, Jonathan, and I went down to the bridge and handed out the rest of the invitations to everyone that passed.

Weekday worship services in homes on birthdays and anniversaries are very common. In these services family and friends are invited and an evangelistic service is always held with an invitation to accept Christ. The accordion was a valuable instrument; anyone that played a guitar was an asset as well. Our children went to most of these meetings. We found the Brazilian Christians very open about their faith in Jesus and eager to share their testimony with others. The common question they ask is: "Are you Catholic or believer (Christian)?" All Evangelical Christians are called *believers*.

Leona Starts Work with Preschoolers

The idea of church workers with small children during the worship service was unknown. The little ones walked around the church at will; some played around the pulpit. Occasionally one would pull on my suit pants. I was afraid I was going to step on one of them. Some parents didn't seem to mind what their children did. One day I asked Leona whether she could do something about taking care of the children during the worship time. By this time Judy had left, but we had another organ player to join our mission.

Soon after the island mission was in the new building, plans were made for us to build a three-room, temporary building for the children. One room was for the kitchen and babies through 3-years old; a second room was for children 4-6 years old, and the third room was for children 7-10. For many years Leona had worked with adolescents, but the lack of attention and provisions for children touched her heart. The mothers took the babies along with them to the auditorium for Sunday school and worship, but the little ones disturbed others.

Leona talked to the women and youth about taking turns caring for younger preschool children during the worship hour. She trained those interested in teaching and not just babysitting. One of the missionaries in Rio had prepared mimeographed booklets for preschool workers; Leona ordered the materials. Leona made teaching materials for the classes. In a short time we had a well-organized preschool class. The regular teachers were elected along with the other teachers, but the volunteers were scheduled to work once or twice a month during the worship service.

An Unusual Door Opens

I became acquainted with the editor of our local daily newspaper. He wanted to see our church building. For one thing Sr. Miguel liked to speak English with me. He was a bachelor and a Catholic. I took him to see our church facilities. He was interested in the small tables and chairs for the children. I explained to him the importance of teaching Bible truths to children. Later that day he ate dinner with us. Then Sr. Miguel did a very wonderful thing. The Catholics had their own radio station and always had all the space they wanted in the local newspaper. Sr. Miguel offered me a weekly newspaper column. I was puzzled, since I was a stranger and not even able to speak or write properly. But what an opportunity! I accepted, but I knew I would need help. I couldn't produce a column each week, because I didn't have time and was gone sometimes. He agreed that I could choose other pastors among Baptists and Presbyterians; that I did.

A couple of years later a lot of grumbling openly was expressed about the slow progress Valadares was making in reaching city goals. I thought I might cheer the people up by telling them of changes for the better that Leona and I had noticed in the years we had lived in Valadares. Sr. Miguel gave half a page to my article.

I began by reminding Valadares residents about the old post

office. In no small town I had ever visited, much less a city the size of Valadares, had I ever seen a post office so rundown. When we arrived in Valadares the post office was tiny, dilapidated, and dirty. When missionary Ronny Boswell tried to rent a box for us, the people at the post office said they had none available, but several boxes did not have doors. Ronny told them emphatically that the Tarry family had moved to Valadares and would be getting a lot of mail—some from other countries of the world. We were important and had to have a box. Ronny asked why some of the boxes didn't have doors. Their answer was that they had been torn off. Ronny asked them why a door couldn't be repaired. He asked whether we could rent the box if we paid to have the door repaired. The postal superintendent replied, "Yes, if you pay for the door, you can rent it!"

Possibly the reason why the post office had no interest in repairing the doors on boxes was that the new post office was to be completed in about a year. I didn't put all about our ordeal in the newspaper but only reminded the people that the large, beautiful post office was a great asset to the city.

Since I am writing about mail service, I will insert this amazing incident. While we were in Valadares, we had a very strange thing happen. One day from the U.S. a letter containing just our name and Minas Gerais, Brazil, on the envelope arrived. How that letter got to Valadares without Governador Valadares and our post-office box written on the envelope I will never know. The letter also was put in the right box. I wanted to think that we were so important to be known in the huge State of Minas Gerais (size of Texas) that everyone knew us. We knew that wasn't the case, but someone in the central post office must have known who we were. This still is a mystery!

In the article I mentioned the city hall in which workers were crowded into small spaces and that the building was dirty and very disagreeable to enter. Now the city had a beautiful, new, three-story building. I pointed out that four years earlier, when we arrived, parking places on the main street were easy to find, but now parking space was sometimes difficult to find because many people were buying cars.

I reminded them that we had noticed more of the downtown streets had *paralelepipedos* (stone) paving. Many of the downtown stores had modernized their show windows. Two more small supermarkets recently had opened. I reminded them that the telephone service was about to get better with a micro-system or satellite system that was soon to be installed on Ibituruna mountain. I complimented them on the improvements of sewer and water that had been extended to several new neighborhoods. A new area had been set aside for a technological college, the airport had an extended asphalt runway, and a terminal building was to be built. On and on I went. I was afraid of what some citizens might say about an American being so frank with them, but I left the impression that we were proud to live in Valadares. I told them that after talking with many people in Valadares and when I traveled on trains, airplanes, and buses, I perceived patience was short in Brazil, but we had seen a lot of progress. In the article I admitted that Governador Valadares was not our first choice among three states we had visited, but God had directed us to Valadares. We loved Valadares; I thanked them for accepting and for receiving us so openly.

Worship Program Grows

As our island mission grew, we had enough musically talented people to start a choir. The Lord blessed our choir all the time we remained in Valadares. The choir helped prepare the spiritual atmosphere each Sunday and during our revival on the island. I, being the choir leader, could choose the songs I wanted for the message. The ladies quartet started by Judy Ritchie continued until we moved to Belo Horizonte. The quartet sang on various special occasions outside our church. As the congregation grew, we added the mission organizations for girls and boys. Leona led in the Girls in Action mission program; I led the Royal Ambassadors. We were moving toward a full program for all ages. At one point we organized a choir of the G.A. and R.A. kids in all the churches in Valadares and were able to sing at some of the churches.

By 1970 Minas Gerais had 90 pastors for about 160 churches. You can see why I believed serving as pastor for churches as well as doing other things was necessary.

Cantaloupes Irritate Airplane Passengers

About the fourth year I was in Minas Gerais, I went to a national Baptist convention in Recife. Ronald Boswell and I had return tickets on the same flight from Recife to Belo Horizonte. Ronny and I took a taxi to the airport together. After we got into the cab, Ronald said, "Let's go by the market and get some cantaloupes." We couldn't get cantaloupes in Minas Gerais. I said: "Ronny, we do not have time for that!" He said, "The market is on the way to the airport; this will take just a minute." I was nervous, but Ronny was a happy-go-luck guy; things seemed to go his way. Nearly every time I rode with him anywhere in Belo, the gasoline needle was on empty. That always made me nervous, but when I was with him, we never ran out of gas. So we stopped at the enormous fruit, vegetable, and "whatever" market. I bought seven cantaloupes; Ronny bought about the same number. In those days the market didn't have paper sacks or plastic bags. People carried their own shopping basket or wire basket that had two little wheels.

When we arrived at the taxi, I put three of my cantaloupes in my suit bag, gripped the other four tightly to my body with my right arm, and held my briefcase in my left hand. We arrived at the airport 10 minutes after boarding time. Of course Ronny probably counted on the airplane arriving late, because that often happened, too. Baggage-handlers always were ready to help with luggage, so we had no trouble getting to the counter with our luggage. When we arrived at the ticket counter, the people there were impatiently waiting for us. All other passengers had been on the plane several minutes; the two engines were warmed up and ready to go. I had to put the cantaloupes on the counter so I could find my ticket, while the baggage people whisked our luggage rapidly to the airplane to be loaded. Running with four cantaloupes on one arm and a briefcase in the other hand was difficult, but I made it.

I was very embarrassed to get on the airplane, with all eyes glaring at the door to see who had been holding the flight on the ground. The only place onto which I could put the cantaloupes was on the floor and then corral them with my feet. The old DC-3 airplane had a small tail wheel that sat on the ground and rose off the ground only after the plane reached a certain speed before it rose into the air. From the start the cantaloupes tended to roll to the tail end of the plane. I managed to get the four cantaloupes under my control until the airplane's nose left the ground and pointed into the sky. All the cantaloupes rolled between the passengers' feet toward the end of the plane. This amused most of the passengers and took away much of their ire at these two Americans who made them leave late because of some cantaloupes. I had to look right into the faces of the passengers who brought me the cantaloupes as they descended from the plane. Ronny and I both descended the plane with our cantaloupes in hand. In Belo I caught a bus for Governador Valadares. Thanks to Ronny Boswell I arrived home and surprised my family with seven delicious cantaloupes. The cantaloupes were greatly appreciated.

Chapter 8

Firm in the Faith

The New Testament is just as full of God's marvelous might—
Not of military conquests but about the spiritual fight,
The conquest of souls wrenched from Satan and his evil bands;
Christ's victorious, perfect life, resurrection, and nail-
scarred hands.

Of the disciples, Zacchaeus, and the woman at the well,
Oh! The power in Jesus to save them from hell!
The marvel of it all echoes in my heart and brain.
I never tire of hearing and telling it again and again.

Saul rose up to destroy all that Jesus on earth had done.
He tirelessly worked and was having such a lot of fun
Until on the road to Damascus He met Jesus face to face.
It changed Him so that He is the best writer
about God's grace.

I'm always amazed to see the expressions of real joy on people's faces the moment they accept Jesus Christ as their Lord and Savior. The experience of seeing joy on the faces makes me aware of the power of God through His Holy Spirit. To God be the glory!

Extra Activities
In the month of May we sponsored for our pastors in the city a clinic on the radio ministry. Missionary O.D. Martin, director of the Radio and Television Board for Brazilian Baptists, led this. He stayed

at our house. Then, for the first time, we had the bi-monthly state mission meeting held at our house. Everyone stayed with us, except our senior missionaries Arnol and Edna Harrington stayed in a hotel. In early June we held our first sweetheart banquet for the youth of all the Baptist churches in Valadares. We held this at First Baptist Church. I invited six-foot-nine-inch Kent Faris, from the neighboring State of Espirito Santo, to be the speaker. He also was a very good chalk-talk artist; Sarah Faris sang at the event. You may remember that when we first visited Governador Valadares, First Baptist Church met in an old reformed house, but 2 1/2 years later it had a three-story building. Part of the upper floor was a large patio; for the next few years this was the location for the sweetheart banquet.

You Have to See This to Believe

For missionaries living in Brazil having an interest in soccer is very helpful. Except for in the U.S. soccer is the major sport in the world. Brazil had won the World Soccer Cup twice and for four years was training to win again. Brazil invited Dr. Kenneth H. Cooper, a former American army medical doctor who designed the program for aerobics and the running exercise program, to help the Brazil team with its physical preparation. During the year for the World Cup, soccer (*futebol*) fever always is contagious. In the 1970 playoffs Brazil advanced to the finals by beating Czechoslovakia, England, Peru, Uruguay, and finally Italy. Brazil played all of its games on Wednesday nights and Sunday afternoons; these overlapped with our night-service hour. Baptists are fans, but most of them believe that God and His work should be first, so during the games we had good attendance but no visitors.

You have to experience the occasion to believe what happens when Brazil makes a goal during one of these games. The cities and towns erupt with thunderous explosions of firecrackers and bursting rockets. Many of the people run out of their houses and into the streets; they leave their TV's and radios blaring while they set off their fireworks. I felt sorry for the dogs. I believed that Brazil needed many dog psychologists to help the dogs recover from their shock. During the games I saw dogs running, running, running and not seeming to know where they were going—just running aimlessly with their tongues hanging out. They were looking for places to hide and to escape the horrific noise.

When the heroes returned home with their third World Cup, the government proclaimed a national holiday. The heroes received a welcome similar to the U.S. celebration in which the astronauts returned from the moon. Dr. Cooper was the other hero for the team. Team members gave Dr. Cooper, with his physical training methods, credit for helping them win. Every time in the following years that Dr. Cooper returned to Brazil, he was given a royal welcome. Running for exercise became very popular; an expression such as "Have you done your Cooper today?" was very common. Doing your "Cooper" meant doing your exercise—principally running.

Preparation for Organization of Island Baptist Church

The island mission decided to organize into a church October 15. This new goal put some extra pressure on us, because before we organized, the building needed to be finished and benches made. The annual mission meeting at Caxambu in July would take some of the pressure off of us, for this reunion with all missionaries in South Brazil bonds scattered missionary families together. The meetings, however, run all day and occasionally last until midnight. Although we lived in the State of Minas Gerais, in which the meeting was to be held, our journey to the meeting took us 15 hours of travel time, while some missionaries traveled for two-and-a-half days.

On the good side, however, the months of August and September 1970 were very good for us. The first good news was that Jonathan accepted Christ. Charlotte followed him, but she was only influenced by his decision. Also, news arrived that the Foreign Mission Board (FMB) was giving missionaries other options for their furloughs. After 30 months on the field missionaries were eligible for a four-month furlough, 35 months a six-month furlough, 40 months an eight-month furlough, and 48 months for a year furlough. These new options changed our minds about a four-month furlough to a six-month furlough and made us eligible for leaving in March 1971 instead of December 1970. Now we had more time to reach our goals before we went to the States.

More good news was that Judy Ritchie's uncle and aunt sent us

$600 from their income-tax returns. This paid off our debts and helped paint our new building in time for the organization of our mission into a church. Judy's home church sent us enough money to buy a pump organ. Then we received another letter that Judy's uncle and aunt were sending us through the FMB another gift—enough to build two large rooms onto the back of our existing one-room worship area. This enabled us also to build a baptistery. This extended our building to the back property line. We rejoiced because God had been so good through friends. We had a month before our organization to get it all done. With God's help we succeeded. These things were falling into place so neatly that I remembered the verse: *Now to Him who is able to do exceeding abundantly beyond all that we ask or think, according to the power that works within us, to Him be the glory in the church and in Christ Jesus to all generations forever and ever. Amen* (Eph. 3:20).

I visited the mayor and told him about our plans to organize our mission into a church and to dedicate our church building; I invited him to be present. I asked him to clean up the block across the street; this block was designated to be part of a huge park. He surprised me by not only cleaning the lot but planting grass and putting up streetlights and nice park benches on which people could sit. This was all ready for the organization day.

During this same time the concrete roof finally had been finished at Fifth Baptist Church. Whenever families have a sufficient income, homes and buildings have concrete-slab ceilings as well as concrete floors installed; this makes them cooler and also safer. A robber easily can remove enough tiles to lower himself into a building but of course can't do that when a concrete roof is present.

A Mysterious Incident Occurs

This mysterious incident happened about an hour before the service for the organization of the island mission into a church. Thursday night, October 15, 1970, was a long-awaited event. Mr. Herringer, a deacon in Central Baptist Church, and I were standing outside near the back of the church building waiting for his truck to arrive with 16 new benches. His company had made the benches. The sun had set in the west, but darkness had not enveloped the island. A gray Rural

Willys stopped in front of the church; a man hurried up to us. He stopped and in a strong voice said, "You are to name this church Holy Spirit Church!" I said: "Would you repeat that, *senhor*? I do not understand what you mean." The man repeated the same thing but added, "*amarelo, verde, e azul*" (yellow, green and blue). I looked at Mr. Herringer and asked him whether he understood what the man was saying. He said he didn't. The man repeated the whole thing again and then turned around abruptly, hurried back to his car, and left.

That night with a packed house the island mission was organized into a church. I had invited Pastor Muryllo Cassete, pastor of First Baptist Church of Belo Horizonte, to speak and also to stay for a three-day revival. At the Sunday-night service I noticed that the mysterious man who had shown up earlier was on the back row near the door. I immediately thought I would speak to him as soon as the service was over and ask him for an explanation. After the preaching I had a filmstrip to show, so the lights were turned out while I showed the film. When the lights were turned on, the man had left.

I didn't talk to Leona about these strange things. A week after our revival Pastor Hilton, Pastor Waldemar, and I went on a week-long trip to visit all the mayors in the 30 towns and villages in the western part of the association in which we didn't have Baptist work. Our goal was to meet with the mayors and to give each a Bible. As usual we traveled in my mission car. On the way I shared with the pastors what had happened with the mysterious man. Pastor Hilton laughed and joked, "Pastor Joe, the guerillas are going to kidnap you." I didn't take this remark as a joke, although I didn't want to let them know that I was worried. You see, the colors yellow, green, and blue are the Brazilian national colors—the colors of the flag. I had thought that a political connection might be involved in the person's behaviors because on November 15 was a national election day. But to order me to name our church "Holy Spirit Church" didn't make any sense. What did the church have to do with the national colors? This person certainly was a nut, but maybe this was a warning.

After I returned home from the trip, Leona told me about a strange thing that happened. I had arranged for a neighbor who was attending our church to take my family to church on Wednesday night. Leona told me that a gray car was waiting in the darkness as they left the church on Wednesday night. The car followed them part of the way home. I had not told Leona nor Judy about the other incident, because I didn't want them to worry. I resolved that when I returned from the next trip, I would go to the army battalion headquarters and tell the people there about these strange things. On Monday I returned home and went to the battalion headquarters. I was sent to the intelligence officer. I told him everything. He said that the situation was very strange but that he had no lead as to this occurrence being related to the guerrillas. But he said he wouldn't be surprised what they might do on November 15, because on Election Day they might do anything to embarrass the military government. However, this Election Day was not to choose a president or even governors; it was just an election of national and state representatives, senators, and county officials. The intelligence chief told me to have all the family stay close to home and not leave the island on November 15.

I went home and told Leona what I had done, because I wanted her to know what had been happening and that I was doing something about it. She told me that at church on Sunday night the puzzle had been solved. The man had done the same thing on Wednesday night, so on Sunday night Leona shared with a group of adults her concern about the incidents. One of our young single men, Nilson, said: "Oh, I know who he is. He lives across the street from me. He is a professor at the university and has been having terrible headaches. Someone in the chemistry department mixed up something for his headaches; this medicine has made him irrational. He had sent a letter to President Nixon asking Nixon to endorse him for president of Brazil." Nilson said we didn't need to worry about the guy.

Leona and I went to visit the mystery man and were well-received. He told us that he had terrible headaches and sometimes didn't know what he was doing. He went to São Paulo and stayed several months for treatments. About a year later he attended Sunday school and later made a public decision accepting Christ as Savior. I began preparing him for baptism, but he had another sickness episode and left town. We never heard from him again.

We organized Island Baptist Church with more than 50 members. We hoped that some of the members of First Baptist Church that lived on the island would join, but none did. One couple joined from Esperanca Baptist Church, which for one year I had served as pastor. A wonderful blessing is that by November 30 we had 97 enrolled in Sunday school and 10 preparing for baptism. The custom is that before they were baptized, all new converts were to go through a doctrinal and discipleship class that usually required about three months to complete. When I was present, I taught the doctrinal class during the Sunday-school hour.

Opening Work in Guanhaes

Guanhaes is an important city because in our association this was the first work west of the Rio-Bahia Highway. This town of about 20,000 people is important to the work in the Sweet River Valley. The mission in Guanhaes was begun by First Baptist Church of Governador Valadares. The Assembly of God and the Presbyterians already had churches in Guanhaes. The Presbyterians had five American missionaries living in the city. This area is basically ranching country. A single Presbyterian veterinarian arrived in Brazil and met a single Southern Baptist woman. They were married and had some kids about our children's ages. The Presbyterian pastor and wife also had some children about our children's ages. An older single woman missionary taught the children of the two couples. The Presbyterians had a beautiful little church building, but after six years they still only had 35 members. I mention this to show that the work in this area was very difficult. After one year the Baptist mission had only 18 members; two of these families had moved from Governador Valadares to help establish the mission.

In Guanhaes we rented a large, empty store on Main Street; I spent a week doing evangelistic preaching. Each night after the evangelistic message I showed a movie. The people were ignorant about the gospel; most were not even interested in a Bible. However we handed out hundreds of gospel tracts and each night preached to between 200 and 300. That was a victory. We found out that some of the tracts and Bibles we gave away later were burned. One young man brought his New Testament back to the mission pastor and said his family wouldn't let him keep it nor attend any more. Later the mission pastor told me that many others had told him their parents or relatives wouldn't let them return to the services. But some seeds were planted.

Our First Trip to Itambacuri

Itambacuri was a town about 65 miles north of Governador Valadares on the Rio-Bahia Highway. No Evangelical church existed in the town. As a project of our churches in Governador Valadares we planned a mission trip made up of members from the seven churches. On Wednesday Pastor Hilton and I went up to get the permit from the mayor so we could have an open-air service and arrange with someone next to the park to furnish electricity for our public-address system. We received written permission to have the evangelistic service on the next Saturday just before dark; after dark we would show a movie film.

A bus was rented for the event; a few of us went by car. We started the service with good music. A man appeared with a note saying that we didn't have the document the city required for us to hold an open-air service and that we would have to leave. The pastors decided this was a maneuver by the Catholics to scare us, so we continued the service. Just as Pastor Hilton started to preach, some people told us the Catholic priest and a mob were on their way to run us out of town. We decided nothing was going to stop us, even though only a few city residents were present for the service; the crowd was mostly just our group. Sure enough the mob appeared, but Pastor Hilton continued preaching, so the mob also heard some of the message.

When he finished preaching, the priest demanded that we leave. We didn't get to show the movie, because the owner of the home that furnished the electricity for the loudspeaker had been threatened, so for his family's sake he was afraid for us to continue and to show the movie. The mayor of Itambacuri wasn't there that Saturday afternoon to prove we had actually made our request properly. A few years later land was bought; a church building was built at the entrance of the city.

Dreaming about Bats

Our first attempt to raise our own chickens didn't turn out so well. In the first place Leona wanted mainly hens, but she didn't know that the salespeople know the difference even when the chick is a baby. One can buy baby hens, but they cost more and one would have to specify hens. The whole dozen chicks were roosters. So we had a lot of fryers but no hens to lay eggs. We should have eaten them while they were fryers, but four became roosters. We had a choir of roosters that sang faithfully at 3 a.m. and again at 5. The whole east end of the island most surely could hear them. Members of the George Brice family, colleagues we met in language school, stopped by for a visit on their way from Rio to Bahia. They wanted to get up at 5 a.m. the next morning to get an early start, but they didn't have an alarm clock. They wanted us to set our alarm clock for 5. Leona told them not to worry, because the roosters crowed regularly at 5 o'clock. When the roosters crowed, the Brices jumped up and started putting their clothes on. But thinking that rays of light should be in the east by 5 a.m. one of the Brices looked at the time; the hour was only 3 a.m. We had to apologize, because we had forgotten to tell them that our roosters were special and also gave a wakeup call at 3 a.m.

We had two roosters left when we noticed that blood was on the chicken-pen floor every morning. The roosters were getting weaker and weaker. I asked our gardener about what looked like blood on the floor. He told me that bats were sucking blood from the roosters' combs, a spot in which they couldn't defend themselves. The roosters were so weak that they could hardly hold up their heads. Since the culprits were bats, for fear of rabies I decided to kill the roosters. I didn't want to bury them in a vacant lot, because if they did have rabies, they might contaminate stray dogs that would dig them up and eat them. *Would the dogs also get rabies?* I didn't know, but I didn't want to take a chance, so I decided to burn them.

While I was burning the roosters at the edge of the dirt street in front of our house, Ronny Boswell drove up with Jeff Pritchard, pastor of Sunny Glenn Baptist Church in Dallas. They had to know why I was burning the roosters, so I told them. In our conversations during the afternoon we told about the snakes on the island, especially the extremely poisonous jararaca snake. That night we went to the

Presbyterian school to speak to the young people during assembly time. I was to introduce Ronny and Jeff. When we went up on the stage, these two big fellows positioned themselves on each side of me. I am five-foot-six inches, Ronny is about six-foot-two, and Jeff about six-foot-five. To emphasize that everything from Texas is BIG, they used my arms to raise me off my feet. I was a little bit humiliated, but the young people thought this planned joke was hilarious! Like short people have to do, I had to rely on my own humbleness to forgive their act of pride.

After the noon meal the next day Jeff went into the guest room to take a nap. We had forgotten to make sure our cat was not in the room. As Jeff was in deep sleep, dreaming about snakes and bats, our cat jumped stealthily on the bed and crept up to snuggle herself near him. Her whiskers evidently brushed against his face. He hit her so hard that she bounced off one wall of the room to another wall and then to the other wall before she hit the floor as she ran out, or so he told me later.

Anxieties—but God Was Working

Preparation for our second furlough brought about another anxiety. One day in July 1970 a young man arrived at our front gate and asked to talk to me. Leona didn't know him, but she didn't know many of my acquaintances that lived in the country towns and villages. I wasn't there, but she invited him to wait inside because I would be back soon. Leona thought the fact that he was dressed in a suit but was barefooted was strange. Leona was busy packing to leave the next day for the annual mission meeting, so she left him to wait for me in the entrance room. After a little while when I hadn't returned, he decided he would not wait and dismissed himself. A little later the milkman passed. Leona needed money out of her purse to pay him but could not find the purse anywhere. First she thought that the purse was on the bed, which now was covered with clothes to be put into the suitcase. At the end of the day when the bed was cleared off, the purse wasn't there. In the entrance room was a bookcase in which we commonly placed things such as car keys and purses.

Her purse contained all of her documents except her passport. We didn't have to carry a passport, because we had permanent resident

163

identification cards (*carteira*). Everyone carries an identification card, which has to be shown if a police officer requests. In Campinas before we left language school, we had registered and received our identification cards (ID). To leave or return to the country we would need to show our ID card along with the passport. We had only about eight months before we were to leave for our furlough. We went to Belo Horizonte to start the process of getting another ID card. When documents are lost, the government has a process to follow in getting the documents renewed. The local police have to be notified and a notice has to be published in a special state paper. Leona had to be fingerprinted and papers filled out; these were sent to Campinas. About three weeks later I was in Belo for something, so I checked at the federal police office at the agency for foreigners, but the agency hadn't heard a word.

Now the pressure was on. The kids were studying at the Brazilian school but were behind with their Calvert Course (English) lessons that Leona was teaching them. They were behind in English and American history. They could read well, but their spelling in English was bad. We were sure that they would do fine in math, because the Brazilian school system was ahead of the American system in the first six grades. Getting them ready to enter an American school added to the pressure.

A state board meeting, the five-day pastors' retreat, a bi-monthly missionary meeting, and the state youth conference took some of the remaining time to get ready to leave for furlough. I resigned as pastor of Fifth Baptist Church, since the first stage of its building was completed. Island Baptist Church found an interim pastor. I had to have all of my reports, including charts and graphs, ready for the annual associational meeting in May. Then the week before we left, we were to have a revival on the island. I had thought that by delaying our furlough we would have more time to get ready, but this didn't happen.

By this time only three weeks remained before furlough. Six times I had been to Belo Horizonte without getting the problem solved about the new ID card. A lawyer in Campinas checked into the process but said he couldn't do anything. The woman dealing with our process asked us whether we had a friend in São Paulo that could check on this for us. I called missionary Amelio Gianetta; he discovered that the original documents were written for us in São Paulo, not Campinas. Probably Thurman Bryant had gotten our first resident documents that we had assumed were made in Campinas.

Naturally we were praying pretty diligently for this problem to be resolved, because our airplane tickets already were in our hands. I had no spare time to go to São Paulo myself.

Three days before we were to leave, by bus I made a special trip to Belo. As always a long line of people was in front of me, but the woman working on our process walked out of her office and noticed me standing in line. She looked surprised and summoned me to her desk. She said, "Can you believe this? Your wife's documents just landed on my desk a moment ago. Did you bring them?" Happily I received Leona's new card and rejoiced all the way home. Praise God again! Yes, an answer to prayer. So many times in our lives things have happened in similar ways. Why do we get uptight when God has told us: "Don't worry about anything!" We were firm in faith, but we were tested to the limit.

I Marvel at How God Brings Things Together

We had asked the WMU (women's mission group) of First Baptist Church in Lovington whether it knew of a furnished house for us to rent for the six months we were be in the States. We had not heard anything. The day after I arrived from Belo with the ID card, (only two days before we were to leave Valadares for the States), we received a phone call from Washington, DC. Dorothy Runnels told us that her mother had a stroke and was in a care center. Her mother's house was only a two-bedroom, but if we desired, we could stay in it in Lovington. Harold Runnels was a New Mexico representative in the U.S. Congress. She said that her mother's things hadn't been moved. Everything was just as it was when she had her stroke. From the dresser drawers and closet we packed her mother's clothes into boxes so we could have enough drawers for our use. Dorothy told us to use whatever was still edible in the refrigerator and pantry—to make ourselves at home! In an unimaginable way God had answered our needs and our prayers. These are a part of the marvel about God's watchcare and provisions of our needs. We have to lean on other people; this expands the circle of friends in our lives.

For this reason I say to you, *"do not be anxious for your life, as to what you shall eat, or what you shall drink; nor for your body, as to what you shall put on. Is not life more than food, and the body than clothing? Look at the birds of the air, that they do not sow, neither do they reap, nor gather into barns, and yet your heavenly Father feeds them. Are you not worth much more than they? And which of you by being anxious can add a single cubit to his life's span? And why are you anxious about clothing? Observe how the lilies of the field grow; they do not toil nor do they spin, yet I say to you that even Solomon in all his glory did not clothe himself like one of these"* (Mt. 6:25-29).

Chapter 9

Spiritual Highs and Disappointments

Stop! Wait! Let the marvel of it all sink into your mind
Until you feel a spiritual freshness, awareness, and you find
Yourself again in the sweet will of the heavenly Divine—
Ashamed, yet eager to do His will the rest of your time.

My conversion experience was so real and satisfying;
I felt lifted into the holy presence of God without dying.
A serene peace and calmness saturated my soul
To make it the most unusual day in life I would ever know.

My salvation experience at 8 years of age has kept me going. This very real experience I never can forget, nor do I want ever to forget it. I enjoy seeing the same thing happen in other people's lives.

Introduction

Our six-month vacation was wonderful but very busy. Furlough is a time of visiting with family and working to promote missions. The FMB wanted me to accept four weeks of world-missions conferences or two camps and two conferences. I enjoyed these events. Leona stayed with the kids. We were privileged to share experiences in 21 churches in five states. We were guest missionaries at Glorieta, NM, for Foreign Mission Week. We went to two Girls in Action day camps and Inlow Camp for girls. Charlotte enjoyed the girls' camp.

For four days I went to a world-missions conference in the area south of Lafayette, LA, in Cajun country, and then moved to the Houma area. The church near Lafayette didn't have a pastor, so a deacon was my host. He picked me up for my meals and also took me to the churches. I got to know him well. Until a few years earlier he had been a devout Catholic. He had a plumbing and air-conditioning business that God had blessed so much that he was able, at very low costs, to help several new missions and churches with their plumbing and heating and cooling systems. On the last day we were together, he took me to the new mansion he was building. As he showed me around this very large house that had an indoor, Olympic-sized swimming pool and a huge barbecue grill, I was puzzled about one thing. Everything absolutely was beyond anything I had ever seen, except that electrical wires suspended the light bulbs hung from the ceilings. I guess he noticed that I was puzzled about this, so he explained that he and his wife could not make up their minds about the chandeliers. I thought to myself, *What a strange problem. My friend and his wife can't decide on chandeliers! My problems are so much simpler in Brazil. We cannot afford ceiling fans.* In some places we had only hard benches with no backs. On that furlough I began to understand how much God was blessing America financially. But this financial blessing brought unimagined problems to solve.

The other world-missions conference was in West Texas around Plainview. I had the opportunity to be in the association in which my cousin was the associational missionary. On Sunday morning I went to a nice, new Baptist church building in the country. The pastor and I discussed what I would do in the service. Just before we went into the worship area, he told me about a problem that was occurring in his church. He said the choir normally was late getting into the service because choir members had three sets of choir robes and wasted time deciding which choir robes to use. Again I thought to myself, *What a strange situation prosperity has brought to this materialistic America!* What trivial problems arise when God has blessed America with so many things which 30 years ago didn't even exist. About 1940 that church and her sister churches in that whole area had only one-room church buildings as did most of those with which I was working in Brazil.

The last Sunday in the States we visited with Leona's older brother, Wayne, and family in Dallas. On Sunday morning we attended the second service of First Baptist Church in Dallas. That evening at

Sunny Glen Baptist Church in Dallas we spoke and showed slides of our work in Brazil. Dr. Jeff Pritchard, a tall, impressive preacher, was the pastor. He was the pastor that had the dream about snakes and bats and knocked our cat across the room when she nestled up close to him in Governador Valadares.

On Monday night Wayne took us to the Billy Graham Crusade in the new Dallas Cowboys football stadium before a football game had been played in it. What a great way to end our furlough! The next morning we flew out of Dallas and back to Brazil.

A New Car

About two years after we arrived in Brazil, General Motors and Ford had built factories there. That gave us other options for automobiles. Billy Frazier, a missionary in São Paulo and chairperson of the mission's transportation committee, had made a deal to buy at a good price heavy-duty station wagons that factory personnel had used for a year. The Brazilian Chevrolet Veraneio was the forerunner to the modern-day SUV. These big cars were only for field missionaries. When we arrived from furlough in 1970, Billy had one of these automobiles waiting for us in Rio de Janeiro.

I was spoiled to the United States' wide, level roads, so driving for 11 hours on the winding, narrow Rio-Bahia Highway to Governador Valadares was very tiresome. For about a week everything seemed strange again. *Wow!* The U.S. was so nice and English was so easy. When Brazilians speak Portuguese, it is a beautiful language, but I found myself struggling to speak.

When we arrived back in Governador Valadares, we were royally welcomed. Two neighbors brought us Brazilian puddings, another brought a cake, and another brought flowers and a box of candy for the children. The neighborhood children visited Carl, Jonathan, and Charlotte. Then on Saturday night the island church had a surprise welcoming service and social. We were overjoyed!

So Quickly in Trouble Again

On Saturday after we arrived on Friday, a lay preacher visited our house to invite me to spend the next weekend with him at his country church at a place called *Pega Bem*, which means "catch well". I had never been in his area before, so as associational missionary I believed I should accept his request. He wanted me to have a Saturday-afternoon baptismal service, the Lord's Supper, an evangelistic service on Saturday night, and an early morning message on Sunday.

We were in the dry season, so the roads were very dusty. I went through Vai Volta, which means "go and return". After about three hours traveling I arrived at a river that had no bridge — just a small barge. That was scary putting the new mission car on the raft along with a Rural Willys, with only inches from my back tires to the end of the raft. Men pushed the long raft by putting long poles on to the bottom of the river; each pushed in rhythm. As we crossed the river, I did some praying. I still remember that when we reached the other side and I drove off the raft, a group of pigs at the bank of the river squealed and scattered in every direction.

I went by the lay preacher's humble home; he and a daughter went with me to Pega Bem. This 14-year-old daughter was barefooted. The lay preacher farmed a small plot of ground to supply food for a big family. He was one of our Bible institute students. As I saw the poverty of this humble preacher's situation, I again remembered how fortunate Americans — even the poorer ones — are.

Pega Bem had only a few houses, all made of adobe mud bricks; most had only dirt floors. The people had the very minimum of material possessions. When we arrived in Pega Bem, about 20 to 30 people had arrived from the mission 10 miles higher up in the mountains. I assume they brought their food; I suppose they slept in the church building. Most of them had walked, but to get to Pega Bem a few had ridden horses or donkeys. About 3:30 p.m. we gathered at the river at which I was to baptize several new converts. In a house nearby those baptized and I changed clothes; then we made our way up to the church. Before I entered the one-room church building, a very strong smell of what I thought must be really rank wine irritated my nostrils. I was right; oh, what an obnoxious smell was inside the church building! I led the business meeting and then administered the Lord's Supper. That was the first and last time I ever took a sip of wine in Brazil. The wine was as terrible as it smelled. Years later Leona and I took the Lord's Supper in a Romanian church; this church had wine because one can't buy plain grape juice in Romania. I suggested that the next time someone went to a store in the city, he or she should buy a supply of bottled grape juice to use for the Lord's Supper.

Some of the members wanted me to take them to visit a sick member about four miles away. The road was so narrow that a back wheel once slipped off the edge of the embankment. Most of the roads are hand-cut out of the side of a mountain, with an embankment on one side and a dropoff on the other side. I drove to the end of the road; then we walked about half a mile to the man's house. On the way back to Pega Bem a donkey blocked the road and stubbornly insisted that the road belonged to him. Finally he moved over some for me to pass but still put a dent in the side of the car. By the time we returned to Pega Bem, darkness had settled in. We had time only to grab a bite to eat before the evening service. A lantern was used for light for the evangelistic service.

I sent the associational newsletters to a deacon of the church. I stayed in his humble house. The kitchen had an adobe-made, wood-burning cook stove with a grill large enough for three pans. Black beans, husky rice (home-grown), and a piece of pork or skinny chicken made up our evening meal.

After the service I was tired and ready to go to bed. The bedroom probably was the one in which the deacon and wife slept. I had a crude, handmade double bed with solid board bottom and a thin, corn-shuck mattress for padding. The walls were adorned with an old, cross-cut saw, an old bridle, and some spurs that hung on a rafter. Two or three sacks of rice or beans were on the floor in the corner. The small living room area had two benches and two small tables. Two other rooms had double beds.

Under the faint glow of a little oil lamp made from a tin can, I lay on my bed and observed the things in the room. When I blew the lamp out, I could see through the roof in some places. This house was like some I have described before—the walls were about seven-feet tall to divide the rooms but with no ceiling to keep one from seeing the roof or to keep out the sounds of other noises in the house. I saw stars in spaces in which the roof tiles didn't touch or were broken. I thought to myself, *I hope no rain falls tonight.* I always have been a light sleeper, so I could hear the sounds in the house. Grandma was sick in one room. Her moaning and groaning made me feel sorry for her. I could hear the others in the house talking. I could also hear a mother hen clucking to her little ones.

I was tired, but I couldn't sleep. Yes, the mattress was hard, but they had given me the best they had. I was very appreciative. My mind was also going over the things I had experienced recently in the U.S. I thought what a contrast my furlough had been to this experience that I was having! Just two weeks ago, when I was in Dallas, on Sunday morning we attended First Baptist Church. In my mind I contrasted that enormous and luxurious church plant to this tiny, crude little church house. I wondered whether anyone at First Baptist Church of Dallas would walk 10 to 12 miles to participate in a baptism, Lord's Supper, and an evangelistic message with me as the preacher—especially if most of those people had been barefooted! I remembered the exhilarating thrill Leona and I had experienced in participating in the first service of the Billy Graham Crusade in the new Dallas Cowboys stadium with thousands of people present. We had about 50 attending in this most humble situation, but God was present just as much as He was at the Billy Graham Crusade. To those people that gathering was just as important as a Billy Graham Crusade was. On these Brazilians' faces you could see their joy and could spot their enthusiasm. Yes, I was glad to be in Pega Bem.

Reminiscing About My Early Childhood

My mind wandered back to my past on the farm. I had thought we were poor. We lived in a wooden house that was pretty cheaply built. The house had three bedrooms, a living room, a kitchen, and a small room in which the milk separator sat. Mama made butter to sell along with eggs. We raised about everything we ate except flour and sugar. More or less 70 yards to the back of the house were the corrals and a small barn in which dried corn for the animals and storebought cow cake were kept. Behind this small barn were the stacks of winter feed that Daddy raised; in the fall bundles of maize were stacked high for winter "fodder" for the cows and horses.

Daddy farmed about 60 acres and had about 100 acres in pasture. I can remember when he did his farming with two big horses. He usually had three or four cows and milked at least two of these. He also had some hogs. Off to the left of our house about 50 yards was the chicken house. A chicken-wire fence surrounded the hen house to keep badgers, skunks, and coyotes out.

I thought my dad and mom had a pretty neat setup. Eastern New Mexico has a lot of wind, so on most days our windmill pumped a lot of water. The fresh, cool water went through a trough (wooden, I think) inside the well house and out into a dirt tank. Daddy made this tank for holding water to irrigate the garden but also to raise catfish and carp. To me the tank seemed pretty big. Once my older brother, Bill, made a tiny raft. While my daddy and mother were working in the field, we tried the raft out. Now I am glad the raft turned over immediately, because one or two of us might have drowned. I didn't like the oozy, black mud on the bottom of the tank either. In the spring and summer, between rains, my mother watered her garden from a pipe that went from the dirt tank into the garden. She raised green beans, blackeyed peas, butter beans, okra, squash, pumpkins, cantaloupe, and probably a thing or two that I am forgetting. Watermelons and corn were grown in the field.

Many times I heard about my severe bout with pneumonia that I had when I was about 2-years old. My parents were very concerned about me. I also heard about my sitting and playing with the red ants on top of their den between the backyard fence and the stock corrals. My older sister, Helen, didn't try to rescue me because she was afraid of getting stung, but she did run to tell Mama. I was severely stung; my condition worried my parents.

I remember our play life was pretty simple. When Mama didn't want us walking on the plants in the garden, she told us to play in the shade of the house. Many times I made tiny mud bricks and built a house with rooms. An old wooden shingle served best as the roof for the house. Our house had a tin roof, so the wooden shingle wasn't from our roof. I had one toy car; I made roads in the dirt to visit my sister or brother's little houses. When one of us got irritated with the other, often the irritability was taken out on the other by destroying that person's tiny mud playhouse.

As we grew, one of the games we played was Anti-over. One group would get on one side of the house and one on the other side. The joy was to tag one on the opposing side after catching the ball.

Back and forth the ball was thrown over our house. Other popular games for entertainment were jump rope, jacks, spinning tops, marbles, and hopscotch. We didn't have bicycles or tricycles, but we did have a little red wagon. Such were the simple things that children did to occupy themselves.

We were given chores such as watering and feeding the chickens, cleaning the hen house, and gathering the eggs from the hen house. In the summer all of us were involved in shelling blackeyed peas, English peas, snapping green beans, shucking corn, and preparing other things for canning. Mama cut the kernels off of the cobs and canned the corn. Mama also planted Irish potatoes and sweet potatoes. I still can taste Mama's sweet-potato cobblers. She spiced them up with sugar and cinnamon, put a layer of dough on top, and baked it until the dough turned brown. Sweet-potato cobbler—yummy, yummy! Daddy also planted enough peanuts to last us a year. Mama had pint and quart jars that were filled with vegetables or fruit and put into the canning cooker to seal the lids. After they were cooled, these jars were put on shelves in the well house. As kids we often tired quickly from our chores, but as I look back, chores were very important for us to learn to help our mother and father. The corn cobs were saved to burn in our pot-bellied stove in the living room. The animals that ate corn on the cob left the cobs for our stove. We had to shell corn for the chickens.

We had 14 cherry trees and three prune trees. During cherry-picking time I enjoyed helping pick, especially when I could climb the trees. After we picked the prunes and pitted them, we put them up on the tin roof of the house, on which the hot sun was even hotter. Other pitted fruit also were put on the tin roof to dry. Of course some of the birds enjoyed a few of them before the fruit dried. Mama swapped off cherries with neighboring farmers that had plum and apricot trees. We went to a neighboring farm and picked plums. Mama canned these in jars and stored them in the well house also. This small, white native rock house was called the "well house" because the water pumped by the windmill passed through the trough along the end of the well house. When the trough was full, the water emptied into a pipe that poured into the dirt holding tank on the outside.

That night in Pega Bem these things flashed through my mind much faster than I could have written them down. After a while I realized I couldn't see any more stars through the cracks in the roofing. The wind began to blow and thunder began to roll. I couldn't hear Grandma moaning and groaning in agony. Neither could I hear the hen clucking to her little ones somewhere in the house. The pitter-patter of rain began; I just knew I was going to get flooded out. I knew that everyone else was asleep, because no longer could I see the glow of their little tin oil lamps over my walls. With cloudy skies, no moon or stars could penetrate the pitch darkness! I moved around on the bed until I found an area in which rain was not dripping on me. Yet I couldn't sleep because of the contrast between the U.S. and this part of Brazil. My thoughts again wandered back to my childhood days. I guess this happened because those days were similar to what I was experiencing at the moment, yet we had so much more on our farm than these people had.

Winter was harsh enough, although we lived in Southeastern New Mexico, which was warmer than Northern New Mexico. Occasionally we had snow and sometimes a blizzard. Besides the kerosene-oil cooking stove that heated up the kitchen and cooked our food, the only other heat in the house was a pot-bellied stove in the living room next to the kitchen. We spent long winter days close to that stove, which warmed our front sides but left our backsides cold. Sometimes I turned my back to the stove to warm it. Eventually the stove managed to warm up most of the room; life was better. We each had only two or three toys. I had a teddy bear, a rubber ball, and a small car. Each year by mail we received the Sears, Roebuck catalog and the Montgomery Ward catalog. We kids fussed over those catalogs and many times looked them over. The sales catalogs had all the new toys on the market. We dreamed and wished that we would get some of those new toys for Christmas. Each year our mother saw that we got at least one new toy or new shoes or something new.

If that pot-bellied stove could have talked, it would have many things to tell, for as I said, the room was so cold that we all stayed as close to the stove as possible. In Eastern New Mexico trees were few, so we didn't have wood to fuel the stove. Daddy usually didn't have money to buy enough coal for all winter. He usually started the fire

175

with corn cobs and corn shucks. In early fall Bill and I went over the whole pasture and looked for dried cow chips (cow patties). Cow chips were better than nothing for our living-room stove. I felt good about having brought in some of those cow chips in a toe sack. Daddy usually sat a little distance from the stove after he cared for the animals on those cold and sometimes snowy days. Roasting Spanish peanuts that were grown in the garden was a delightful time for us.

One corner of the room was set aside for Mama's quilting rack. The big wooden square was the size of a double bed. First of all my mother sewed together pieces of scrap material that she had left over from making her own dresses as well as Helen and Margaret's dresses. These pieces had to be put together in a design to make the quilt top pretty. Colorful, 50-pound flour and sugar sacks with many kinds of patterns furnished material for most farm women to make dresses, aprons, curtains, cuptowels, and tablecloths. After cotton was ginned, Daddy always kept some of it for Mama to use for quilts. But to get the cotton in a smooth thin layer she had to "card" the cotton with two hand-carding boards. These two boards were about four-inch-by-10-inch rectangular shapes with handles. The inside of the carding boards were thick with one-fourth-to-one-half-inch, stiff wires made like a brush. I enjoyed watching my mother moving those boards back and forth together with cotton. A layer of carded cotton was placed between the colorful, pieced top and the solid bottom; this made the quilt warm. Then Mama put the quilt in the quilting frame to quilt together the three layers.

Once a week for two or three hours on a designated afternoon other women usually would help; the quilting rack was lowered from the ceiling to a comfortable height for the women to work as they were seated around the quilt. Each worked with needle and thread on the same design; they sewed the top to the bottom cloth of the quilt. This kept the cotton in place so it wouldn't become lumpy when it was washed. Mother also participated with neighbor women when they were making their quilts. This was a good time for fellowship among ladies in the farming community. When we kids were too small to hoe weeds in the field, we went to play with other kids.

Christmas was exciting, although I knew that we would not get many presents. Our little community Baptist church always had a

Christmas party for the children. Santa Claus usually brought all the kids a small bag of colored hard candy, a few nuts, and an apple or orange. This poem expresses my feelings about Christmases on the farm:

MY CHRISTMAS STORY

Christmas Eve was different on the New Mexico plains
From many parts of the World from Europe to Maine,
But I was as excited as a boy anywhere
When mother tucked me in bed with gentle care.

Sugarplums did not dance around my head
On Christmas Eve night as I lay in my bed,
But my mind was filled with curious fascination
About Santa and His reindeer covering the whole nation.

Our stockings were not hung by the chimney with care
Because, without a fireplace, we hung them on a chair.
I am certain that our house was not quiet as a mouse,
For the mice never were quiet at night in our house.

Santa and his reindeer on our roof could not pause,
And down through the stovepipe could not enter Santa Claus.
Neither was there room for a sleigh and reindeer on our rooftop,
Or Rudolph and some others over the end of the house would flop.

Santa would land, of course, in our front yard,
And to open the door he would not find it hard,
For Mother and Dad said they would leave the door unlocked.
That way he could enter and the stockings be stocked—
Stocked with fruits, nuts, and also cookies
Because he had a great supply of all kinds of goodies,
But I worried about him bringing me toys,
Because I had not been a very good boy!

My knowledge about toys Santa would have in his sleigh
Was from hours of looking at the catalogs every day.

That was my favorite pastime on cold winter days and nights—
Studying carefully the catalog by kerosene lamplight.

But somehow I perceived that Santa's generosity
Somehow must be linked to my folks' prosperity!
I could not expect more than one or two toys
Even if I had been an exceptionally good boy!

Nevertheless Christmas Eve night was very exciting.
All efforts of the sandman to put me to sleep, I kept fighting.
Finally he would win and I would sleep very sound
To awaken the next morning and to the living room bound.

Sure enough, Santa always visited before the rising sun.
He always left something for me to have fun.
But not from that Sears, Roebuck famous wishbook—
My favorite book where I liked to look!

Christmas came and went when I was a little kid
Hoping to get boots and lots of toys, but I never did.
Nevertheless, whatever the reason that Santa had,
I accepted what he gave me and was no longer sad.

The Rest of the Story

Suddenly morning had arrived! I did finally get some sleep; the movements of people in the house awakened me. The aroma of fresh coffee was strong in the house. The coffee beans were homegrown, home-roasted, and ground. The coffee was sweetened with homemade sugar called *rapadura*. For our breakfast Sunday the wife prepared some sweet cornbread called *broa*. Most people put about half milk and half coffee, but since I never liked milk, I just asked for some hot water to weaken mine. I let them think that I was "odd". We also were served the few pieces of scrawny chicken left from the night before. Since I was the guest, I was offered a piece first; I willingly took it. The rain had stopped; activity outside the house reminded me that the early morning service was to start at 7 a.m. This early service was to aid those from the mission to get back home before dark.

Since our service was to be over by 8:30, I decided I could make the 11 a.m. service at Alvarenga, a church I had visited before. I didn't know whether I could get to Alvarenga if I went on the road on which I had arrived, so I asked the people whether they knew of a shorter way. I was told, "Yes, just go over that high hill. You will find another road on the other side." The high hill was very high and had been cleared of all trees and shrubbery to graze cattle, so I could see a road winding back and forth up to the top of the high hill. I didn't look very enthusiastic, but some men assured me I could make it and that Jeeps do this all the time. I guess I am too gullible or maybe stupid.

The lay preacher wanted me to take his teen-aged daughter with me and let her out after we crossed the river. He explained that after I got to the top of the hill, I could go straight down the other side to the river. The road I needed was just on the other side of the river. His daughter and I said goodbye and away we went. Well, this big blue Chevy wagon could hardly make the sharp turns as we went up the winding, narrow road to the top. If I had met anything on the road, I would have been in a predicament, because the incline was so steep, I didn't think I could get started again if I stopped. When we reached the top, to my dismay the road didn't go straight down to the river below but went along the top of the ridge. My instructions were to go straight down to the river, cross the river, get up on the dirt road, and take a right. That would take me to Alvarenga. I told the teen-ager that I thought a road would go to the river. She said, "No road, but just go straight down to the river." Steep hillsides where cattle graze are very rough because the cattle cannot graze with their heads pointing down, nor do they graze with their front legs planted upward and their back legs on the downward slope. They make trails parallel with the top of the hill and graze with their front and back legs on level ground. That way they graze to the right and left, or if they are going to the river to drink, they follow their little trails zig-zagging down the hillside. I started bouncing down the steep hill in first gear and pressing hard on the brakes. I tried to pass over those trails as softly as possible. I barely could control the car. I thought to myself, "I will never take the word of anyone again about shortcuts anywhere."

When I arrived at the river, I had a thought that made my heart

179

sink. *How am I going to cross this river? Just as they said—no bridge in sight! What have I gotten myself into?* The river was about 75 yards wide and didn't have a dropoff to get into the water nor to leave the water on the other side. That was very unusual, because the raging rivers after heavy rains usually cut deep gorges into the riversides. I asked the teen-ager whether she would walk across the river (she was barefooted anyway) so that I could see how deep the water was. I also asked her to observe whether the riverbed was very rocky, sandy, or muddy. As she descended from the car, I thought, *How stupid I am. If I cannot get across this river, I surely cannot go back up the hill. Here I am with a new car—new to me, at least, for it had only 10,000 miles on it. What if I couldn't get across the river? What if I got halfway across and couldn't get out? I never would want the South Brazil mission or missionaries to know about this.* I prayed as that girl stepped carefully into the river until she had crossed it. She returned with her report that the riverbed was very firm and had no big rocks. By her skirt I could tell that the depth of the river was about running-board deep. So we eased into the river; I carefully crossed as the water washed the undercarriage of my car. I had no problem pulling out of the river and onto the road. I was amazed, along with the fact that no fence was on either side. I don't know what kept the cattle off the road.

I thanked the girl and told her goodbye. Her home was somewhere down the road to the left; I turned to the right. I arrived in plenty of time for the 11 a.m. service in Alvarenga. Because it was a ranching area, the church had Sunday school at 11. This was followed by preaching; then the people ate and visited for another two hours before they returned to their farms and ranches. I arrived home about dark. I was a relieved missionary and thankful to God for the experience I had. I asked God to give me more wisdom or good sense. He had helped me out again.

Disappointment at Island Church

I had rather not write about this, but this subject was a big problem for our church and the Minas Gerais Baptist Convention. One of our Southern Baptist missionaries, a widow, went to the States for furlough in the early 1960s and was in contact with and strongly influ-

180   Rosalee Mills Appleby

enced by the charismatic movement. Soon after she arrived in Brazil many years before, she had lost her husband, but she and her small son stayed in Brazil. After her husband's death she became even more involved in prayer and sought a deep spiritual life.

After becoming acquainted with the charismatic movement she returned to Belo Horizonte and began encouraging some of the preachers along the charismatic line. As far as I know, she never spoke in tongues herself, but she was in favor of them. The Baptist school in Belo was one of the largest Baptist schools in all of Brazil and eventually became the largest of all South America. On its property this school had a very nice church building. Our Baptist missionary was a member of that church. She had started a radio program and began having as speakers pastors that were interested in the charismatic movement. She invited two well-known North Brazilian Baptist pastors who were interested in the movement to move to Belo. She promoted their success in implanting the movement in Belo Horizonte.

Neither the staunchest Baptists of the church nor the other pastors in the city could comprehend what was going on. The members that didn't agree with changes in Floresta Baptist Church on the school campus began moving their memberships to other churches. Assembly of God people began to join Floresta Baptist Church. No one could foresee the outcome of what was going on, because nothing like this had ever happened before. Many of them highly esteemed the missionary that was promoting this change in doctrines. Many Baptists were puzzled, dazed, and didn't know how to react.

The leadership of the Brazilian Baptist Convention also didn't know what to do. Soon the majority in Floresta Church was in the hands of the charismatics or those sympathetic to the movement. By this time the activists for the movement had been sending or taking some of the charismatic printed materials to other areas of the state, especially the Sweet River Valley Association, the most fertile area of the Minas Gerais Baptist Convention. Wherever a church was without a pastor, a pastor or laypeople from the charismatic movement in Belo were sent to offer their help to that church. These Charismatic leaders disguised themselves as true Baptists. The unsuspecting churches accepted them and allowed them to preach, so eventually these men in sheep's clothing were able to take 20 Baptist churches without pastors into their charismatic fold. By the time we arrived in Governador Valadares, those 20 churches had been lost to the movement in the Sweet River Valley.

The FMB recalled the missionary that instituted this movement; by the time we arrived, she was gone. However, among many Southern Baptist churches in the States she continued to raise money for the movement. Until she died many years later, she wrote books and tracts and became known as one of the most spiritual missionaries in Brazil. She was loved by Brazilians and especially in the State of Minas Gerais in which she served. Baptists, who could see the fallacy of the charismatic movement, were disappointed, yet they were thankful for the spiritual help she had given them before she instigated the charismatic movement.

The damage had been done; finally about 1968 the Minas Gerais state Baptist convention broke ties with the charismatic Baptists. This was sad and disturbing, because many of the churches lost had profited from Baptist funds to help them buy property and build their first church buildings. The deeds for most of these properties still were held by the Brazilian Baptist Foundation. The Brazilian government had never had anything like this to happen; therefore, they didn't know legally how to deal with the problem. One of the longtime Baptists, a judge, was in Brasilia working with the government. He had become a charismatic and led a movement to block the Minas Gerais state convention from gaining back the beautiful Floresta Church building on the Baptist school campus.

Because of the seven-year ruling the original Baptist group, linked with Southern Baptists, lost its case over Floresta Church. If a church or other entity doesn't get the problem settled in a space of seven years, the occupying group gets the right to keep the use of the property. So to this day the Floresta charismatic group has use of the church that sits on property that still belongs to the original Brazilian Baptist Convention. Of all the churches lost only three or four buildings were regained for original Baptist use. I use the word *original* because the charismatics continued to use the word *Baptist*. Because of this problem, eventually the convention churches began putting in their bylaws a clause which states that if the group ceases to follow original Baptist doctrine, the building returns to the convention. Now if a church becomes charismatic, the original Baptists are able to get the property back if they get on the case quickly, but still these cases usually take years to clear up.

When we arrived, Governador Valadares had a vibrant charismatic Baptist church with three or four missions. After we began working in the neighborhood, one of its mission churches was started in the Santa Rita neighborhood close to Fifth Baptist Church. One of our young men became enamored with the charismatic worship style; nothing I could do persuaded him otherwise. This forced me to diligently study the Book of First Corinthians, especially chapters 11-13, to answer my own questions and the questions of others.

The first case in the island church was our children's Sunday-school teacher. She recently had married a Catholic young man. He finally visited church with her and almost was ready to make a decision to accept Jesus. However, she began to be interested in the charismatics. She and her husband wanted a baby so badly that she went to a "prophetess" that lived in the slums on the Carapina neighborhood, the hill near downtown. The "prophetess" told the Sunday-school teacher she would get pregnant and have a son. The teacher was enamored by this prophecy. We tried to persuade her not to fall for the charismatic movement and not to be enamored with the prophetess. She did get pregnant. However, the "prophetess" failed to tell her that the baby would die before it was born. After this tragedy we couldn't persuade her to stop seeking miracles from the charismatic people. She dropped out of church; soon she and her husband divorced.

Charismatics and other Pentecostal groups were spreading throughout the whole state and much of Brazil their enthusiasm of miracles, signs, and wonders. Miracle-workers were popping up frequently. Every weekend busloads of miracle-seekers were leaving Governador Valadares for towns near and far to visit the works of a miracle-worker. The spiritists also had their miracle-workers in the form of doctors. These usually did all kinds of operations by using dirty knives and other strange medical tools. The mania for these miracles or signs and wonders was rampant and made me search my own heart for answers. If they were right, I was wrong and needed to go their way. But I couldn't abandon my salvation experience I had as an

8-year old. I knew that the Holy Spirit had led in me making my decision to become a part of His kingdom and knew that the Holy Spirit also was in me. Yet they taught that speaking in tongues and having a definite outstanding gift of ministry, mainly casting out demons or performing miracles, was something to be SOUGHT immediately after one was converted. They believed these were the most important gifts and were signs of the Holy Spirit's presence and power in a believer's life. If such signs were proof that the Holy Spirit occupied a believer's heart, I did not qualify as a saved person. Therefore, I prayed, studied, and even more patiently waited and watched what was going on in their lives.

My observation was that they were haughty and arrogant and performed as if they had control of the Holy Spirit instead of the Holy Spirit having control of them. In the large Calvary Baptist Church (charismatic) of Valadares, a barber that left our church for Calvary Church confessed to me the following case. He told me that a certain "prophetess" in Calvary Church prophesied that God had told her a certain married man should not have married his wife. God revealed to the prophetess that the couple should get a divorce. This prophecy caused the couple to get the divorce. Then the prophetess told the man that had divorced his wife that God had told her he was to marry a relative of hers (the prophetess). So they got married! Would God do a thing like that? Many events similar to this were happening within charismatic churches.

One scandal after another was making newspaper headlines in our city. This became embarrassing to some pastors in our city's ministerial alliance, of which I took part. Mostly the Presbyterian, Methodist, and Baptist pastors held the offices in the alliance, so we decided to stop calling meetings for a while and later to start over without those that were embarrassing the cause of Christ being invited to participate. However, some of these pastors had difficulty seeing that the charismatic movement was going to split their own churches. Once in front of the post office I met the pastor of First Presbyterian Church. He knew that Baptists finally had separated from the charismatics; he told me we had done the wrong thing. We should have had patience and love for those people, he said. I knew more than he did about what soon was going to happen in his own church, because our home was surrounded by some of his most faithful members. A few months later several prominent members had left his church for the charismatic movement. A charismatic Pentecostal church was started about a block from our house; members of one of his most prominent families became leaders in that church.

Before we left for our second furlough, a talented young husband and wife in the island church troubled our hearts by their change in doctrines. She was our organist and had a beautiful voice. He was the young people's Sunday-school teacher. Before Leona and I left, we had a long talk with them. We gave or sold to them some of our children's best things. Very bluntly I told them that if they maintained their position (doctrine), to please just leave our church for one with whom they agreed. They assured me they were going to stay Baptists. About three months later we received a letter from members of the island church telling about this husband and wife holding charismatic studies in their home. They hadn't kept their word. Before we returned to Brazil, they became members of Calvary Charismatic Baptist Church.

I was at seminary in California when the charismatic movement started in California by the Episcopalian minister, Dennis Bennett, rector of St. Mark's Episcopal Church in Van Nuys, CA. This was the beginning of the charismatic movement in the U.S. The movement spread rapidly; the pastor and wife of my hometown church soon were involved in it. The pastor first tried to get rid of the body of deacons so he would be able to change the doctrines of the church. Many of the members left First Baptist Church for the Jackson Avenue mission. Thanks to God, Pastor Phillips was forced to leave and didn't succeed in changing First Baptist into a charismatic church. The charismatic movement in North America had very little effect in persuading the majority of the members in denominational churches to change their loyalty. Charismatics who tried to take over some denominational churches did not succeed. Those that left the denominational churches united to form interdenominational charismatic churches. Brazilian Baptists, Presbyterians, or Methodists should have done the same and not tack denominational names to their movement. Keeping the denominational names was dishonest and confused lost people as to who were the true Baptists, Presbyterians, or

Methodists.

The charismatic Baptist churches in Brazil had as their goal to turn all Baptist churches into charismatics. Therefore they carried on a very active visitation program among Baptist church members. They worked against us much more than did against any other religious group, including Catholics. This vicious lack of mercy and love on their part helped me to take a firm stance against them.

As we returned from furlough, we found the island church had lost three families who contributed financially and leadership positions in our church body. Our treasurer also had borrowed church money for his own personal use. Attendance was down; the people were discouraged. Naturally we felt a letdown. Mrs. Runnels sent us $300 that I divided between the island church and Seventh Baptist Church.

The Floods

September is the beginning of the rainy season in central Brazil. Many times we saw rain fall for 15 days without stopping. I took Carl with me on a trip into the country to visit two churches. We arrived at the first church, Natal Baptist Church, but rain fell constantly. The situation was miserable for Carl, because he had to stay indoors around adults all the time. We met an old-time *colporteur* (traveling Bible and Christian-book salesman) that helped open up the Baptist work in the Sweet River Valley. I enjoyed hearing his experiences. The next day we couldn't get to the second church, so we visited a church on the highway and went home. Not long after our visit to Natal Baptist Church, I heard that the old *colporteur* had died. These men were very important, because many people otherwise didn't have access to a Bible. I was glad that I got to visit with him. His stories of traveling over long distances on horseback or by foot made me feel as though I hadn't sacrificed anything. His love for the Lord Jesus was expressed in his eyes and expressions on his face. Praise God for him!

Every year flooding caused disasters over areas of Brazil. Minas Gerais got its share. Governador Valadares had flooding along the little river tributaries that flowed into the Sweet River. The homes would be flooded or washed away, but the poor people had no other place to go, so they would return and rebuild with scraps of whatever they could find. The small islands near the big island would flood, too. Two of these smaller islands had social clubs on them. A few times the water flowed over the lower parts of the big island on which we lived.

We had been doing some house-to-house visitation along the tributary that is near Seventh Baptist Church. One of the converts we visited had a very thin and crooked leg. Her name was Maria; more than 50 percent of the women have the name *Maria*. We started helping her financially. When floods occurred, most of those people lost what little they had. The reason that floods are so disastrous in Brazil is because nearly all the towns and cities are built along the rivers. For several years we followed Maria until she was able to receive a lot and a little shack in a new neighborhood. She felt blessed.

Exchange Students
Governador Valadares received two American exchange students. The girl was from Las Vegas, NM, but she wasn't interested in us. The Jewish boy from New York became our friend. He visited our home various times and played the piano and organ very well. He even knew a few hymns and enjoyed playing them. As a present he brought us a bottle of apple cider. He didn't know that the apple cider wasn't just cider but a stronger drink.

Baptist Conventions
Vacation times are in January, part of February, and the month of July. Brazilians usually get a month for vacation; missionaries are allowed a month. However, most missionaries are like us—too busy to take a month's vacation. The Brazilian national convention is in the month of January; missionaries are encouraged to attend. Many missionaries are chosen to work on committees on the national level. Missionaries are shown appreciation by our Brazilian brothers and sisters; Brazilians desired to involve American missionaries in leadership roles, which was an honor for the missionaries.

Associational and state youth organizations also had their camps and retreats. Since I had organized the Valadares city youth, I was chosen to help on the associational planning committee for the youth of the Sweet River Valley. I took youth from our church and sometime other churches in the city to those meetings. I also promoted the boys' mission organization, Royal Ambassadors, in our church and in the city. I began taking boys from our church and Central Baptist Church to the state retreats. So our vacation normally was only one week, because we didn't have time for more; we could only afford one week. We usually went to a beach in the State of Espirito Santo or Rio de Janeiro. For a couple of years during the last week of December and the first week of January we went for a two-week vacation to the beach.

The state conventions always met in July during the mid-year vacation month. If the schoolteachers had been on a strike the first months, then most of July was used to make up for the strike. July is mid-winter—a little too cool and breezy for the beach.

Chapter 10

Spiritual Strength
and Physical Weakness

Many times I have marveled about my salvation day.
So close to God I was that I did not want to play.
That afternoon I spent under a tree drinking
from the spiritual well—
Rejoicing, at 8 years of age, to have been saved from hell!

The birds seemed to sing prettier than ever before
And the sun seemed brighter as I drank in even more.
As my brother and cousins rolled old tires down the road,
I rejoiced that Jesus had relieved me of a heavy load.

I wonder why God ever called me into the ministry
Or why He even called me to be a missionary,
For a more timid or introverted kid could hardly be found.
More talented and gifted young people were all around.

I could never have dreamed I would finish college or
seminary—
Live in California and then go to a foreign country
Nor adjust to the teeming thousands in a great city
And brush shoulders with multitudes who were without identity.

God's amazing grace goes far beyond the salvation experience.
Along with God's love His amazing grace has encircled me; each year
that goes by I keep experiencing The Marvel of It All. Praise God my

heavenly Father, Jesus my Savior, and the Holy Spirit that dwells within me.

What Would Life Be without Problems?

The last week of April 1972 I made a trip with a man who was pastor of a church in a town as well as of three country churches. The four churches together didn't pay him a decent salary. He had a big family, which was part of the problem. He couldn't furnish shoes for the children or medicine when they were sick. I wanted to visit his churches and see whether I could encourage them to support him better. I took some clothes with me and hoped that they would fit some of the family. I picked him up at his humble home; we began our journey to a big country church that I had wanted to visit ever since I began working in the Sweet River Valley Association.

The last three miles after leaving the main road narrowed down to almost the width of the car. The last mile was even much smaller; only horses and buggies used it. I drove through seven-foot-high grass that folded over the car on each side. I hardly could see ahead. Then about 400 yards from the church we entered the gate that went down into the property of the deacon's house. A big embankment was on our right; the rains had cut a gully on the left side of the road very near the edge that dropped sharply about 30 feet. I almost scratched the right side of the car as I descended down to a level area at the farmer's house, because I had to keep the car close to the embankment to keep the left wheels from getting into the gully on the left.

The deacon and family had nothing whatsoever of conveniences. You cannot imagine how these dear country folk get excited about guests—especially an American missionary—visiting them. This is something that I never will forget. They didn't have enough plates, knives, and forks for everyone, so the guests ate first. The knives and forks were so used that they appeared to have been from an earlier generation. They gave the best they had to offer and wouldn't eat a bite until their company had been well fed. When a Brazilian has had all he wants to eat, he says *estou satisfeito*, meaning "I am satisfied". They didn't even have an outdoor toilet. They just went to some banana trees behind the house. That was very uncomfortable for me. The rain made going outside very difficult, but they did have urinals in the house at night.

After supper we went to the church for a worship service. During the service rain began falling. Because they lived in the country, at night most people carried flashlights to follow the trails to their homes. The pastor, the deacon and family, and I started down the already muddy trail to their house. We crossed a little creek on only about a 10-inch plank. I took off my shoes and rolled up my pants legs, because the mud on my shoes made the narrow plank dangerous to cross. We finally reached the house. Hot coffee was made, but I refused it so that I wouldn't have to get up during the night. We talked a little while before the pastor and I retired to our room. I was not accustomed to going to bed at 9 p.m., so I had to entertain my mind for a while. The steady rain also bothered me, because I was sure the next day I would have a difficult time getting the vehicle out of that hole. We had planned this trip because we thought the rainy season had finished.

The lonely situation naturally provoked a return to memories of my childhood. My mother ironed clothes with a "smoothing iron". This type of iron—including its handle—was made of solid iron metal. Usually two were used at a time. While Mama was using one iron, the other one was heating on the kitchen stove, so when the one being used cooled down, she would put it on the fire and take the hot one to continue ironing.

We must have had at least three or four irons, because on the coldest nights before we went to bed Mama would heat the irons on the stove. She wrapped each one in several layers of paper or cloth and put one under the covers of each bed to warm our cold feet. My brother, Bill, had bigger feet and seemed to take up more than his share of the iron. I had to slip my head all the way under the cover to reach the iron, because Bill was older and taller than me.

The old-fashioned way to separate cream from milk was to let the milk cool; the cream would rise to the top, where it could be skimmed off and put into a big jar. But one day Daddy bought a modern machine that separated the milk immediately after he milked the cows. This milk separator was one of the most fascinating machines on the farm. On top this machine had a big bowl into which milk would be poured. A hand lever turned the inner system of cogs; somehow the cream separated; it went through one spout into a container. The raw milk went into another. Mama made butter to sell in Lovington on Saturdays. She also sold eggs to customers. The proceeds from these sales was Mama's spending money.

When we just had a pickup truck, we kids had to ride in the back. That meant we didn't get to go to town in the winter, because the weather would be too cold for us to ride in the back. We stayed at the neighboring farm of our grandparents. We kids enjoyed going to town, because Lovington had a nice courthouse lawn. Many big trees made good shades; farmers' kids such as us were allowed to play on the grass. Usually we had a picnic, too. Sometimes Daddy or Mama bought hot chili and crackers for us to eat for dinner on the lawn. Occasionally my Grandfather Tarry bought us kids an ice-cream cone, which was the biggest treat. He died, however, in 1940 when I was 5-years old. One time my grandfather's bachelor brother, who was visiting them, went with us to town. He was in the back of the pickup with us kids. We had some live chickens that we were taking to town to sell. They had their feet tied, but one of them was able to jump out of the pickup. My great-uncle jumped out of the pickup to catch the chicken. At the time Daddy was going about 20 miles an hour. We were thankful my great-uncle didn't break any bones. He was more used to riding in a wagon than he was in a moving vehicle.

After Daddy bought a car, we had a place to stay when the weather was cold while Daddy and Mama shopped or delivered butter and eggs to customers. Even so, waiting in the car was cold. I wanted Mama to buy the groceries as soon as possible, because I liked to suck on one of the corners of the sugar sack. I didn't get away with that for very long.

To me another fascination was the radio; on Saturday nights our treat was to listen to it. We didn't have electricity, so Daddy drove the vehicle up to the window of the living room and hooked the radio wire to the car battery. A small, beautiful green light glowed when the small radio was turned on. We listened to the Grand Ole Opry, with Minnie Pearl the star on that program. The other program to which we listened was the Amos and Andy show. They sure were funny. I tried to see the teensy-weensy people performing inside that radio. The only place I could see into the radio was from the back panel, but I could see only the bulbs that transmitted electricity from the car battery to the working part of the radio. The radio got pretty warm; I thought those tiny people inside must be sweating a lot. After those two programs we all went to bed. Daddy did not want to drain the car battery by using the radio.

In times in which Mama helped Daddy in the field, we had specific instructions about what to do or not to do and knew that Bill and Helen were to take care of me and Margaret. Among the things not to do was not to get into the attic of the house. This directive from our parents made us curious and made us want to explore the attic. The opening to the attic was outside above the door that went into the kitchen. I guess we used a ladder to get up, but once we were in the attic, the tricky part was to stay on the rafters. Nothing heavy could be put in the attic, so we found only empty boxes and empty food containers such as cocoa and peanut-butter cans. The farther one went from the entrance hole of the attic, the darker and dustier the attic became. We three older kids had made the attic off-limits for Margaret, because she was only 4-years old. One day she said she would tell on us if we did not help her up. That was enough to persuade us to help her up. She was instructed to stay on the rafters; this was pretty difficult to do. Well, she fell through the sheetrock ceiling onto the dining-room table; fortunately she didn't get hurt badly. A razor strap administered punishment to us two boys. In those days men shaved with a long razor, which was much like a knife. Swishing the cutting edge of the razor back and forth on a thick, leather strap sharpened the straight razor. These straps were about two-feet long and three-inches wide. Daddy did not whip the girls with this strap; he used his hand. But when we disobeyed, Mama used a switch from the orchard. Each spring Mama told us to go to the orchard and bring back a new switch. If we didn't choose one to her pleasing, she went to get the switch herself. My sister, Helen, says I was the only one that ran from Mama to keep from getting a switching. Mama surely could make the switch sting; I didn't like pain. I always knew I would get the punishment sooner or later and knew that it would be more painful than if I had taken my licking at her timing.

Everybody said I was stubborn, but I didn't know what they were talking about. I thought I was acting normal. The only time I remember being stubborn was one Sunday afternoon in which a neighbor arrived to help Daddy and Mama kill a badger. Every night for several nights the badger got into our chicken house. Daddy had set a trap for him, but the badger was too smart and evaded the trap. This particular Sunday afternoon they were going to try to get him out of his hole and didn't want any noisy kids around. I wanted to see that badger, so I fought Bill and Helen, who were to keep me in the house. I got loose from them and took off to see how that badger was going to be caught. Daddy, Mama, and the neighbor had crept quietly to the badger's hole in the ground so he wouldn't hear their feet. They had some buckets of water mixed with some chemical to make him struggle to the top of the hole to get air. Well, what I had done was trouble for me; all I remember was my punishment. I don't know the fate of the badger, but my fate was almost as bad, I thought!

Why do kids want to grow up? Why are kids not smart enough to want to stay kids? I wanted to go to the field and hoe the weeds that Daddy said were taking over his crop of cotton, watermelons, and feed for the cattle. Bill got to leave the house with his water jar, hoe, and a little snack of something. Why couldn't I be like him? Finally one day daddy brought new hoes for Helen and me. The handle was smooth and pretty and the metal part was bright red. Both hoes were just alike. Each had a pretty green brand name on the lower part of the handle. How would I know which was my hoe? So I had mine marked. This was MY hoe! If I saw a snake, I would be brave. I would clean that whole field of all the weeds. I fantasized about all I would do with that beautiful new hoe. Early the next morning we three walked to the field. Behind some higher plants Bill found a shade that would keep our water cool for a little while. We chose our rows; I began chopping the weeds on my row. About 9 the sun was getting pretty hot. I began to sweat; I already was hungry. All I had for a snack was a biscuit with some jelly and peanut butter; the ants had already found it, too. I scattered the ants as best I could and ate my snack. Then my sweat attracted the gnats; those tiny little flies were trying to get into my ears and up my nose. They swarmed around my head; I guess they were trying to get out of the sun. This nearly drove me crazy. Boy, I had not counted on this! I was ready to go to the house, but I couldn't.

Every day was miserable. The plants grew higher, so I decided I could make the time go faster by taking a toy to the field with me. My toy was a small piece of wood that I could use for a car. When daddy was on the far side of the field, I would hide behind the taller plants and play for a while. One day when I knelt down to play, a snake was eyeing me and sticking his tongue out at me. In and out went the snake's tongue. I froze as he stared me right in the eyes. I had put my hoe, my trusty weapon, down out of reach. I was losing my breath and thought I was about to be charmed by the snake. I had heard adults talk about cats and dogs being "charmed" by snakes. Once I had seen our cat charmed by a snake. A big bull snake could swallow big rats. Anyway, I was almost speechless and breathless before I could get my eyes off the eyes of that snake and move for the hoe. I called Bill and we killed the snake. The snake actually was harmless, but we were taught to have a fear of any kind of snake, because rattlesnakes were in our part of the country. I was getting firsthand experiences of the dangers of growing bigger. I realized that things big people had to do were not as exciting as I had thought.

I wanted so badly to guide the horses pulling the wagon. One day Daddy said he would give me the chance if I would shock feed while he worked all afternoon in the field. This was in the fall; Daddy had a one-row binder. The machine would cut stalks of feed and bind them in a bundle with twin string. These bundles were stood up against each other in a manner called "shocking" so they would dry out. They looked as though they were an Indian teepee. We shocked a lot of these bundles. After they were dried, Daddy loaded them on the wagon real high. Daddy let me guide the horses to the barn. I tried to use the horse language like Daddy did. At the back of the barn he made a great big stack with the bundles; the stack was fun to play on when Daddy was in town or helping some neighbor do something. During the winter this feed served as feed for the stock. Driving the horses was a lot easier than hoeing was. I offered to be his wagon driver.

I often wondered whether I would have been able to work in an area such as the Sweet River Valley if I had not had some growing-up experience in the country. Most of the homes in which I stayed, such as this current one, had less than we had on the farm.

The Biggest Mud Hole

The next morning we awoke to more rain. A dark, gloomy, and cold atmosphere prevailed inside the house. The pastor and I decided we could stay until noon and still make the trip to the next church for the night service. I was afraid we would be forced to stay longer. The farmer also recognized the predicament and sent word to nearby farmers that our plans were to leave after lunch, so men began to arrive to help. He had 18 men digging (shaving) off more of the embankment so the car had more space away from the gully. We ate lunch about 11 a.m. and got in the car to see how far we could get. I had not been able to find chains for this car, so the situation was a little worse.

We didn't get but about 50 yards before the car bogged down and we could go no further. The deacon went to get two oxen and fastened chains to their yoke. They began to pull. Together with all the power of the motor we were able to get to the beginning of the road that went up to the gate. The embankment now was to my left (driver's side); the gully was to my right; I could not see it well. With the two oxen and the motor roaring we were making no progress. The men stopped to think about the situation. They already were soaking wet; I felt for them. I began to do some serious praying, because if the car slipped into the gully, we might have to have a wench truck to travel from Valadares to get the car out of the abyss. That might not be possible for a week.

The men decided they needed to hack off more of the embankment to make the road a little wider. These 18 men worked about two hours with big heavy hoes. Then the deacon brought two more oxen and hooked them up ahead of the first two. About seven of the men braced themselves against the right side of the car to try to keep it from sliding into the gully. That was dangerous, because if one of them had slipped into the gully, he might have been hurt, or the car could have slipped and knocked some men into the gully and then car fallen on top of them. I was thinking of all the things that could go wrong and praying that God would bless their efforts to get us out of this big mud hole.

The deacon gave the command for the oxen to start moving. The chains tightened on the front bumper; I pressed the accelerator. The back wheels began spinning. The four animals strained harder; gradually we began moving. Two or three men also were pushing from behind and were getting covered with mud from the spinning tires. Gradually but surely we were making progress up the hill. The compassion on the part of the six men that went with us the three miles to the gravel road shows the depth of country folks' love. They had to push several times. Then they trudged the three miles back home. I hoped they didn't catch pneumonia.

When we finally arrived at the gate to the next church, darkness had settled in and rain was still falling. The gate was closed and locked; this indicated that no one had entered to attend church that night, so we drove three hours to get back to the pastor's house. Because of the rain our plan to visit the other churches was changed.

Satan Is Always at Work

Satan seemed always to keep us on our toes. A nightclub opened at the end of our block; the music was so noisy that no one could sleep until 2 or 3 in the morning. The law said that after 10 p.m. the loud noise had to stop. We joined with our neighbors in calling the police to get the club to stop the loud music, but that didn't produce any results. The police officers would drive by and stop for a little bit but didn't do anything. I used my space in the city paper to protest for our neighborhood. Weeks went by without success! Before this restaurant/nightclub opened, we had a very wonderful street. Now the street was very dusty and was not safe for the neighborhood kids to play in the street in the evenings.

As some people parked their cars, they blocked the driveways; this made the residents mad. We acquired a lawyer, but the nightclub owner still was defiant. I thought about putting a loudspeaker on the roof of the residence next door and use the loudspeaker to preach to the people at the club; perhaps that would stop them. The one good outcome was that we got acquainted with our neighbors. We finally had results; the business had to close and move to another location. Later in a brawl at the new location the owner was shot.

The Mission in Campanario

At the same time as the evil presence of the drinking and dancing crowd at the end of our block bothered us, our spirits began rejoicing over the progress at the island church. Better results began after we began early Sunday-morning prayer services. Only a few weeks later we had nine new converts.

A deacon of the church supplied groceries to Campanario, a village about 50 miles north of us on the Rio-Bahia Highway. Each week he went to Campanario with his truck loaded with food and household items. He wanted to start a preaching point, so we went together to Campanario. I found a Presbyterian woman that allowed me to rent her garage. I had a few simple benches made, so we were in business. One day I took a car full of youth to hand out a notice about the beginning of the Baptist preaching point. On Sunday afternoons we would go up for services at 3 and return in time for church training and evening worship at 6.

How Hepatitis Affected Me!

In chapter 12 Leona gives details about my bout with hepatitis, but I want to tell some of my emotions about the consequences of the eight weeks of recuperation. This illness occurred about three weeks after I returned from the muddy trip on which I probably contracted hepatitis. Our little dog, Spit-Spot, gained my total admiration. She was really the kids' dog; however, she always seemed to respect me very much even though I didn't give her much attention. Spit-Spot usually stayed outdoors, but now she had special visitation rights. She was just the size to put her chin on the edge of the bed and watch after me. Her eyes had a sad, pitiful look as if she was suffering with me. I couldn't help but appreciate her to the bottom of my heart, because she could sit for hours—not wanting to play but just to sympathize with me.

I often had thought that if I had about a month to rest, I would catch up on a lot of things. That included reading the Bible more intensely, reading other books in my library, reviewing my Portuguese-language study books, and catching up on correspondence. Well, for four weeks I didn't feel like doing anything; this was frustrating to me. I was happy when our portable typewriter that my brother, Bill, had given me could be brought to my bed. That way as I sat up in bed, I could start doing some writing.

Of course I had many, many hours on which I could reflect on my past. The television reception was terrible and therefore most of the time not worth watching. I wasn't worried about dying, although this was a possibility, but I just believe God had more for us to do. I spent much time reflecting on all my past experiences, especially those on the farm.

I was born on August 3, 1935, in the middle of the Great Depression between 1929 and 1939. The adult folks talked about this all the time. Sometimes the government forced farmers and ranchers to kill some of their livestock; I guess this happened because few people had money with which to buy meat. Along with the stock-market crash of 1929, over much of the West and Midwest a terrible drought devastated the crops. By the thousands poor farmers from Oklahoma, Arkansas, Kansas, and Texas moved to the fruit-growing areas of California. Terrible dust storms thickened the air so much that dust-pneumonia killed some of the people. One of Leona's grandfathers and a great-uncle died at Roy, NM, from dust pneumonia. I remember some terrible dust storms on our farm in the spring. Although times were difficult, because of our irrigated garden we usually had food. Gradually Daddy, a very diligent worker, began to prosper. About 1940 he traded off his horses and bought an old, red Farmall tractor. He kept that a year and then bought a new, two-row John Deere tractor that was nicknamed "popping Johnnie" because it had very little horsepower and because the engine made a *pop, pop, pop* sound. Yet this was a great material advancement. He also had a feed-grinding machine that helped him make better feed for his cattle. Daddy was pretty good at trading things and making a little profit. The last two years we were on the farm, we had a good 1938 Ford car and a not-so-old pickup.

Saturday was the day to take baths in an aluminum tub that held about 10 gallons of water. The tub was filled by buckets carried from the windmill. All of us kids took baths in the same water. In the wintertime this water was heated on the stove. We usually took these baths on Saturday nights unless we were going to town; then we took them earlier. The term, "Don't throw the baby out with the bath water", was derived from this way of bathing. If the baby was the last one to have its bath, the water was so dirty that he or she might not be seen in the water and therefore be thrown out in the dirty water. Those were the good ole days if you don't like taking baths every day.

Our church was very important in our lives. Our farming and ranching community had a one-room church house. I can remember it being situated in two places. At first the building was southeast of our house about a half of a mile. From our home we could see the people when they arrived at church. For some reason the building was moved about 400 or 500 yards into another man's pasture—about the same distance directly south of our house and across the road from our grandfather's house. The village of Plainview, NM, with three or four stores in the past had existed maybe 300 yards southeast from the place onto which the church building was moved. Occasionally some-one who walked around the area in which those buildings had been would find a penny, nickel, or dime lying on the ground there.

My dad was the song leader for the church; my mother was the adult Sunday-school teacher. I think my parents were happy being active in the life of the church. Because it was a one-room church house, a heavy wire was strung from the east wall to the west to divide the church building in half. A strong wire also was stretched from the north to the south; a curtain could be hung to block off the pulpit area. These two curtains divided the adults from the young people and older children. The curtain that could be drawn to block off the pulpit area also was used for dramatic presentations put on either by adults or young people. However, I remember that we little children had a place by the side of one of the windows on the stage behind the cur-tain. I especially remember springtime, in which the window was open and a breeze passed through and cooled us from the heat. The church building had only one tree near the window. The sound of the birds singing in the tree added a beautiful background to Bible stories. I still remember hearing stories about Jesus loving little children, Jesus healing the sick, and other stories about Jesus. As I heard these, I also heard the birds twittering in the trees. These stories began to touch my life.

Most of the community social life took place in this little church building. We had no dances, but box suppers and pie suppers were held to help raise money. Young women would make a pie or prepare a lunch and put it in a decorated box. The young men interested in her would bid for the box; the highest bidder would eat the contents as he sat with her. An element of curiosity prevailed about the food in the boxes. During the summer we often had dinners outside on Sundays after the morning service. The children ate and played while the adults visited.

I don't remember having a pastor at this church. We often had visiting preachers; my folks would invite them to eat Sunday dinner with us. Guests always were first to serve their plates, so the preacher got to choose his favorite piece of chicken. We children were taught to respect adults and say "yes ma'am" and "no ma'am" and "yes sir" and "no sir". Adults were served before the children were. However, this meant that kids sometimes just got a chicken foot instead of the better pieces of chicken. In many Brazilian homes the adult men sat around the small table, the children sat on the floor, and the wife stood up to eat. As the years went by, I visited in many wealthier Brazilian homes in which the whole family sat around the table. In the Brazilian homes I was reminded about my childhood experience and felt honored to be served first. I didn't take the best piece of chicken but didn't take the chicken foot either.

Hog-killing day was an exciting day for me. After I was about 5, Daddy let me watch him kill the hog. Some neighbors always helped Daddy. As I remember, hog-killing usually occurred in the fall just before the crops had to be brought in. Daddy and Mama also helped two or three neighbors on their hog-killing days. Helping each other made the task more enjoyable.

After the hog was shot and the throat cut to drain the blood, hot water was needed to pour over its body to make scraping the hair off easier. A hand wench then lifted the pig or hog by its back legs; it hung at the height easy for the men to cut the hog up in pieces.

Nearly every part of the hog was used for something. Most farmers used the hog's ears, tail, and brains in some way. Since we didn't have electricity, the meat had to be "cured" or canned. Curing the meat meant spicing and salting it down. The women already had little round sacks made for sausage. As the meat not proper for bacon, hams, pork chops, or roast was brought to the women, the hand meat grinders began turning. We had our meat grinder, but Grandma Tarry brought hers, too. I liked to help put the pieces of meat into the meat grinder and watch ground meat squeeze through the holes at the front of the grinder as if they were two dozen worms emerging at one time. I once stuck my right forefinger into one of the holes from which the ground meat was pushed out the holes; the blade sliced the tip of my finger off. For many years I had a scar on the tip of that finger. Kids have to learn some way. From that time on mothers who knew what I had done could make real believers out of their children by telling them to look at my finger to see what a meat grinder could do to a kid's finger. For sausage the ground meat was seasoned with salt, sage, and other spices. The sausage meat was stuffed into the long, skinny sacks that Mama had made.

By noon the smell of fresh pork frying on the stove permeated the whole area inside and outside the house. One hog wouldn't be enough to get a family through the winter, so many times more than one was killed. This was a long day's work. Mincemeat was made from some of the ground pork. The ground meat was cooked and sweetened with raisins, brown sugar, and spices and then canned in jars to be saved for future use. For most people mincemeat pies represented a delicious treat; I was one that liked them. The hams were covered with a special curing mix that was rubbed on the outside of the hams until they were covered well. The skin was left on the bacon slabs with the streaks of lean meat. These were not smoked at our house but just were covered with salt to cure. From the rafters in the well house all of this meat was hung on hooks to cure. The fatter sides of the hogs were salted down to what was called "salt pork". The rest of the skin was cut into smaller pieces and fried or baked until all the fat was rendered out and they became cracklings. Cracklings were good to eat but were not so healthy.

The windmill pumped water into the trough which passed through the well house; when the trough was full, the water overflowed to the earthen tank outside. This water always was cool. Into the water we could put small watermelons, bottles of milk, and other things that needed to be kept cool.

I guess all of the farmers' wives had a big black kettle. This kettle was used to heat water for washing clothes. Daddy bought a gas-driven washing machine for Mama, but hot water still had to be heated in the kettle. The big kettle also was used to make homemade lye soap. The ingredients for lye soap are equal parts of lard and water and a can of lye. This is stirred and cooked until it thickens. When the soap is cool, the lye soap was cut in blocks about the size of small bricks. This was before refined detergents that we have today. Farmwives made their supply of soap for a year. Nice hand soap was a luxury that I do not remember having.

Miscellaneous Experiences

We had two cows with horns; neither one seemed to like me. I didn't like their milk, but that should not have been a reason to dislike me! I had to keep on the alert, or ole Betsy or ole Horny would charge me. Ole Horny had the sharpest horns. One day I was watching her new calf at the back of the pen. She was nearby in the pasture; I was not harming her baby calf at all as I stood outside the corral. I didn't hear Old Horny until she was very close to me. As fast as I could, I took off running around the back of the haystack and barn. She was so close that she was able to bump me with her horns; this made me nearly lose my balance. I had to increase the movement of my legs not to fall flat on the ground. If I fell, I knew I would be a goner! From my mouth a frightened cry of "Help! Help!" got the attention of my mother, sisters, and brother. My goal was to reach the gate of the back yard, but how would I have time to open it with Horny so close to me? I was grateful when I saw that someone had opened the gate. *Would I make it though? Bump, bump* went the cow's head against my backside. Each time with the force of the bump I almost fell. I sailed through the gate; ole Horny gave up the chase.

We had a big tomcat. Often during the night another cat visited our house. Nothing chills my body or curdles my blood more than does the sound of two cats fighting. I couldn't go to sleep for a long time after I heard the cats fight. They begin their fighting with the most mournful moaning and groaning one can imagine. Then suddenly one would attack the other; their cries were so loud and vicious that I thought surely one of them would be dead soon. When this part of the battle began, I almost sat up straight in bed from the suddenness of the attack. The best thing I could do was to put my head underneath the covers. One year, after several nights of cat-fighting, Daddy took his 22-caliber rifle and shot in the dark toward the cats. The fight stopped. The next morning he went out to see what had happened and found a dead cat. Guess what? He had killed the invading cat, not our cat. Boy, that was luck!

At the dining table we kids had a bench on which we sat. When Margaret got too old for the highchair, she needed a place to sit. Daddy used a 10-gallon can to hold sorghum syrup that he made from sugar cane. Mama filled the syrup pitcher from the can. The can was a little higher than a bench or chair. Mama would put Margaret on that can at the end of the table. In that can we had enough syrup to last a year. One day Margaret turned over the can; the lid popped off. The can was about two-thirds full of syrup. Before Mama or Daddy could get to the can, about half of it had run out on the floor. That was a sticky mess! Of course that was the last time Margaret sat on the syrup can.

Some neighbors moved from the farm that joined us on the north. They had some children about our ages. I think they had every toy that was featured in the Sears, Roebuck catalog. They had windup bull-dozers or caterpillars, cars, trucks, and all kinds of toys. When they moved, outside the house they left a medium-sized toy dump truck. The truck was dirty and maybe a little rusty, but Daddy brought it home and painted it green. Daddy gave it to me on my birthday. I was so proud of that truck. I enjoyed putting dirt in the bed and dumping it again on a pile of dirt. One day the family returned to visit their old friends and visited us. We kids went outside to play; the boy recognized the truck. When they were ready to leave, the boy cried because he wanted to take the truck with him. Mama insisted that he take the truck. You know who cried then? Yes, I was heartbroken! I had only one or two cars; that boy had so many, he didn't take care of them.

Primary-School Days

During my recovery days about the only thing I could do was think about my past. This is a part of The Marvel of It All! I was very excited about starting first grade. I would get to ride the school bus. My Aunt Susie, also our neighbor, was the bus driver. I still was embarrassed about an incident that had happened a few weeks before. I had heard someone use a very vulgar word and I had called my Aunt Susie that word. I had no idea what it meant, but I got a terrible lashing over it.

I enjoyed riding the small school bus. The bigger kids, two of whom were Aunt Susie's kids plus my older brother, Bill, and sister, Helen, made up nearly half of those riding the bus. The classrooms had a coat room in which everyone in the wintertime put their lunches and coats. The first three grades got out of class 30 minutes before the older kids did, so we had 30 extra minutes to play on the playground.

I was embarrassed because another boy and I were the only ones that wore overalls. These were the blue bib coveralls or striped ones that for the last 25 years—even in Brazil—have become popular again. But in my early days they were going out of style; nearly all the boys wore waist pants with a belt. Overalls stigmatized us as poor kids.

Another thing that stigmatized me as a poor kid was my lunch. Most kids' mothers made sandwiches with storebought loaf bread, known as "light bread". My lunch usually was a couple of cold biscuits with mustard spread and a piece of salt pork bacon in them. Many of the others' lunches had apples, bananas, or oranges; I rarely had any of these. Some had a piece of pie or a piece of cake; I rarely had these. Mama did make butter rolls for Friday's lunch. I didn't like butter, but with a lot of sugar on it, I managed it. My lunch pail was a peanut-butter can; its lid had holes for a little ventilation.

I had a friend, Joe Phillips, whose daddy was the manager of the White House Grocery on Main Street beside the Lea County bank. He was kind enough to share some of his goodies with me; I always appreciated him for that.

Sometimes a city kid left part of a lunch that he or she had not eaten. After school, with no one else in the coatroom, I would go through the sacks or lunch boxes to see if some goody had been left. Sometimes I found a prize such as a piece of cake.

I was a very bashful boy, especially around girls. In the first day I had one very embarrassing thing occur. The girl behind me gave me a piece of licorice candy (black was the only color of licorice then); I put it in my mouth. Before long I had black around my mouth. Eating candy or chewing gum was against the rules. The teacher called me to the front and asked me whether I was eating candy. I said, "No ma'am!" "What is that all over your mouth?" she asked. Everybody laughed! Licorice was made in a long, skinny, twisted form about the size of a pencil. She said, "OK, Joe, just stay up here and eat the rest of it before the class." I liked my teacher very much. She knew this would be an effective punishment for me, because I was so easily embarrassed and bashful. Especially since I had lied, this punishment was torture.

I made pretty good grades, but I excelled only in one thing—that was wiggling my nose. In the Easter play I got to be the bunny rabbit, because I was the only kid that had that gift. The last day of school was memorable because Aunt Susie bought each of us a "milk nickel" ice cream on a stick; the ice cream was covered with chocolate. It was something new and then cost only a nickel.

My second year of school while I lived on the farm ended almost before it got started. At the end of October my mother died; in January we moved to Lovington. This is enough reminiscing for now.

Annual Mission Meeting

As a family the big question in our minds was whether we would get to go to the South Brazil annual mission meeting in July 1972. This always was the greatest week or our lives, since we got to meet with about 300 missionaries and their kids. Vacation Bible School was for the MK's (missionary kids); the week held a lot of other fun things for them. I prayed that I would be well enough to go.

Leona later gives the details about the promise we had to make to the doctor about our participating in the annual mission meeting in 1972. I was so grateful to God that because of my recent illness I had not caused the family to miss this wonderful event. I tried to keep the doctor's advice and just fudged a little to hear our special invited speaker a time or two.

One night at mission meeting a revival broke out. About 10:30 one night Carl and a friend knocked on my door. They excitedly told me about how the Holy Spirit had melted the hearts of the missionaries and how sweet the fellowship was. Missionaries were hugging each other; some were crying for joy. Carl and his friend wanted my pocket New Testament that I used for personal witnessing; they went out to witness to some hotel-staff members.

When we left Caxambu, Leona was sick, so I was forced to drive some. I felt sorrow for her, because I think she had reached her physical limit. Caxambu, in the southern mountains of Minas Gerais, was cold in the wintertime, but this year it was colder than usual. The hotel had no heat. After we arrived home, Leona was so exhausted that she spent most of a week and a half in bed with bronchial pneumonia. To make matters worse, while we were in Caxambu, our maid got married, so when we returned, we didn't have a maid. But God looks over His people. One of Pastor Hilton's daughters arrived to help. Leona was giving her free piano lessons. A neighbor and member of First Baptist Church also helped clean the house.

The Rest of 1972

To get my energy back to sort of normal took about a year. For a good while I was so tired by noon that I spent most of the afternoons in bed. My sickness delayed my plan to visit some churches to promote the need for them to contribute more for opening up missions in the western part of our association. The western area had 60 cities, towns, and villages with only one church and one mission—that burdened my heart. My spirit rejoiced with the August baptism of nine people on the island; we had four more waiting to be baptized. The whole month of August we had the Bible institute. Twenty-five students were studying seven subjects a day. The institute was a blessing for Leona and me.

Brazil was celebrating 150 years of independence from Portugal; the Evangelical churches were asked to participate in this celebration. We were surprised the government would ask Evangelicals to do something special. The Brazilian Baptist Convention led in a campaign called "Independence and Life". In Governador Valadares we had night prayer meetings before we held a three-day revival in the local churches. Our special for the 150-year celebration of Brazil's independence was to hold our second citywide revival the last week of September. We wanted to win as many Brazilians to Christ as we possibly could.

Our preacher for the second citywide revival was ex-priest Anibal Pereira Reis. In chapter 2 I told about this man. He was my close friend and during the revival stayed in our house. We had a citywide Baptist choir comprised of choirs from the seven churches. Leona played the organ for the hymns and special music brought by the guest singer. I had arranged for the army band to play the first night to kick off the service after the Brazilian, state, and Christian flags were brought in. A crowd of 2,500 people stood to the music of the Brazilian national anthem.

Our biggest attendance was on Sunday night, with about 4,000 people in attendance to hear ex-priest Anibal tell about his salvation and why he left the Roman Catholic Church. During the week more than 800 decisions were recorded. Only 22 of these were from the island, but all of the seven pastors and churches were jubilant over the results. By this time Anibal had written 13 of the more than 40 books he wrote before his death in about 1995. He was a very courageous man to write so openly about catholicism. One of the books that he wrote was adopted by the military as a required book for all military officers to read. He had death threats because of the book *Can Priests Be Trusted?* I happened to be in his home in São Paulo when that book was "hot off the press". I asked him, "Anibal, are you not afraid for your life for publishing a book like this?" He said, "Yes, but if they kill me, I have already published enough of the truth to compensate for the loss of my life." He said that as a priest he carried a gun but as a pastor he did not.

In 1971 the Catholic Church took him to court; Anibal, having a law degree, defended himself and was acquitted. This made the Roman Catholic hierarchy angry enough to send out a letter to bishops and priests to somehow stop Pastor Anibal. Agnelo Rossi was the archbishop of São Paulo until the end of 1970, when he was transferred to Rome to work in the office of the Sacred Congregate for the Evangelization of the People. This archbishop in the Vatican sent a letter on November 12, 1971, to Dom Paulo Evaristo Arns, the bishop of São Paulo. The following is a translation of that letter:

"We have knowledge of the judicial sentence that turned out to be favorable of Father Anibal Pereira dos Reis. Certainly he will take measures to proclaim and amply spread this decision on his side because this interests him. I lament that luck went his way. Now, for certain, he is going to inflame still more his stubbornness as a protestant preacher.

208

"As his old professor, former Bishop, and observer of his activities, I recognize him to be one of the most educated priests in all Brazil. His enormous capacity as a worker is admirable. He is intelligent, educated, yet a stubborn worker. Now he is the most noticeable heretic in Brazil and the one that disturbs the advance of ecumenicalism the most. We would have already accomplished much more if Anibal had not defected! Had it not been for him we would have already accomplished much more. His books and his preaching are causing enormous difficulties for our plans there in Brazil. We fear that this literature will be translated into other languages; this would spread the evil into other countries.

"The Holy Father, informed of all this, is apprehensive, he solicits you, through me, that you insist in the Brazilian Bishops Conference meetings to study ways to destroy, hamper and neutralize the works of this priest. If we have lost him as a priest, that is a great loss, now we must curb his influence.

"What shall we do? As I have already said, you devise an adequate plan! Maybe promote something to demoralize him among the Protestants themselves.

"The Brazilian Bishops ought to convince themselves that Father Anibal is the priest that actually caused Paul VI the most worry; he is expressly interested in an urgent solution. Send me cuttings of newspapers and magazine articles. Send me also information about the measures to be taken by the Counsel of Brazilian Bishops concerning the subject of Father Anibal Pereira dos Reis so that I can inform the Holy Father." (A friend that worked inside Bishop Arns' office gave to Pastor Anibal a copy of this letter that contained the Vatican letterhead.)

After the big campaign, Monday was a busy day as we made sure that all the churches took their benches back, knocked down the big board podium that elevated the choir, pulpit, and organ, and saw that the big floor area was swept. That night at our island church we had a thanksgiving service for the ingathering of souls. During the service a young man had an epileptic convulsion. He recently had moved to Valadares with a man that had managed a hotel in Ipatinga, 50 miles from Valadares, at which the big steel mill is located. This hotel manager had taken pity on him; in the hotel he gave him a job of ironing sheets and pillowcases and then brought him with them to Valadares. Adam was from the little town of Iapu but had no living parents to provide him with medicine for his epilepsy. He also was deformed in his shoulders and chest, because his mother fell with him when he was 1-month old. The couple helping him moved near our church; Adam began attending. At our church this young man recently had made a profession of faith. The husband and wife moved their letter to our church.

This epileptic attack was violent, so we took him to a room at the back of the auditorium and for an hour worked with him. We took him to a hospital at which he spent the night. We knew that neither Adam nor the couple could pay a hospital bill. Leona and I didn't have extra money for this either. I resolved to take him to the Evangelical Hospital in Belo Horizonte. Kathy Richardson made reservations for him at the hospital. The hospital didn't really want to take him either but did. Our whole family had to go to Belo with Adam, because Leona had to help drive. The kids would have to miss school. We laid him in the back of the car in which I had lain when I went to Caxambu. This big car was a blessing. The doctor gave Adam a strong shot, so he slept all the way. We left home about 3 p.m. and arrived at the hospital about 10. At about 1 a.m. Leona and I left the hospital to go to the Boswells' home for the night. We stayed a couple of days because the next day I had a state board meeting.

For seven weeks Adam stayed in the Evangelical Hospital. I brought him back home, but he soon became worse again. I discovered that the man helping him hadn't told his wife that Adam had seizures; this soon became a problem in their marriage. Adam also was having terrible pain in one foot. I tried to get him in the only hospital in Valadares that dealt with charity cases, but that hospital didn't treat epileptics. What a problem we faced now! He was converted in our church; we couldn't abandon him. What would God do with him? Finally his aunt in Iapu offered to take care of him, so I took him to her. This hurt me, however, because at that time we had no Baptist church in Iapu to help him.

210

Leona's Volkswagen Beetle

Leona needed a car. Twice an American family, the Julian Flints, had been to Brazil to work on engineering projects with the Brazilian government. The Flints were unusual in that they tried diligently to learn the language and become involved with Brazilian churches, except when they were in Rio, they went to International Baptist Church. They took part of their vacation to attend the South Brazil Baptist Mission meetings and paid their own way. Many of the missionaries knew and loved them. When Julian, Eve, and their two children decided to leave Brazil, we offered to buy their 1970 white Volkswagen bug and a few other things.

The Volks Bug was the most popular car in Brazil and was great for parking in the city. For traveling on muddy roads the Volks also was greater than you might think. With chains I could go anywhere until the ruts in the road got so deep that the car dragged bottom. When I traveled by myself, I enjoyed taking the Volks—even to Rio for quarterly executive mission meetings. It didn't use as much expensive gas. Nearly all the time we were in Brazil, we paid more than $2 for a gallon of gasoline.

During the time we used it, the car was a blessing. Before we left for furlough in December 1975, we found a buyer for the car and used the money to buy a lot for a church in Virginopolis. So that has continued to be a blessing in the work.

Chapter 11

Preaching Points, Missions, and Opening a City

Faces of hundreds of Brazilians flash through my mind—
People who, through our ministry, Jesus they could find—
Of those the Holy Spirit made different and kind—
What a tough time I'll have someday leaving them behind!

I marvel about it all because I was not at all bold.
I just tried to put myself in Jesus' hands to mold—
Preaching points, missions, churches, and opening up a city—
Praise Jesus, Hallelujah, and to God be the glory!

I am not boasting, for I would have been used even more for God if I had had the experience early in my ministry that I had in 1988. I tried to do many things for God by my own force and didn't always allow Him to do the work through me. Part of The Marvel of it All is that God permits us to use our energy until we run out of gas and have to depend totally on Him.

Traveling First Class

On our second furlough we had brought a car air-conditioner in the States. I found no one in Governador Valadares to install air-conditioners in automobiles. All the instructions with diagrams for mounting the air-conditioner were in the box. I found a mechanic that knew some English; he thought that with the diagrams he could install it. However, when he finished, no place in

212

Governador Valadares had equipment to put in freon gas.

On a shop on the road leaving Rio de Janeiro we had seen an advertisement about car air-conditioners. We spent Christmas with the Laings in Rio de Janeiro, so I took our car to the shop and left it. The next day I happily brought our car back to the Laings. The next morning, however, all the freon gas had escaped. I took the car back to the shop; the people there said they wouldn't guarantee the air-conditioner, because they had not installed it. They really didn't want to mess with my car, but I pleaded my case; they had mercy on me because of the heat in the Sweet River Valley. They tried to find the leak and again filled it with Freon gas. Two days later the Freon again had escaped. Since we were on vacation because of Christmas, for the third time I took the car back. Two days later we returned to Valadares in the comfort of cool air. As far as I know, we were the only family in Valadares that had this luxury. Because the Chevrolet Veraneio was large, the air-conditioner didn't cool the back of the car well, but it sure made traveling a lot better than did driving with windows open— especially on the dirt roads when we followed trucks, buses, and cars.

While I was in the shop in Rio, I met a man that lived in the beautiful city of Petropolis on top of the mountains that overlook Rio de Janeiro. He was Catholic but wanted me to pray for him; he was concerned about his teen-aged children. His name was George Bocas. He did not have a Bible. Many rich people in Rio have summer homes in Petropolis because of the cooler climate. Portugal's governor in Brazil, before independence from Portugal, had a summer palace in Petropolis. A few months later we went by George's house and took him and his family a Bible. I witnessed to him and have the pleasure in knowing that he was presented the plan of salvation. He didn't make a decision that day, but I trust he later made his decision and that I will meet him in heaven.

1973 Flying By

And the Peace of God, which surpasses all comprehension, shall guard your hearts and your minds in Christ Jesus (Phil. 4:7). From March through June I took time to visit 20 of the 58 churches in the Sweet River Valley. I am ashamed to say that I visited some of these for the first time, even though I had been serving the Lord in this area for nearly seven years, except for the 10 months we spent on two furloughs. Most of those visits were to clarify for the people our state and national programs of integrating all Baptists into active Christian service through prayer, witnessing, and contributing financially. The motive behind this effort was "spreading the gospel over Minas Gerais and Brazil faster".

I was pleased with the reception that I received in the churches. I was aware that I still was a stranger and that "Mineiros", people of Minas Gerais, are like Missourians—the "show-me" state in America. Mineiros want to know how long a missionary will be with them: four years is a little short for some of them to wholeheartedly want to cooperate. When they see you are one of them and plan to stay with them, their confidence rises. Many times Brazilians deeply humbled me. For instance on one short trip I was at a church not far from the town of Tarumirim. About 15 people walked eight miles to hear me. This visit was made in the winter; in the hills and mountains of that area the temperature was cold. Some people had no shoes; some had no long-sleeved shirts; I am sure they would have worn them if they had. My visit was at night; that meant they wouldn't get home until after midnight. They knew very little about Minas Gerais and much less about Brazil and the rest of the world. But they knew Jesus as their Savior and needed to know that Brazilian Baptists had their state, nation, and the people of the world on their hearts.

I have mentioned that Pastor Hilton, Pastor Waldemar, and I visited many of the cities and towns and gave Bibles to the mayors in the western area of our association. Of those we visited, Virginopolis' mayor was the only mayor that wouldn't accept a Bible. I made time to do some traveling in that area also. We finally had a little church in Guanhaes that I have spoken of as well as the little church in Pecanha, sponsored by a church in Belo Horizonte. Pastor Waldemar had told me that Virginopolis had a woman that was a believer. He also told me of an understanding between the city council and the priest that no "believer" could buy properties or buy building materials for construction. This was the strategy for keeping all Evangelicals out of Virginopolis.

Sixty cities, towns, and villages were in this area. In April I stopped on the city square in Virginopolis; I simply was hoping to meet someone that would become a friend. Almost immediately four or five men surrounded me; they wanted to know who the stranger was and what I wanted. I had decided that I would never try to cover up my identity. I told them I was a Baptist preacher from Governador Valadares. One of the men blurted, "We do not want believers in our town. They are worthless and a big problem to us. We have no use for people like you." They told me that I wouldn't be permitted to work in their town. I found that Pastor Waldemar's analysis about the people in Virginopolis was true. A young military policeman stayed after the others left. I asked him whether he knew about a believer in Virginopolis; I hoped he would know about the woman Pastor Waldemar mentioned. To my surprise he said he was a believer but didn't want anyone to know. He was a charismatic Baptist from Valadares. This police officer told me that the woman Pastor Waldemar had heard about lived in the first house on the curve entering Virginopolis from Guanhaes. With this information I went back to the entrance of Virginopolis and pulled up beside the first house. As I got out of the car, a man appeared at one window and a teen-aged boy at another window. I asked the man if whether a woman who was a believer lived in the house. The man replied, "Well, if a believer lives in this house, I have no knowledge of this." I immediately realized I might have caused trouble for the woman of the house if this was the correct house. The man and his son wouldn't accept a gospel tract and slammed shut the windows.

I left Virginopolis with a heavy heart. As I suffered over what had occurred as well as the lack of believers in these areas, I decided I would have to return and spend some time just making friends. I needed to prove that Evangelical Christians weren't so terrible. I went home resolved to give more time to the Western part of our association.

Altinopolis Mission Started

We had a converted spiritist and his wife to join our church when these individuals moved to the island. They had been members of First Baptist Church of Valadares. After about a year he had a job taking care of a telephone tower (Satellite Telephone Company) on the top of a high hill about 60 miles north of Governador Valadares. Yes, a better communication system was beginning to arrive in our area. Geraldo and his wife, Conceicao (Conception), moved back to Valadares and located on the island. He had won to the Lord a poor farm hand and wife who lived at the foot of the mountain on which the Satellite Telephone Company was situated.

One Sunday morning this farmhand, Mario, his wife, a teen-aged daughter, and a son about 11 years of age visited our church. They had sold all their meager goods, moved to Valadares, and bought a tiny space on the side of a hill in the Altinopolis neighborhood, a new development. The former owner had dug out a space on the hillside and built a small, two-room house. Mario and his wife wanted to follow Jesus; no one lived in the area around Embratel (Satellite Telephone Company) to continue discipling them. They moved to the city.

Naturally Leona and I paid them a visit and discovered a neighborhood in Valadares we didn't know existed. Mario's tiny house consisted of a bedroom with one double bed and the living and dining room. In that room they had one small table with four chairs. The floors were dirt. The cooking was done outside over a small wood stove made of mud brick. The water faucet also was outside and had one spout that went into the concrete tank that served for washing dishes, hands, and also their clothes. The inside front of the concrete tank had grooves like a rub board that served for rubbing the dirt out of the dirtiest clothes. A little rack inside the eating room door served for hanging pots and pans. As I remember, these were all of their earthly belongings. Their clothes were hung on nails in the bedroom. After I visited with them, I immediately recognized we needed a Baptist presence in this neighborhood. Soon we were holding Sunday-afternoon services in their front yard in the hot sun.

As new converts Mario and his wife attended my discipleship class that I taught during the Sunday-school hour. Seeing how destitute they were, because Mario did not have a job, the church began giving them basic food items. I paid him to hoe and cut the grass on the island church property. But this was temporary. In our discipleship class that was principally to prepare them for baptism, we began to pray that he would find a job. One of the members of Fifth Baptist Church worked for a small iron-ore smelting plant that was not far from the place in which Mario lived. The Lord arranged for Mario to work there.

Mario, however, was very frail and sick with an ulcer. The only work they had for him to do was loading heavy blocks of crude, smelted iron onto flat truck beds to be taken to a large iron-works factory. These blocks of crude iron weighed about 100 pounds each. A few days after he began working, I visited the smelting plant to observe how he was doing. He didn't know I was there. All of the other men doing this work were young and very strong. I watched Mario struggle to lift those iron blocks up to the truck bed. I thought to myself that he wouldn't last one month. We thanked God for the job, but I told the discipleship class that surely God had something better for Mario. We began praying for a better job. One of the lessons in the class was about tithing. Since I knew Mario's financial situation, the devil suggested I just leave Mario out of those needing to tithe. Most of our church family barely got by from month to month, but Mario's case was much worse. I struggled with Satan's suggestion, but my convictions on tithing won out. I taught Mario and his wife that tithing was for all people.

A Day I Never Will Forget

My family usually was among the first to arrive for worship on Sunday mornings; sometimes we were there before the janitor was. The Sunday morning after Mario had received his first paycheck, he and his family arrived before anyone else. Mario entered the auditorium through the front door and was almost shouting with joy. He blurted out, with one hand high in the air grasping his tithe, "Pastor, here is my tithe". He wanted to give it to me, but I explained to him that part of his worship experience is giving his tithe when the other worshippers put tithes and offerings into the *gasofilacio* (money box) at the altar.

I want to tell you how prayer and tithing works for the poor. Mario worked about three months loading the heavy blocks of crude iron onto trucks. One day the manager of the plant called Mario to his office. He said something such as this, "Mario, I have observed how you are dedicated to your job. I have watched you struggle to get every block of iron onto the bed of the trucks. Now I have something

217

else for you to do. I want you to be in charge of cleaning the offices and keeping the company grounds clean." You can never outguess God! I had thought about God opening up a job in some other place.

Mario was learning to put God first and carefully use his money. First Mario put a concrete floor in his two-room house. Mario bought beds for his two children. The next project was to build a small room at the back for cooking and washing at the tank. As time went on, he bought a radio and other things. Mario and his family never will be rich, but God was blessing them more than they had imagined. After some months working he had medical benefits that would pay for an ulcer operation. After the operation his health began to improve.

I Get Ahead of God

Recognizing that the Altinopolis neighborhood was becoming populated in a hurry, I began looking for lots to buy for a future church. I couldn't find anything for sale in the Altinopolis neighborhood but did in an adjoining neighborhood. Throughout a three-year period I bought two lots, because no money was in the strategic property fund. The lots were situated about halfway up a high hill from which you could see most of Valadares. The road was dirt; during the rainy season each year it almost would wash out. The location I had chosen was not the best. I got ahead of God!

We continued having Sunday-afternoon services in Altinopolis. We arranged for Geraldo, the man who won Mario to Christ, to be in charge of working with Mario, family, and neighbors at Altinopolis so I could begin work in Campanario. Every Sunday afternoon I took a carload of young people to have a service in a Presbyterian woman's garage. We left Valadares at 2 p.m., started services at 3, and returned to Valadares barely in time for church training at 6. We were having between 20-30 people to attend the service in Campanario. After a while Seventh Baptist Church of Valadares became interested in helping at Campanario by taking responsibility for services twice a month. After a about a year, Seventh Baptist Church made me happy by taking responsibility full time of that preaching point.

Some months later two nice lots about a block and a half above the Catholic Church and school were put up for sale in the Altinopolis neighborhood. The only problem was that when the road was cut around the hill, it left those lots about four feet above the road. That meant we would have to cut an entrance up into the lots. By this time the strategic property fund had money; I received $4,000 to buy the lots. Normally the first thing Brazilians do when they buy lots is to put a fence—barbed-wire if they can't afford anything better. Our two lots had barbed-wire fences on the back and side divisions, but the front was open, although the four- to five-foot embankment made the lot difficult to enter. The city required fencing, or the property owner paid higher property taxes. I bought prefabricated cement slabs to build a fence in front. We wanted to get something built as soon as possible, so I had electricity and water hooked up and bought some materials to build a storage shed to store tools, cement, and smaller building materials.

We were unloading some building materials when the priest from the school and church below walked by. He asked what was going to be built. I told him we were preparing to build a Baptist church. His response was: "Why are you going to build a Baptist church? Baptists have built enough churches in Valadares already! Why do you not help us build the school for our community? That is what this community needs more than another church! Why do you not cooperate with us?" Then I began my rebuttal. I said: "You know, sir, many centuries ago the Roman Catholic Church was begun by the Emperor Constantine. Soon everyone was forced to cooperate with the Roman Catholic Church; they had no more liberty. Anytime people who simply wanted to worship Jesus according to biblical teaching were found, they were killed and their properties sold or given to the church. During the Inquisition, times were even worse. Only in the 15th century Martin Luther, the Anabaptists, and John Calvin were able to break free from bondage to worship as the Bible teaches." The priest broke in by saying: "But that was many years ago. Now we are brothers. Many community projects have financial needs more than we need churches. Why don't you forgive and forget the past?" I didn't try to answer him on this line any further, because I knew what he was referring to. Since the Second Vatican Council, Catholics were allowed to own and read the Bible. They were having Bible studies in their schools and churches. Also the Catholic churches had begun offering their schools as dormitory needs for our Baptist associational meetings. I knew this warming-up maneuver was an attempt to stop us from witnessing to Catholics. I said, "I hope no one steals the building materials that we are putting here tonight." The priest replied, "Well, if they do, the reason is because they need the things more than you do." I replied, "Sir, your response is exactly why we are going to build a Baptist church in this neighborhood! We want to teach this neighborhood biblical values which include honesty; stealing is a sin!" The priest left with nothing more to say.

God protected our building materials; we finished our plans. We built a simple meeting place for Altinopolis. We economized by putting a foundation strong enough for two stories, although for the moment we just built two restrooms and a covered an area that would seat about 75 people. I envisioned this area across the back of the lot to be a small part of a future, large building. Today the back end of a large two-story worship center sits on that foundation.

Once we finished this initial piece of construction, we started meeting under the "shed" with the two sides open; we met on the concrete floor. People on the street and neighbors could hear and see what went on. I began going to Altinopolis early for its worship service, which was during the Sunday-school period at the island church. Then I went to the island church to lead the worship service and Altinopolis had Sunday school. By this time I had trained someone to teach the discipleship class at the island. Now Altinopolis could begin regular Sunday-morning and -evening services.

How Altinopolis Opens the Door
to the Palmeiras Neighborhood

Geny was a Baptist that recently moved to Valadares from a small town in the interior. Geny and her four children lived in a little house adjacent to the back of the Altinopolis mission. She wasn't attending any church, so she was very happy a church was at her back door. She was a widow and was struggling to make a living by washing clothes by hand, ironing, and working at a hotel or whatever she could find to do.

Geny had a sister that lived in the Palmeiras neighborhood on the opposite side of the Rio-Bahia Highway. Geny's sister wanted us to go to her neighborhood and start a mission. Geny's sister's husband wasn't a Christian; he made very difficult her effort to start a work, but in her yard we were able to start a children's Sunday school. This was added to our schedule on Sunday afternoons. Soon two Contaiffer sisters in the island church took responsibility for the work with the children in Palmeiras.

Laisete and Genilda Ribeiro da Silva

At First Baptist Church in Valadares I became acquainted with Laisete. He had surrendered for the ministry; he and Genilda were engaged to be married. He was very good at cutting and polishing precious stones; as a young boy he started doing this. After they were married, they lived on the island. Island Baptist Church invited Laisete and his wife to help with the Altinopolis mission; this helped me a great deal. Laisete was my true son in the faith, as Timothy was to Paul. He spent hours with me on the books I wrote in Portuguese and traveled many places with me. Through most of the rest of our ministry in Brazil this family remained our friends and helpers in other mission work. We have several pieces of his stone artwork that are treasures to us.

A Priest Becomes Interested in Changing

Central de Minas was a special place for me. The first Brazilian home in which I stayed was with a young couple that lived there and owned a store in the town. The Baptist church was a good, strong one. I received a notice that the Catholic priest was interested in the true gospel and was even making an effort to change the baptism of babies. Pastor Hilton and I visited him first; he made some positive statements that he was interested in making a change. The priest knew he was being watched closely by his parishioners, so we planned that for only one of us to visit him at a time was best. Pastor Hilton drove a Rural that had the name of First Baptist Church of Valadares painted on the side. This wouldn't be good, so the next time I went to visit him by myself. He showed me some of the church documents. He said they pushed the tithe, but that most of the people were dishonest about tithing. He kept a record of the members' gifts and that some of the ranchers only gave a calf or bull now and then as an offering. I discussed with him again the plan of salvation; we talked about Christian

221

growth. He seemed to have made a sincere decision. That was the last time I saw or heard from him because he immediately was transferred to some other place. He was afraid that this was going to happen to him.

My First *Pingela*

A *pingela* is a bridge of only two wide boards about as thick as railroad ties crossing over a small river. This type of bridge was made only for vehicles such as small trucks and automobiles of regular width. One thing for sure is that a horse and buggy could not cross over a pingela, because the horse would fall into the river below.

I took a load of pastors to an examination of a lay preacher whose church was seeking to ordain him to the ministry. The ordination was to follow the examination if the council of pastors approved him. When I arrived at this *pingela*, I was pretty scared to have to cross the river. I asked the pastors whether we had any other way to get to the town in which we were going. The only other way was so far that we wouldn't arrive in time for the examination. The *pingela* bridge sloped up because the road on the other side of the river was higher.

We made the trip fine, except my hands were trembling. While we were at the meeting, rain fell. As I returned down the hill, I was more concerned than ever because my tires were covered with mud. Slowly I descended the hill approaching the river so I wouldn't have to brake as I started over the *pingela*. Of course, I wanted to think I was as good of a driver as Brazilians that traveled that road often were. I could feel the tires slipping a little. I can assure you, without disgrace, that I was very nervous. The river was small, but the water was roaring swiftly. The square logs were upheld by huge square beams that went into the riverbed. When the front wheels touched the muddy road on the other side, I gave a sigh of relief, but at that moment the back wheels slipped off of the boards. The car's forward motion was enough that the back wheels bounced onto the road, but I heard a strange noise in the rear. I got out to see what had happened. The end of the tailpipe was smashed; thus the exhaust was closed off. I took out a tire tool and pried the end of the tailpipe open so we could finish our journey home. I didn't like crossing *pingelas* in daylight; my blood pressure ascended even more at night.

When we traveled the country roads, we had to open many gates. A boy often was present to open the gate for us and of course to receive a coin for his help. In my pocket I always carried some small change for tips. A few times instead of a gate we would find cattle guards called *mata-burros*, or burro killers.

Jose Maria

The name *Jose Maria* literately is Joseph Mary, a common name for boys. *Maria Jose* is a girl's name. One Sunday Jose Maria attended church. This 26-year-old man was an alcoholic. Leona and I went to visit him and his family. He lived with his mother and three older sisters. Domingas was a very good friend of the family. (The story of Domingas is in chapter 5.) She had witnessed to Jose Maria and tried to help him quit drinking. Jose Maria previously had studied to be a priest. The mother and sisters clearly indicated that we were not welcomed in the house, so we left.

Jose Maria continued to visit our church. With interest he listened to the messages; sometimes he was able to control his thirst for alcohol. One day I had a young man, Gerson Januario, to preach in our church while I was away. Gerson was a little boy from the village Central de Santa Helena, where Central Baptist Church had a preaching point. The pastor saw potential in the young boy and brought him to Valadares and sponsored his schooling. While I worked with the young people, I had much contact with Gerson. While Gerson was studying his high-school material at night, during the month of September each year he attended the Bible institute during the day. He had a rich, bass voice. On the night Gerson Januario preached for me at the island church, Jose Maria made a decision for Christ.

Finally Jose Maria's mother and sisters allowed us to visit Jose Maria only because he began to overcome his alcohol problem after he started attending the island church. They were clear, however, that they were staunch Catholics and didn't want us to bother them with our religious beliefs. After we moved to Belo, Jose Maria married Enedina, Leona's helper with GA's and in the children's department at the island church. Jose Maria started an accounting firm but later went into the ministry. Before his mother died, she as well as all the sisters accepted Jesus. All of these family members became workers in a

Baptist church.

Opening Up the Town of Virginopolis for Christ

In early August I returned to Virginopolis with the plan to spend Friday night and Sunday night in the hotel to see whether I could make friends. I arrived at the hotel just before the evening meal, which was served family style. A sergeant of the police sat at my table. Before I started to eat, the sergeant asked me who I was and where I was from. I told him I was a Baptist missionary from Governador Valadares. He said, "I guess you know you will not be allowed to preach on the streets in this town. Furthermore, you need to know of an ordinance in this town that does not allow believers to purchase property or building supplies. You see, therefore, that you have no reason to stop in this town with those intentions."

I bowed my head and prayed silently for the meal and the sergeant. About halfway through the meal I asked him about his spiritual position. He said he was baptized a Catholic but really he was an atheist. He didn't believe in God. I asked him, "Suppose that you are wrong? What will you do in this case?" He didn't give me an answer. I asked him whether he would permit me to go to my room to get my Bible, for I had something to show him. He said he would. This surprised me! I went to the room and brought back my Bible and began a study on John 3:1-16. I took him through every verse and explained every phrase and the meaning of some of the words. Some of the other men began to listen. One man who was a pharmacist in town began to interrupt me; he tried to distract me by his knowledge of the Book of Revelation. As I went through the study, I clarified the passages. About an hour later Sergeant Milton said to me, "I have to go to the office and work now, but would you pass by the office and see me on Monday morning before you leave town for Valadares?" I had told him my plan to go to the city of Santa Maria de Suacui on Saturday and would be back in Virginopolis on Sunday afternoon.

At 10 that night I was at the second-floor window in the dining area; I watched the young people pass by on their way home from school. The hotel owner's wife approached me and said, "You know, I heard your Bible study with the sergeant tonight. I never have heard anything like it. The priest has been teaching Bible studies, but he has never taught anything like you taught." I said to the woman, "Very well, would you like to have more Bible studies? I will be back here Sunday afternoon at 3 p.m." The woman agreed!

On Saturday morning early I headed north to Agua Boa to browse a little and return to spend the night in Santa Maria de Suacui. A few miles farther north from Agua Boa is a little place called Mother of Men; the saying is that a woman that gave birth to 21 sons once lived there. She deserved to have a place on the map, I think. I milled around Agua Boa a couple of hours; I was just trying to make a special contact with someone. I returned to Santa Maria de Suacui, the larger town in the area, to walk the streets a little. Only a few people were around, because Saturday at noon merchant activities close down. I met a few people in the hotel, but I didn't have the luck I had had in Virginopolis.

I left early Sunday morning to get to Pecanha for a 7 a.m. service; then I drove on to Guanhaes to be present for the 11 a.m. worship hour there. These two places had the only organized Baptist work in the large area. I told the state missionary pastor that I was going to have a 3 p.m. service at the hotel in Virginopolis and invited him. He went with me; we arrived by 3 p.m., but the hotel woman didn't appear, so finally the pastor returned to Guanhaes. I was disappointed, but God still had much more for me later—more than I ever could have imagined.

Can you imagine with me the situation I was in? This was Sunday night; I had no church to attend. This was the first time ever for me to be in a place that didn't have a Baptist church. Worse than that, no Baptist existed in town—in fact no Evangelical Christian as far as I knew. At the evening meal I was the only one eating at that table. The police officer that had told me how to get to the home of the Christian woman appeared in the hotel to see me. He had seen my car at the hotel. He told me he knew a man that he thought would like to see me. *Wow!* He told me exactly how to find the house but he didn't want to go with me.

I found the house and was invited in. The man went by the nickname of Sr. Nem. In his humble kitchen at the back of the house Sr. Nem, his wife, and eight children stood neatly arranged from the youngest to the oldest. They listened for 30 minutes while I told them

225

the plan of salvation. After I finished, I had them to close their eyes while I prayed. I prayed out loud for them to have the courage and faith to trust Jesus as their Savior. I asked them to do something that is very difficult in a family group. I asked them to admit that they were sinners and to ask Jesus to forgive them. After some silence Sr. Nem confessed his sin and asked God to forgive him. A strong smell of cheap liquor surrounded Sr. Nem, so I was surprised that he was the one to confess before the others. The relief on his face was encouraging to me, but I wanted to be sure he had understood, so I asked him where Jesus was. He replied in his heart!

I took Sr. Nem aside to talk to him about growing in the Christian walk. In a new Bible I carried with me, I marked some special Scripture verses and gave it to him. The Bibles I had to give away were provided through the literature fund provided by Southern Baptists. His reading was very slow and unstable, but at least he could read. I also gave him a Sunday-school quarterly and asked him to read some of it each day. Before I left, I asked him whether we could have a worship service in his home. I was thrilled with his response. "Yes," he said. I marked our return visit for September 7, the national holiday for liberation of Brazil from Portugal.

I walked on Cloud Nine as I left the house. Back at the hotel I asked the owner himself (for I didn't find his wife) whether I could show a religious filmstrip to the people in the lounge. He said *yes*, so I showed the film, gave my testimony, and then happily went to bed.

The next morning I went to the police headquarters as I had promised Sergeant Milton. I found out he was the highest police officer in Virginopolis. We had a good visit, but I didn't push him to accept Christ. One thing was certain: he no longer was an atheist or an agnostic toward the Bible. Furthermore, I felt as though he was a friend. As we were leaving the building I saw the jailhouse. I asked him whether the priest ever gave the prisoners any spiritual help. He said *no!* I asked him whether I could talk with them a few minutes and he said *yes!* He continued by saying, "You need to know, however, that all 13 men in those cells are incarcerated because they killed their wives or tried to!"

I went into the entrance room and met the police officer on guard duty. The Holy Spirit was strongly with me, for I didn't know why I asked to see the prisoners or what I would say. I was simply amazed that I found myself in front of those 13 men who seemed to be hardened criminals. I read them the Scripture of Paul in the jail at Philippi. I explained the Scripture and prayed for the men. I never have felt the power and presence more strongly anywhere in all my life than on that morning. When I finished praying, I asked whether any of them would like to make the decision that the jailer in Philippi and his family had made. Eight or nine of them raised their hands; those men were choked up, some were crying, and all had tears in their eyes. The jail had only three cells; I later found out that one cell was reserved for women but was empty at the time. I asked the men in the first cell whether any of them knew how to read. One man said that he could read, so I showed him through the bars where I had marked key verses in the Gospel of John and gave the Bible to him. I told him to begin with the book of John and read to the other men one chapter a day. After he had finished reading, I asked him to have the guard pass the Bible to the second cell, in which a man would read the same chapter to those men.

The hotel owner had business in Valadares and had asked me whether he could go with me instead of on the bus. I picked him up; we headed for Valadares. I had some time to talk with him, but I didn't tell him what had happened at the jail or at Sr. Nem's house.

We stopped in Sardoa, where I visited the mayor in that city, because I had known him since our first trip with the other two pastors. He also wanted a ride to Valadares, so I took him.

The First Evangelistic Service in Virginopolis

A few months earlier we had met an Independent Baptist family at the English-Speaking Baptist Church in Rio de Janeiro. Glenn Auctaun wanted to see some mission work in its beginning. Their children and ours would be out of school for Brazilian Independence Day (September 7), so I invited them up to Valadares; we all would go to Virginopolis.

They arrived on September 6; on September 7 we attended the Valadares Independence Day parade of some schools and the military band. We didn't stay for all the parade, because Glenn and I left after an early lunch for a trip into the country. We went to a village church in which I preached and administered the Lord's Supper. I thought this trip would be a beginning for Glenn to get accustomed to country life. Before we arrived at the village, the road became a trail. We had to put the car on a barge to cross the river that was hardly big enough for the car, just like I did when I went to Pega Bem. We had to get back before dark, because the barge didn't run at night and also because I had scheduled to be at the small town of São Vicente do Rio Doce about 7 p.m. We arrived in time to eat; I preached. That night São Vicente was having its independence celebration, so the noise was so loud we could hardly have the service. About 11 p.m. we arrived back in Valadares.

On September 8 we drove to Virginopolis. I had made arrangements to stay with the American Presbyterian missionaries in Guanhaes. I didn't think that Glenn, his wife, and two little boys would be comfortable in the hotel in Virginopolis. The hotel was very crude for city folks. Also, our kids hadn't met the Presbyterian missionaries' kids; they were about the same age as ours, so I thought this would be good for them. The third reason for not staying in Virginopolis was that I didn't know how our welcome would be in the hotel, if anyone caused an uproar over holding a service at Sr. Nem's house. I invited the Presbyterian missionary to go with us, but he told us that we were inviting a stoning; thus he didn't want to go.

I had suggested that Sr. Nem invite friends from around his house, which was far from the central square. That night we had 35 people crowd into Nem's tiny living room. How does a missionary start a work where no one has a Bible nor knows a verse of Scripture or a song? With Leona playing the accordion we started out with the first stanza of *What a Friend We Have in Jesus*. That night we sang that one verse many times. On the trumpet I played a hymn that brought a lot of people from the street close to the open window. We tried to teach a chorus. While we were singing, both Leona and I realized that our backs were right up against the open window. We would have been easy targets for someone to throw a rock. I taught the people John 3:16 and expounded on that. I presented Pastor Genedier de Frietas, the mission pastor in Guanhaes, and set up Sunday afternoons for him to conduct a Bible study with them. He did this for about six months and then accepted a church in the State of Espirito Santo. We thanked God we had no uproar from the street people and that no stones were thrown.

This story covers more than two years' time. I had to concentrate on Virginopolis as much as possible, so I went once or twice a month. I didn't feel the need so much to be at Sr. Nem's house every time as I did to be with the prisoners, so I never failed to stop at the jail when I passed through Virginopolis. No matter the time of day the prisoners always were there. I was pleased with their Bible studies; they learned many spiritual choruses and several hymns.

One day when I arrived, two new prisoners were in jail. Two young men, both 19 years of age and both with the name of Jose, were present. These two men had killed a man on a bus. The bus had a back door where passengers entered, like the city buses had, so they entered from the back and saw their enemy, pulled their guns, and blasted him in the back. Both young men played the guitar, so they enjoyed learning the music for the choruses. Both soon accepted Jesus as their Savior. They learned the music quickly, so now we had music to make our singing better. I gave copies of Billy Graham's book, *Peace with God*, for them to read. If I was in Virginopolis at night, I went to the jail after the service in Sr. Nem's house to show them a movie film or filmstrip. The hour of my arrival didn't make any difference to Sergeant Milton or the guard; I always was welcome. One reason for this was that the prisoners were changing their foul language, were more cooperative, and had better attitudes.

Several months later I arrived at the jail for a service and noticed that the man in charge of the Bible wasn't there. I asked the guard where the man had gone. The guard said that he had escaped. I asked where the Bible was; the guard said that he took the Bible with him. I was told that he escaped because he knew that when he finished his time in that county, another county was waiting for him to do time. I got the impression that the guards had helped him to escape. Why? Most of the men had made a great change. When I began going to the jail to talk to the prisoners about their spiritual lives, the walls of their cells were covered with pictures of naked women. One day I arrived, and all those pictures were gone. This encouraged me very much, because I had not suggested to them to take the pictures down.

I had tried to find someone that would rent a house to me, but no one would. I knew that the priest was watching me carefully. Sometimes when I was walking down a street nearer to the center of town, I would look back; the priest, who was spying on me, would duck into an open door. Most of the houses in the country towns and villages were built on the street and had no front yards. When you opened the front door, you stepped out on the narrow sidewalk and then directly into the street. You could walk along the sidewalk and easily see into the bedrooms, because the "windows" were shutters which usually were open. The older houses had back yards with fruit trees, a small garden, chickens, a dog or dogs, and maybe a pig and other things. So the priest easily could step into anyone's door, because on hot days the doors also usually were open. I had decided that if he ever confronted me, I would stand my grounds on the fact that I had as much right to be in Brazil as he had, because he was from Holland. The Brazilian Constitution allowed "freedom of religion", although Evangelicals certainly didn't have equality with Catholics. I did nothing, such as trying to preach on the downtown plaza, to deliberately antagonize the priest. I didn't talk against him.

After about a year, one morning I arrived at the jail; the guard on duty asked me whether I had met the new *delegado*, or Sheriff Geraldo Alves Pinto. He had responsibilities over the county. I hadn't met him or the sheriff before him. The guard told me that the sheriff was reading his Bible and that I needed to visit him. After the jail service I went to see him. I talked to his wife, Maria, and found that she recently had been saved in an Assembly of God church in Ipatinga. After we had a Bible study together, I asked whether he had heard about what I was doing in the jail. He said he had. Then he told me he believed that he was sent to Virginopolis to "liberate the prisoners"! I was puzzled and asked him to explain what he meant. He was a little vague, but I understood he was speaking in the spiritual sense. He wanted to be involved in the liberation of the citizens of the city. Yet Geraldo himself at that point had not embraced Evangelical Christianity. I asked him what he thought would happen to the two young men that had killed the man in the bus. He told me the man killed was a *pistoleiro*, or hired killer. He had killed the father of one of the boys and was looking for them because they knew who he was. Their killing actually was in self-defense, so Geraldo didn't think they

230

would have to spend time in prison after their case had been tried. This explanation made me feel a lot better, because I really believed they were good young men.

God Opened New Doors

Geraldo told me he was going to protect me and that the next time I visited Virginopolis; he wanted me to preach on his street. *Wow,* how wonderful that things were changing! When I left his house, I was on Cloud Nine. Surely if God had opened so many doors for us up to this point, God certainly had a lot somewhere for us to buy for a church. A huge paper mill between Governador Valadares and Ipatinga was being built. Thousands of acres of eucalyptus trees were planted to supply the wood pulp for the new mill. A new neighborhood was being developed in Virginopolis; houses were being built for workers that planted, cut, and cared for the trees in the area. This plant was a joint venture between Brazil and the Japanese government, just like the Steel Mill in Ipatinga was. I found the man that was selling the property in the new neighborhood; I thought he might have some property I could buy. The new area was the nicest side of town.

I went into the man's office that was a few doors down the street from where we had eaten our meal with Mrs. Coelho earlier. This man turned out to be a relative of Mr. Coelho, owner of the service station in Valadares, and therefore related to Mrs. Coelho. This man didn't seem to know about me, though. I entered his office; he asked me what I wanted. I asked him whether he had any more lots for sale in the new subdivision. He happily spread out the blueprint of the sub-division so I could see what still was for sale. Then he asked me why I wanted to buy. I told him I wanted it for a Baptist church. He immediately and nervously began rolling up the blueprint and emphatically said; "I don't have any property to sell for a Baptist church. Maybe the Japanese will buy some more lots, but I don't have anything for you."

About two weeks later I arrived in Virginopolis to preach my first open-air service. Geraldo, the sheriff, had arranged for me to use for the loudspeaker the electricity from a bar. I told Geraldo that I wouldn't preach at that place unless they closed the bar while I preached. The bar owner agreed to close the bar for this first-time event.

With the help of the loudspeaker I began inviting the neighbors. I played a trumpet number or two. The hour of the day wasn't good, because the sun was very hot and I was in the open with no trees. I don't know how many listened from their windows, but very few except those that had been in the bar were in the street. As I preached, some heckled me. Of course the sheriff was present, so they weren't going to get far out of line. I realized I hadn't been very smart about this first service. I should have waited until a Saturday night and brought with me some young people or a men's singing group. To be in Virginopolis on Saturdays and Sundays was almost impossible, because on those days I had other activities. When I could, I worked Virginopolis into my schedule. Anyway, with the protection of the sheriff I was able to preach on a street, something no other preacher ever had been able to do. I didn't use this privilege any other time except in front of Sr. Nem's house, at which we could get some big crowds.

Two Women Incarcerated

One day I arrived at the jail to find that the female cell had occupants. A mother and her 21-year-old daughter were in the cell. When she was 18, the daughter had married an 80-year-old rancher. The rancher had three ranches. The mother was happy for her daughter to marry the old man, because certainly he wouldn't live too much longer; her daughter would be the heir to at least a part of his inheritance. About three years after the marriage, the old man still was as spry as ever. *Would the man never die?* Impatient to let death overtake him naturally, the mother and daughter, with the help of a male relative, decided to help the old man die. As he slept, they suffocated him. They weren't successful in proving that the old man had died a natural death, so for their suite the mother and daughter were given the third cell.

These women had to listen to my messages; I am sure that when I wasn't there, some of the men also talked to them about the Lord. To the women I gave a Bible and other materials. The daughter seemed to be repentant, but I didn't see much evidence that the mother ever had a spiritual experience.

Another Surprise

In first part of 1975 the state board invited me to promote stewardship and the Brazilian Cooperative Program over the whole State of Minas Gerais. I first thought we could continue to live in Governador Valadares and do the state work, but the Lord led me to see that such an idea was not the best or practical. *What would I do about Virginopolis? If we moved to Belo Horizonte, who would or could carry on the work?* We began to pray more earnestly. We knew the work was God's, so we trusted that He had it all planned out.

The Miracle of Purchasing a Lot

One day after a service in the jail in Virginopolis, the guard told me he knew of a young man, Francisco, who might sell me a lot. He went with me to Francisco's house. Francisco soon was going to get married and needed money. Francisco took us to see the lot; to my amazement the lot was right in the same area in which the real-estate man wouldn't sell to me. For the lot he wanted the equivalent of $3,000. He said his dad had an adjoining lot that he might sell also and that I might pay about $6,000 for both. We went to see Francisco's father, but he said that he wanted $8,000 for his alone. After we left Francisco's father, I looked Francisco in the eye and said: "Francisco, I will be here one month from today with the money, but I want to know, are you going to back out of this deal because of pressure from the city?" He gave me his word that honestly he would sell me the lot, so I returned to Valadares a happy man.

I had one major problem, though: we had no more money in the state strategic property fund. Furthermore, Leona and I didn't have the money and didn't know anyone in our churches that had that much extra money. I wondered how we could arrange to get the money. We had Leona's Volkswagen that, though we both used it, we could sell since we soon would be going on furlough. She consented to sell the Volkswagen bug. Leona, having a true missionary heart, recognized that God had opened this door and knew we had to take advantage of this opportunity.

I had another problem: the island church couldn't accept the responsibility of Virginopolis and build a church building on the property. The island church had three other missions: Altinopolis,

Palmeiras, and Gonzaga. First Baptist Church of Valadares had organized Ninth Baptist Church with about 70 members; some were well-off financially. I talked to Pastor Wilton Franca of Ninth Church about accepting the responsibility of Virginopolis. The new church accepted this challenge.

On the day to meet Francisco with the money for the lot I took Pastor Franca with me so he could become acquainted with Sr. Nem, those that met in his house, and also the jail ministry. I first had thought I could put the property in the name of Ninth Baptist Church, but it had not registered officially yet and couldn't receive property. We decided to put the property in the name of a deacon of Ninth Baptist Church until the church was registered officially.

Pastor Wilton Franca and I arrived in Virginopolis and checked into the hotel. We had hardly put our bags down when we heard a knock on our door. When I opened the door, Mr. Coelho, the real-estate man that wouldn't sell me the property, was standing in front of me. His face was red with anger. He blurted out, "Did my nephew promise to sell you a piece of property?" I said, "If his name is Francisco, yes, he did." He angrily responded, "He shouldn't have done it! We have an understanding in our town that no one is to sell property without others knowing what is going on!" I knew about which he was speaking, so I thought to myself, *I guess this is the end of our deal.* For what seemed as though it was several minutes, he stood before me. I looked at him and he looked at me. *Well,* I thought, *If the deal is over, just say so, Mr. Coelho.* Finally he said, "We are a people of our word. I will give you the deed to the property!" He turned around and walked away. *So Francisco didn't even have the deed in his own possession. His uncle still had it. Wow!* What a miracle! Mr. Coelho had said he wouldn't sell me a lot in the best neighborhood of town near the high school and also the police station. *God, you are an awesome God!* So that is how we were able to open up the city for the preaching of the truth in Virginopolis.

Only one time did we seem to face real trouble. One night I was showing a film on the wall of the house next door to Sr. Nem's house. We had a crowd of people partially blocking the street. A passing car stopped; two rough-looking men pushed and shoved themselves angrily through the crowd and up the two steps of the porch. They

234

demanded that we shut off the projector. That is when the Holy Spirit took over. I was scared—more for the projector than for anything else. The only light was from the projector and the film being shown on the wall, but I could tell these two men were the trouble-making type. I didn't know what to say, so I just stood firm and didn't move to turn off the projector. My heart beat rapidly as I thought sure I was going be knocked off of the porch with one of their fists. Again they demanded that the projector be shut off. For some reason—certainly not out of courage, for I was shaking—I didn't turn off the projector. Suddenly, they turned around and walked off.

About a year later Pastor Wilton Franca died; his church changed its name from Ninth Baptist to Memorial Baptist in honor of its deceased pastor. While we were on furlough, Memorial Baptist Church built a small church building on the lot in Virginopolis, but the people weren't able to buy another lot, so they had to build a small parsonage on the same, small lot. As the years passed, I kept up with the struggle to maintain a lay preacher or pastor in the city. Under extreme hardship one very young couple—Oswaldo, as lay-preacher, and his wife, Neuza—labored for the Lord in Virginopolis. Oswaldo recently had been saved in Guanhaes mission; Neuza, only 16-years old, was a Presbyterian. A book could be written about their struggles in Virginopolis. They confronted difficulty in buying staple foods and a lot of opposition in many ways. At one point a young Christian doctor and family lived in Virginopolis, but the persecution was so strong that they finally moved back to Victoria, Espirito Santo. Maria Pinto, along with Geraldo the former sheriff, led in establishing an Assembly of God church almost directly in front of their house. Two of their daughters, however, preferred to be Baptists. Soon after the property was bought, Sr. Nem moved to Belo Horizonte.

Years Later

About 15 years after we left Valadares, Leona and I went back to Virginopolis for a four-day revival. We had planned to stay in the hotel, but because this was the same weekend as a big festival, the pastor thought we should stay in a home at the edge of town. When we arrived at the house, I recognized it as the same one I had asked whether a woman believer lived in that house. *Dona* (Mrs.) Zelia had invited us to stay with her. By this time her husband had died and two daughters and a grandson were living with her in the house. We listened to the amazing story of her conversion 15 years earlier. *Dona* Zelia was visiting her brother, sister-in-law, and her mother in Ipatinga about 50 miles away. They had been converted; after she attended a Baptist church with them, she was converted. She was overjoyed but knew she couldn't share this joy with her husband. Later her brother visited them and had the idea to witness to Zelia's husband (his brother-in-law), because their relationship had been as close as brothers. Zelia's husband became infuriated and ordered him out of the house; he never allowed him in his house again. Zelia hid her Bible, because she knew her husband would burn it. She read it only when no one was in the house. She remembered the day that I had stopped at her house. Since she had made no sign of being a believer, her husband didn't know the truth. For nearly 15 years she longed to attend the Baptist church and secretly kept up with what was going on there. She lived on the outskirts of Virginopolis, about a mile from the Baptist congregation. The Sunday after her husband died, Zelia was in church and soon was baptized. Even though she had to walk, she didn't miss a service on Sunday morning and night and when other services were held.

Zelia had a grandson that always had lived with her because his mother had died in childbirth. At this point his father had remarried, but the boy, now 10-years old, continued living with the grandmother. At various times during the four-day revival we talked with him; he made a decision for Christ. On a later visit we found out that his father was very angry because the boy had accepted Jesus as his personal Savior. He took the boy to live with him. His father wouldn't allow him to continue to go to church.

Every night the Assembly of God pastor's daughter attended the revival. She was about 12-years old and enjoyed the chalk talk, trumpet, and the puppet I used in my presentations. I hoped she also enjoyed the message. Every night she invited me to visit her daddy. Finally, on Sunday afternoon, Leona and I visited her dad. During the visit he told me about a woman that recently had visited his church — a former resident of Virginopolis. She told her testimony about being in jail with her daughter and about an American man that visited them in the jail. She told of her conversion in the jail. That was such a blessing for me. I told him I was that man. If I had not gone to visit the Assembly of God pastor, I never would have known about that conversion experience. This was the woman that helped her daughter kill her 83-year-old husband. At the time she had seemed to show no emotion or to indicate to me that she, as her daughter had, had made a decision for the Lord, but she told the pastor that she made her decision in jail. She was traveling around and telling her story to the Assembly of God churches in the area. So, we can believe in planting seed that brings a harvest. I often wish I had news about all the other men who accepted Jesus in the jail. I trust they are scattered around the area in some church and that some day we will meet in heaven.

Two or three years later Leona and I went back for another revival. This time Zelia had sold her small ranch at the entrance of the city and bought a nice home close to the church. A daughter, about 45-years old, still was living with her. The daughter hadn't accepted Christ and showed no signs of changing her lifestyle. She was friendly but not because she had any love for us. She just tolerated us because of her mother. We were overjoyed that Zelia was happy because she was close to the church and could be at every meeting.

In 1998 we were in Virginopolis for the last time. The church was going well but still was small. I met with Geraldo (the former sheriff) and Maria because I had told the story many times, but I wanted to verify some things with him. We had a delightful time together. He could have written a wild Brazilian (Western) book about his sheriff's criminal cases with which he through the years was involved. Geraldo told us some things that we didn't know. He said that the pastor of Ninth Baptist Church (later Memorial Baptist) had been told by a lumberyard manager in Virginopolis that they would sell all the materials they needed for the construction of the church. When the carpenters arrived from Valadares to start the building, the lumberyard man told them that he wouldn't sell them the material. So they had to go back to Valadares and have the lumber brought in from Valadares. Geraldo said that soon after this, the lumberyard went broke. Geraldo said he knew the hand of God was against the owner of that construction enterprise for not selling the materials.

Disaster-Prone

In late August I was helping Leona paint the nursery rooms at the island church. I must admit I did a foolish thing when I climbed to the top of the ladder without anyone around to keep the ladder from sliding on the concrete floor. I was almost finished with the project when I felt the ladder slipping. I hit the concrete floor with one foot under the ladder and with my weight on the ladder. I thought my foot was broken, but it wasn't. I had paint all over me and the floor.

I was getting over that accident when in late November I had another accident. The rainy season had arrived; our house was leaking. The high point of the roof was at the front; it slopped gradually to the back of the house. The roof was made of long, thin sheets of a hard substance—corrugated as tin was but too fragile to be used for walking. When walking one had to be cautious to step only on the rafters. Sometimes the rains were so hard that the water built up faster than it could drain off. Near the back end of the roof leaves fell from the large trees and kept the water from running off fast. That evening I had to travel to Rio de Janeiro for a quarterly executive mission meeting, but I had time to get some of the leaves off the roof.

I am thankful that when I lost my balance, I was on the low part of the roof, as I was trying to stand on a rafter and reach farther out to push more leaves off. For two weeks we had been waiting for a man to clear the leaves and repair the roof, but he hadn't arrived. I was working over the service area when I fell through the corrugated material. I didn't land as professionally as Batman or Superman might have. I first landed sitting down on the corner of the clothes dryer. My weight buckled one side of the machine. From the dryer I splattered on the concrete floor. Charlotte and Leona were in the kitchen and heard me fall. My head and all my right side hit the cement hard. I hurt my cheek and temple area; this gave Charlotte the biggest scare. I could tell I had no serious bone injuries, but the taste of blood and a headache worried me some.

By the time I was to go to the bus station, I realized I couldn't go to Rio. I was hurting all over. My right wrist and hand had swollen; I hardly could walk on my right foot. On the rafter and broken roofing I had skinned and badly bruised the back of my left leg. My whole right rib area as well as a hip also were hurting. My tailbone had hit the edge of the clothes dryer; when I sat down, I was in misery. I was so thankful I had no serious injuries. I didn't fall from grace, but I know what one experiences in falling from space. I decided that for a while I would keep my feet on the ground.

Chapter 12

Missionary Wife's Work

Araujo Island had a population of about 10,000, with a Catholic and a Presbyterian church but no Baptist church. Our goal was that after our first furlough we would begin a new church on the island. But while we were on furlough for four months, Central Baptist Church started a preaching point in the home of some people that had moved to the island. After we returned from furlough, we attended at their home, but the house was too small, so we invited the group to our house for regular Sunday services, with Central Baptist Church as the mother church. Joe offered to be the pastor of this new work on the island.

Our house was built in three sections. The three bedrooms and baths were on one side of a long hall and the kitchen, living room, and breakfast room on the other. The long hall would seat about 40 people. Each Sunday morning we put in the hall every sort of chair we had. To have everything picked up and the chairs lined up ready for "church" by 9 each Sunday was a hassle. Joe requested that Central Baptist Church let us keep all of our tithes and offerings; we would buy our own literature and pay our own bills. We reported to Central Baptist and used its baptistery. One of the members was an ordained deacon and a Sunday-school teacher. We were blessed with good church workers and teachers.

On the first Sunday of September 1968 we had the first worship service in our home. After one month we had 49 enrolled in Sunday school and 52 people attended preaching. We had Sunday-morning and Sunday-evening preaching services. The children met in the garage; in one of the bedrooms I taught those under 6. In the living room Joe taught the teens and young people; the adults met in the cen-

240

ter hall. The piano was in the living room, but I couldn't see Joe when he directed the music. When our journeyperson, Judy Ritchie, arrived, she played the piano. While she was with us, we formed a women's quintet. We sang at various places—even the Minas Gerais Baptist Convention.

One Sunday Joe preached a message from Luke 7:36-38 about the sinner woman that washed Jesus' feet with her tears. However, instead of using the word for *washing* (*lavar*) he used the word for *carry* (*levar*). The sound and spelling are similar but have a world of difference in meaning. I sat at the front and had a difficult time keeping a straight face, but no one in the congregation made a sound. Each time he explained that the woman carried Jesus' feet but never told us where she carried them. Many times we have laughed about that message. Another funny mistake was the message of the prodigal son in Luke 15:11-32. When the son returned home, the father prepared a great feast with the fatted calf, except Joe used the word *besouro*, meaning *beetle*, instead of *bezerro* for *calf*. Another common mistake made is telling that Jesus is the only way for salvation. The word for *way* is *caminho* and *truck* is *caminhao*. Too frequently the message becomes: Jesus is the only *truck* to heaven. Joe wasn't the first one to make these mistakes. When words are so similar, we were better off not comparing them, then forgetting, which is easy. I'm sure the Brazilians could tell about other funny mistakes, but they are too kind and wouldn't want to hurt our feelings.

A Rabies Emergency

A group of women from the island mission visited each week in the homes of those interested in learning more about the church or of those who were sick. One day I was headed home from an afternoon of visitation and felt a strong urge to go to the home of Jandyra, a church member that lived near the church. When I reached the house, various neighbors were in the street talking. Jandyra as well as her neighbor were very upset. She told me they had just been advised that a dog that had bitten their two boys had rabies. They didn't have a car, so I took them to a doctor. They needed the vaccine. The doctor had enough to begin the treatment for the two boys, but he needed to order more from Belo Horizonte. Joe was in Belo for a special conference,

241

so the doctor gave me the needed information; I called Joe to pick up the medication from the secretary of health's office. The next day Joe arrived with the vaccine packed with ice to keep it cool until he arrived by bus. This was sufficient for both boys. Many times since then I have remembered that when God nudges me to do something, he has a reason. I will never forget how He used me to help these two families.

Visit of Family

Our dream and prayer had been to have some of our family visit us in Brazil. Mother, Daddy (Tony and Irma Isbell), and daddy's sister, Ruby Redus, visited us in December 1972. Phone service was not easy; Internet service didn't exist, so we weren't able to help my folks decide where to land. They looked at the map and decided Brasilia was as good as Rio, so they chose Brasilia. They didn't realize Brasilia was a 17-hour trip for us. However, that gave them an opportunity to see the new capital of Brazil and more of the country. In 1960 the national capital moved from the coast in Rio de Janeiro to Brasilia in the interior. Brasilia is a showcase of modern Brazilian architecture. Our mission car was a Chevrolet Veraneio, the forerunner to the SUV. We were thankful for a car large enough for eight people to travel comfortably; usually one of the kids sat on the luggage (we didn't have seatbelts then).

Daddy was fascinated by the rolling hills of western Minas Gerais. He wished he could be a young man again, for he would have liked to have a farm on some of those hills. Years later Brazilians began farming many of those hills—especially to raise soybeans. In 1972 the area principally was for ranching. Before Daddy and Mother left Brazil Daddy gave his hat to Laisete. Years later, Laisete was still wearing that hat and proud to tell others where he got it. This trip was a lifetime experience for both them and us, for they never returned to Brazil. The heat in Governador Valadares was very difficult for my folks. They had left New Mexico in the middle of winter to arrive in the middle of summer in Brazil. It was sweltering hot and humid.

We planned our travels so my folks could see the maximum of Brazil in their five-week stay. We traveled to the north area of our Sweet Valley Association for them to see the ranch land and small villages. The weather was perfect and the road, considering it was dirt, was in good condition. The Baptists had one mission in a town farther north, but we didn't go there this trip; our goal was Virginopolis.

Joe often bought gas from a man who had a Shell gas station in Governador Valadares. One day we were talking with Mr. Coelho (the word *coelho* means *rabbit* but is a popular family name); he said he was from Virginopolis and that his mother still lived there. Since we were going to Virginopolis, the man wanted us to visit his mother. He was a very strong Catholic and wasn't asking us to talk to his mother about her spiritual life but only to meet her as friends. The man contacted his mother about our trip and about the day and hour we would arrive. Since Daddy was a farmer, he especially was interested in the sugar cane fields. Along the road to Virginopolis we stopped to see a man using oxen to tread around a machine made all of wooden parts. These oxen turned a sugar-cane press in an old fashioned way — squeezing the juice from the cane into a vat. The man was making homemade liquor. He was friendly, but we could tell he was very busy putting sugar cane into the press, so we didn't take up more of his time.

The Coelhos' home was in the center of town about one block from the cathedral and hotel. They received us warmly and insisted that we have lunch. That was a great experience for all of us. In its center the round dining table had a smaller, round, rotating table. The bowls of food were placed on the rotating table and the serving plates on the lower stationary table. The food was very tasty and the fellowship sweet.

Joe later visited the widow Coelho, who made clear the fact that she was a staunch Catholic and wasn't interested in hearing anything from the Bible but respected the friendship. Well, that was a partial victory, because she was one more among a large number of our Catholic friends. I was building up friendship of another person in that town.

Virginopolis was a typical Catholic town with no Evangelical witness; the people there didn't want any. This story is told in chapter 11.

After our traveling Daddy said the Scripture had more meaning: *For every beast of the forest is Mine, The cattle on a thousand hills* (Ps. 50:10). He believed they had seen cattle on the thousand hills in Brazil.

No one should visit Brazil without seeing the beautiful city of Rio de Janeiro. Missionaries Don and Barbara Laing with their four children were living in Rio. Don and Barbara grew up in Hobbs, NM, just 20 miles from Lovington, but Joe and Don met in Brazil. They graciously took all eight of us in to spend Christmas with them. We visited the usual tourist sites: Sugar Loaf, Corcovado (statute of Christ), and the beaches. Daddy needed to take their tickets to the airline office, so Don, Joe, and Daddy went to downtown Rio. The traffic was something else as the cars darted in and out of the lanes. The sidewalks were filled with people walking in a hurry. Everyone seemed to be in a hurry. Daddy had never seen anything like that. When they arrived back at the Laings, Daddy said he knew how to better pray for us all.

When we left Rio de Janeiro, we took a different route back to Valadares. As we drove up the high mountains out of Rio and got close to the resort city of Teresopolis, the car's fan belt broke. Shops were closed because of the day being Saturday afternoon, but Joe carried a new fan belt for a case such as this. We were able to get to a station and were delayed only long enough to put the new fan belt on.

In Valadares we visited several churches, missions, and open-air services and did the work we would have done had they not been there. In our church Joe asked Daddy to share his testimony. For many years Daddy had been a deacon and a Sunday-school teacher but never had been asked to tell about his salvation experience. Tony and Irma moved to Vaughn, NM, soon after they married in 1931. They received one of the last homesteads in the area—about five miles north of Vaughn. Their only transportation was the horses and a wagon. A family had lived there a short time and had dug out an area to build a one-room house in which to live. Tony and his brother Andy finished it, built up the sides a little above the ground, and put on a roof. Later they built a small adobe house.

Daddy's parents and family followed them to Vaughn to homestead as well. Daddy and Mother were working together in the fall of 1933 to harvest the feed while their 2 1-2-year-old son, Gene, was playing with the dog. A rattlesnake bit Gene in the face. Tony ran to a neighbor's house to borrow a horse to ride the five miles to Vaughn to get a doctor. The doctor couldn't save Gene because he was bitten on the face. A Christian neighbor was a great help and comfort to them. This helped Tony and Irma think about their spiritual lives. They both grieved over Gene's death. At that time neither Tony nor Irma was a Christian, nor was anyone in Tony's family.

Rabbits and other small field animals were eating their garden, so Tony bought some rat poison to put around the edge of the garden. He became very sick from the fumes of the poison and went into the dugout to lie down. He was so sick, he couldn't get up, so he prayed to God for mercy. He was alone because Irma was visiting her folks in Roy. The dark dugout suddenly became bright with light. He looked toward the door; a brilliant figure stood looking at him kindly. Tony understood the figure to be Jesus. From his head to his feet Tony felt a surge go through his body. The sick feeling was gone; he stood up.

From a Sears, Roebuck catalog Tony and Irma ordered a Bible. Sometime later Tony bought a model-T Ford truck without doors. He was able to get a contract to pick up the garbage from the Harvey House Restaurant at the Santa Fe railroad terminal in Vaughn. Daddy raised pigs; the garbage provided food for them. He made ham, bacon, and sausage to sell; he sold some to the Harvey House. This job helped support the couple during the Depression. Time passed; Tony and Irma marked a Sunday on the calendar to start going to church. They awoke that morning to find snow on the ground, but they promised they would go. The old truck without doors got them to church. Most of the members stayed at home, so the pastor was amazed to see visitors. During a springtime tent revival Tony and Irma were saved. Daddy's mother, two sisters, and their husbands also made decisions; the seven were baptized in Vaughn Baptist Church. The loss of Gene brought about the decision for salvation of these seven plus another sister and her husband plus most of their children. Like a rock thrown into a pond makes ripples, so have the effects of the death of their child and the ripples continued through the years. Out of sorrow God brought victory. After Tony had given his testimony, Joe gave an invitation. Seven people accepted Jesus as Savior and Lord. Tony was amazed!

Evangelical Sports Club

A Presbyterian family had the idea of forming an Evangelical club so Christian families would have for recreation a place free from smoking or drinking. We became members of the club. The club had a swimming pool, areas for different types of sports, and a playground for the smaller children. Our kids enjoyed the play area and swimming pool, since no public pools existed. The club had a structure built like an old fort and teepees; the kids enjoyed playing cowboys and Indians. We could take friends there for picnics and allow the kids to play. Since the Christians didn't go to the movies and the schools had no sports programs, the club provided the kids with recreation or socials outside the church life.

Visit to Paraguay

In 1975 we had a New Year's missionary retreat at Palma Camp, at the Latvian colony. In the early 1920s some Latvian leaders had a vision that God was leading them to leave their country. They sent some men out to various places to see where God was leading them. The group that visited Brazil believed this was the place that fit the vision. A large group settled in the western part of the state of São Paulo and set up their colony. They were Evangelical believers; some of the outstanding leaders in the Baptist convention were of Latvian descent. As the young people grew up and left home, the colony was diminishing to the point in which they knew some day none would be left. The Latvians had given the land to the Brazilian Baptist Convention with the understanding that the older people would be taken care of until they all died. The Baptists had built a camp there to be something like a Ridgecrest or Glorieta, the Southern Baptist assembly grounds in the U.S. To help financially support the camp director Fred Hawkins had set up a silkworm farm. We had a wonderful missionary retreat there.

From Palma we visited Charlene and George Oakes and boys Philip and Tim. Their boys were near the same ages as Carl and Charlotte. Charlotte had a chronic stomachache problem that seemed to be more problematic at mealtime. We had taken her to various doctors and even a pediatrician in Belo Horizonte. They did various tests but found nothing, so they suggested a pill just to ease the pain. When Charlene Oaks saw how Charlotte cried with a stomachache, she told me what their doctor had prescribed for their son, Tim. That same day we bought the medicine their doctor prescribed. Sure enough, after the treatment, Charlotte quit having the daily stomachaches. Because Brazil doesn't have a freezing climate to kill various parasites that live in the dirt, they become a common problem for people. Children especially have difficulty avoiding stomach problems. We were so thankful that Charlene had helped with Charlotte's problem.

We had an enjoyable time with the Oakeses. From their home in Maringa, Parana, we traveled to see the Sete Quedas (Seven Falls) on the Paraguay river. With the Brazilian government, getting out of the country almost was as difficult as getting in was. We followed the many walking trails to see the seven different falls. One of the bridges over a wide gap was a wooden swinging bridge. The bridge had safety nets along the sides, but we still were a little scared to look so far down. The falls were beautiful; the kids enjoyed these falls more than they did Iguacu Falls. We were glad we visited the Sete Quedas, because a few years later they were covered with water when the huge hydroelectric dam Itaipu was built near Foz do Iguacu. At the port on Brazil's side we took a boat on which we didn't have to have documents and crossed the river into Paraguay. We took a taxi and went into the little village to the headquarters of the Brazilian missionaries working in Paraguay. We took the boat back across the river and drove down to town of Foz do Iguacu (Iguacu Falls). We drove out to the falls. The force of the waters falling sent a fine mist into the air; before long we felt as damp as the air. The rainbow was as gorgeous as it was at the Seven Falls. The Iguacu Falls plunges 237 feet (higher than the Niagara Falls) and is more than two-miles wide. The falls border Brazil, Argentina, and Paraguay. Because of the distance from the coast many tourists never see these beauties of Brazil. The location of the making of the movie *The Mission,* which tells some history of the Guarani Indians, was near the falls.

Family Sickness

As in all families, from time to time we also had sickness in our home. The most serious and difficult time was in 1972. Joe had been out in a country church and stayed in a deacon's home (the visit to a deacon's home that Joe reported in chapter 10). A few days after he arrived home, he thought he had the flu because his body ached and he had a chill. He went to the pharmacist for a shot. The shot didn't help much, so on Saturday he got another shot, spent the day in bed, and didn't go to the revival. He didn't think he had time to be sick. He had a full schedule of activities—one being a weekend revival in our church on the island. Pastor Hilton of First Baptist was the preacher; he could also lead the music in Joe's place. Joe had noticed that his urine was dark but thought the cause was from the Vitamin B12 shots. On Sunday afternoon he felt a little better, so we went as scheduled to Campanario, a preaching point in a city about an hour and half north on the paved highway. I drove so he could rest, but he preached at the open-air service. Then for Pastor Hilton he preached at First Baptist. By Monday he felt really bad and went to the doctor. The doctor was sure Joe had hepatitis but requested blood exams to confirm his belief. Finally after the third blood exam hepatitis was confirmed, but by now Joe was very ill. His blood coagulation went very low; the doctor was concerned about internal bleeding. Joe was allowed to get up only to go to the bathroom.

Joe's eyes and skin were yellow and the sheets and his pajamas were yellow from his sweat. In the next 10 days he lost all appetite and lost 15 pounds. I learned to cook without using any oil. The first week he just lay in bed with his eyes shut, because the light hurt. We had a tape player; he spent his time listening to sermons and music.

We gave Joe a bell to ring if he needed anything. Fortunately for the family I always had washed separately the dishes of any sick "patient", so we wouldn't pass on any sickness one might have. For the next six weeks I moved to Charlotte's bed. The children could visit with Dad but could not stay in the room. Even Spit-Spot, the dog, knew that Joe was sick. She would put her head on the side of his bed and look up at him very sorrowfully.

The doctor wanted Joe to drink lots of liquid, so I bought for him a jar of concentrated cashew juice. This is made from the fruit that produces the cashew nut. Whether he had a reaction from too much of the juice or from a medication, we never knew, but after about three weeks in bed, one morning Joe awoke with an itching rash that start-

248

ed at the top of his head. Every pore on his forehead was breaking out with a pus pimple. The rash spread gradually down to his face and inside his mouth. Joe thought he could understand how Job must have felt. I called our doctor and barely caught him, because he was leaving for the hospital with his wife who was in labor. We waited all day for him to call back. Finally about 9 p.m. he arrived. By this time Joe really looked bad; his head and face were swollen and covered with rash. When the doctor saw him, he was quite worried, too, because the rash was in Joe's mouth and throat also. No pharmacies were open at that hour, so the doctor asked whether we had any anti-allergic medicine. I found a bottle about half full, but it was full of tiny ants. He said to strain them out and gave Joe a dose. He stayed with Joe until the medication began to take effect. Early the next morning the doctor returned with a shot to subdue the allergy.

People of Fifth Church were very concerned. Many people had a remedy for hepatitis; some of them went out into the pastures to gather a plant called *picao*, pronounced *pikone,* to make a drink to cure Joe. He drank it frequently. The doctor did not have faith in its curing effect but said it would not hurt.

About three weeks after Joe was diagnosed with having hepatitis, Jonathan complained about an itchy, red rash on his neck. We had been in church both morning and evening. At first I thought he had the measles and went for my medical book. By God's guidance the book opened to scarlet fever. I read it quickly and then turned on to read about measles. On Tuesday Charlotte complained about a sore throat; her throat glands were swollen. *OK, must be mumps,* I thought. The doctor stopped by the house to check on Joe, so he looked at Jonathan and Charlotte. He thought that Jonathan probably had the measles and Charlotte the mumps; he advised them to stay in bed and rest. After a week Charlotte seemed OK, but Jonathan's rash continued to spread without a sign of going away, so I went to the medical book again; this time I re-read about scarlet fever. The doctor confirmed that Jonathan had scarlet fever, so now our son as well as Joe had to stay in bed away from others. Jonathan missed a month of school; when he returned, he wasn't to participate in any active sports for another month. All the old skin over his whole body peeled. We never knew where he picked up scarlet fever; as far as we knew he didn't pass it on to anyone. Carl, the maid, and I were thankful we stayed well.

I was really busy taking care of the sick and doing other things. Carl recently had started studying at a new school, Polivalente, farther from home, so twice a week in the mornings and five days a week in the afternoon I took him to school. Charlotte had to be at the Presbyterian school from 1 until 5 p.m. I had the church activities, Joe's secretarial work, and the house going. We were so thankful to have a maid, or my task certainly would been much more difficult. During the six weeks that Joe was confined to bed, I learned to do many things that Joe always had done. I learned to watch the gas gauge of the car so that I wouldn't run out of gas. At least the gas stations gave full service; I didn't have to learn how to put gas in the car until we were back in the States on furlough.

Joe tried to explain how to withdraw money at the bank. I never enjoyed even writing a check. On my first trip to the bank I was very nervous and forgot most of what he had said. I waited in line and at my turn I gave the teller my check; he gave me a number. I just waited at the window for my money. Normally the person steps back once a number is received and waits for the teller to call the number. That gives the bank time to check the account to see whether money is sufficient to cover the check; then, when the number is called, the person returns to another window to receive the cash. The teller was very kind and gave me the cash without my waiting in the other line. Joe was surprised and decided I should be the one to go to the bank each time.

We had prayed that Joe would be able to go to mission meeting, because if the doctor didn't give his consent, none of us would be attending. The doctor wanted to make sure the hepatitis wasn't contagious. Joe had spent six weeks in bed. Our prayers were answered. The doctor gave his consent: Joe could go to annual mission meeting in Caxambu. In the back of the Chevrolet van we made a bed for Joe. At mission meeting he stayed in our hotel room most of the time, but at least the rest of us were able to attend the much-looked-forward-to gathering. Mission meeting, along with Christmas, was a highlight of the year. During the week the children had Vacation Bible School while the adults that weren't teaching in V.B.S. had meetings. Mission meeting was a time of worship and fellowship for everyone; all activities were English.

Injuries

We had a small, plastic wading pool in which the children loved to play, especially on hot days. To give the pool a solid base we had set it on the concrete. Without thinking Carl jumped in with too much force and bruised his knee badly. It swelled up and became very painful. Without giving any anesthesia the doctor had to lance the knee to relieve the pressure and let the infection drain. I hurt deeply for Carl, because this was such a painful experience.

All the children in the neighborhood loved to play in our yard. The tree was perfect for climbing. Jonathan liked to hang by his legs upside down. One day he jumped and intended to land on his feet but instead landed flat. His arm hit the cement slab Joe had made for the basketball goal. We took him to the doctor; he confirmed it was broken. I was thankful Joe was home, because the sight of suffering made me feel faint.

Later our children were playing at a neighbor's. They were playing on the hammock; the hook holding the hammock worked loose from the wall and hit Carl in the head. The father was a doctor; before he let us know what had happened, he rushed Carl to his office and took stitches. The family felt bad about the accident, but we were all thankful our son wasn't hurt worse.

Parasites

Parasites are a constant threat, as we mentioned already about the little children with bloated stomachs. Besides the intestinal types we encountered a few others. Carl was running down the hill from our house to the Richardsons' and hit his arm against the rough, plastered wall. We didn't clean it properly, so impetigo set in. Impetigo is one infection that must be treated quickly, or it spreads and is very contagious.

One parasite, *bicho-de-pe* (footworm), commonly is picked up in places in which pigs have been. Carl had a strange sore on his toe; it was swollen and itchy. After a few days of his suffering, I decided to pick it; inside I found a sack full of tiny eggs. The sack peeled out nicely and left a clean hole. Later I removed these from others of our family. One did not have to be barefooted or wear open-toed shoes to pick up these parasites; they know how to work themselves through the socks all the way down to the toes. They usually dig down beside the toenail and lay their eggs.

Another strange parasite we encountered is a worm that people and animals get from a large fly that stays around cattle. In fact we have seen cattle with large sores on their backs; these sores are caused from these flies. The fly stings and plants the larva (eggs) under the skin. After a few days the area begins to itch; it swells and becomes quite sore. As the vermin grows, so does the spot until it looks much like a boil, except the secretion is clear. Carl and Jonathan had been with our neighbor boys at their ranch; Carl was stung there. A young woman from church helped me in the house. She immediately knew what Carl had and how to remove it. The worm has hairy rings down its body. When one tries to remove it, it expands itself; the rings of hair keep it from being pulled out. It will break off. The whole worm has to be removed, or the sore won't heal. Years later, after Carl was in high school in Belo Horizonte, he had another round with the worm. Carl had a sore just above the ankle; the sore caused the ankle to swell and was so sore he could hardly walk. I had forgotten what the worm he had in Valadares was like, so I took him to a doctor at the Evangelical Hospital. The doctor thought it was a boil that was not quite to the point for lancing. He asked me to return in two days. Later Carl showed the Brazilian cook at the American School his foot; she recognized the problem. She suggested that instead of trying to pick it out, we seal the hole with clear fingernail polish and cause the worm to suffocate. Once the worm was dead, it would be easy to remove. I tried this and it worked. This also would be the case of other parasites such as chiggers or ticks.

Home Duties

From the States we had brought a secondhand push lawnmower, because we couldn't find one in Brazil. We had a large yard and had to have gardeners use large scissors to cut the grass. As the boys became the size that they could mow, especially between school sessions the lawn became one of their chores. When we were without a maid, they took turns washing dishes. Each morning they were responsible for making their beds. According to their ages we gave the three allowances for doing chores around the house; we helped them manage their money to buy birthday and Christmas presents or things for themselves. Of course the tithe for the Lord's work was taken out first. They were responsible for giving God His part.

Chapter 13

Pressing On!

I (we) press on toward the goal for the prize of the upward call of
God in Christ Jesus.

Year 1974
I have learned through experience that when things are going well,
Satan begins to release more devils from his infernal hell.
I have seen the battle raging in the hearts and lives of men.
I have seen some dear people succumb to the power of dreadful sin.

Many are sad and burdened under a heavy, heavy load.
I witness daily weak ones stumbling along the Christian road.
Of course I myself am not immune from the darts Satan hurls
At all Christian men, women, boys, and girls!

Joy and sadness are a part of life. But in Christianity we have
more victories than disappointments. The sad part is that Christ has
given the opportunity for the betterment of every life, but wrong
choices lead to tragic mistakes. New Christians are vulnerable to
Satan's deceitful nature and often linger on the edge of right and
wrong. Some Christians are very slow to grow enough to take a firm
position for Christ; sometimes they drift back into the world. This is
sad.

In 1974 inflation was 30 percent a year; the minimum salary that
the majority of the people received was $50 a month. Despite high
inflation Brazilians had made great progress in the nine years we had
been in Brazil.

Mount Ibituruna Excursions

In an earlier chapter I mentioned that the Richardsons and we tried to go to the top of Ibituruna peak that was on the eastern side of the Rio Doce River, right across from downtown Governador Valadares. We had a neighbor that was pioneering the hang-glider sport. This peak later became one of the most famous hang-glider peaks in South America. Unfortunately our neighbor was killed from practicing his favorite sport.

The mountain was not ready for tourism, although a Catholic shrine with a statue of Mary was at the tip-top. We were told that we needed to put the car in first gear, get a run near the bottom, and never let up on the accelerator until we reached the top. Well, after being in Valadares about three years I got up the courage to try again. The sharp turns in which I thought I ought to slow down, I knew I couldn't. The chugholes invited me to slow down, but I didn't dare slow down, for I wasn't going more than 20 miles an hour anyway. My biggest concern was meeting a car descending the mountain; that would have been a disaster. When we reached the top the first time, I was sweating; my heart was pounding. Our second car was a Chevrolet SUV, a more powerful car, so we had no problem and many times went up the mountain.

The view was spectacular as one turned around 360 degrees and observed the panorama of beauty that stretched in every direction. As it sprawled below, Governador Valadares looked small. The road going east to distant Mantena soon was lost between the hills. The Sweet River wound like a snake between hills and mountains in a southeastern direction until the river looked the size of a thick thread. To the south, hills and mountains swallowed the Rio-Bahia Highway so that soon its historic path was lost from sight. Somewhere over a thousand curves and hills, toward the northwest the city of Belo Horizonte rested behind the great mountains rich with iron ore. It was very similar in appearance to the mountains east of Albuquerque, NM.

The shrine dedicated to Mary was a lot larger than the appearance of it from our house on the island. Under the base of the statue was a room in which people could leave flowers and light candles. The area was good for picnics and Bible studies, so the island youth also had an outing of hiking to the top of the mountain a couple of times. After we bought the Volkswagen bug, we took both cars to the top of the mountain and let the boys and girls, including Charlotte, hike to the top. We used the cars to bring the group down. The rainy season practically made a gully out of the road. When the weather permitted, we took a number of missionary friends to the top to appreciate with us the fantastic view. After the road began to be used for hang-gliders, the highway crew made the road wider and kept both roads in better condition.

A Disappointment

The Bible teaches that we are not to get the glory for anything here on earth, yet, when one labors to help a person or family, a natural desire is to want the person to remember the kindness. When we were building the church building on the island, we hired a very poor man to help the bricklayer. He had a big family and lived in a one-room house. After a while he and his wife made a decision for Christ; I baptized them. Later two or three of the older children accepted Christ also. They had a boy with a clubfoot. We sought help in a hospital in Belo and finally found one that would take his case. For surgery I took him to the Belo hospital. At least once during his recovery I took the father and mother to visit him. Finally I brought him home in much better condition.

We bought a cheap lot near the Altinopolis mission and had a small, three-room house built for them with the intentions that their presence would bolster the membership at the Altinopolis mission. One of the girls was a teen-ager and helped with the children at the Altinopolis Mission. Aunt Ruby, that visited us for Christmas, sent a gift to help pay for the house. After about a year a Pentecostal group persuaded the parents to change churches. We were very disappointed! Several times during our missionary career, similar situations happened. In our humanity we just have to admit that we were glad that at least they were with an Evangelical group, but we and our church had done so much for them that we were hurt when they changed churches.

More Country Experiences

On many of our trips to the country something unusual happened. On many occasions people would request a ride. On one trip as I entered Sardoa, a police officer stopped me. He wanted me to take a woman and her son down the road toward Valadares and drop her off at the entrance of the ranch in which they lived. They had gone to the health clinic and didn't have money to catch a bus back home. This mother and son were illiterate; their Portuguese was difficult to understand. The boy wasn't going to school; no one in the family was literate. I felt sorry for them. They didn't even have a radio at home. They never had heard of nor seen a Bible and never had heard of any religious group except Catholic. I gave them a Bible but only could pray that they could find someone to read the Scriptures I marked for them. The whole family worked arduously on the ranch yet didn't receive enough money to live on.

One day in a neighboring village, Conceicao de Tronqueiras, a police officer stopped me because I had violated a traffic sign. I was tired when I drove into this sleepy little town in mid-afternoon. No cars, buggies, or people were in sight, so I felt no necessity to go around the town's little plaza; instead I made a sharp left turn. In about 30 yards I was on the road that went out of town toward Valadares. A police officer blew his shrill whistle. The officer gruffly asked me for my documents. He also gruffly asked whether I could read signs. I simple had no excuse, but he demanded an answer. I was so embarrassed. I finally said I was tired and just wanted to cut off a few seconds to get home. Then he gave me a hot lecture on obeying the traffic laws. Included in the reprimand was his complaint concerning the wrong attitude city people have about village traffic laws. The sign said to go around the little plaza; he said that is what the sign should mean to city drivers as well as country drivers. I was so embarrassed about what I had done and the scolding I had received that I didn't give him a gospel tract. I congratulated him for his alertness, but inside I believed he was proud of himself because I was probably the only one all that day that he had to discipline. That day I think he earned his pay.

Seventy-Eight Dead Mosquitoes

Mosquitoes regularly tormented us during the summer and rainy seasons. For the annual Sweet River Valley Associational meeting in Resplendor, Bill Richardson and I checked into a hotel. We hurriedly ate and left for the night meeting without lighting the mosquito spiral to kill the mosquitoes. This was the only vacant room in the hotel; it didn't have a window to the outside. It had only a window for ventilation and light for rooms in the middle of the hotel.

I was very tired and not feeling well, but I attended a little while at the meeting then returned to the room. A swarm of mosquitoes was in the room. I turned out the light and went to go to bed, but immediately I was attacked so viciously that I thought they hadn't had a taste of human blood in several days. I turned the light on and started swatting them with a newspaper. I killed 78 thirsty mosquitoes; the walls were covered with their tiny remains. No fan was in the room, so I spent a miserable night in the heat and lack of fresh air, even after the mosquitoes had been silenced.

Beginning Mission in Gonzaga

Gonzaga is a small town about 55 miles from Governador Valadares, a three-hour drive on a winding dirt road on the western side of the Rio-Bahia. When I drove through the small towns, I always looked for houses or stores that were vacant that would serve to start a preaching point. One day I was returning from Virginopolis on my way to Valadares when I noticed a large store had closed. I asked around until I found someone that knew the owner of the vacant store and where he lived. I located him and rented the store. I also found a carpenter and paid him to build six simple benches. The next Friday I returned. Gonzaga had very weak electricity from a generator at the river. I cleaned out the store that was very dusty and dirty. I went to get the six benches, but they weren't ready. I put the portable loudspeaker on the car and went through the streets announcing the evangelistic services that would start at 7 p.m. We had electricity, but I borrowed a little table from the boarding house (*pensão*) for my slide projector. The electricity wasn't strong enough for a 16-millimeter movie projector, but I could run the small filmstrip projector. I showed the people a religious filmstrip and preached a short message to about 70 people. Everyone had to stand; some were women with babies. I started by teaching them John 3:16 and one stanza of *What a Friend We Have in Jesus.*

I learned a lesson that I should have already known. The custom is that when you ask a carpenter to make something, you pay for the lumber then and pay for the labor when the job is finished. But the man made a plea for me to also pay for his labor, so I agreed, which was a mistake. We didn't have benches for the second service or third service. I was amazed that the people continued to attend, especially the women that were pregnant or had to hold their babies. Some women had little children who most of the time hung onto their skirts and wanted to be held. Finally, for the fourth service I was able to pick up the benches.

One night a shaggy, barefooted man entered. His hair and beard were long and matted. His clothes were filthy. The people didn't want him near them. At the end of the service I asked for all those that had understood the message and wanted to make a lifetime commitment to Jesus as their Lord and Savior to meet me at the front. This dirty man went to the front. He reeked with the smell of liquor and body odor. As I was loading my equipment into the car, he approached me and tugged on the back of my suit coat, so I turned around. He said to me, "Pastor, the next time you are here, will you visit me?" I told him I would. Because of his drunken state I didn't take him seriously. I didn't think he would remember asking me. I didn't even remember to pray for him during the week.

My regular day for visiting Gonzaga was Friday, but I almost didn't return to Gonzaga the next Friday. The Kent Faris family in the State of Espirito Santo was on furlough. Someone had informed the chairman of the property committee that the mission house had a bad leak in the roof. No other missionary lived in Vitoria to take care of housing problems. Since I was the closest missionary to Vitoria, Espirito Santo, the property chairman wanted me to assess the problem and authorize someone to fix it. I drove the tough, seven-hour drive to Vitoria on Wednesday and back on Thursday. I was so tired on Friday that I contemplated skipping my trip to Gonzaga. However, my mind finally persuaded my body to go. Somehow I believe I had to keep my appointed time with the people or they would lose confidence in me. Right after the noon meal on Friday I left for Gonzaga to arrive a couple of hours early to drive around the town with the loudspeaker announcing the service. Then I went to the meeting hall to clean the room and got ready for the service.

The service went as normal, but I noticed a young man that I hadn't noticed before. At the end of the service, as I was loading the car, this young man approached me and said, "Pastor, you promised to visit me at my house this week." I hadn't recognized him as the young, shaggy drunk. He still didn't have on any shoes, but he had shaved and had a haircut and clean clothes. He was young, only 26-years old. I had given my word. What was I to do? I had no way to communicate with Leona that I wouldn't be returning home that night, but I had to stay. He told me how to get to his house the next morning. I stayed in the boarding house that night.

Early the next morning I went to the end of the village and found the narrow road that he had said would go past his house. Barbed-wire fences were on each side of the narrow road. I met a man who was leading a burro. The burro had large straw baskets on each side; they made him nearly as wide as a car. We had a tough time getting by each other. The man was a little perturbed because the road, according to him, was made for buggies and burros but not cars.

Following directions I found the entrance to Sebastian's house. By the time I had opened the gate, he was hurrying up the narrow footpath. We met; he gave me a hearty Brazilian hug. Almost out of breath he said, "Pastor, guess what happened to me last Saturday night." I said: "I can't imagine, Sebastian. Tell me!" He said, "Last Friday night you know I gave my life to Jesus. Well on Saturday my drinking buddies forced me to go to the bar with them. I did not want to go! When we got to the bar, they bought a bottle of cane liquor and set it before me, but I would not drink it. Then they bought me a Coca Cola and set it before me. They said, Which of these drinks is the better? They thought that I would certainly choose the liquor that I had loved so much." I said to them, "Friends, last night I found what I have been looking for. Liquor is no longer a temptation to me." I took the Coca Cola and drank it. They chided me and could not believe it. They said, "Sebastian, you cannot mean what you are saying. We are your friends and have had so much fun together. You cannot do this to us!" I walked away from them!

We walked to his humble house. The house was made of adobe brick; three small rooms still stood; one room had fallen in. Sebastian presented me to his wife, Socorro. For me she made some tea from avocado leaves. I could see that things were not very sanitary, but I knew I needed to drink the tea. The ceiling and rafters were black with smoke from the homemade wood cook stove. A piece of iron grill fit over the brick; the kettle was on that piece of iron. The room was smoky, for not all of the smoke went out the chimney. A little naked boy and a girl in a little dress played on the floor. The floor was a pretty green color; it was made to look that way with fresh cow dung— amazing how cow dung can make the dirt floor hard and colorful!

After we had tea, Sebastian left his wife alone with me so I could talk to her. She told me that what had happened to her husband was amazing and that she wanted what he had. I took 30 minutes to tell her what she needed to do; I quoted Scriptures that became powerful as the Holy Spirit worked. Then I asked her whether she wanted to make a definite decision to give herself to Jesus as her personal Savior and Lord. I had her to voice her own prayer, as I normally do; surprisingly she just began talking to God. Her tears and expressions of joy confirmed in her heart that she had made a genuine decision.

Even before she had finished, I heard someone running down the path to the house. As Socorro finished, her younger sister, Fatima, that lived down the road burst into the room. She was out of breath, but she said in short phrases between breaths, "I do not know . . . what has happened . . . to my brother-in-law . . . but I want . . . what he has!" I felt goosebumps of joy as I felt the Spirit of God surging through me. I had never imagined anything such as this! How could God be so good? He was sending people to me because a drunk man that I didn't even believe was sober enough to understand had made a sincere decision to accept my precious Jesus as Lord and Savior. Now he had been witnessing of his changed heart and life. I took another 30 to 40 minutes to give the plan of salvation to Fatima so that she would know what she was to do. At the end, in tears of joy, she confessed her sins and with her mouth asked Jesus to save her.

Sebastian did not have a regular job but told me that he had been a hoe hand for several of the ranchers in the area. I gave him some tracts and Bibles and challenged him to just go to all of them and tell them what Jesus had done in his life. I told Sebastian to tell about Jesus just as he had done to his drinking buddies, his wife, and his teen-age sister-in-law.

With an exceptionally happy heart I went back to Governador Valadares. Leona had not been worried too much, because she knew I had decided to stay. She rejoiced with me!

The next week when I returned, Sebastian had a good report to give me. He had spent the week talking to the ranchers where he had worked and telling his testimony. He also knew how to play a guitar a little. Sebastian had lost his worker's card (like a social security card) in São Paulo two or three years before and never had money to get another one. I gave him money to get another worker's card so he could get a better job.

The only churches in Gonzaga were Catholic and Assembly of God. A Presbyterian rancher lived in town so his children could go to school. At our services two of his children were saved. He was very happy and interested in helping the Baptist church get started in Gonzaga. In town he had property that he offered to sell to me, but I didn't have the money.

I baptized Fatima and her fiancé; later I also performed their wedding. Leona and I talked to Socorro and Fatima's mother about accepting the Lord, but she would not make that decision.

About 30 years later we visited Gonzaga to see the beautiful new church building. In the nearby villages the church also had two missions. What a joy to see the crowd and especially one man! The man I had contracted to make the first benches had been converted and now was active in the church. Praise the Lord!

Another Mysterious Experience

I planned to spend a week visiting some churches and wanted to take Carl with me. I also was hoping to fish a little. We planned to go the week between our annual mission meeting and our state convention. At the beginning of the year our local newspaper ran a notice about a change in the system for registering automobiles. The new system required that we register our cars according to the final number on the car tag. Every month I called the transportation department for information about when this plan was to go into effect so I could be sure to get the car registered.

We went to our annual mission meeting and had two or three days before Carl and I started on our trip. I didn't take time to read the newspapers because of other pressing matters. Carl and I left on Monday afternoon about 3. After we traveled about 40 minutes, we were stopped at a police checkpoint. We were told that we couldn't continue our trip because the license plate had expired. The last number on my license tag was a six; we were in the seventh month. This was the reason that I had checked every month about the date this system was to go into effect. I told the officers my story that I had planned this trip for months, that the churches were expecting me, and I couldn't disappoint them. The principal officer of the two lived in Belo Horizonte; his wife was a Baptist. He told me they would let me pass if I would promise to return the same way. If I got on the Rio-Bahia Highway, my car would be impounded. My plan was to make this long trip through the country and return on the Rio-Bahia Highway. If I returned on the dirt back roads, I would need an extra day and would not be able to get necessary things done before I left for the state convention.

I decided to go to the first church and then drive back after the service to a small hotel in Conselheiro Pena. Tuesday morning I would get up early and arrive in Valadares by 8 a.m. I would hope to get the car registered by noon and then hit the trail again to get to the second church. This would be a miracle, because normally two days were necessary to register the car. In the past I had to stand in a line at one place to pay a county tax, go to another place to pay a state tax, and stand in yet another line to pay a federal tax or something. Then I would need to stand in a line to get the license. Of course this process was the reason for having the motorists spread out their registration throughout the whole year, with not everyone's expiring at the beginning of the year. I hoped the new plan would work smoothly.

We did as planned. We left the first church about 9 p.m. This area was still known for *pistoleiros* (gunmen) that robbed cars or trucks occasionally, so normally I didn't travel these roads at night, but this time was necessary. Carl and I both prayed before we started back. We had traveled about an hour and had just gone through a little creek near a ranch house when the motor suddenly stopped. I turned the key and heard only the grinding of the starter but no sign of wanting to start. I had gone very slowly through the water in the creek, so I had not drowned out the engine by water. I took my flashlight and raised the hood of the car. I checked the distributor cables; they all were tight on the spark plugs.

The night was beautiful and had a full moon. We could hear a cow mooing nearby. I tried to start the car again but did not experience the slightest sign of the engine wanting to start. I said, "Carl, let's pray." I began telling the Lord all about the necessity to get back to Valadares the next morning to keep our word to the churches. I told him all the things I knew He already knew. I told Him that we were humanly bound to failure because I was not a mechanic, although I had some tools in the car. I reminded Him how many times He had helped us in the past. Then Carl prayed. When we finished, I turned the key; the motor fired up beautifully. Away we went with joy and thanks in our hearts. In fact I believed that the car was running better than it had before.

I drove about a mile and met a black Rural stopped by the road facing me—it was a state official car. I asked the man whether he was having car trouble. He said that for some strange reason, his car had stopped running. I offered to take him to Conselheiro Pena, in which he could get help the next morning. I turned on the inside dome light so he could see that I had my young son with me, for he seemed to be nervous. I told him I was a Baptist missionary; I thought that might ease his fear of my being a *pistoleiro*. He still didn't want my help. I didn't tell him I had had the same experience and that I had prayed and God was the answer to my problem, for I was sure that he would think I was crazy.

I resumed my journey and had gone about another mile when I met another black state official car also stopped. The officer told me the same story. I told him that one of his buddies also was stopped about a mile back and that I had offered him a ride to Conselheiro Pena if he wanted to spend the night. Again, I showed him that only my son and I were in the car. I cannot explain this strange experience, but I can tell you that Carl and I were impressed. I know that God answered our prayers; I have wondered whether I should have prayed for those fellows. On the other hand, I offered those guys help and they wouldn't take it. Their reaction to my offers made me think they wouldn't have believed in prayer as a solution. My conclusion is that God wanted to give us a very unusual experience to strengthen our faith.

We checked into the little hotel about midnight and got up about 6 a.m. and left for Valadares. By 8 a.m. we surprised Leona, Charlotte, and Jonathan by arriving for breakfast. By noon I had the car license renewed; we went on our way to a church at or near Quatituba, a few miles beyond Resplendor. The next day we arrived at Assarai and did a little fishing in a nearby stream. We made the trip as planned.

Four Associations

By the end of 1974 the one large Sweet River Valley Baptist Association had divided into four associations. The first one to officially organize was the Northern Sweet River Valley area; next was the Eastern area, and last was the Steel Valley Association. The towns around Governador Valadares chose the name of *Central Rio Doce Association* (Sweet River). That meant four associational annual meetings to attend. I was not the actual associational missionary of all four, but I was a consultant. My big concern about the associations forming independently was that they would not be interested in starting new work in the towns in the Western area that had only four weak Baptist missions: Pecanha, Guanhaes, Virginopolis, and Gonzaga. By this time 64 churches were in the area, whereas in 1966 when we arrived, we had 48. However, we had several missions strong enough to organize into churches soon. But I was right that the load for beginning new work in the west fell on the Central Rio Doce Association, or principally Governador Valadares. First Baptist Church of Governador Valadares continued to lead the way into several towns. The Steel Valley Association was doing well to just keep up with the growth around the big steel mill and paper mill. The Northern and Eastern areas were mainly rural areas and did not have any booming towns.

What Voodoo Can Do

Manuel and his wife sent a message to us that their teen-age daughter was acting very strange. This family helped start the work in Altinopolis neighborhood; he worked at the small smelting plant. The daughter was in a trance of some sort, was stiff as a board, and stared at the ceiling all the time. She was not eating. They told us that she had been dating a boy that was a Macumba spiritist.

We talked to her, but she hardly reacted. We prayed with the family and had little advice to give. For about two weeks we visited her frequently; she continued in that strange state of mind and body. Manuel and his wife were very distraught. Finally we found out from the brother that the girl's boyfriend had stolen the radio from Manuel's house. He put a voodoo hex on the girl so she wouldn't tell her parents. This scared the girl so much that she was in this distraught situation. The girl evidently had seen or heard some terrible things that happened to people that crossed the whims of people that practiced this African spiritist religion. Manuel and his wife didn't know the boy had been taking her to their séances, a spiritualist meeting to receive spirit communications. The island church as well as the Altinopolis mission began praying.

Leona and I read Scripture to the girl and talked to her calmly. We prayed with her even though her mind seemed to be in a faraway place. After several weeks she began to improve and gradually returned to normality—a scary experience to see the nature of a girl that had been attending church to become so immobile and unnatural as Manuel's daughter had become.

Mission Leadership Responsibilities

The South Brazil mission organization was made up of 10 states and the Federal District. At sometime or another nearly every missionary served in some position. Each state also had a president and other officers to facilitate resolving necessary things. Minas Gerais had from three to eight couples and one or two single missionaries. One of my terms as president of the Minas mission station was in 1973 and 1974. This position required filling out forms requesting new missionaries, strategic property funds, and other things and sending them to our South Brazil mission office about two months before annual mission meeting.

Each unit that received funds had to keep records on all money received and spent. I was lucky because Leona likes bookkeeping and I don't. We also had to send in monthly reports on all monies received and spent for housing, transportation, literature, small equipment, and strategic property. I was greatly relieved that Leona took care of this and also prepared and sent in the annual report to be audited by the South Brazil treasurer. While their children still were at home, the missionary wives usually didn't assume many of the state and South Brazil mission administrative responsibilities. After the children left home, they were called on heavily to share in the major responsibilities. During our last years in Brazil the computer made this job much easier.

State Stewardship Director

In July 1974 we received our 10-year service pen. We had been very happy in what we were doing. We thought that for the rest of our lives we could be happy in Governador Valadares. However, one day our executive secretary for Minas Gerais, Jose Alves da Silva Bittencourt, shocked me. He wanted me to work on the state level to promote the Brazilian Baptist Cooperative Program in the way the Southern Baptists of the United States did. In 1982 Brazilian Baptists would celebrate 100 years of Baptist work. The Foreign Mission Board was pushing the conventions by 1982 to become totally self-supporting; Brazilians were happy to comply to this. Most of the older states still received 50 percent or more of their state expenses from the Southern Baptists through the Foreign Mission Board. This went for salaries of the state leaders who were Brazilians and all other expenses. We now had 201 churches in our state the size of Texas. To become self-supporting would be a big task, because most of these churches were small and were not even sufficiently supporting themselves.

Pastor Bittencourt liked what I had done in getting the churches in the Sweet River Valley Association to improve their giving to the Cooperative Program regularly. This meant I had succeeded in getting most of the churches to send 10 percent of their monthly budgets to the state convention office, where 70 percent of all that was given by the churches was kept for state use and 30 percent was sent to the

Brazilian convention headquarters. The national office divided that money between the three major seminaries, publishing house, Brazilian Foreign Mission Board, and the Home Mission Board.

When I received this request, I was surprised and told Pastor Bittencourt that if I accepted it, I would want to stay in Governador Valadares. The first thing he wanted me to do was to work up a chart for the giving of all the churches in the way I had done in the Sweet River Valley Association. Pastor Bittencourt was in no hurry for me to make a decision, but I practically accepted. I needed to get several things done, however, before I could start working on stewardship on the state level. Nearly a year would be needed before I could bring to the next annual mission meeting the request to change my work assignment, so I had some time to get things in order.

The three associations that had organized themselves out of the Sweet River Baptist Association had capable pastors for leadership, so this was a relief. I didn't have to give them regular time but just to help them if I was asked. Even the Central Association was very capable also of directing itself. But Altinopolis, Palmeiras, Gonzaga, Virginopolis, and the island church in a short time needed to move forward at a faster pace.

The Billy Graham Crusade

Once before we arrived in Brazil, Billy Graham had been in a crusade. In October 1974 he would be in Rio de Janeiro for the second time to hold a revival in the Maracana Soccer Stadium, the largest stadium in the world. We decided to take our children out of school so our entire family could attend. This might be the only time the kids would have this opportunity. The Laings in Rio invited us to stay with them for the week.

The first night of the Crusade I was asked to help with our car to gather the offering. I was to drive around the stadium on the third floor to collect the offerings at the various entrance doors. I was happy to do this for two reasons. The first reason was that I would have a part in the Crusade, and second, we had special parking privilege. This meant we would need to arrive early, but we would park under the stadium and not have to walk for blocks. The Laings and we —all 10 of us—piled into our car. That meant our group members always sat near the same entrance door on the third floor so I could find them after I had delivered the money to an office on the ground floor. By the time I joined them, the message was just beginning. The drivers received a message by telephone as to the moment we would start. Two police officers got in the back seat of the car; we went up the ramps until we reached the third level. I drove slowly to the first entrance from the ramp. The police officers got out of the car and took the money that had been given on level three; then I went slowly to another entrance and so on until we had gone all around the stadium. Then we went down to the ground floor under the stadium. The policemen took the money to the counting room and I was free. During the day some special meetings occurred; one day Billy Graham addressed our missionaries.

The Crusade was a great success. The last service was Sunday afternoon. When the last message was preached, buses still were arriving from surrounding areas. I felt sorry for those that couldn't get in. The stadium was packed with an estimated 120,000 people; the smaller Maracanzinho was filled, with no room for the late-arrivers. We were all blessed by the experience. We stayed a couple more days for the quarterly South Brazil mission meeting, in which I was involved. We returned to our beloved Governador Valadares rejoicing; we were spiritually uplifted for the continuation of our busy schedules.

Closing Out 1974
At our Central Rio Doce Associational monthly pastors meeting in September I presented a reformed structure for the association to operate without me. The pastors still wanted me until I left to be the coordinator, but we divided the work through committees. I ended up keeping the treasurer position, serving as pastor of Island Baptist Church, chairing the stewardship committee and planning and directing clinics of various sorts. I no longer was responsible for most of the evangelism and church-development projects. Most churches in our region were very evangelistic and mission-minded. Personally I learned a lot from them. My desire was to develop a strategy for the association to work together to open up some towns in the west. I encouraged the churches to pledge at least two percent of their month-

ly income to associational expenses for new preaching points and missions beyond the missions they already were opening on their own.

I want to express my admiration and appreciation for most of the Brazilian pastors with whom I have worked and especially for those that had traveled with me. I found that many of them know a lot more about the Bible than I do; they are certainly better preachers. They seem to be more dedicated to their prayer lives and Bible studies than I was.

Our fourth annual revival at the island church was especially good. Four-day revivals, Thursday through Sunday, are most common in Brazil because many students work during the day and go to high-school classes during the weeknights. Some students often skip classes on revival nights, or at least the Friday night—not that this is encouraged, but many don't want to miss out on anything. They want to receive the same spiritual blessing as the rest of the church does. During the service I painted a picture with chalk; to the person that brought the most visitors each night I presented the picture. One night one of the newest members brought 28 visitors. Missionary Kent Faris used this method to increase attendance, so I copied him.

While I made some visits in the Altinopolis neighborhood, I discovered a family that had moved to town from the country. They had been farm and ranch hands and were very poor. They were living in a shack and had only one bed. The father and mother made decisions for Christ but weren't married. Neither the couple nor the four children had birth certificates. According to Brazilian Baptist customs I couldn't baptize them because they weren't married; they couldn't get married without birth certificates.

Soon after the island revival I held a four-day revival at the Altinopolis mission. The last night we had about 80 people present and six conversions. This boosted our regular Sunday-night services to about 50 since the revival. The blind mother of the poor ranch hands attended the revival and accepted Christ. Such dear people as these, not knowing how to read or write, needed a lot of help. To get a decent job without being able to read or write was very difficult, but to get a good job without a birth certificate was worse. To go to school next term their two older children needed their birth certificates. I began searching for a job for him as well as trying to get birth certificates. Birth certificates have to be sought from the county seat town in which the person was born. This can get complicated and take time. If a Baptist church existed in the county seat town, I would contact the pastor and get his help. We would send money for the people to pay for the certificates and for having them mailed. If no church existed then, the process became more complicated; I had to find someone to go to that town.

Meanwhile at home we had two little girls staying with us for the rest of the school season. We kept the first- and second-graders. Their parents moved to another neighborhood; at such a late date of the school year they couldn't transfer to another school. The 12-year-old girl stayed with another family and cleaned house for the people. The good part about this was that the mother was overwhelmed by this kindness. She attended church to see the 12-year old baptized and also accepted Christ. How the Holy Spirit uses efforts to be Christian witnesses through kindness is amazing.

Chapter 14

God Cuts a New Facet in Our Lives

"Things which eye has not seen and ear has not heard, and which
have not entered the heart of man, all that God has prepared for
those who love Him." For to us God revealed them through the
Spirit; for the Spirit searches all things, even the depths of God
(1 Cor. 2:9-10).

Surely Satan has unleashed all he has in our own age—
Divorce, liquor, drugs, pornography—he spreads with violent rage.
To weaken the Christian as much as he can is His master plan
Until more and more we only are pawns in his deceiving hand.

Are we all from Christ fast falling away—
Fulfilling the prophecy of Scripture before His arrival day?
Have you lost the sense of wonder, awe, and spiritual mystery
That spurred God's people to faithfulness throughout history?

Are your offerings and sacrifices abominable to our Holy Lord?
If the worship service passes the hour, do you get bored?
Would you miss days of work or complain when standing
at a game?
Why are you impatient and slack about what you do
in Jesus' name?

If you stop often to ponder, marvel, and meditate about it all,
Jesus will strengthen you afresh before you ever fall
And Satan will be on the defensive side time and time again,
And we will be warriors on the side that is sure to win.

272

Oh, the marvel of it all
Began when I was very small.
But the greatest marvel yet to be
Is when Jesus will come for me!

If anyone reading this does not know the way,
Repent of your sins; invite Jesus into your heart today.
He is knocking longingly at your very heart's door.
He died for you as well as for me and all who have lived before.

With this chapter we arrive at the end of our direct ministry in Governador Valadares and the Sweet River Valley. Since then many times we have returned to Valadares for different types of ministry. The end of the poem expresses my understanding about the value of faithfulness to God and his purpose for us until we die.

1975
Called to Help a Demon-Possessed Girl

One morning about noon the owner of a bakery on the island called me to go to a house about three blocks from our home. The bakery man sent his children to our Sunday school, although he and his wife did not attend our church. A teen-aged girl working for him became ill at work and was taken home. He told me where she lived. I took Geraldo, a church member and former spiritist, with me. This is the same man that had won the couple to the Lord that lived at the bottom of the mountain at which the telephone satellite tower was located.

When we arrived at the house, the street in front of her house was crowded with people. Inside the house the girl was screaming in agony. I went into the house and in the living room met the father and mother. I asked them whether she recently had been attending any spiritist sessions. He said that she had. I went into the room where four men were trying to hold her down; each one held a foot or an arm. The fright in her eyes was indescribable, but I will try to explain it. An interesting—and at the same time, terrifying—thing to me is how a person's eyes can show the depth of his or her inner being. Her

273

eyes were red where they naturally had been white. They expressed the horror of an inner turmoil! Her eyes flashed and moved back and forth constantly.

The four men were arguing among themselves. Geraldo immediately began acting as the faith-healers do, with a forceful voice demanding the devil to leave her immediately. I told Geraldo not to do that; I wanted to talk to her. I asked the men to be quiet; they did. I looked at the girl in her eyes and began talking softly to her about Jesus. I do not remember what I said, but I was thinking how Jesus might deal with a situation like this. As I talked softly, I exalted Jesus; she calmed down and listened intently. All was going well until the men began talking again. One was a Catholic, another Pentecostal, another charismatic, and the fourth a spiritist. Each had his opinion as to where she should be taken. The girl began screaming and struggling again so fiercely that those four men had difficulty hanging on to her constantly moving arms and legs. I could not do anything else, so I left.

On Sunday afternoon Leona and I went to the girl's home. We were invited into the living room, so we talked to the mother first. The girl's mother said that she had been taken to a charismatic faith preacher and seemingly returned home better, but on Saturday she had another attack. The mother called for the girl to visit with us in the living room. The girl said that she remembered me being present and talking to her. She felt peaceful while I was talking to her, but when those men began arguing again about to whom she should be taken, she saw evil in their faces. To her, one had a huge nose, another had big ears, and another big eyes; their disfiguration added to her fear of them. When we had finished a good visit with the girl and her mother, we stood to have prayer. As I closed the prayer in Jesus' name, she fell stiff on the couch. Neither the father nor her mother were saved or interested in our type of Christianity. We invited them to church and offered our assistance if we were asked. We were never asked. However, about five years later, Planalto Baptist Church youth in Belo invited the youth of Island Baptist Church to direct a weekend youth-led spiritual emphasis. The girl that had the problem was with them and at that time was a member of Island Baptist Church.

Young People and Adult Activities

More than half of the population of Brazil is youth. In Brazil, however, a person is considered young until he is 35. Single youth make up a large part of those considered young. These young people in the Baptist churches use Saturday nights for special spiritual meetings. Young people like to surprise each other on birthdays. Several of them sometimes formed a group and go to a youth's house at midnight if the church earlier hadn't been invited for a special celebration.

The two vacant lots with grass at Island Baptist Church formed a good place for young people from other churches of Governador Valadares to meet occasionally to play ball. We also had at least two associational youth rallies at Island Baptist Church. Once we had a big tent for the rally, but the wind and rainstorm blew part of the tent down.

Young people also enjoyed surprising the pastor and wife on birthdays and anniversaries. Once they arrived at our house at 6 a.m. on Sunday morning on Pastor's Day. Standing at our gate they woke us as they clapped and sang beautifully. They brought a big cake and soft drinks. I enjoyed the surprise, but a piece of cake before breakfast was not the best thing for my early morning appetite. We invited them to return that afternoon for cutting the cake.

Many times a carload of young people went with me to Campanario, Altinopolis, Gonzaga, and Palmeiras on Saturdays or Sunday afternoons. In fact some of the young people kept the Palmeiras mission going for a long time.

Most Baptist churches had prayer meetings every night of the week before business meetings. Business meetings usually were held either on the second Saturday night or on the second Sunday morning during the worship hour; this omitted the preaching hour. I didn't agree with this and usually had our business meetings on Wednesday nights. A large percent of adults and some children also enjoyed having a special evangelism service on their birthdays; these activities usually took up one or two nights a week. These services brought the church closer together as a family. What if our churches in the U.S. were like this?

Trying to Maintain U.S. Customs

Brazil had nothing like Halloween; however All Saints Day is November 1 and Day of the Dead. The first two years we were in Valadares, we had Halloween parties only for our children. We had something special or scary in each room of the house; but we soon saw the evil in this holiday and for many years have been totally against the American emphasis on the hallowed or holy evening that is the night before the catholic All Saints Day.

The World Book Encyclopedia tells how and from where Halloween was derived. "The Irish are responsible for spreading the idea of the 'jack-o'-lantern'. They told the tale of a man named Jack that was unable to enter heaven because he was so miserly. He could not enter hell because he had played practical jokes on the devil. So he had to walk the earth with his lantern until Judgment Day. The Druids, priests in ancient Gaul and Britain, believed that on Halloween, ghosts, spirits, fairies, witches, and elves existed to harm people. They thought the cat was sacred and believed that cats once had been human beings but were changed as a punishment for evil deeds. American descendants from Great Britain brought this over to America. In the 700s, the Roman Catholic Church named November 1 as All Saints Day. The old pagan customs and the Christian feast day were combined into the Halloween festival." With all the superstition from spiritism (Spiritualism) and Catholicism, Halloween did not exist in Brazil until a few years before we left but is not yet anything similar to the U.S. celebration.

We celebrated Thanksgiving and Christmas as important holidays. Brazil had a Thanksgiving Day on its calendar, but the idea was not practiced. I think Brazilians got the idea from Americans but didn't have an incentive to observe Thanksgiving as America did. For this holiday we usually met with some missionary family or families. Sometimes we invited a Brazilian family to observe an American Thanksgiving with us.

Christmas in Brazil is a big celebration but has become commercialized as it is in the U.S. This holiday is not nearly so important for Catholics as Easter or the month of June that has St. John's, St. Peter's and other saints days. The days before Easter the Catholics try to simulate the death of Jesus by parades, painting of streets, and the burning of a stuffed figure representing Judas Iscariot. This seems to be the most sacred of religious holidays. Little is said, however, about the resurrection of Jesus.

The Crusade of the Americas

In 1975 all of South American Baptists held evangelistic revivals. The main campaign for Brazil was in the month of May. We held our third citywide campaign at the same large shed that was almost downtown. Again, the revival was a great success. We had an outstanding preacher and singer. Later on in the year each of the nine churches and the missions had revivals in their own neighborhoods; we also worked to get those who had made decisions in the citywide crusade to attend the local neighborhood crusade.

Jonathan Gets a Cow's Skull

One day, when Jonathan was about 10-years old and we were traveling to Belo, in the distance on a hill he saw a cow's skull with the horns. The skull looked as though it was about 12 inches in size. Jonathan wanted the skull, but I didn't want to turn around and go back. I told him that if he was awake when we returned to Valadares, I would get the skull for him. Of course, I didn't expect him to be awake when we returned. I even forgot about my promise, but he didn't forget. He kept watching. When he saw the skull, he immediately reminded me what I had said. I stopped the car and went into the pasture to get the skull. The closer I got to the skull, the bigger and bigger it became. When I picked up the skull, it was more than a yard wide from the points of the horns. I tried to talk him out of taking the skull home because it was so big, but I had made a promise. We put the skull on the steps in front of our house in which it would have probably been put if we had been in the States. A few days later, our Presbyterian neighbor friends got up the nerve to tell us what a skull meant to a lot of Brazilians. Many Brazilians are superstitious; they believed the skull at the door kept evil spirits away. We immediately removed the skull from sight because, as Evangelical Christians, we didn't want anyone to think we were superstitious. For us the Holy Spirit kept evil spirits away.

Decision to Move

Do you not know? Have you not heard? The Everlasting God, the LORD, the Creator of the ends of the earth does not become weary or tired. His understanding is inscrutable. He gives strength to the weary, and to him who lacks might He increases power. Though youths grow weary and tired, and vigorous young men stumble badly, yet those who wait for the LORD will gain new strength; they will mount up with wings like eagles, they will run and not get tired, they will walk and not become weary (Isa. 40:28-31). God moves in mysterious ways His wonders to perform; this is how God persuaded me that time had arrived to move to another level in our missionary ministry. Pastor Bittencourt, the state executive director, liked what I was doing in promoting stewardship in the Sweet River Valley Association and asked me to do the same thing on a state level. I had told him I would but only if we could continue living in Governador Valadares.

One day I went to Rio de Janeiro to a South Brazil quarterly meeting. On the way home, about halfway on that nine-hour drive, the Lord spoke to me. This was another rare time in which God talked through my mind so directly that I was startled. He said: "Joe, what is your problem? Can't you see that I have everything ready for you and the family in Belo Horizonte? The house in which Cathryn Smith is living is too big for her. She wants something smaller. An American school is in Belo Horizonte for your children. Belo Horizonte is situated in the center of the State and would be better for your work as Stewardship director. What are you waiting for?" This word from God was all I needed; I was ready to go. God had spoken directly to me again! This is convincing!

For months we had been discussing what we would do about Carl's education after his graduation from middle school. We didn't want him to continue in the Brazilian school system for high school. In Campinas the mission had a hostel for teen-age MK's (missionary kids), or we could see whether he could stay with one of the missionary families in Belo. We would be taking a year's furlough; then we would have to make a decision.

The other problem was that in the dry season I was very allergic to the dust. I could sing only one stanza of a song; my voice would be gone. I took Sinutab often; I had done this since college, but I was a lot worse. Non-drowsy Sinutab didn't exist in Brazil, so much of the time—especially while I drove—I was miserably sleepy.

When I arrived home, I said to Leona, "Let's move to Belo." She spontaneously replied, "No, I do not want to even talk about it!" My reply was, "Well, when you are ready to talk let me know." As the weeks passed, God worked in Leona's mind and heart. She began to understand that, for the best of the family, we needed to move. The kids could stay at home and for their high-school years attend the American School. A mission house already was available for us in Belo. And Belo was more centralized in the state; I would be able to have better contact with the churches. God was able to show her that He would go with us to Belo. She still had some fears to conquer: she was scared to drive in what seemed to be wild traffic and scared of getting lost in the city of about 2-million people. The traffic seemed to have that many cars.

By July we had to submit to the personnel committee our request to move. After much prayer and thought, together we made our decision to move. Many things had to be completed before our furlough date. In July we would complete four years on the field, so we were due a year's furlough. We tried to get permission from the state education board to approve the boys doing double classes to get the year's credit into the first semester. We thought the boys could do that by having classes all day instead for the regular half day. The board didn't approve, so we didn't want to leave in the middle of the school year if the kids were going to lose the year. They would lack the second semester of the grades they were in; the schools in the States would be starting the first semester. We decided to let them finish the school year in December.

We had difficulty leaving Valadares because we had such good relationships in the city. I enjoyed the fellowship among the pastors. I knew the mayor personally and had been invited to special occasions at the city council. I also had a responsibility in the pastors' alliance. We had great plans for Governador Valadares—especially among the Baptists.

The move also was difficult for the children. They had an ideal recreation area in our yard and had many friends in the neighborhood. In Belo they had no place for a basketball goal or any kind of recreation. The back yard was very small and was all concrete. The front yard sloped down steeply to the fence; this made cutting the grass difficult to even bend over head-forward to cut the grass. On the other hand, they would be on the same block with the Richardson boys and be able to participate in athletic events at the American school. This school had been started principally by Southern Baptist missionaries but included various denominations. This school had become an international American school. I thought that being near the Richardsons and going to an American school might compensate for the disappointment our kids might have in leaving Valadares, although our kids were perfectly happy in the Brazilian schools.

God Answers Again a Desperate Prayer

The day that we were to leave for the first leg of our journey to the 1975 annual mission meeting was a busy day. On Sunday I preached at Altinopolis and then went to the island church to preach again. At 2 p.m. we had a special meeting with the examination of the candidates for baptism from the Altinopolis and Gonzaga missions. I baptized six people—two from Gonzaga were Sebastian and Socorro. The baptism was followed by the observance of the Lord's Supper. We left Valadares at 4 p.m. for Belo Horizonte, at which we were to spend the night with the Richardsons. I drove the first 60 miles to Ipatinga; we bought gas. Being winter, darkness was settling in. I asked Leona to drive because I was very tired. I lay down in the back of the car to take a nap. When we were about 10 minutes out of Ipatinga, the car motor started sputtering. At first I thought we might have bought some bad gas, but when I lifted the hood and saw sparks dancing over the coil, I knew we had to get back to Ipatinga and get help. On a Sunday night our getting help would be only a miracle of God.

Leona turned around; we sputtered back to Ipatinga, with all of us praying silently. Soon after we crossed the bridge over the Rio Doce River, we knew of a truck stop and across the street a mechanic's shop. We stopped at the mechanic shop; of course the shop was closed. I drove across the street to a gas pump; the engine stopped completely. The motor had gotten us back to Ipatinga and seemed to say, "I got you this far; that is all I can do".

What were we going to do? We had told the Richardsons we would arrive about 10 p.m. We would have to find a place to stay — perhaps at the truck stop about 50 yards behind us — but we were praying for a quicker solution so we could get to Belo that night. I got out and raised the hood of the car. While I was observing this, a drunk man asked me what my problem was. I told him; in his drunken drawl he said, "I think I have an old coil that would get you to Belo Horizonte. My shop is behind the truck stop. I will go get some tools and the coil." I didn't know whether to believe him; for some reason I said I would go with him. Actually the truck stop was an ideal place to stop because it was open 24-hours a day; on the second floor it had rooms for truckers; on the ground floor it had a snack shop, a restaurant, and other stores.

As we walked in front of the first store of the truck stop, two men crossed our path immediately in front of us. One man stuck his key in the door of a car parts store. He opened the door; he and the other man went in. *Wonderful,* I thought. *Maybe he will sell us a new coil.* I asked the mechanic to go in with me. We went into the store and bought a new coil. We all left; he locked the store again. I think God staged that exact day, hour, and moment for us to see God at work. The mechanic went to his shop to get the tools to put a new coil on our car. The gas pump at which we had stopped was not under the truck-stop canopy; therefore we were almost in the dark. I had to use my flashlight to help the mechanic see what he was doing. Since he was under the influence of liquor, several times he dropped his tools down through the engine to the ground. Getting his tool from underneath the car slowed his work, but even this perhaps was God's working, because I had a good chance to talk to him about his misguided spiritual life.

We went on our way and praised God for His wonderful way of blessing us with experiences in times of our utter helplessness. We arrived at the Richardsons about 11 p.m. and apologized for our delay. We had no way to call them and let them know about our problem, but of course they were happy we hadn't been in an accident.

The next day on our way to Serra Negra we had a flat. We hadn't driven far when the spare tire blew out. I was thankful I had two spares, which I often did on long trips.

281

At this annual mission meeting we requested permission to transfer to Belo Horizonte and also approval for me to work as the state stewardship director of Minas. We were approved. Dr. Frank Means, area secretary for South America, was at that meeting. He publicly said something such as this: "I cannot think of anything more exciting and rewarding than Joe Tarry taking the position of state stewardship director for the State of Minas Gerais." His approval of such a move at that time in the development of that great state made me feel sure I had done the right thing.

No Rest for the Weary

I had diminished some responsibilities, but I was amazed at the unexpected things that filled the gap that I thought would give me more time for preparing to leave Valadares. For instance, four days after we returned from mission meeting, we went to our state convention for four days. A week later a couple of new missionaries, Tom and Libby Roebuck, visited our field. We showed them around our city and took them to meet a few pastors and their wives. They stayed only a day and a half. On Tuesday, Manuel of the Altinopolis mission called because his brother had arrived from the country and had a bad case of tuberculosis. Manuel, in whose home we started Altinopolis mission, by now had a three-room house, but the problem was lack of room for his brother to stay without contaminating the whole family. We explained the plan of salvation; the brother accepted Jesus. Twice during the week I took the sick brother to the county clinic. We did not know what we were going to do with him. I and another member went to Manuel's aid; the only solution was to take him to the state hospital for serious cases. I had already done this for a man of Fifth Church, but I had to find out whether this hospital had a place for him. Every day he was weakening.

On Friday of that week I received a call from Geny of the Altinopolis mission. Geny's teen-age daughter had given birth to a boy, but the girl had hepatitis and was near death. Leona and I went immediately to the hospital. This 17-year-old girl had been witnessed to by an aunt, another member of our church, and had attended First Baptist Church some but not the mission. We explained the plan of salvation to her and she accepted Christ.

The next day we received another distress call as I was walking into the house with luggage of missionary couple Dennis and Alita Blackman, who were interested in visiting our field of service. This time the news was that the young mother with hepatitis had died. Leona and I went to the home where the girl's body had been taken; we heard the story of her husband's life. Sr. Gastao had been married three times. His first wife was a Baptist; she lived only 11 months after their marriage. His second wife gave him four children before she died after 15 years of marriage. She had died after four years of battling cancer and only a year and a half before he married his third wife that had just died at 17 years of age. This third wife, Geny's daughter, had been the maid that had been taking care of his children during his second wife's illness. Sr. Gastao had become an atheist because of his many problems.

The next day, Sunday, I showed Dennis and Alita Blackman around the island while Leona prepared dinner. As I was arriving back at our house, Manuel was arriving to tell us that his brother had died. I took him to find a church member to help him get the funeral arrangements made for his brother. Bodies have to be buried within 24 hours because Brazilians don't embalm. Funeral homes are open on Sundays. Manuel didn't know even the first step to be taken for burying a person; I didn't have time to help him much. For the extremely poor the county pays the expenses and gives a very thin coffin made with wooden slats. Soon after dinner I went to conduct the funeral for the young mother, Sr. Gastao's third wife. Leaving the cemetery, I went to Manuel's home to comfort the family and then to our home to show Dennis and Alita around the city. We hurried back home to grab a bite and then on to the island for church training and worship. We had cancelled the evening service at the Palmeiras Mission. The next morning we arose at 4:30 a.m. to take the Blackmans to Belo Horizonte, where they could catch a plane back to language school in Campinas. Neither of these two missionary couples felt led to move to Valadares to replace us.

Returning from Belo Horizonte the next day, Tuesday, I visited Sr. Gastao; he accepted the Lord as his Savior. That very night he went with us to revival services at First Baptist Church. The next night I visited Manuel's sister-in-law, the wife of the man that had died with tuberculosis. She had stayed a few days in Valadares after her husband's funeral. She accepted Jesus as Savior.

One week after the young mother was buried, I was conducting the "Campaign of the Americas" revival at the Altinopolis Mission. While I visited in the hospital, I had met a great-aunt of the young mother who died. The great-aunt was in the service and joyfully accepted Jesus as her Savior.

The Campaign of the Americas Revival on the island was a great success, with 17 decisions for Christ. Some of these were young people. In August we continued to work on getting ready to move.

September was busy as usual with the Bible Institute. The students were suppose to review the material throughout year; then we always spend the first four days reviewing and giving tests on the last year's material. The rest of the month we covered the new material.

God Brings Together the Loose Ends

One loose end was to buy some property for the Palmeiras mission. I never like to buy only one lot, but I found a lot that was unusually large and bought it. I made the down payment plus seven monthly payments of $33 a month. These extra payments were to cover the payments while we were on furlough. Two of Leona's aunts helped provide this money. Over and over again through other people God was providing our needs. The mission in Gonzaga moved into another building that was adequate, but the rent was less. I arranged for Geraldo and his wife to be responsible to go every weekend and conduct services. The last Sunday I went we had 65 people present with some ranchers showing interest. The last time I visited the prisoners in Virginopolis, they were very sad because I wouldn't be seeing them for a year. I assured them that Pastor Wilton Franca of Ninth Baptist Church would be visiting them. I took several good books for them to read.

Unwanted Woes

During August we had a new roof put on our house. This roofing was supposed to be made of better material. We were anxiously waiting for rain, not just to settle the dust of the dry season but also to test our roof. Before we left, we wanted to be sure the mission house had a good roof. In late September we were at the dinner table when an early rain poured down in a torrent. The rain was so hard that suddenly water began pouring into nearly every room of the house. We scrambled to move beds around and to put pans and buckets under the leaks. We couldn't get to all of the leaks fast enough. Water was pouring in on some of my books in the study, on the electric typewriter, and into one of the desk drawers that was partially open. Did we have a reason to be unhappy? Not until five or six days later did the man return to fix the roof. We were glad this wasn't the beginning of the rainy season, when rain sometimes falls for two to three weeks without stopping. Our old leaky roof that the mission had become accustomed to hearing about was not as bad as the new one.

The men created another problem while they were working on the roof. Somehow they had knocked some pieces of plaster into the water box that was over the bathroom (between the roof and ceiling); this stopped up the water pipes. This caused another headache. These things seem to happen during the busiest times.

During the same days, however, we had some good things about which to rejoice. We baptized 10 into the fellowship of our church—eight from one of the missions and two from the island church. I resigned as pastor of the church to be effective on November 17. This was very difficult to do, but we had arrived at another milestone in our lives in which we expected exciting things to continue to happen.

Closing Up and Saying Goodbye

Fifth Baptist Church, Esperanca Baptist Church, Central Baptist Church, First Baptist Church, and the city Women's Missionary Union had special going-away services for us. Brazilians enjoy giving lasting presents; we were given beautiful silver serving trays or bowls with the name of the church and date engraved on them. They truly have lasted; each one carries a memory of those that gave them. We were overwhelmed at their generosity. We were humbled. These programs were difficult for all of us, because we loved the people and the work in Governador Valadares.

The program at Island Baptist was the most difficult. The group wanted to surprise me. They asked Leona to delay the family's arrival at church on the last Sunday night we would be in Valadares to give time for people to arrive. They wanted our arrival to be after dark. I carefully had planned my last sermon for the church. That last Sunday was a very busy day. I went to Altinopolis for early service and then to the island church for the morning worship service. After lunch I went to Gonzaga and passed by Palmeiras on the way back. When I arrived at home, I expected the family to be ready for church. Just as I arrived, Carl was taking a shower. He never has been in a hurry when he gets in the shower; this time he really took a long time. I was frustrated because they always had been ready to leave. Darkness was closing in; I challenged them by saying that by my watch, we already should be at church. They showed me their watches and clocks in the house and proved my watch was wrong. I couldn't believe it! I was getting upset about our arriving late, but they kept thinking of something to delay a little longer. Finally they decided we were late enough; we all got into the car. When we arrived, the church was dark, but many cars were parked in front. I thought the electricity must have gone off. By the number of cars I imagined that the church was packed and, of all things, we were late. As soon as we arrived at the door of the church, the lights were turned on. My anger melted because the church was full and the choir began singing *We'll Never Say Good Bye* (in Portuguese). A light was focused on a big poster which was a painting of the front of the church; in the doorway was a picture of our family. How clever and appropriate! Brazilians are professionals with surprises and praising those whom they love and appreciate. The pulpit was not at the center of the platform but instead five chairs for our family were there. My sister Helen had sent pictures and incidents about my life. Without my knowing it Leona helped them put the program in Portuguese. I wondered why Pastor Samuel de Souza Leite was there. I discovered he had been invited to preach that night. I didn't get to preach that wonderful message of thanks I had planned for the church.

Besides the beautiful silver tray with cobalt blue glasses the island church had a huge white cake with a small Brazilian flag crossing over the small U.S. flag; this symbolized the ties of our two countries with our presence in Brazil. A member of the church had hand made the two flags.

Extra Activities

Carl represented his school in the city Olympic chess tournament and won third place. Now in this busy time the junior chess tournament also was being held; Jonathan was one of four to represent his class. He really wanted to represent the school on the swimming team, but his coach put him in the chess tournament instead.

Moving Day

Moving was sad for the neighborhood kids as well as for ours. The swing on which they had swung so often was gone. For safety purposes I tore down the platform in the *caja mango* tree. They had enjoyed the platform just as much as if it had been a house.

We marked the date for the truck to load up our things to move to Belo. Our poor dog Spit-Spot was so confused. She knew when she saw a suitcase that someone was leaving, but to have boxes all over the house was too much. We had arranged for a couple of the church to stay in the house and look after Spit-Spot. When everything was loaded we couldn't find Spit-Spot. We looked in all the rooms and finally found her inside the boys' closet.

We needed to go to Belo to see that the things were unloaded at the house on Ponte Nova—everything was to go into one bedroom, because Cathryn Smith would stay in the house until we returned from furlough. We returned to Valadares to spend a couple of days with Pastor Jopencil Machado and family of Esperanca Baptist Church. When we returned to the house in Valadares, the kids immediately looked for Spit-Spot. They finally found her in the closet again. We attended Carl's graduation from Polivalente (eighth grade) and the piano recital for all three with D. Dulce. Jonathan completed the sixth at Polivalente and Charlotte completed primary school (fourth grade). We had completed everything and were ready for furlough. We drove to Rio to fly to the States. Our car was given (sold) to the Women's Training School (IBER) for its use.

An Excursion on the Way to the States

In December 1975 our dear friend Ideir Silva dos Santos went to the States with us. We had been friends since our arrival in Valadares in 1966. We planned our trip to stop over first in Manaus. We stayed two days at the mission guest house, across the street from Lonnie and Janelle Doyle. Manaus is situated near the area in which the Negro River meets the Amazon River. We took a boat trip up the Amazon River, ate in a floating restaurant, and visited the area in which the Negro River meets the Amazon River. After we visited the famous areas of Manaus, we flew to Bogota, Colombia, and spent three days visiting the Baptist work and other interesting sights. From there we flew to Clovis, NM, to spend Christmas in Portales.

Chapter 15

1976—An Amazing Furlough Year

On furloughs God always had wonderful surprises for us. We learned that we never were to guess what the next furlough might be like, because God always blessed us. The United States Bicentennial year was far more exciting than we could have imagined.

We arrived in the states just before Christmas 1975. A Brazilian friend, Ideir Silva dos Santos, was to spend six months with us. Ideir never had seen a winter in which all non-evergreen trees looked "dead". We planned to rent a house in Portales, but after three months on the farm with Mr. and Mrs. Isbell we still hadn't found a place. The farmhouse was crowded with Tony and Irma, our family of five, and Ideir. Leona had grown up in Portales and knew that Mrs. South, a member of First Baptist Church, had a real-estate business. Leona called to see whether Mrs. South had any houses available for rent. Mrs. South had retired but said she would see what she could do. She called back later and offered to sell us her own house at a good deal. Since we had no money for a down-payment and had no credit rating, the bank would loan us only part of the money. Mrs. South agreed to carry the rest of the loan at seven-percent interest, whereas the bank interest was 10 percent. This turned out to be a good deal, because being in a university town and with a military base near, through the years we never had problems keeping it rented. In 1979 we lived in it again.

Leona and I had many opportunities to speak about our work in Brazil. Leona participated in three world mission conferences and went to Glorieta with Ideir for an Acteen mission conference (teenage girls). One of our opportunities was a church in Phoenix, AZ. Ideir was surprised when we drove down into the valley of Phoenix and saw the grass and trees so green. What a change in scenery!

I had eight week-long speaking engagements in six states and spoke in 90 different churches. Leona and I had the opportunity of being responsible for the foreign-mission booth at the New Mexico Baptist State Convention in Carlsbad. I also had the privilege of being one of the main speakers at the New Mexico Baptist State Women's Missionary Union Convention.

Our Trip East

As soon as school was out for the summer, we loaded the car and headed east. Our first goal was Washington, D.C., to visit with our Lovington friends, U.S. Representative Harold and Dorothy Runnels. During my last year in college and the year in Maxwell, NM. Harold helped me financially. Their New Mexico home was a block from my dad's home in Lovington. What a blessing to be able to stay in their Arlington home for three days and nights as they were staying in another house outside of Washington. Harold took us to a noon meal in the Congressional Dining Hall and presented us to the other New Mexico congressmen. He gave us a royal tour through the Capitol building and the legislative room in which congress meets to make decisions. We stood in the place in which the President of the United States makes his speeches to congress. We had our pictures made with Harold on the steps of the Capitol. Harold also got tickets for us to visit the White House. All this was a wonderful experience.

Since this was the Bicentennial Year, crowds of people were everywhere. We were in line going up the steps of the White House when to our surprise we met Bernard and Margaret Dougharty descending. We had known the Doughartys since 1957 when he was associational director (DOM) of Northeastern Association and I was pastor in Maxwell. When Margaret saw us, she pointed her finger and said in a loud voice, "You look just like Joe Tarry." I was shocked and replied, "Well, I am Joe Tarry." That was a pleasant surprise to meet familiar faces in a crowd of thousands so far from home. We also visited the Lincoln Monument, the Washington Monument, Kennedy's Eternal Flame, and a small part of the Smithsonian Institute.

By this time six busy months had passed since our arrival in the States; the time had arrived for Ideir to leave. We took her to the

Washington airport for her to fly back to Brazil.

From Washington we went to a five-day meeting for furloughing missionaries and families by the FMB at a camp near Lynchburg, VA.

Leona's cousin Clyde Redus was stationed at the Norfolk Naval Base; we visited him and his family. Clyde was a navigator on a plane that had flown many missions in Vietnam. Clyde took us to see his plane and even let the kids sit in the cockpit. His kids were about the same ages as ours, so our kids stayed with them while we went to the Southern Baptist Convention at Norfolk, VA. Later we took Clyde's daughter, Mindy, with us to visit Williamsburg. What a history-filled day!

From Norfolk we stayed a couple of days in Baltimore, MD, with Leona's cousins, Ken and Maudine Saunier, and family. From Baltimore we went to Boston, MA, to visit my Uncle John and Aunt Hattie Sheriff. Our children had been weak in American history, but this trip taught them more than if they had been studying books, since they actually saw some of the most famous historical sites. They took us to see the church from which Paul Revere started his famous ride. We saw the ship *Constitution* and then went to Bunker Hill. We went into the country to the spot on which the first shot of the Revolutionary War was fired. Time didn't allow us to see all that we wanted. We had to hurry our trip, because in the last week in June both of us were scheduled to be the missionaries for a week in G.A. and R.A. camps in Alabama.

We spent only one night in New York City. We arrived at our hotel about 3 p.m. and were given directions how to catch the subway that would get us to the ferry that took visitors to the Statue of Liberty. At the Statue of Liberty we climbed the inside stairs to the head of the statue. We had a wonderful view.

As we returned to downtown New York City, someone on the subway suggested we see the city at sunset from the top of the Empire State Building. So we hurried to get to the top of that building just before the city lights were turned on. The next day we drove back to Baltimore for a couple of days before we left for Philadelphia.

In Philadelphia we were able to see the Liberty Bell and the building in which the American Constitution was written. From Philadelphia we went to Huntsville, AL, for two nights to visit a family that was related to a sister-in-law. The husband worked at the NASA Space center in Huntsville, so we saw the areas designated for tourists.

I was the missionary speaker for the Royal Ambassadors (mission organization for boys) and Leona for the Girls Auxiliary (mission organization) camps in Alabama. Since both of us were from the West, we considered that God had blessed us with this opportunity to speak for these two camps in the southeastern part of the U.S. Leona and Charlotte had a special treat at the girls' camp. Albert and Thelma Bagby, whom our children had not met, were retired missionaries to Brazil and now spent their summers at the camp. Albert was the son of the pioneer missionaries that started the Southern Baptist work in Brazil. This visit with the Bagbys blessed Leona and Charlotte, because the couple had many stories to tell. We left on Saturday morning, July 3, for Clinton, MS.

We planned to be at Marjean Patterson's home in Clinton, MS, on Saturday afternoon of July 3 so we could go to church with her on Sunday, July 4. We had met Marjean, Mississippi's WMU state leader, in Belo Horizonte in 1975 when she was visiting Mattie Lou Bible. We told her we were scheduled to be in Alabama, so she insisted that we plan to stay with her for July 4. When we arrived at her home, a note was on the door for us to get the house key at a neighbor's home. The neighbor explained that one of Marjean's dearest friends had died and that she had to leave, but she wanted us to make ourselves at home. We believed this was a strange situation, but we were so glad to have her nice home in which to stay. All day rain had fallen on us; that made for a tiring trip.

Sunday morning we went to First Baptist Church in Clinton, at which Marjean was a member. In the men's Sunday school class one man mentioned that he had gone early to the post office in Jackson to get a special stamp put on some $2 bills. For some reason I had bought five new $2 bills in New Mexico, one for each of the family, and I had them with me. The man told me that the post office would be open until 1 p.m. for the purpose of selling the special Bicentennial stamps.

The people at First Baptist were very nice to us and made us feel at home. That morning we heard beautiful patriotic music and a great message. Along with many other bells throughout the nation the church bells were rung for several minutes at noon. We were invited to eat the special Fourth of July meal at the church. We hurried through the meal so we would have time to get to the Jackson main post office to get the special stamps on the $2 bills. Jackson is very close to Clinton; we arrived at the post office just a few minutes before closing time. We returned to Marjean's house, where we enjoyed, from her nice, big, color TV, watching hours of Bicentennial celebrations throughout the United States. From Clinton we stopped in Dallas at Leona's brother's house before we returned to New Mexico.

Later we drove to Barstow, CA, to visit my sister and brother-in-law, Helen and Tom Hare. They took us to Disneyland. We literally had been from Boston on the East Coast across the States to Los Angeles on the West Coast. We shared our Brazil experiences with the Hares' church, First Baptist Church of Barstow. We also visited First Baptist Church in Porterville, in which we had lived and worked before we went to Brazil.

In the fall, deer-hunting season was a highlight of the year for Tony, Leona's dad. He began preparing with his group for camping out in the mountains near Mayhill, NM. Carl, Jonathan, and I were excited about this trip. The boys took a hunting course offered by the county rifle association; the course was necessary to get their first hunting licenses. When we lived at Maxwell, I had killed a deer, but this year I didn't get one. Tony nearly always killed a deer. He made steaks from the best cuts and the best chili con carne from most of the rest of the meat.

Three years later Jonathan and I went with Tony and his hunting buddies on our second hunting trip. Carl was studying at Hardin-Simmons University and wasn't able to go. That year we camped near Cloudcroft, NM. One night a fierce wind hit; it almost blew the big tent down. After the windstorm, a foot of snow fell; it made the trip a real hunting experience. The storm also reached Portales; Irma was staying with Leona and Charlotte in town. Jonathan had the thrill of shooting at a deer, even if he didn't kill it.

Furlough Homelife

For MK's to adjust in the Stateside schools is difficult. The kids know they are there for a short time; usually they don't know any other students, so they must make new friends. Making new friends is difficult; for teen-agers breaking into the "gang" is even more difficult. Charlotte didn't have that problem later, because she did all her high-school work in Belo. We tried to furlough in locations in which our kids, from past furloughs, knew others their age. The boys were able to get "into the crowd" because of the chess teams. Through the church and school Charlotte had friends that she had made during our first stay in Portales. We felt as though our youngsters fit in with their crowd and enjoyed the months in the States. Our children made good grades in the Stateside schools. In an exceptional fashion they made adjustments from Brazilian schooling; we were very happy about this. On the first furlough they had only eight weeks of American school. Besides all three making excellent grades, in the sixth grade Charlotte won first-place prize on her science-fair project. She did have a little supervision from her Uncle Alton. Carl moved up to the third board on the varsity chess team; Jonathan made the junior-varsity chess team.

All three studied piano with Eunice Schumpert in Portales. They had opportunities to get a little farming experience by riding the tractor and with their Grandfather Isbell seeing firsthand the irrigation system. The three were able to do the fall semester in Portales—Carl in the 10th, Jonathan the eighth, and Charlotte the sixth grade. When we arrived back in Belo, Carl and Jonathan enrolled in the American school and Charlotte enrolled in the Baptist school in front of our house.

Our Return to Brazil

I had visited the Tampa Bay Baptist Association for a world-missions conference. Northside Baptist Church of Ruskin, FL, wanted to sponsor our family and invited us to stop by so the church could meet the whole family on our way back to Brazil. At the Miami airport the pastor met us in a van. Our luggage, however, didn't arrive with us, so we went to Ruskin with only our carry-on baggage. We were glad we weren't leaving for Brazil that night without our luggage. We had a wonderful time meeting the church family. Their adoption of us as their missionaries consisted of sending us special cards on all of our birthdays, our wedding anniversary, and other special times of the year. The next day we were thankful to receive our luggage in Ruskin. We learned we always should put in our carry-on baggage pajamas, a change of clothes, and other necessities.

Most airline flights for Brazil or returning to the U.S. usually left about 11 p.m. By the time the plane reached 36,000 feet, the flight attendants brought hot, wet hand towels for passengers to clean their hands. Soon after the towels were taken up by the attendants, a big two-course meal was served. We always enjoyed those delicious meals. After the meal one could choose to watch a movie or sleep. On this return flight I did not even try to sleep because I was too overwhelmed by the number of events that God had put together for us. On a plane sleep always was difficult for me anyway. The year's furlough made possible a visit with all our siblings and their families. We now were entering a big change in our ministry—a responsibility in the whole state of Minas Gerais. A move to Belo Horizonte, third-largest city of Brazil, would take some time for adaptation.

Chapter 16

1977—Our Missionary Career Changes

Oh, the depth of the riches both of the wisdom and knowledge of God! How unsearchable are His judgments and unfathomable His ways! For who has known the mind of the Lord, or who has become His counselor? Or who has first given to Him that it might be paid back to Him again? For from Him and through Him and to Him are all things. To Him be the glory forever, Amen (Rom. 11:33-36).

Ready for Another Term

On Friday, December 30, 1976, we arrived in Rio de Janeiro. Missionaries Don and Barbara Laing met us at the airport and told us to start praying about our crate, because the government had just passed a new customs law putting a limit of $300 per family unit. We discovered that inflation in Brazil was 46 percent per month.

The next morning at 10 I was at a Chevrolet car dealer's to buy a new car. I really didn't expect to buy a car that day, because everything closed at 1 p.m. on Saturdays. To my amazement the dealer prepared all of the paperwork by noon; I drove away in a new Chevrolet Opala, made in Brazil. The car was similar to the Chevrolet Nova. The car cost $5,000 but without any extras; it did not even have a radio, because the mission didn't pay for any extras.

We spent New Year's Day with the Laing family. Charlotte enjoyed playing with Deretha and Sonia; they were about the same ages. The boys played with Paul, even though he was a little older. Jan was older than all of them, so she entertained herself or helped her mom. Our families had a lot in common and enjoyed the fellowship together.

Don was supervisor of the print shop for the Baptist Publishing House. At the time of our arrival he also was the interim pastor at the English-speaking Baptist Church in Rio de Janeiro. Don asked me to preach the following Sunday morning at International Baptist Church. Sunday night I interpreted for a pastor from Alabama in Niteroi. I quickly realized that after a year away from Brazil, I was rusty in Portuguese. On Tuesday, January 3, we left for Belo Horizonte, our new home.

Belo Horizonte, meaning *beautiful horizon*, was the third-largest city in Brazil; in 1977 it had about 1.8 million people. We dreaded moving to Belo Horizonte because of the traffic. The traffic circles caused a lot of congestion. Belo Horizonte was patterned after Washington D.C. The streets run like spokes from a hub; they angle off from the downtown area. If you started off on a wrong street, soon you could be far away from the place in which you wanted to go. Belo is mountainous and is nestled at the base of a large mountain range similar to the Sandia Mountain Range at Albuquerque, NM. The mountain range that overshadows Belo is composed mostly of high-grade iron ore. Because so much iron ore is in other mountains in Minas Gerais, no economical need exists to scar or destroy that beautiful mountain range by mining the ore. On the other side of the mountain range is the deepest shaft gold mine in the world.

Water, Water, Everywhere!
We arrived in Belo right in the middle of the rainy season. This was not a good time to arrive! That year Belo experienced the worst floods in 30 years. The river that divides the center of the city from the high hill on which we lived overflowed and entered hundreds of businesses and hotels. Many other neighborhoods in Belo as well as many other towns in Minas Gerais were underwater. Rain fell for two weeks without stopping. We had seen rain fall for three weeks at a time with only occasionally relaxing to just sprinkles for short periods but nothing like the downpours of this year. When the rains are gentle, the danger of floods isn't so great, but when rain pours, the rivers flood.

The American School

The American School began in a house and basically was begun for missionary kids. Southern Baptists had the largest group of kids, but other denominations increased the need to enlarge the school. Finally a Church of Christ family purchased land on the outskirts of the city; the school bought a piece of property next to this family's home. When we moved to Belo, the school was operating in a new building at its new location. About 150 students from kindergarten through 12th grade were enrolled. The American School really is an international school, run on the American system, with students from United States, Japan, Australia, Great Britain, South Africa, Bangladesh, and Brazil. The administrator and the teachers are Americans, except the teacher of Portuguese was Brazilian. Carl enrolled in the 10th grade and Jonathan in the eighth grade. The boys caught a special bus at 7 a.m. and arrived at home about 5:30 p.m., when they had sports practice three times a week. Being an international school this school was highly competitive; a lot of homework was given. Charlotte completed sixth and seventh grades in the Baptist school across the street. From 7 until 11:30 she attended the morning session. Her two more difficult courses were Portuguese grammar and math.

Finding a Church Home

Since our kids had been only in small-church situations, we thought they might like being in a larger church that had better facilities for youth. We wanted them to enjoy church and not rebel against their parents' being full-time church workers. So we visited some of the larger churches. Starting missions and growing them into churches was very difficult; I was hoping we could settle into a well-organized church. But God arranged a situation that would weigh heavily in our decision about where to serve Him.

Missionary Cathryn Smith asked us to visit an exciting mission that her church sponsored. First Baptist Church in the São Benedito neighborhood, in the extreme northern edge of Belo Horizonte, was one of the mother churches that started Planalto mission. Soon after we arrived in Belo, I was invited to be pastor for the Royal Ambassador Camp. We had only one car, so Cathryn offered to take

Leona and Charlotte to visit their mission on Sunday while the boys and I were at camp. The camp had 120 boys; two brothers were friendlier to Carl and Jonathan than the others were. When we returned home, Leona and Charlotte were very excited about the Planalto mission. To top this off, that Sunday was Leona's birthday; the mission surprised her with a bouquet of flowers. Of course Cathryn had planned that surprise. The next Sunday our family went to the Planalto mission; to our surprise the two friendly boys at camp belonged to that mission.

The Planalto mission met in one small storeroom in a building that had a much larger storeroom on the ground floor and two apartments on the second floor. The small room was crowded with about 50 people. Can you imagine having Sunday school with classes for adults, young people, school-age children, and the little ones all in the same room? Everyone was very excited that our family was visiting. After the service the people there gave me an invitation to serve as their pastor. I didn't want to be the pastor, because I was supposed to work in the whole state in stewardship. I knew a mission would take a lot of time and effort to growing it into a church, finding a lot and raising money to build, getting a blueprint drawn up and approved, and the many other details and problems. Most missions also had several people who needed special help.

The Planalto mission impressed me, however, because it already had some good leadership and well-qualified teachers plus the help of a seminary student. The mission already had the mission organizations for all ages. The Planalto mission was unique and not the same as other missions we had started with all new Christians that needed training. Three churches that had members living in or near the Planalto neighborhood had joined together to start this mission. The Planalto mission wanted a response from me as soon as possible. I knew that Leona and Charlotte believed God was in this proposal. An idea entered my mind: "I will put out the fleece! If these people are sincere, I will challenge them. If they accept, I will accept." The challenge to them was if they would rent the larger store space, I would accept. I didn't tell them this, but I hinted when I asked them why they hadn't already rented the larger store space since they were so crowded. I put out the fleece and tested them and also searched to know

299

what God wanted me to do. I told them I would give them my answer the next Sunday.

By the next Sunday the people at the mission had rented the larger store space, so I accepted. I believed this was God's answer for me. The Planalto mission had started in October 1976 in Nair de Maria's garage a few blocks away. It soon moved to the little store space, about 15-feet-by-20-feet in size, in which it was meeting. Then seven months later the mission had a room that would seat about 120 people. Seven people were waiting baptism; soon six more converts were added to them. All the Sunday-school classes, except the children's class, which remained in the smaller area, met in the larger area.

Another aspect that excited me about this mission was that *Planalto* (which means *high plains*) was situated in a middle-to-upper-middle class neighborhood. The rent was equivalent to $275 a month, a big increase. In this neighborhood the price of a lot ranged from $10,000 to $18,000. Leona was a real asset in the area of music. She used her accordion, which helped make the singing more vibrant.

My plan was to give two weeks a month to the church, make one long week trip each month, and on another Sunday visit two churches nearby to promote stewardship. At the time Brazil was rationing gasoline, so no gasoline was sold on Saturday or Sunday. One could not travel more than 250 miles on a 40-liter gas tank. I soon did what some other people did, which was sort of illegal. I had another 40-liter tank put on top of the original tank inside the luggage compartment. This gave me the capability to travel about 500 miles.

The Terrinha Family

The two brothers that befriended Carl and Jonathan at R.A. camp were Luiz Paulo and Marcos Terrinha. They had two sisters that became friends with Charlotte. Their mother, Nely, was not in good health but was very active in church. Their father, Amelio, worked as a painter but was an alcoholic. He was very nice when sober but very abusive when drunk. Nely was an extremely talented person and, through arts and crafts she made, helped supply food and clothes for the family. She didn't have a high-school degree but was a very good teacher and also counselor. Perhaps because she was converted through the work of the Baptist Women, she was a strong leader for the mission organizations. One important activity group carried out by the Baptist Women is the Baby Roll. When one of her babies was born, the Baby Roll leader of a church near Nely's home asked whether the group could conduct a baby service for Nely in her home. Because of this home service Nely accepted and was saved.

Woes Over the Problem at the Customs House

Jesus said: "*Do not lay up for yourselves treasures upon earth, where moth and rust destroy, and where thieves break in and steal. But lay up for yourselves treasures in heaven, where neither moth nor rust destroys, and where thieves do not break in or steal; for where your treasure is, there will your heart be also. The lamp of the body is the eye; if therefore your eye is clear, your whole body will be full of light. But if your eye is bad, your whole body will be full of darkness. If therefore the light that is in you is darkness, how great is the darkness! No one can serve two masters; for either he will hate the one and love the other, or he will hold to one and despise the other. You cannot serve God and mammon*" (Mt. 6:19-14). This advice from our Lord reminded us to put the spiritual things higher than the physical. In mid-December we had put several electrical household items in a crate to be shipped to New Orleans and then transported by ship to Brazil. On December 23 Brazil passed a new law that allowed only $300 per process of imported electrical things to enter the country duty free. That meant a family of five would be allowed only $300 of duty-free items. The law, like many laws in Brazil, went into effect immediately and without warning.

We had brought about $2,000 of items that would last us for years and would modernize our life considerably. We could do without the electrical items, but we did want them. If the customs officials felt as though the law was being abused, they could confiscate what they wanted and sell them at an auction. I went to the customs house myself to see about our household things. After the customs woman finished examining our crate, she said that because of the new law she couldn't release any items. Missionary Fred Hawkins and I went to the sub-inspector general of the customs house. He felt as though the new law was unjust, especially because our things were in New Orleans for shipment before the new law was passed. He seemed to be very sorry for us but couldn't release our household items.

I went home and asked the other missionaries to pray for us. We also sent word to friends in the U.S. to pray about our situation. We had brought our limit of cubic footage of clothes, Christmas presents, and electrical things. How would we ever choose which items worth $300 dollars would be the best thing for us? If customs wanted to charge import fees on the shipment, what could we afford to pay? With the Lord working on the situation, the South Brazil mission lawyer and Fred Hawkins finally got everything out of customs just under the three months' limit.

Saudade—A Difficult Word to Describe

Saudade is a Portuguese word that has no equal in English. This word expresses a longing with sadness and emotion. Every time I returned to Governador Valadares in which we lived the first 10 years, I felt this mixture of lonesomeness, love with sadness, and joyful emotion, which caused the aspect of longing. I felt some sadness because we had been called to another place and missed the people we had loved. But I felt joyful emotion because our experience had been positive and a blessing that we had so many people that equally blessed our lives. They were so appreciative that we almost cried when they hugged us and expressed their *saudades* for us.

Frequently I returned to Valadares. The house in which we had lived had to have some repairs so it could be sold. Also I needed to make payments on the lot we were buying for Palmeiras mission, which was still meeting under the trees in a yard. Although the island church had a pastor, I needed to help him get ready to build at the Altinopolis mission. A man had given a lot to the Altinopolis mission, but the document was in my name. Three new pastors were in the city, so I met with all of the pastors and presented them a plan for entering the new neighborhoods as soon as they began to develop.

A Great Disappointment

My heart was broken because of the attitude the new pastor of the island church had about the Gonzaga mission. While we were in the States, I had sent money to the church to pay for Geraldo and his wife to go to Gonzaga each weekend and to spiritually nurture the young

Christians. The pastor had stopped them from going to Gonzaga; I presume he used the money. I believed he didn't want to go outside the city to occasionally visit that mission. He seemed to believe the Altinopolis and Palmeiras missions were all he could manage other than the island church. I expressed my dismay about his attitude; I said, "But pastor, you had no reason to stop Geraldo and his wife from going to Gonzaga! They were capable of taking care of that congregation!" That was the end of Baptist work in Gonzaga for a while, but I couldn't forget about that village. In a short time that group of people could have been an organized church.

An Exciting Experience

One day I took missionary Cathryn Smith's car to a garage to have an electrical problem resolved. I couldn't keep from noticing the many poster girls on the walls; some were practically nude. Just before I wrote out the check for the car repair, I told the owner that if Cathryn Smith had brought her car into his shop, she would have been very embarrassed about those poster girls on the walls. Very few Brazilian women drove cars in those days, so he didn't have much to worry about a woman entering his shop. I also told him that I was offended since I was a missionary. The mission's general mechanic had recommended that I take Cathryn's car to him for electrical problems. I would like to recommend his shop to other missionaries.

When I finished writing out the check, he noticed that I signed it in name of the South Brazil Baptist mission. He asked me whether I was connected to the Baptist school. I said, "No, but I live across the street from the school." He excitedly told me that he had five children; all were or had been in the school. He excitedly called two of his sons that were working with him and presented me to them. He explained that just a few days before, his 16-year-old daughter Rosangela had been converted in a religious assembly at the school. Before her conversion she was very rebellious, treated her younger brother and sister rudely, and brought great concern to her parents because of her actions. He explained that they were Roman Catholics and had given careful attention to their home life. Suddenly Rosangela had completely changed. Now she was bubbling with affection for all of the family. She told them about her beautiful experience with Jesus. Her attitude about life had changed.

After he told me about Rosangela, he told me that he was a good man. The family members attended church often and lived good, moral lives. But he asked me: "What else do I need to do to be saved?" I was happy to tell him; he was grateful. He invited me to return and visit with him.

The next Sunday, just after our noon meal, Rosangela called to invite our family to their home for a *culto*, or home worship service, to be held at 3 p.m. The young people of Grace Baptist Church were to direct the service. Leona and I went; also the director of the Baptist School and member of Grace Church attended the service. They insisted that I bring the message. After the message I gave an invitation; Rosangela's father and mother accepted the Lord. We went back two times to answer their questions. The next time I was in the electrical shop, I noticed that the nude posters had been removed from the walls. During the next 20 years I took automobiles to that shop for electrical repairs. The aging grandparents, being firm Roman Catholics, harassed the family members because of their evangelical decision, so by the time we left Brazil they had not broken completely away from their Roman Catholic ties. A great loss occurred to the family one day when one of the adult sons died unexpectedly. I believe, however, as I often have seen, they will make the change after the death of their aging parents.

Some Christians are afraid to say things such as I said about the pin-up pictures on the electrical mechanic's walls. I took a long time to have the courage to make such statements, but I felt as though I was doing this for the sake of his business and also God's sake. The Holy Spirit leads in guiding Christians to say things that elevate spiritual principles above secular principles. In his letter to the Romans the apostle Paul said: *For I am not ashamed of the gospel, for it is the power of God for salvation to everyone who believes, to the Jew first and also to the Greek* (Rom. 1:16).

A Heart-Rending Plea

One day our doorbell rang. As I opened the door, I was surprised to see the rancher Jose from Gonzaga. I invited him in and wondered how he had found my address. He had made the trip to Belo to beg me to return to Gonzaga occasionally to reestablish the mission. He reminded me that he would sell a lot near his house in Gonzaga for the mission. He also reminded me that he was a Presbyterian but would be glad to become a Baptist if I would return to reopen the mission. To make the case more urgent he reminded me that under my preaching his three teen-agers had accepted Christ; they needed spiritual guidance. This was a very difficult decision to make. He had taken the effort to travel all the way to Belo for this purpose. *What could I do?* About half of the distance from Belo to Gonzaga was dirt and would take six hours to make the trip one way. I finally told him that I would not be able to help Gonzaga personally, but I hoped that the association would soon be able to help them. He left a burden in my heart. At every opportunity I pressed the Central Sweet River Association to reopen work in Gonzaga, which it did.

Filling in for Another

September was the month for the Bible institute in Governador Valadares. During the furlough of Dr. Bill Richardson I was requested to direct this year. Bill had directed it for about 10 years. Leona and I always had taught classes. However, not living in Valadares made a different situation. I stayed in a cheap hotel on the same block as First Baptist Church.

The administration of the institute involved more than I had expected. The first three days the students, mostly older men, reviewed the material studied the year before. They all had the syllabi from the previous year; each had been given 50 questions to answer from their study material, from which the questions of the final exam were taken. A graduation service was held for those finishing the four-year course after the final exams. After the final exams were taken, the rest of the month was spent on the study of the new material (new syllabus).

The institute was the highlight for these men and a few women. Some hadn't finished more than the fourth grade. They were eager to learn, although some didn't read very well. Most of them, however, were good singers. They loved to sing into the night; the harmony was beautiful. I wish you could have heard them. They joked a lot, but most of the time they were praising the Lord. Jeronimo arrived three days late this year because he had been sick. He was an amazing man at 64 years and was very skinny. He was a beloved lay-preacher that served a country church. On an old typewriter he had pecked out the answers to the homework questions. He was one of the most loving, considerate, gracious, and humble humans I have ever known. He had to walk about 18 miles to visit some of his members. People such as him remind me about something Jesus said: *"But the greatest among you shall be your servant. And whoever exalts himself shall be humbled; and whoever humbles himself shall be exalted"* (Mt. 23:11-12).

The good side of spending the month in Valadares was that I could finish some things that I had left undone before we moved. I noticed new neighborhoods were springing up all around the city. I have mentioned about selling the mission house. An empty house always needs attention. Also I wanted to help get the construction started on the Palmeiras mission, for much of the money passed through us. The island church insisted that I be on the building committee. So we drew the plans and prepared the way for building. I visited people in the churches and missions we had started.

I acquired a 16mm movie projector that a man from Ninth Baptist Church was giving to our state Baptist board to be used in the leper colony on the outskirts of Belo Horizonte. Baptists had a church in the colony.

A Vision for New Neighborhoods in Belo
In the capital city of Belo Horizonte many new neighborhoods were developing. Every month by the thousands people were moving from the country to the city. Living just a few blocks from the center of the downtown area, I went almost daily into the heart of Belo. My main reason was to pick up our mail at the post office, but I usually needed something else, also. I noticed men on the streets with handouts about new neighborhoods opening or about to be developed. In one year I collected 75 handouts about new neighborhoods.

In Valadares I had discovered that a down-payment and monthly payments on property were cheap. Also I learned that once a new development had electricity, water, and sewer, the price for the lots was several times higher. One day at a pastors' meeting of the Central Baptist Association in Belo I informed them of how many new neighborhood developments had been launched in the past 12 months. They were amazed! They made me the chairperson of a committee of pastors and laypeople to devise a plan to start buying properties in new developments. Because of the lack of enough pastors laymen were used as leaders in many of our churches.

This committee designed the Barnabas Plan. Besides the 75 new developments, the city already had 185 neighborhoods (called *Bairros*) without a Baptist church or mission. Just to buy a lot in these outer neighborhoods cost from $8,000 to $12,000; closer into the center of the city it cost up to $50,000 to $60,000. If we could just keep up with the new neighborhoods, in a short time we would experience a tremendous growth. Another thing all the pastors knew was that residents in new neighborhoods are more easily interested in their spiritual lives than are those in the older, established neighborhoods. The newer developments often are occupied by poorer people, who are moving from the country and small towns to larger cities. They have left their parents and their traditional ways and seek the answers of a better life spiritually as well as physically. Family ties and traditions often keep people from leaving their traditional church and accepting a new one.

I will not give the details of the Barnabas Plan, because the plan didn't get off the ground. Most of the churches were struggling to make their own buildings adequate and to pay a decent salary to their pastors. Most of the pastors didn't receive adequate salaries, but the convention helped them because their children didn't have to pay tuition at the Baptist school. The majority of the students at the Baptist school was Roman Catholic, as in the case of the electrical mechanic I wrote about, who proudly informed me that he sent his children to the Baptist school. Hundreds of other Roman Catholic parents sent their children to the Baptist school instead of Roman Catholic parochial schools because the Baptist school had such high educational standards. Although the Roman Catholic schools were good, the Baptist school had the best reputation for academics and discipline.

Although the Barnabas Plan was premature for its time, the pastors became aware of the harvest fields surrounding the city. As a pilot project I convinced two men to join me in buying three joining lots in one of the new neighborhoods. Jadyr Elon Braga and Paulo Popov were members of First Baptist Church in Belo; their church later started a mission on those lots. About 15 years later that neighborhood had become a very prosperous neighborhood.

Renewed Interest in the Baptist Men's Mission Organization

Some isolated groups of men that organized to promote fellowship and missions were scattered throughout Brazil. These organized because of the success of the strong Women's Missionary Organization, but not as much interest existed among most of the men. In the 1940s Pastor Francisco Nascimento organized the men on a national level, but his dream had fizzled out. In 1963 the Department of Baptist Men in Missions was organized again on the national level. This was accomplished by American missionary Alvin Hatton, but this also didn't last. Alvin also organized the Royal Ambassadors (*Embaixadores do Rei*), which translates as "Ambassadors of the King" for boys. The R.A. organization has continued to be strong. Then in 1978 some men again pushed for a reorganization of the men's work. I was asked to promote the third Pan American Layman's Congress in our state of Minas Gerais. This congress was to be held in Niteroi, State of Rio de Janeiro. To promote this I met with some men in the Central Baptist Association in Belo. This led to the organization of Baptist Men in that association. I hoped they would be an integral part of making the Barnabas Plan work. I also was interested in getting the men organized so they would help support the boys' mission organization, Royal Ambassadors. For four years I had been involved in the state R.A. camps; only two pastors had supported the boys' organization.

Long Bank Lines

All countries have ways to do things that make a person impatient. To stand in long bank lines of up to 20 people was difficult for me to accept. Every bank in this large city always was busy. Depending on the bill, electric, water/sewer bills, taxes, and most other bills had to be paid at a state or federal bank. I usually took a book or magazine to read. On the other hand I had plenty of time to get to know the person in front or behind me in the lines. During those frustrating occasions we found a way to spread the Good News, because everywhere we went, we always carried gospel tracts to hand out or leave.

Paying the bills became more complicated when we believed the amount on the bill was incorrect. The company always charged the equivalent of $15 or more for going over the basic limit. If I took the time to make the trip across town and spend an hour or two waiting in line to challenge the electric or water bills, the company usually gave me a refund. However, on the first trip I made to complain about the water bill, I had to return home and read the meter, then take the meter reading back to the company and wait again. I learned to take the meter reading, whether for water or electricity, with me every time I had a problem.

Time to Marvel about the Past

In October of 1977 I made one of my longest and loneliest trips of the year. I spent nearly two weeks visiting 17 churches. Most of these churches were weak in their participation in the Cooperative Program. The trip was good, but at nights I had a lot of time alone to reflect on my family and my life.

Many times I marveled at all that had happened in my life. When my mother died late in October 1942, my father moved the family to Lovington, a small town of about 3,000 people. Lovington was the county seat of Lea County, a farm and ranch community. Hobbs, 21 miles southeast, had grown more because of oil that was abundant all the way to New Mexico's eastern and southern borders with Texas. All of this area is flat country; the southern part of the county mostly is sand hills. The only trees anywhere were those that pioneers had planted in the area.

Our new home in Lovington was situated at the south end of town. We had a windmill, an outhouse, and plenty of space, because the block on which we lived was vacant except for the house Daddy bought. Daddy had bought three lots; one was a corner lot. The block east and south of us had no houses; only one house was on the block to the north. Therefore, these vacant lots became useful in providing grass for our cow.

My father had promised my mother that he would keep us together. His mother, our Grandma Tarry, lived with us since Grandpa Tarry died about two years before Mama died. I later admired my Grandma Tarry, for without complaining she accepted the responsibility of helping our family. By the time we moved to Lovington, Tommy (we called him "Skeeter") was 9-months old, Margaret 5, I was 7, Helen was 9, and Bill was 10. As soon as spring arrived, Daddy went back and forth to prepare the farm for another year's crop. When school was out, we all went back to the farm for that summer. After the fall harvest in 1944 Daddy sold the farm and all but one cow, some pigs, chickens, and our cat that he brought to town. He also brought the bundles of dried maize for the cow, dried corn for the pigs, and grain for the chickens. We lived on the edge of town, but I am sure that some people didn't appreciate the animals in the city limits. Daddy's first job in town was as janitor at the Lea County Courthouse. Daddy was doing the best he could.

Soon after we moved to Lovington, Bill and I went to First Baptist Church. I am sure Daddy was still grieving, or he would have taken us the first Sunday. First Baptist Church met in a basement, which was the first stage of a much larger building that the church planned to build. I remember the Sunday-school teacher was very friendly. Soon my father and the rest of the family were attending regular worship services morning and night. I think this was partly because of Mother's fervent prayers for the family before she died. On the other hand Daddy realized that he needed God's help in rearing five children. Both Mother and Daddy had been active in the Plainview country church.

A few days after we returned to town from the summer on the farm, our cat disappeared. About two weeks later, my uncle who was living on grandma's farm that joined ours told us that our cat, old Tom, had returned to the farm. The farm was 12 miles from Lovington. We knew that dogs at even great distances had the instinct to find their way back to their natural habitats, but we had no idea that our cat could do such a thing. Old Tom was brought back to town and soon adapted.

Our New Home and Surroundings

Daddy brought the big black kettle that had been used to make lye soap and to heat water to scald the pigs before he butchered them. Grandma used that kettle to make lye soap for washing dishes and our clothes. The house had the modern commodities of electricity and natural gas. Our house was 10 blocks south of the school and about 10 blocks from the center of town. Especially on cold and snowy days this seemed like a long way.

During the winter the water barrel froze with thick ice. During the summer mosquitoes found places to breed, but the worst thing was the flies. Of course we had the cow, pigs, and chickens that drew flies from the corral area to our house. This situation probably was the reason that a few years later the city officials suggested that Daddy get rid of those animals. However, all the flies seemed to live in our area and found ways to get through the screen doors and into our house. Once a week we covered all the dishes with a tablecloth and used fly spray to spray the inside of the house. For a day or two we diminished the fly population. I mention these things because having experienced them first-hand as I grew up, I could cope with some similar problems I faced in Brazil.

Daddy didn't smoke or chew, but both of my grandmas dipped snuff. Grandma Tarry turned the snuff can up so that as much as she wanted could fall into her mouth. Grandma Cox used a twig from a tree branch. She chewed on one end of the twig until it spread out some and then dipped the twig into the snuff can many times a day. Dipping snuff was a dirty habit. The only leisure Grandma Tarry had was when she went to bed at night and read detective magazines. As I grew older, I reflected about Grandma Tarry's life; my appreciation grew stronger. When she should have been able to enjoy her retirement, visiting her other sons and daughters, getting to know the other grandchildren, she was stuck with helping rear five grandchildren. Grandma believed she had to fix Sunday dinner and therefore didn't get to go to church to worship God. She was too tired to go to church at night.

Heavenly Sunshine in My Heart

Children pick up more than adults think, even though they don't

311

seem to be listening. When I was 7-years old, I began to understand that I was a sinner. I knew that when I wanted to be good, something within me urged me to be bad. I hadn't lived long enough to do anything really bad, but I just wanted to be better. I saw people trust Christ as their Lord and Savior and accept Jesus publicly after the preacher finished his sermons. I began to understand that Jesus was what I needed in my heart.

For weeks I felt the urge to make a public decision, but Satan presented me three reasons for not making that decision. The first reason was: "Joe, you are too young to accept Jesus. What will the adults think of you? They will think that you do not know what you are doing. They will not believe you!" The second reason Satan gave me for not trusting Jesus and accepting Him for dying for my sins was: "Joe, what will your friends that don't go to Sunday school or church think if you accept Jesus as your Savior? They will ridicule you and make fun of you. You don't want that to happen, do you?" Well, that made the decision more difficult, because I guess everyone is concerned about what others think. The third reason was: "Joe, you are just a kid. You have the rest of your life to accept Jesus. You will have a long life, so wait a while!" This, I knew was a lie, because I had known two or three children who had died.

Every Sunday during the invitation the battle waged in my heart and mind as to accept Him or not. After a few Sundays I took my seat on the second row by the aisle so that only a few steps were needed to meet the pastor when he gave the invitation. During the hymn of invitation when the Holy Spirit tugged at my heart, Satan responded with the objections he always presented. I stuck my right foot into the aisle; that act threw my weight in the direction of my foot; that put me in the aisle, and I went to the pastor in front. At that moment joy flooded my soul. I felt as though I was lifted into the presence of God. In four or five steps I was in front of Brother Hardcastle; he warmly received me. I was weeping with joy and in broken words told him that I was trusting Jesus.

World War II was raging. An Air Force base had been built between Hobbs and Lovington; some airmen attended our church. One of those airmen was overjoyed with my decision and gave me his military Gideon's New Testament. I went home very happy. While I was waiting for dinner (noon meal), I lay on my stomach on my bed and read from the Psalms.

After dinner we all went to the country to see Uncle Lester and family; Uncle Lester was farming Grandma's place. We didn't have many playthings, but old car tires became a favorite toy for us boys. My cousins Junior and Kirby, my brother, Bill, and I rolled the tires; we pushed them with our hands. Junior and Bill, being the oldest, always got the two white-walled tires which were Cadillacs, mine was a Chrysler, and Kirby's had to be a Ford or Chevrolet. But that day of my salvation experience I didn't want to play. I didn't want to lose the wonderful feeling inside me. Most of the trees had lost their leaves by late October. The songbirds such as mockingbirds, meadowlarks, and scissortails had left. About all that stayed for the winter were the sparrows; they chirped more beautifully than ever before. That afternoon the sun seemed to shine more brightly than I ever had seen it.

Pastor Hardcastle visited Daddy and me and quizzed me about the sincerity of my decision. When both were satisfied that I knew what I had done and knew the reason for publicly accepting Jesus, I was ready for baptism. Baptism was on a very cold November night. The water was icy cold, but I was happy that I had identified myself publicly with my Lord and Savior, Jesus Christ.

Adapting to Home Life without Mother

We had a sense of someone missing in our house. Several years passed before the absence of our mother seemed to become a natural thing. We didn't talk about it among ourselves, because this subject was sad, but the feeling of our loss was among us. Many nights before I went to sleep, I begged God to just let me see Mother in my dreams, but I was rejected; I am sure He knew best. One thing, however, brought joy to our hearts: our little brother. Sometimes we called him *Skeeter Bug*, because (similar to a mosquito) he could be here and yonder so fast. He helped us to forget about the loss of Mother and entertained us a lot. Grandma never had much time to give him as a mother should, so we brothers and sisters had our special times to entertain him. I will never forget the first time he held my finger when he was learning to walk well. His little hand wrapped around one of my fingers felt wonderful.

We all had our chores. Daddy went to work early and returned home late. Helen and Margaret were doing what they could do in the house, while Bill and I helped take care of the animals. In the spring Daddy plowed up a large part of one of the lots and planted a garden. Daddy, Bill, and I were responsible for that garden until we found other work in town. Our chores and homework didn't allow any time for play with neighborhood kids except on Saturday afternoons and in the evenings during the summer. Actually Sunday school and church activities were a part of all of our lives.

Daddy worked for a year as janitor at the courthouse and then got a job as a mechanic at a service station. Daddy made more money as a mechanic. He had experience working on his own cars, pickups, and machinery.

The Effect of World War II

The United States entered World War II after the attack on Pearl Harbor by the Japanese on Dec. 7, 1941. Gasoline, shoes, clothes, sugar, and other staples were rationed. Each one in the family had a book of stamps for buying shoes or other commodities. When a person used all of the stamps in his or her book for certain items that year, she or he couldn't buy any more of that item until another book was issued for the next year. Everyone reduced his or her traveling because gasoline was rationed; also tires and spare motor parts were limited.

Scrap-metal drives were held until not a piece of scrap iron or tin could be found anywhere. Occasionally the school had special scrap drives by classes. I remember the third-grade class going from house-to-house within an area and seeking permission to pick up scrap pieces of iron. We picked up the small pieces and placed them in a pile, but the larger pieces were picked up by a truck. This scrap iron was used in manufacturing war equipment.

To be ready if we were attacked in the United States, the schools had air-raid drills. These were different from fire drills in that we stayed in the hallway of the school. Another thing was the stamp drives. Each student received a little booklet of 10 pages; each page had a space to stick 10 10-cent war stamps. A book of stamps was worth $10; these were traded for war bonds. The kid that bought the most stamps was recognized through the loudspeaker to the entire grade school. Seldom did I get a dime to put one stamp in my booklet.

The Hobbs airbase had B-25 bombers and then B-17's. These planes were flown day and night. The young pilots were at the base for about three months before they were shipped overseas to combat duty. Until this day, when I hear the motors of propeller airplanes, my mind goes back to World War II. The airbase brought the war closer to us. I had nightmares of invasions by Germans or Japanese. This fear was increased by the news of men from our little town of Lovington and Lea County being killed in battle.

Grandma Becomes Ill

Most of the time she was helping us, Grandma was sick. After about five years her feet looked bad; the sores on them wouldn't heal. She finally went to a doctor that diagnosed her problem as diabetes. Her condition worsened so quickly that she couldn't stay with us. Grandma had sold her farm in 1945; Uncle Lester and family moved into town to a house about two blocks from us. Grandma had a new four-room house moved onto a lot beside Uncle Lester and Aunt Susie. Aunt Susie gave her the daily insulin shots. Our home life had changed again!

Returning to Reality—The Santa Cruz Preaching Point

Laisete and Genilda Ribeiro had helped us at the Altinopolis mission in Governador Valadares. The year we were on furlough, Laisete attended South Brazil Seminary in Rio de Janeiro. Then they moved to Belo Horizonte to the Santa Cruz neighborhood. Laisete and Genilda didn't have a car or a church near their home, so we picked them up each Sunday and took them to Planalto with us. With the two families we had 10 people in our car. Genilda's mother lived with them and usually went to church with us also. Fortunately their two boys were small, but we were packed into that car like sardines.

Laisete was a gem stonecutter by trade but believed God had called him to preach. He wanted to start a preaching point in his home. He and I talked to the pastor of an older church that was closer to Santa Cruz than Planalto; we discussed with the pastor about supporting the preaching point. The pastor wasn't interested, because his church already had tried to start a mission in the Santa Cruz neighborhood. Renascenca Baptist Church even had purchased property for a mission at Santa Cruz, but the neighborhood people were very indifferent to the gospel: Roman Catholicism and spiritism were predominant. The church sold the lot to start another mission on the fringe of the city. Even though Planalto still was a mission, it agreed to sponsor the Santa Cruz preaching point.

Laisete and Genilda started this preaching point in their small living room. The group soon grew too large for that space, so they rented a larger room below their house. In the past this room had been used for a spiritist meeting place. A circle on which the medium was to sit was painted on the floor. The presence of the Holy Spirit expulsed the evil spirits when Laisete began his preaching point under his house!

A Big Bang

One particular Saturday evening we picked up Laisete and Genilda in the Santa Cruz neighborhood on our way to the Planalto neighborhood. We were going to a monthly business meeting at Planalto Church. Laisete would give his report of the work at the Santa Cruz mission. We were traveling on a dirt street when a terrific bang startled us. We heard a scraping noise under the car; suddenly the back of the car rose off the ground a little bit. This forced the car to stop. Laisete and I got out of the car to investigate the damage.

The driver in the car behind us was very frustrated about the situation, because we partially were blocking the road. He finally pulled around us and yelled some words as he sped past. I didn't know what he said, so I just waved at him. Laisete said: "You don't know what he said, do you?" I replied, "No! "He was cursing you." That was one time I was glad I hadn't learned Portuguese curse words. In fact my curse-word vocabulary remained very weak!

The muffler and tailpipe had separated from the manifold. The muffler dug into the dirt street. It hit a rock or something; this caused this section of the exhaust system to fold backward under the back axle. This messed-up muffler and tail pipe situation was weird, because it elevated the back of the car so the right back wheel was off the ground two or three inches. All passengers descended from the car. With the jack I raised the car higher. Laisete and I worked and worked until we finally succeeded in getting the tailpipe section freed from under the car. Behold! The jack broke and wouldn't let the car down. With everyone lifting the car higher off the jack Jonathan was able to pull the jack out. Since we had no muffler or tailpipe, we had the loudest car in the city for our transportation to church Saturday night and twice on Sunday.

The São Bernardo Preaching Point
Vila Oeste (West Village) Baptist Church started a preaching point in the São Bernardo neighborhood after we had begun working in Planalto. Vila Oeste was a thriving neighborhood in Belo on the west side of the city. The Vila Oeste neighborhood was made up mainly of people from the interior parts of the state. São Bernardo was a similar neighborhood. Vila Oeste Church rented a house for the mission. This was in a bad location because a small river flowed along the side of the house; this flooded during heavy rains. During the dry season the river stunk because the water mostly was sewage from the houses. A young couple of Vila Oeste Baptist Church led this humble preaching point. After about five months the church asked Planalto to assume the leadership of its mission. Since at least 14 people were walking from São Bernardo neighborhood to our Planalto mission, the Planalto group accepted because it could envision having a church in that area before too long.

Planalto Mission Becomes a Church
On December 8, 1977, the Planalto mission organized into a church with 59 members. Nineteen had been members of Fifth Baptist Church in Governador Valadares, the first congregation at which I was pastor. Of course, our family made up five of the 19, but the rest had settled in the São Bernardo neighborhood and joined Planalto. About 200 people attended the organization service. The first month we had 81 percent tithers; also about $500 dollars was given to the property fund. We could say that now we were a proper church to be the mother of two missions. We had some wonderful people in this little church. I would like to mention all of them, but space doesn't

317

allow. Two men were sergeants in the Brazilian Air Force. An Air Force base was near Belo. Gediel led the boys' mission work and was one of the pillars of the church. Vera, Gediel's wife, among other things was the leader of the girls' mission organization and a Sunday-school teacher. Floriano was a sergeant; he had surrendered to preach and was studying at the seminary at night. His wife, Blanca, was not a Christian but attended church. One day I visited Blanca; she accepted Jesus as her Savior. From that day on she always called me her pastor. They moved to Natal, a city far north, after Floriano finished seminary. Floriano left the Air Force and was pastor of a church. Later they returned to Belo; for a while he was pastor of a church in Belo, but Blanca continued to call me her *pastor*. That warmed my heart.

Family Concerns

The only concern we had at this time in our family was the suffering that Charlotte had with her teeth. After her near-death (told in chapter 1), each time she had a cold, we took her to a doctor. Tetrex was a very good antibiotic to cut the infection, but for young children it also disfigured and turned teeth brown. She had nearly all of her baby teeth filled before her permanent teeth grew. We were blessed to have had a wonderful dentist that was very patient with her. The front permanent teeth were badly distorted and brown. Charlotte was self-conscious of her teeth until she later had major dental work done. That dental work was painful but made her teeth look normal.

1978

In January 1978 the camp was without a director. I was responsible for the two R.A. camps. Pastor Bittencourt asked Leona and me to help with the camps until a new camp director was hired. Now both of us were involved in another new responsibility!

Living near the state camp gave us an opportunity to participate in more of the activities. For more than a year Leona and I were responsible for getting the cooks, planning the meals, and buying the groceries for most of the camps. We were so thankful that our area director, Dr. Thurman Bryant, visited us during a time we were busy buying supplies for the camp and saw the need for a state camp director. He soon found Leo and Dorothy Weatherman to fill that position.

God sent them to be our camp directors; how thankful we were!

Developing Another Gift

Missionary Kent Faris was a good artist and used illuminated chalk talks to promote his evangelism work in the adjoining State of Espirito Santo. I bought film-developing equipment from Kent when he and his family returned to the States for a few years. I also bought from his artist supply his tripod, black light, and a supply of colored chalk. I had painted with watercolors and oil but never with chalk. I began practicing and chose several scenes to paint, along with a couple of my own design. Since Kent's evangelistic message presented by painting was accompanied by Sarah's beautiful voice, I would have to do something different. Leona had a good voice, but she usually wouldn't be with me when I traveled. I took almost-completed paintings with me to the churches. After the message I finished the painting. When I was finished, I asked to have the lights turned off so the black light would bring out the illuminated colors. I gave a picture to the person that brought the most people. I never imagined that I would be doing this kind of work for our Lord!

Carl Suffers a Physical Blow

Carl had his heart set on going to the Air Force Academy. This was a worthy goal, so we began the process to get him into the Academy. His grades were good enough; New Mexico's Congressman Harold Runnels agreed to present his name to the academy. One problem that we hadn't worked out was a place at which he could take the military physicals that were necessary for the Academy. We were not in a hurry for the physical, because when the problem arose, he was finishing his junior year in high school.

The American School was putting the final touches on the gymnasium. The P.E. teacher decided that a contest between the boys would be good. The boys were given options of a list of exercises from which to choose. Whoever won in his area of exercise would have his name in bronze on a plaque in the hall. The first problem was the lack of proper preparation for a contest in any of the physical exercises. Carl chose push-ups. The rule was that the boys would do as many push-ups as possible and then rest 20 seconds between push-ups until they could do no more. The concrete floor of the new gym was still "green" (still damp) and cold. The boys didn't even have a mat or towel on which to lie; their hot sweaty bodies were directly on the cold cement, plus the weather was pretty cool. Carl did 151 push-ups.

When Carl arrived home, his arms were swollen up like those of "Popeye" in the comic strip. His arms swelled so big that he couldn't bend them. Fortunately the other boy didn't have the same reaction. Leona took Carl to the Evangelical Hospital; the doctor was horrified. He told Leona that she should take him to school the next day and show the teacher the results of the contest. The doctor thought that lying on the damp concrete might have caused Carl's body to have such a reaction. His blood pressure was very high; other body functions weren't normal. For more than a week he couldn't bend his arms. Two weeks passed before he could use his right arm. For a while he continued to have high blood pressure. Now the difficulty was telling Carl he couldn't qualify for the Air Force because of the high blood-pressure problem. I suggested that he go to college and that if he still wanted to go to the Air Force, he could apply. He later did this but didn't have the joy of going to the Air Force Academy.

Property for Planalto Church
Praying, believing, and expecting God to work is a sure way to see God open up the doors to spiritual success. We finally had an opportunity to buy a lot on the opposite side of the block from the place on which we were meeting. The lot was a triangle with the point touching the main avenue, Cristiano Guimaraes. We had a total of $11,200 from the church savings strategic fund, Minas Gerais special strategy property gift, and SBC Bold Missions funds. We lacked $1,700. At this time Planalto Church had 74 members; the monthly budget was $800. We also were paying rent for two mission points. With the sacrifice of the members and with God's help the money necessary to buy the lot of our dreams was provided.

Joao Batista Mordomo Presented
Since stewardship doesn't interest Baptists as much as it should, I decided I could use a doll to create enthusiasm in my teaching on the subject. I acquired my first ventriloquist doll and at the state conven-

320

tion in July presented him as "John Baptist the Steward". I wrote a chorus about stewardship. John Baptist the Steward began teaching this chorus to the churches.

I'm a steward for Jesus!
He's worthy of all I can be!
My time, talents, tithe, and things!
Through my testimony I honor His name.
Glory to Jesus, my Savior and Lord!
Because through Him I am who I am.
I'm a steward for Jesus.
I'm happy in all His blessings.

John the Baptist Steward became more beloved than I was. Once when John finished his song and comments, a little boy proudly walked to the front of the church and handed him an offering.

General Things
We had a lot about which to rejoice! Carl and Jonathan had finished their junior and freshman years with excellent grades. They both participated in soccer, basketball, and volleyball. A few times in Belo we had seen them play against Brazilian teams but never attended the tournaments between the American schools because they were out of state. Charlotte was doing better in the Brazilian school. Living so close to the school was convenient because she could get to class in less than 10 minutes. She would go to eighth grade in the American School next year. All three children were blessings in Planalto Church.

At the South Brazil mission meeting I was elected the chairperson of the Self-Support Committee. In August I made a trip to Rio de Janeiro to familiarize myself with the self-support files. South Brazil had a total of 11 conventions receiving support funds; all had started with total support from the FMB. The FMB was pushing for all states to set dates for total self-support. Gradually some states had assumed some of their own support; São Paulo and Rio de Janeiro almost were self-supporting. Each mission station was urged to help the leadership of its state to set a cutoff date for FMB support. I was to visit some of the states and explain the reason for their assuming financial responsibility.

I also went to São Paulo with a team of three from Minas Gerais to help plan the second national evangelism campaign to be held in 1980. This campaign would be working up to the Centennial celebration of Baptist work in Brazil in 1982. After these trips I went in September to Valadares again for the Bible institute for a month.

Travels in the Country

The car in front of me, going too fast, had hit a dry powder dust spot; that threw dirt over his motor and stopped up the carburetor. I had done that before, too; I was afraid this would happen again. We were driving in dirt up to the running board. This was the first time I had stepped out of the car into powder dirt above my ankles. Can you imagine what a road like that would be if rain were to fall? Instead of being stuck in dry dirt one surely would be stuck in high mud. As had always happened, God provided a way out. The next car was driven by a Baptist man that I knew well; he had three friends with him. They soon had the carburetor cleaned in the car in front of me; we were on our way again. The problem is you cannot judge the depth of the dust on the road bed.

The last few miles I traveled to arrive at a country church were worse than I had expected. I was glad I had stopped in a neighboring town, because one of the Baptist men agreed to go with me. Soon darkness engulfed the region; the road became very narrow. In places I had to be careful I didn't scrape the side of the car on the embankment or scrape stacks of wood on the other side of the road; the wood was to be picked up by a truck. The Baptist man was very helpful to open the gates, but he was the biggest help crossing a *pinguela* (two thick planks used for a bridge). He guided me across those planks. Up steep hills, down into valleys, we slowly bounced along the narrow road. *Would we arrive in time for the service?* I was concerned about the heavy, low-hanging clouds that all day threatened rain. Occasionally rain does fall during the dry season. The feeling of separation, loneliness, and distance always reoccurred in situations such as this. My joy returned when we pulled up to the little country church in which the lantern light glowing through the windows gently overpowered the heavy blackness that hugged the church on that starless night.

The next day the weather still was cloudy and threatening rain. To get to the next church I had to climb a very steep mountain on a road with narrow, twisting curves. "Oh, Lord, please don't let it rain or I will not get out of these mountains for days," I prayed. As I pressed the accelerator, I broke out in a nervous sweat as I tried to keep up the momentum and at the same time dodge chuckholes and miss gullies left from last season's rains. Reaching the top of the mountain I was enthralled by the beautiful sight. Oh, the amazing wonder of God's creation; how fabulous the Creator's imagination is! What a spectacular view I beheld! Joy and gratefulness invaded me so much that I stopped the car just to gaze at what I saw. I thought, "Thank You, Lord, for directing me to visit New Alliance Baptist Church, for I perhaps never would have seen this sight. Oh, Lord, so few people in this world have seen this view. I am glad I am one who has seen this part of the world with my own eyes. The surroundings are beautiful, gorgeous, and RARE." I often just stopped and waited a while, since I was enthralled with the view, and wished I didn't have to hurry on the journey. Happily I began the descent on the narrow, rough road. I traveled around curves and down, down into the valley. Sometimes I was partially shaded by high grass or totally shaded by mango and other trees. Often the road passed between a house and a barn from which usually children ran out to see who was going by; I usually scattered chickens right and left as I made my way with the car through their playground.

All the churches I visited were happy that I made the journey to see them. Two of the churches never had been visited by anyone from the state office. Most of them never had had an American missionary visit them. Now I felt so glad that I went. I am not worthy to have had the blessing of being touched by the lives of many simple, honest, and sacrificial people that make up God's kingdom. Many of these people walked miles to get to church. "Thank you Lord, that You didn't allow me to seek out the easier churches to reach on this trip," I prayed.

Brother Wilson Dies
The first time I met Brother Wilson was the Wednesday night

after our first visit to Planalto Mission. We arrived a little late; Wilson was leading the prayer service. His baggy, wrinkled suit didn't appear to have been washed recently, his hair wasn't combed well, and his shoes were dirty. Yet, Wilson was leading the prayer service in which all the others were cleanly dressed in that middle-class neighborhood. I discovered later that he arrived at church directly after he had worked all day.

I admit that I wondered, "What is this man doing leading the service?" I just didn't know Brother Wilson. He was present every Wednesday night and sometimes on Sunday as representative of the mother church. I soon learned how much the people loved Brother Wilson. He was instrumental in the start of the mission when it began in Nair de Maria's garage. I heard about his brilliant testimony for the Lord as he sang and preached as he laid brick in his daily work. The first time he announced he wanted to sing a solo, I almost cringed and wondered what would happen. I was amazed at the simplicity and beauty of his untrained voice. I also was ashamed about my judgmental feeling about his singing, for he sang with joy, sincerity, and authority from his heart. I heard so much about this man that I was ashamed of myself.

On November 29 Brother Wilson died of Chagas, a disease caused by a beetle bite that affects the heart. We went to his funeral.

Joy at the End of 1978

The São Bernardo neighborhood mission attendance was running 40-50, the Santa Cruz mission 25, and Planalto Church 70-80. The Planalto Church was running around 100 the year before, but several of the members lived in the São Bernardo neighborhood and now attended that mission. So between the church and its two missions together we were averaging about 145 in the morning services but more in the evening services.

At the end of 1978 my doctrinal class was made up of an interesting group. One was an elderly woman who had been the president of a spiritist center. Another woman in the class had contemplated suicide on the same day a church member invited her to attend our revival. She attended, accepted the Lord, and began rejoicing in her walk with Jesus.

Chapter 17

Leona's Story

Our New Home

Our new home in Belo Horizonte was a mission house on the corner of Ponte Nova with Saldanha da Gama streets. Missionaries James and Jewel Lunsford built the original home; then missionaries Jack and Jean Young added to it. The house had four bedrooms, two full baths, a nice kitchen and breakfast room, dining room, and living room. The garage, long enough for two cars plus an area large enough for a ping-pong table, was under the house. Stairs led from inside the garage up to the kitchen. The garage door opened to the busy Ponte Nova Street. A city bus stopped beside our house; this was convenient but also very noisy. The preschool playground of the Baptist school was across the street. The front yard of the home was small; it had shrubs, flowers, and a small area of grass which sloped sharply down to the fence. The fence was about five-feet above the sidewalk and a cobblestone street. The height of the yard plus the grated metal fence helped keep unwanted people from entering the yard. The back yard was small and was covered with concrete except for a narrow strip for flowers. This surely was a disappointment for our dog, because in Governador Valadares she had a big grass yard. A room for Joe's office, an area for washing clothes, a small maid's room and bathroom, and a storage room were at the back of the house. All nicer homes had a maid's room and bath. We used the small storage room as a darkroom for Joe's new hobby: developing film. Why is a nice four-bedroom home important for missionaries? Most missionaries have many visitors.

Minas Baptist School

The Baptist school complex, across the street from us, covers two entire city blocks. In 1918 Dr. and Mrs. O.P. Maddox began the school in their home and then moved it to First Baptist Church. In 1925 a valuable, large piece of property on a mountain near the downtown area was for sale. Dr. Maddox led a prayer campaign for the purchase of the property and sent in a request for $25,000 to the FMB. He trusted that the FMB would see the vision of the missionaries and Brazilian Baptists in Belo. Two to three months was normal for transfer of money from the States to Rio de Janeiro. A few days before the date set for the auction of the property, without knowing for sure the money had arrived, Dr. Maddox went to Rio de Janeiro. He brought the huge sum of money (for those days) back in the money belt that Mrs. Maddox had made for him. Dr. Maddox trusted in God to protect him riding in second-class on the train with $25,000 in cash back to Belo Horizonte.

Since Evangelical Christians were considered poor and undesirable people, Dr. Maddox had a lawyer that was sympathetic with Baptists to do the bidding for the property. The auction began with a low bid, but several bidders made exciting the challenge to buy that valuable property. Finally only two men were bidding for the property. Just as the bidding reached $25,000, the opposing bidder quit. Evidently he thought the lawyer was representing a firm or someone very wealthy. After the bidding stopped, Dr. Maddox stepped forward and in cash paid the price for the land. Gasps and exclamations of surprise were heard from the bidders. "Where did this tramp get so much money?", some asked. Dr. Maddox had bought several acres of hills rising high adjacent to the center of Belo Horizonte. The area was called *Floresta* because it was covered with trees. As time passed and as the school grew, most of the property was sold. A large complex of buildings for all grades, including kindergarten, was built on two large city blocks.

If and when they were allowed to enroll in state schools, the Evangelical students were persecuted there. One reason missionaries bought land for schools in the state capitals was to provide a school for Christians and especially for preachers' kids. For about 60 years the school also had a dormitory for preachers' kids or for Christians from the interior to stay and study. By the time we arrived in 1977, the school had more than 7,000 students in the morning, afternoon, and evening sessions. It was one of the largest Christian schools in South America.

Importance of the Missionary Prayer Calendar

The Mosaic, the women's mission magazine, and *Open Windows*, the Baptist daily devotional magazine, both have a birthday prayer list of missionaries. Sometimes one might think: "I don't know these people; what is the use of reading their names?" As missionaries we recognize the value of prayer for us on our birthdays. God honors all the prayers, even if they don't specify a particular need. On the afternoon of one of my birthdays I was on my way to visit a group of women in the Planalto area. I was traveling on the new, divided boulevard that went past Planalto. I needed to turn left, drive a short distance, and exit right up into the Planalto neighborhood. I saw the huge truck descending in my direction, but I thought I had plenty of time to get across in front of him. What I didn't calculate correctly was the speed this heavy truck would gain as he descended. As I turned in front of him, I realized I didn't have time to get into the right lane as I had planned. I stayed in the inside left lane; this forced him to move over. To avoid hitting me he exited up the hill I had planned to ascend. My next problem was that I was going in the opposite direction and had to drive about a mile to turn back. When I finally arrived back at my turning point, the poor truck driver still was trying to back down the hill to get back on his way. He didn't realize he could have gone to the top and down on the other side to get back on the boulevard. I hoped he didn't recognize my car.

The experience left me feeling weak. The huge 18-wheeler truck would have flattened my little Chevette. God had His hand on me and guided me to stay in the inside left lane. At that moment I had forgotten the day was my birthday. That evening I told Joe my experience; we realized the date. Thanks to all that prayed for me that day, even though you didn't know me or my needs.

Women's Missionary Union

Soon after we moved to Belo Horizonte, the state Woman's

Missionary Union board asked me to be leader of the Baptist Women's group. In that position I planned with the state executive director various state women's activities, which included a camp. This two-night camp was at the state camp near Ravena, about 20 miles out of Belo. The women had a great time of fellowship and spiritual renewal.

The state leadership team, made up of leaders for each age group, from time to time was invited to teach the manuals for the various age groups.

I served 18 months as interim executive secretary for WMU. That was a very busy time for me, because our three kids still were at home. I was responsible for the financial payments and reports. At the end of January I took a 10-day trip, my longest period away from home. Another state worker and I went to the national convention in Recife; afterward we attended a workshop of the national WMU. The women's workshop would help me in my promotional work and planning for Central Association women's camp, the state women's camp, and the pastors' wives camp. Joe and the kids did well in my absence, since a seminary student was helping with household chores.

For the annual report at the WMU convention I had John Hatton paint posters for me in the form of various road signs; each sign presented some part of the report. John is an MK (missionary kid) married to Monica, a Brazilian; they were living in Belo across the street from us. (Today they are with our IMB and serve in Chile.) State Executive Secretary Bittencourt really enjoyed the visual annual report I gave at the state convention; this perhaps was the first time a visual report was given.

Our local church, Planalto, had a mission organization for each age group: women, men, youth, G.A., R.A., and Mission Friends (children). For two years we had mission fairs to promote Brazilian world missions. One year the fair theme was "Mission Trip Around the World in 60 Minutes". We assigned to each mission group a country in which Brazilians had missionaries serving. The group was responsible for the research on its country and for decorating its room accordingly with items such as maps, flags, and pictures. The group dressed as its country and served a typical food. Everyone got involved. One year we had a couple from Angola present to help with the celebration. Everyone attending received "tickets" and a passport to visit the various countries. Our goal was accomplished, as the whole church got acquainted with some of the countries in which their Brazilian missionaries were serving.

Documents for Travel

Time for furlough arrived; Brazil required documents to get exemptions or pay $1,000 per person to leave the country. At times we believed that getting out of Brazil was almost as difficult as getting in was. Golden Gate Seminary had sent me a document stating I had studied there for two years. We gathered the documents we needed to send to Brasilia, but my seminary document was missing. We looked everywhere we could think of and couldn't find it. I prayed God would give me an idea of a place to look. I believe nothing is too small to request of God; He knew where that document was. I did find it but not where it should have been. I praised God for answered prayer.

15-Year Celebration

Paul and Carlita Popov both were born and grew up in Brazil, but as a teen-ager Paul had gone with his older brother to the States. He wrote to a pastor friend and asked him to find a GOOD Christian girl for Paul to marry. Carlita was a daughter of a pastor friend of the friend of Paul. The pastor friend suggested to Paulo that Carlita would make a good wife. Paul wrote to Carlita; after an exchange of letters they were engaged. They never had met personally until Paul arrived to marry her and take her to the U.S. They had four daughters born in the States: Mary, Rosalee, Myriam, and Rachel. About 1974 they decided to move back to Brazil to Belo Horizonte. Carlita took the girls to visit friends in Governador Valadares, where we first met them. When we moved to Belo, our friendship grew. We enjoyed fellowship, either in our home or theirs. In our home I taught Mary and Rosalee piano.

I was invited to play the piano for Mary's 15th birthday celebration. For Christians these services are similar to a wedding to honor the girl and usually occur with the participation of a group of 15 girls. The 1st birthday and the 15th birthday are the most important and call for a big party. The practice for the program was Saturday afternoon, so Carlita invited our family to bring our clothes to change for the program after a barbecue at their home. Joe was away at a conference, so the kids and I gathered up our "church clothes" and my music and piled into the car. Joe was very faithful to buy the gasoline or at least remind me to do so. I knew I needed to buy gasoline on our way to Progress Baptist Church, but in our haste I forgot. Because of city traffic the drive from our house to the Popovs' normally took about 45 minutes. After the practice at the church, we went to the Popov home to eat. We dressed and returned to the church for the program. Everything went well; we headed home about 9:30; then I realized the gas needle was almost on empty. We arrived home at about 10. As we pulled up to the garage door, Carl noticed the garage light was on in the area of the ping-pong table. He jokingly said, "I hope no one stole the ping-pong table". Carl unlocked the garage and I drove in; everything looked normal and quiet. Everyone was loaded with his own change of clothes as I led the gang upstairs into the kitchen. The house was dark, but enough light was shining through the kitchen window for me to see my way across the room to the light switch. Carl was close behind me. As I reached for the light switch, a gruff voice from the dark hallway said, "Don't move." I froze—I couldn't even have screamed. Thoughts ran through my mind—*Could Joe be home? No, Joe wouldn't do this to me.* I don't know how many seconds passed before the person in the dark hallway started laughing and turned on the light—Laisete, Genilda, and sons Junior and Jonathan stood there. Since Valadares days Laisete's custom was to reach for the doorknob at the same time he reached for the doorbell. This time he was surprised that the door opened but no one seemed to be home. Their first thought was that someone had broken into the house and had exited the front door and left it unlocked. They went throughout the house but found nothing wrong, yet they couldn't leave without locking the front door. So they waited for us but did not know where we had gone or what time we would return. I was very embarrassed, because I couldn't even offer to take them home since I had forgotten to buy gasoline. I did give them money to get the bus home.

Friends from Lovington

A couple from Jackson Avenue Baptist Church in Lovington visited us. Mr. and Mrs. Deese had been visiting their daughter that was serving as a journeyman (two-year term) in North Brazil and were on their way back to the States. They spent one day and two nights with us. We took them to the bus station to go to Rio de Janeiro for their plane. Joe let them out at the entrance of the bus station, and they removed their luggage. Joe was going to park the car while they made their way to the right terminal. Joe's door was still open and he thought Mr. Deese had stepped away from the car; he didn't know Mr. Deese had his hand on the ridge of the doorpost. Joe shut his door at the same time he heard a gasp and I screamed. I pointed to the closed door. Joe looked to his left and saw Mr. Deese's fingers inside the car near his left shoulder. Immediately he opened the door and imagined that all of the man's fingers had been broken. The good thing was that modern cars had a thick puffy strip of rubber around the door to keep it from rattling but also making a cushion. Joe was shocked! What could we do now since their bus soon would arrive? We know he must have been in great pain but we had no time to take him to a doctor. He insisted that his hand was OK, so Joe parked the car; we saw them off on their bus. Joe felt very sorry for him and very stupid!

Home Worship Services

Brazilians love to have parties, so a very common method the Christians have to evangelize their friends, neighbors, and family members is to have a birthday party/worship service in their home. Nearly every week we had a home service in someone's home. For years I took the accordion for the musical instrument, since neither Joe nor I play a guitar. Music is a universal language that everyone knows and enjoys. When the electric keyboards became popular, we bought one to use in the missions and also in the home services. The first keyboard ran on batteries so it could be played at any location.

At one time or other we had a service in nearly every home of every member of the church and missions. Sometimes the rooms were so crowded with people that one hardly could wiggle, but we never had complaints.

Our 25th Anniversary

Our 25th wedding anniversary occurred in the middle of April, but with other activities happening, we celebrated it on May 1. Charlotte planned the celebration as a come-and-go event at our home. To accommodate everyone we had two celebrations: one day we had friends and missionary colleagues; the next day we invited the church family. A member of one of our missions worked as a cake decorator in a bakery. Charlotte ordered two different cakes from him. That gave him the joy of participating in a special way in the celebration.

Zenaide and Manuel Family

For a while in Sunday school I taught preteens. Because of the R.A. program Moses started attending and became involved. His father, Manuel, worked for one of the richest men in Belo Horizonte, but he paid Manuel one minimum salary a month (about $60) for doing full-time general yard work at the employer's mansion near Planalto Church. However, he allowed the family to live in a large, wooden storage shed he had built across the boulevard from the building we were renting. The family members carried water from a neighbor and paid part of the neighbor's water bill. The family was large— 11 kids, with five still at home. To supplement the income Manuel's wife, Zenaide, washed and ironed clothes for others. One Sunday Moses brought me a gift wrapped very simply in brown sack paper. I treasured that gift—not because of its worth but because of his loving heart and appreciation. Moses was faithful to R.A.'s and other church services; soon his sister, Marta, attended with him. We visited the home and saw the situation. The place they lived had not been piped for water or sewage. The church agreed to pay for and install water and sewage pipes; the men laid these pipes out to the street. Zenaide and Manuel were very grateful for this.

Zenaide was very interested in the Bible study and started attending with the two younger children. Manuel wasn't interested; he said that church was good for his wife and kids but not for him. When Zenaide accepted Jesus, joy filled her life; she became a bubbling witness. Joe requested that Luiz Paulo Terrinha, a member and seminary student, have doctrinal studies with her; then Joe baptized her. Only later did Joe find out that she and Manuel weren't legally married. About three years passed; Manuel finally accepted Jesus. He didn't want to be baptized, but he decided they needed to get married in a civil ceremony. Thirty-five years earlier they had married in a Catholic service, but a civil wedding was necessary to be legal and recognized by the state.

None of them had birth certificates, a requirement for buying a marriage license. They had moved to Belo from Teofoli Otoni, a city about 100 miles north of Governador Valadares. Joe wrote Pastor Jonair Monteiro to see whether he could get copies of birth certificates for Manuel, Zenaide, and the children. The certificates arrived; we made plans for the wedding. Some church members paid for the wedding. I gave Zenaide material to have a new dress made for the wedding. Another friend volunteered to make a cake. Her married kids and grandchildren all were excited about the wedding; this was a big celebration. Manuel and Zenaide were as excited as two young people who were marrying.

Everyone loved Zenaide; I don't believe she had any enemies. She was very bold with her Christian witness. She spoke to everyone she met about her new faith in Jesus. As she washed clothes or worked, she sang loud enough for all the neighbors to hear.

Soon after this, Joe found out that this rich man had two smaller lots not far from our church. Since our lot was larger than normal and was on the main avenue, he thought the man might trade his two lots for our one lot. The rich man had an office in a hotel that he owned in the middle of the city. Joe went to town twice and waited for hours to see him but without success. This man had several low-income housing projects and always had problems. Every time Joe went to talk to him, people—most of them poor—were waiting to see him about something.

Finally Joe reached the rich man by phone and told him what he wanted. The man invited Joe to visit him at his mansion; not many people ever had such an invitation. After he presented himself at the gate, Joe drove down to the beautiful home surrounded by trees and beautiful gardens. Because the rich man was sick that day, Joe was taken into his bedroom. The man first said he was interested in Joe's request to trade for his two vacant lots. He said he would like to do something for the church. Joe thought to himself: *Wow! This guy is not as bad as people say he is*. Joe thought the trade was going to be easy. The man wanted to see, on paper, the lot that Joe was offering him. Joe already had seen his two lots and frankly didn't like the location much but was eager to know his offer before we ever built anything. The rich man finally said: "I'll tell you what I will do. I will trade you one lot for your lot, but you will have to pay me for the other one." Joe was puzzled and disappointed. Joe immediately saw that he had no plan to help the church. Joe wasn't going to beg him. Joe's conclusion was that anyone who treated his hired hands as he had and was treating Manuel and Zenaide wouldn't help a church.

Later Pastor Laisete and family moved to Prudente de Morais, a small town that had no Baptist church. Laisete and Genilda started a Bible study in their home. This new mission was under the umbrella of Planalto Baptist Church. As the group grew, Laisete found a lot with a small house to buy. The house wasn't much, but Laisete fixed it up; the group had a larger place to worship. After the mission was established, Laisete found a lot and small house that really was cheap, so we bought it for Manuel and Zenaide. They had never had their own home and needed a place to live when he quit working for the rich man in Planalto. The idea was that Zenaide and the younger kids would be a blessing for the work in Prudente. We got them moved to their location, but that didn't last long. She was homesick for their grown children and grandchildren; the kids wanted them to be closer. Manuel and Zenaide were able to sell the property in Prudente and, with the money, bought a nice lot and started building a house in a new development on the far southeastern edge of Belo Horizonte. This was close to a married daughter and family. Joe and I were disappointed about this, but after a year we could see that this was a good move. The neighborhood was growing, their lot was large, their home was near family, and they were being a blessing to a new Baptist church in that neighborhood.

Before we left Brazil in 1999, Manuel asked Joe whether he would baptize him. Praise the Lord! The church building was new; water wasn't hooked up in time for the baptism. In a pickup truck they carried barrels of water and then used buckets to fill the baptistery. The baptistery hadn't been tested; by the time we arrived for the service, much of the water had seeped out. The water level was so low. Joe thought, *How in the world can I baptize Manuel and six other people?* Joe suggested they cut about eight inches off the legs of a chair so the candidates could sit low enough to be under the water when Joe baptized them. The church was packed with family and friends. Many of Manuel's family members were present for the first time in a Baptist church. What a testimony to the family and a blessing to us after so long!

The Lowrie and Jenkins Mission Teams

For about 14 years we had the privilege of working with Pastor Dwight Lowrie of Texas and Pastor Wayne Jenkins of Louisiana. For many years they took evangelistic, medical, and construction teams to Brazil. Our first experience to work with them was in Teofilo Otoni, just north of Governador Valadares. This was a city of about 30,000 in the heart of gemstone mining; all this area was very traditional Roman Catholic. Baptists had three churches. We had many wonderful experiences as we did home visitation with these groups. On Saturday afternoon the pastors had planned a service in the city park. Taxi drivers always were parked around the plaza and hoped they could get passengers. This Saturday was the day of Saint Christopher, saint of motorists, so the taxi drivers had planned a parade that would be about the same hour as our service was scheduled. The evangelical musical group was playing and singing when the motorists started honking and others on the plaza made all types of noise to disrupt the service.

The most successful crusades with the Lowrie/Jenkins teams were in Governador Valadares and Juiz de Fora. Joe and I took our cars, both mission and personal, so we could get our teams to the church and back to the hotel. Many people still didn't own cars, so our cars were helpful. The church's responsibility was to contact people in the neighborhood, explain that the visitors were Americans, and set up a day and time for a visit. Each team was made up of about two members of the local church, about two American volunteers, and a translator.

I was working in Juiz de Fora with a team at a mission. The members had a well-planned schedule for us. At one home the woman

335

invited us into her little house. The living room also was her bedroom. The dresser had about 10 different statues of various saints; two statues were of Mary Aparecida, the patron saint of Brazil. We used her Roman Catholic Bible for the Bible study. After I translated the plan of salvation for the volunteer, the woman assured us that she confessed her sins every day. Most all Brazilians I have witnessed to have expressed their confidence in Mary, mother of God. With all the "saints" on the dresser I knew her idea wasn't the same as ours. I explained about Isaiah 44:9-19 and then turned to Psalm 115:4-8, but to our surprise that page was missing from her Bible. She couldn't believe someone had very carefully removed that page! She read from my Bible about the idols made by men: "they have mouths but cannot speak, eyes, but cannot see; they have ears, but cannot hear, noses, but cannot smell; they have hands, but cannot feel, and feet, but cannot walk." Little by little she understood that she needed to put her trust in Jesus alone for salvation. She prayed to accept Christ. The Brazilian Christian asked her about the saints on the dresser. She decided she would just box them up, but the Brazilian suggested she get rid of them. I asked for one of Mary Aparecida, so she gave me the prettiest one. I wanted to show what many Catholics pray to with faith—a simple porcelain doll. Maria Aparecida's cathedral in the state of São Paulo is enormous, second only to St. Peter's in Rome.

That same week at one of the homes we were scheduled to visit, no one answered the door. Rather than waste our time I suggested we visit any other home that would welcome us. We clapped at the gate of a house at which we could see a girl about 10-years old. I explained who we were and asked whether her mother was home. She disappeared inside and we waited. Finally an older woman appeared in the door and invited us to enter. When we entered I knew this was different, I discovered she was a spiritist medium. I guess she thought we wanted some spiritual advice. I explained who we were and why we were there. Her "throne" and worship items were at one end of the room and a dining table and chairs at the other end. She invited us to sit down around the table. She explained that she had attended a Christian church until she was a young adult but never found peace. I felt sick at heart to think that somehow the Christians she had known had failed to lead her to Jesus. We left that home with heavy hearts but with a prayer that the testimony she had heard would cause her to reconsider her spiritual life before Jesus.

A few times I helped with a medical team. I always had fun working with one dear nurse named Billie. The medical teams worked at the church every day, so all they saw was the route from the hotel to the church. On Sunday afternoons we would take the groups around to see the city. The chapel built during the week also would be dedicated. I took my medical group out to the dedication; Billie was in my group. The road to the church was dirt; since we were in the dry season, the road was very dry and dusty. At one spot a mother goat was near the fence with her baby twins. The owner had put what looked like nurses' masks over their noses, so I told Billie: "Look, the babies have masks on, just like yours." She remarked: "Isn't that cute! I wonder why?"

I replied, "Must be to protect them from the dust." She took me seriously; I let it ride for a while and then confessed that the owner didn't want them to nurse from their mother.

Danger during Rains

One Sunday afternoon in the rain Carl, Jonathan, Charlotte, and I were on our way to Planalto. Earlier Joe had gone to Planalto for a meeting. This was during the rainy season; the rain had caused many chuckholes in the streets; these were difficult to see when they were filled with water and because so much water was running down. One stretch of the street/highway was only four lanes (two lanes each way) along the top of the dam of Pampulha Lake. Near the beginning stretch over the dam was a big chuckhole filled with water. The back left tire hit the hole; the noise sounded almost like a blownout tire— except the tire kept rolling. I couldn't stop at that spot, but just beyond the dam was a street onto which I could turn and get out of the traffic to stop. I checked all the tires; they looked normal, but from the noise I knew something was wrong. I drove up a short way; Carl and I looked again. This time I had stopped just at the right spot for the air to escape quickly from the tire. Carl and I started preparing to change the tire when a man pulled up behind us and insisted on helping. The rain was pouring down, so I held the umbrella over him as he jacked the car up and changed the tire. When he finished, we all three were soaking wet, but he wouldn't accept any money for his work. All I could do was thank him for his help. We thanked God for sending us an "angel" to help us.

Thinking it had a nail, Joe took the tire to be fixed. He discovered the tire was OK, but the rim had been bent; this allowed the air to escape.

Chapter 18

Spiritual Challenges that Test and Strengthen

You are our letter, written in our hearts, known and read by all men;
being manifested that you are a letter of Christ, cared for by us,
written not with ink, but with the Spirit of the living God, not on
tablets of stone, but on tablets of human hearts. And such confidence
we have through Christ toward God. Not that we are adequate in
ourselves to consider anything as coming from ourselves, but our
adequacy is from God (2 Cor. 3:2-5).

1979-1980
Introduction

Our family took a two-week vacation; it was the longest vacation we'd had since we moved to Brazil. We spent the last week of 1978 on a beach at Rio das Ostras in the State of Rio de Janeiro and the first week in January 1979 at a beautiful mountain resort in the same state. These places were at our timeshare club we had joined. Since our kids were old enough to see the mysterious and diabolic way the spiritists (spiritualists) worship, we all went to the beach on New Year's night. The spiritists groups had gathered on the beach; all the people were dressed in white garments. Each group made a small fire; the people did not do this to stay warm but as part of their worship ceremonies. The mediums all smoked pipes or cigars as a part of their long rituals that would last until midnight.

The amazing thing that I observed this time was a man preaching in one of the groups, just as if he were an evangelical preacher. This stunned me; I listened intently to his message. He even used a few

Bible verses. At the end of the message, however, they began their worship of their spiritist saints. Most were from African deities but now were identified with a name of a Roman Catholic saint. My impression was that spiritists felt threatened by losing some members through Evangelical preaching. The spiritist preaching was trying to adapt a little of Evangelical preaching to keep their members away from Evangelical churches. As time passed that night, some people were overtaken by a spirit or spirits that caused gyrations and frightful facial expressions as I described in chapter 2. At midnight each group carried its two- or three-foot boat laden with fruits, flowers, and other things into the ocean until the people were waist-deep in water. They set the boat free to go into the high sea to appease Iamanja, their goddess of the sea.

During the week we spent several hours on the beach each day. We had our beach umbrella and mats. Someone had to stay with the things while the others walked the beach looking for shells or were playing in the water. Since I couldn't take much sun, I usually was the one to stay under the umbrella. We were a little cautious about eating food from vendors, because we didn't want to get food poisoning, but we did enjoy the spit of grilled shrimp doused with lime juice.

Jonathan spent hours building sand castles that later were washed away. The beach in that area didn't have the waves that were good for surfboarding. The water usually was calm. Charlotte was a good swimmer, but Leona had trouble even floating. Even so, the two enjoyed playing in the water. Something about ocean water made it easier to swim or float. I usually went far enough out to have a good swim; then I was ready to stay in the shade the rest of the time. Usually a small group of gypsy women walked the beaches and wanted to read someone's palm.

At night we had our family worship time, which included a study of a book of the Bible—usually a choice of the kids. Then we played games together. The second week we didn't have the beach, but we found other recreation activities.

Jardim Guanabara Preaching Point

Some have asked how we started a new work. At times we started a new work through strategy planning—to reach out into an area without an Evangelical witness. By the Holy Spirit's guidance we went into any situation that opened up. At other times we had the door to open by people that attended our church but lived in a neighborhood with no Baptist church. That was the case with Jardim Guanabara mission. We had some members that walked a good distance to our church from the Jardim Guanabara (*Bairro*) neighborhood. Tupi Baptist Church had a mission/preaching point in the edge of Jardim Guanabara, but our members didn't want to attend there, especially at night, because the street had no lights. I found a house for rent in the center of the neighborhood. With the help of the Baptists living in the area, we started a preaching point. We soon had a full house—more people than the Tupi group. I respected the Tupi church and told the church, since it also was renting, it could be in charge of our preaching point in which we had started and we would help pay the rent. The people there didn't want to do this. So I told them that whenever they moved to a better location, our group would join them so the work in the neighborhood could be stronger. So we continued; some of our Planalto members went to the Jardim Guanabara mission to lead the Sunday-school and worship services. Their Sunday school was after the preaching, so occasionally I would preach at 8:30 a.m. and then preach at Planalto at 10 a.m. This is the same thing we did at São Bernardo. From the beginning Laisete was at Santa Cruz, so I didn't have to be responsible for preaching at Santa Cruz.

Terrible Floods in Minas Gerais

Floods are the most frequent disasters in most of Brazil. Poverty-stricken people suffer more damage and death from the floods than do others because they build along the rivers; their houses usually don't have foundations. In late February and early March 1979 the heavens opened and dumped an unusual amount of water on four states; the worst hit was Minas Gerais. Most towns, villages, and cities in Brazil are built along hundreds of rivers. Since most of Brazil is a tropical and semi-tropical area, a normal amount of water is a lot of water. During the 36 years we lived in Brazil, I never saw the newspapers refer to how much water was normal or how much water fell during any time of the year. The normal rainy season, or *monsoon* (a term not used in Brazil), must have had more than 40 inches in the semi-tropical area in which we lived. I am just guessing, but I know a lot of water fell from the middle of November to the end of April. Several years during a 21-day period we saw rain that did not stop. At times the rain would slow to a drizzle but then go back to torrents of rain.

In the summer of 1979 about two-thirds of Minas Gerais was flooded. Although I don't think a final total was ever given, at the height of the flooding parts of 191 cities and towns were under water. Fifty-five of these were cut off from any communication with the rest of the state. Ninety roads and highways were impassable; 200 bridges were destroyed. Our state reported about 300 deaths, these mostly were from mudslides in the slum areas and a few that covered automobiles on the highways. More than 200,000 people were driven from their homes; 6,500 houses were destroyed. Between 800 and 1,000 Baptist families were directly or indirectly affected.

When the city officials of Governador Valadares were warned that water had to be released from the dam above, they sent trucks and buses to the island. They drove up and down the streets and blew their horns and with loudspeakers warned the people about the danger so they could get off the island. The wall of water inundated all except one small part of the island. For seven days the mission house in which we had lived and hadn't sold had four feet of water inside it. Island Baptist Church was filled with eight feet of dirty water. For a pastor's home we had built an apartment above part of the building. The pastor and wife left the church just in time. The priest at the Roman Catholic Church refused to leave, but two days later he had to be rescued in a boat from the gallery of his church. One cannot imagine the force of rushing water until he or she sees the final result. So much water was going into the drainage system from the city streets that the heavy metal lids covering the manholes were forced off; this left open holes in the ground. More than once swirling water around the open manholes sucked a person into the open hole.

Several interesting God-things happened in Island Baptist Church. The pastor had left his Bible on the pulpit. The pulpit rose with the water and floated for six or seven days before it settled to the floor again. The Bible didn't get wet. After we had built the building in 1970, we were given a huge desk. The desk wouldn't go through

342

the door into the office in the back room. The only way to get the desk into that back room was through the front door and then through the baptistery. Well, that big desk floated out through the baptistery again and into the worship area. I suppose the benches floated, too, but how the Bible didn't get knocked off the pulpit or the pulpit didn't turn upside down is phenomenal! The pump organ was soaked and ruined. We realized how blessed we were that God had moved us to Belo; otherwise, we would have lost everything.

Two-and-one-half weeks after the flood I went with Pastor Bittencourt, our executive secretary, to assess the damage and make contact with the churches that had suffered from the flood in Valadares. The concrete bridge connecting the island to the center of the city had tilted a little. Even after more than a thousand truck loads of mud and trash had been removed from the island, most of the streets still were impassable. Of the more than 10,000 that had lived on the island, only a few people had returned. We took some money from Southern Baptist disaster relief to help buy mattresses and essential things for as many as could be served, not just the Baptist people. Island Baptist Church suffered the most, because all of its members had to leave the island and for about three months were scattered throughout the city. After the island residents had recuperated, many built a second floor so that they could avoid losing everything in another flood. Already some three-story apartment buildings existed. Now 20 years later the island is the showcase of Valadares.

Pastor Bittencourt and I went to several other towns and cities and offered Southern Baptist relief funds. The pastors were instructed to have for us a list of church members and friends who were very needy.

Tragedy at Planalto Baptist Church
The last week in March was a very, very difficult time for Planalto Church. Sunday was promotion day in Sunday school. Cesar, 5-years old, had stood up on a table in the children's room and said: "This is the happiest day of my life; let's sing *Satisfied.*" All week he had been singing that chorus. We had no warning that the Lord would use this little boy to open the doors to visit many neighbors and friends in the area. That afternoon Cesar was playing with other kids and darted

from behind a car into the street. At that moment Sr. Nilton, a banker, was driving by and ran over Cesar. Yeda, the mother, saw the accident; she ran into the street and picked him up in her arms. She knew then that he probably wouldn't live and instantly gave him to God. He was rushed to a nearby hospital. Yeda stayed at home, because she was about two weeks away from giving birth to another child. After I taught a class at the São Bernardo mission, I arrived at the church for the evening service at Planalto and heard about Cesar's accident. I went to the hospital, but they wouldn't let me see the boy. He died soon after I left. I went back to the church to get Leona, Charlotte, and Jonathan; we went to see Yeda at their home. The parents, Mr. and Mrs. Araujo, were concerned about Sr. Nilton because he was so inconsolable that he had to be taken to a hospital. That night at church we all prayed for Sr. Nilton. I knew the funeral the next day would be very emotional.

Before the funeral I met with all the family and prayed that the service would glorify God. Sr. Nilton's wife, two banker friends, a lawyer, and about 300 other people attended the funeral. The service truly was a victory for Jesus. With poise and assurance the congregation sang songs. In memory of Cesar the children of the church sang choruses and even sang *Satisfied*. The parents and grandparents, members of our church, demonstrated deep Christian faith and understanding. One of the bankers told the grandfather that before the accident he was an atheist, but now he believed in God. The Lord took control of the funeral. God helped us all to hold back our tears; the many lost people present really saw how God can comfort those who belong to Him. Even after they lost their darling little boy, the family prayed for Sr. Nilton. After Wednesday-night prayer meeting some of us went to visit Sr. Nilton, but we went to the wrong house. That neighbor had heard about the lovingkindness the church had shown and asked us to return to visit him. Then on Friday morning Sr. Nilton visited me at our home; after an hour of Bible study he accepted the Lord.

Early Thursday morning of the same week Cesar died, a man whose wife and children were members of the church died . The man had accepted the Lord but hadn't been baptized. We spent the day getting documents and making other arrangements to bury him that very day. That night we were supposed to start a "Win School", to be led by missionary Jack Young at our church, but we postponed that until Friday night. The Araujo family and the family of the father that died both participated in the "Win School". The next Sunday morning all Sunday-school members went into the neighborhood and witnessed about Christ to friends and neighbors instead of the having regular classes; nine people accepted the Lord Jesus. That week the Lord's presence through the Holy Spirit brought us through great trials. That Sunday night a sister of the man whose husband had died made a decision.

Disaster-Relief Teams Arrive

On Monday after the difficult week at Planalto a group of men from Texas arrived to go to Governador Valadares to help Island Baptist Church clean up and repair from the flood. As far as I know the first disaster teams to take on a project in Brazil were from Texas to help restore the island church and a mission at Aimores, close to the Espirito Santo state line. Olin Miles, Baptist Men's leader from Texas, sent the first team to Governador Valadares. The first team consisted of five men: three from Dallas, one from Tyler, and the other from Lone Star. Four of them arrived together and one arrived in Belo the next day. In the car I could take only three with me in the car because of luggage and tools. Two men had to go by bus. As we were leaving, a torrential rain started; I decided we couldn't leave that day. I told them of the danger of more mudslides and that parts of some roads already had been washed out; the rain made traveling very dangerous. They were unhappy with me, for they would be losing another day of work. On the trip the next day we saw the area in which four cars were still buried with a mudslide. This sight helped them to understand why I refused to travel the day before.

We stayed in the hotel in which I usually stayed in when I went to Governador Valadares, but this hotel really wasn't the best place for them. The beds were not the quality for larger men to enjoy a good night's sleep. This was my first experience with disaster-relief teams; I was sorry I had lodged them there. These five men stayed in Governador Valadares eight days. Milton Schmitt, Royal Ambassador leader from Dallas' First Baptist Church, had brought a set of cooking utensils to prepare the meals; however, each day we were able to eat in a restaurant at a good price.

These men cleaned and rebuilt the furniture that was worth saving. They replaced the destroyed fence and made the lower part of brick and concrete with metal bars on top. This metal work for the fence was ready when they arrived. I spent much of my time buying things they needed. They also repainted the inside of the church. All the electrical outlets had to be cleaned. A few members had returned to their homes on the island, but the only furniture they had were the beds bought with Baptist World Alliance and Southern Baptist funds. These men also pooled some money among themselves to help some buy other things they needed. This experience was good for me. These men, accustomed to electrical equipment, mixed the cement by hand and did all the manual labor necessary.

At night worship services were held in the eight churches in the city; the Texans preached. Ideir dos Santos, the Presbyterian woman that spent six months with us in the States in 1976, interpreted for two of the men in four of the Baptist churches in Valadares while a boy interpreted for the other three men in the other four churches. I went to the two missions, Palmeiras and Altinopolis, to encourage them. The thanksgiving service in Island Baptist Church the last night the relief team was there was a tearful event as Brazilians and the disaster-relief team met for the last time together. Baptists from Texas had provided for all the expenses of restoring Island Baptist Church to its former worshipful look on the inside and enclosing the property with the nice fence.

The second Texas team arrived on May 12. Eight men were to stay until May 24. We decided that missionaries Lawrence Walker, South Brazil business manager, and Fred Hawkins would take the team members by car to Aimores directly from Rio de Janeiro. Lawrence hadn't traveled so far into the interior; by the time they arrived in Aimores, he thought they had reached the end of the world. The 12-hour drive truly was tiring!

When I arrived a day earlier to make sure things were ready, I was very disappointed. Olin Miles, Texas state men's director, had said the foundation for the mission building must be ready before the team arrived. I thought I had made the instructions plain and even had sent money for the foundation, but it was not ready. Of course Olin and the crew members were disappointed, but they went to work. Missionary Jesse Kidd arrived on Tuesday afternoon to take my place as interpreter for the group, because I had to return to Belo for Carl's high-school graduation on Friday. The next Monday was the day for the team's departure from Aimores, so I returned to help take the men to the airport in Belo. The sun had almost set when I arrived; Jesse and his carload were about ready to leave. The others were not ready, so I told Jesse to go ahead of us; we would meet in Manhuacu. I reminded him to be careful not to take the road to the right at a fork in the road, because if he did, he would go to the wrong place. Our plan was to eat and spend the night at a certain hotel in Manhuacu.

The 50 miles from Aimores to Manhuacu was on a rough dirt road. My group began asking me questions about my work; that led to stories about my experiences. About an hour later I arrived at a town I didn't recognize at first. Then suddenly I realized that we were in Mutum, the town that I had told Jesse to avoid. I couldn't believe it! I had taken the wrong fork in the road. If I went back the same way that I had arrived, we would be delayed another hour. I asked a man in Mutum about another road to Manhuacu; he gave me directions. I left Mutum on a dirt road with which I was not familiar—one with no road signs at the forks in the road. Now I was really troubled. I stopped at a couple of farmhouses to make sure I still was on the road to Manhuacu. We finally arrived at the hotel after 10 p.m.; no restaurant was open, so the men in my car had a reason to be unhappy with me. Evidently Olin Miles forgave me, because he invited me to share some of my missionary experiences at the Texas Baptist Men's state meeting in the fall; I had told him we would be going on a short furlough in August

Carl's Senior Year at EABH

In the missions and churches as well as at EABH (American School of Belo Horizonte) our children always are assets to our ministry. Most of his three years at EABH, Carl made the honor roll. Carl played soccer, basketball, and volleyball. In these sports these American school teams played some good Brazilian schools and sports club teams. In soccer the American school was no match for the

Brazilians.

Each year EABH participated in the tournaments between the American schools in Brazil. EABH was the smallest school, so most boys were involved in all three sports. His last year Carl was consistently in second-place in scoring in basketball. He got the most-improved award in basketball, but Jonathan was the hero in the only game his team won in the basketball American school tournament. Jonathan was sent in during the final minutes of the game. In the last few seconds he was fouled and made both free-throws, which won the only game for EABH in the tournament.

At noon once a week Tom Sumerall, missionary for English work, started a Bible study at EABH. The study was well-attended, but Tom was transferred to Brasilia. For the rest of the year missionary Jack Young picked up that responsibility. During his last year at home Carl preached for me a few times when I was traveling. He went to the youth activities in the Central Association and state youth meetings.

Carl's graduation was at the school gym. Only three seniors—three boys of three different nationalities: from Bangladesh, Japan and America—graduated in 1979. We were thrilled and proud to have our oldest child graduate. Each of the seniors gave a speech.

CARL ANTHONY TARRY

I am sorry that we scared you the night when you were born!
We were playing a game about barley, rye, wheat, and corn.
Playing Pit with friends is a very rowdy, noisy game.
For your arriving early, maybe we are to blame!

What's going on out there, you must have thought?
"I'll just get out of here and see, so I struggled and fought."
So as soon as our guests left, your mother exclaimed:
"I am in labor!"
Hastily and prayerfully we went to the hospital to meet the doctor.

By six o'clock the next morn I knocked
at Ken and Beth Glenn's door.
They exclaimed: "It can't be! It is impossible!
We didn't have a clue!"

Since you are partially responsible for the early arrival of our boy,
You get to be the first to see me and share this father's joy!

Remember when you batted the plastic ball so very hard
That it sailed over the house top into the back yard?
For a 4-year-old that was a feat, although the house was small.
And the size of the almond tree Dad pulled up was not so tall at all!

You delighted our hearts as you grew and developed day by day.
Our lives centered on you, as we interacted in childish play.
When Jonathan and Charlotte arrived,
you adapted well as big brother.
As parents we worked to help each of you love one another.

You gave your heart and life to Jesus when you were 7 in Brazil.
You carefully made your decision on your own free will.
I rejoiced in baptizing you in the mighty Sweet River
After you had been cleansed by Jesus' precious blood forever!

Your interest and success in chess showed you had
an analytic brain.
You still analyze thoughts and examine every angle,
as if ideas are a game.
But God has His hand on you and deserves to guide in what you do.
So no matter what the devil does, God will see you through!

Arriving from school one day with arms the size of "Popeye"
Your blood pressure had also soared very, very high!
The doctor and we were extremely worried and "upset"
That the rigid contest your gym teacher suggested had to be met.

Perhaps your determination was to do more pushups than expected
And maybe also do more push-ups than your coach
would have directed.
Sweating and exhausted you lay resting on the cold gym floor,
Causing an extreme chemical reaction
and your blood pressure to soar!

Regardless the reason, the Air Force has its stringent regulations.
Everything for the Air Force was ready; regular blood pressure
is an obligation!
We were disappointed that your dream for the Academy did not
come true,
But we pray that God will give you another heart's desire
as what to do!

You were an asset to mission work in the land of the Southern Cross.
You are leaving home for college; Mom and I feel your leaving
is our loss.
You influenced more people than you will ever know!
For Mom and Dad it is never easy to let their firstborn go.

Dad and Mom

Our motive for taking a short furlough in 1979 was to help get
Carl started at Hardin-Simmons University and also to visit our aging
parents.

A Near-Serious Accident in Lima, Peru

In July we left Brazil for our short furlough. For very little more
money than a straight flight from Brazil to the States would cost, we
had the opportunity to stop in other countries, so we decided to visit
Peru. We paid the extra expense for this stop. Visiting other countries
gave us an education on other South America countries. The furlough
before we had visited Colombia. I had a desire to go to Peru to see the
Andes Mountains, the llamas, and people.

We landed in Lima, Peru at midnight; missionary Elbert Smithen
Jr. met us in a big (old) Chevrolet station wagon. We had advised
Elbert that Carl had more luggage than usual as he was leaving home
for college. We were on our way to Smithens' home when a drunken
man blared through a red light and hit us broadside; he dented the
back door by which Leona was sitting and nearly hit the gasoline fuel
spout. We didn't know Elbert was new on the field and still had difficulty conversing in Spanish. As often happens with drunks, the man
wasn't hurt, but his car sure was. Elbert had difficulty steering the car

and almost swerved into a light pole. After much conversation to settle the legal part, we left the scene and arrived at the missionarys' house about 1:30 a.m.

The next day we left most of our luggage at Elbert and Winnifred's house and caught a flight to Cusco. In the early afternoon we arrived in Cusco and located a hotel. Cusco has an elevation of about 11,000 feet, so normally tourists used at least one day adapting to the altitude. We walked through the street market and were shocked at the poverty of the people. Their wares for sale were displayed on the ground; the items looked as though they were things we would put in the trash. Every kind of bolt, screw, doll pieces, and every used thing imaginable were for sale. We were thankful for our coats, because the weather was cold. We returned to find the hotel very cold, too, because it had no heat in the rooms. We were so cold, we just went to bed.

The workers at the hotel were accustomed to people leaving early on the train for Machu Picchu, so they offered to awaken us the next morning. We had an early breakfast, which was a poor excuse for breakfast; even the coffee was cold and tasted terrible. The hotel cooks prepared lunches for us to take on our trip. In the dark we made our way to the train station and boarded the train for Machu Picchu. Our journey to the amazing ancient ruins of Inca Indians began. A section of the track included a series of switchbacks, because the mountain was so steep. The railroad follows the Sacred River of the Incas (Urubamba River). Actually Cusco is 3,000-feet higher than Machu Picchu.

We arrived about 10 a.m. at the ruins and were supposed to leave at 4 p.m. The ruins in the high, rugged mountains with rich, gorgeous surroundings were more than one can absorb in one day. We were amazed, enthralled, and overwhelmed about the ingenuity those Indians showed in building with huge carved rocks on a rugged mountain amidst surrounding peaks. They also had designed an ingenious water system for their city.

The day passed all too fast; we loaded back on the train at 4 p.m. After we waited a while, we were informed that we couldn't leave because a train had derailed in a village not too far away. The whole group of us had eaten most of what we had brought. The only food to buy was a few oranges that some Peruvian peddlers had; these soon were gone. Darkness swallowed the area and the temperature fell. People were not complaining; rather they started getting to know each other. A family from South Africa had kids the ages of ours, so they made friends. The kids went to visit with the engineers and were permitted to see the engine's controls. About 1 a.m. we finally left Machu Picchu and at 5 a.m. arrived in Cusco. In the dark we made our way back to the hotel. The hotel was closed, but we finally found a doorbell in the dark; the manager opened the door for us. We were happy to get to bed for a few hours.

Rather than sightseeing more in Cusco we decided we would try to catch the afternoon flight back to Lima. As we arrived at the airport, we saw that seemingly everyone was trying to leave on that plane. Our situation looked hopeless, but for some unusual reason a military office helped us get tickets. After I got our tickets, I began to wonder about the wisdom of our plan to leave that day. I never had seen so many restless people. The plane was going to be super loaded. People were pushing and almost crushed each other as each tried to be first in line. Just before the exit doors of the waiting room were opened, word was given that the exit door to be used was at the other end of the room. Since we had been last in line, reversing the waiting line to another door put us first in line to exit. Everyone made a mad rush for the exit and ran for the airplane. *Absolute bedlam* describes the situation. We did get on but were scattered in the airplane in random seats. I did some praying, because the airplane seemed to have difficulty getting off the ground and shook in an unusual way.

The two most impressive things we saw in Lima were the catacombs of the cathedral and the Inquisition Museum. Under the cathedral thousands of human bones were arranged: skulls were interestingly laid out in one area, arm bones neatly arranged in a pattern in another area, leg bones were arranged in another, and so forth. Only God, since DNA was not known in those days, could rearrange those bones into their original bodies.

The torture chamber in the museum was very vivid; it used very real-looking people made of molding material. In a wall, about three-feet above the ground, a hole with bars over the opening contained a human-sized man doubled up as tight as he could be; a mouse was looking at him with intense interest. Another type of torture was demonstrated by a man setting with his wrists tied by wire to the arms of a chair. This wire could be tightened with a big screw on each chair arm; the screw was similar to the kind that tightens violin strings. The idea was that if the person didn't confess to his accusation correctly, to tighten the wire around the wrists until the veins burst. Another method used during the Roman Catholic Inquisition was to force water into a human until the person looked as though he would burst. The man being tortured this way was lying on his back. His eyes bulged out to show his misery; his stomach was horribly bloated with water. Yet two human figures were forcing more water into his mouth. Another memorable method of torture was the "rack", which showed a man's body being stretched apart. This was a painful torture method. I was amazed that this historical museum, showing methods of torturing objectors to Roman Catholicism, is situated across the street from the huge cathedral.

Getting Carl into College

Housing during furlough (now called *Stateside assignment*) can be a problem because the missionaries arrive in the States with just their suitcases. That means they need to find a furnished house that includes linens and kitchen items. The national WMU has promoted the idea of churches, associations, or states furnishing a place for furloughing missionaries. For many missionaries this has been a real blessing. Three times during our 36 years with the board we were able to take advantage of this offer. In 1979 we lived in Portales, NM, in the house we had bought in 1976; WMU groups of the local churches helped with linens and kitchen things. The other problem the missionary faces on furlough is buying a car and selling it before he or she returns to the field. On this furlough our dear friend Jack Gregory from Lovington furnished us with a good Chevrolet.

Carl wanted to play soccer on the Hardin-Simmons University team, so that meant arriving in Abilene, TX, early for the practice season. We bought the necessary items for Carl to stay in the dorm and took him to the university to get settled. We were determined not to cry as we said our goodbyes. That was most difficult, but we held the tears until we drove away.

About two weeks later we returned to Hardin-Simmons to attend an orientation session with Carl. Dr. Jesse Fletcher, formerly with the FMB but at the present time president of the university, earlier had written a personal letter to Carl. In the letter he stated that Hardin-Simmons would be the only university at which he could call the president "Uncle". That showed Dr. Fletcher's personal touch with the MK's (missionary kids); this was greatly appreciated. Dr. Fletcher had led the university board of trustees to give work scholarships to MK's. The WMU also gave MK's some very valuable monetary help; for each of the children we had a college savings account of about $1,000. So all we had to give was his spending money. Carl's first job on campus was in the cafeteria.

During the first summer vacation time Carl stayed with his Uncle Pat and Aunt Doris Bowen in Roswell. During his college years the Bowens' home became his second home. At a restaurant he found a job washing pots and pans. The job didn't pay a lot, but he received one meal a day and was able to pay a little on his room and board. At the end of the summer he was able to buy a used car.

Our furlough was for only five months, but we were able to attended Foreign Mission Week at Glorieta and speak in a few churches. We had time to visit our parents and siblings.

Christmas with all the gang was at the Isbell farm. We had a wonderful time together. However, packing suitcases to leave for Brazil along with preparing for the family Christmas get-together was too much stress. Leaving the day after Christmas was not such a good idea. On December 26 we left for Brazil to begin another term.

1980—Another Job Change

Once we were on our way, our return trip to Brazil was smooth. Our hearts beat with joy when at the airport to greet us we saw about 15 of our church members and the missionaries who lived in Belo Horizonte. We were more than two hours late because of bad weather, but they waited for us. One of the little Brazilian girls presented Leona with a bouquet of flowers. This was a moment of intense emotions, similar to what we experienced each time we left for the States and had Brazilians and missionaries present to send us off.

While I was in the States, I had received a letter from our executive secretary. The letter told me that the Baptist men in the state wanted to organize; they had requested that I be their leader. I was surprised that Pastor Jose Alves da Silva Bittencourt would agree to their request; this would pull me off of the stewardship responsibility to work with the men. But, on the other hand, who furnished most of the financial needs in Baptist work? The men! So I returned to a different job assignment. If the state convention believed this was more vital than stewardship was, I believed I should do what it wanted me to do. I already had designed a chart for every association in the state convention; this chart easily could keep the financial record of every church for a 10-year period. With this chart anyone easily could know which churches were weak and which were strong. Strengthening our men and boys in the Lord's work was the new challenge.

Planalto Church ended 1979 with 100 members and about 215 enrolled in the three Sunday schools. By the end of March 1980 we had grown to 119 members and 230 in the four Sunday schools. Planalto and her three missions all needed more space, especially for Sunday school. We needed to make a decision: should we use the money saved to buy another lot for Planalto or use it to build on our property, thus saving rent, or should we rent one of the apartments above the place in which we were meeting? One of the apartments above became vacant, so we decided to rent; this would give us more space for the children's work. We had five classes in our worship area. Can you imagine how noisy that was? The children met in the smaller store (original worship area) downstairs. Renting one of the apartments above us was a great blessing. Praise God for problems and for God's surprises that were happening nearly every week.

I must give Leona credit for many things. She was busy as state Baptist Women's leader and was on the Central Association's planning committee. She was preteen teacher in Sunday school, G.A. leader, church WMU program chairperson, played the accordion (our musical instrument) for the church worship and home services, and every week visited in the neighborhood with me when I was in town and with the women when I was out of town. Always unexpected cases of helping people in need happened, especially in two of the missions. She also had her home responsibilities. We usually had a seminary student who helped with housework.

Living in the State Capital

When we lived in Governador Valadares, we were the only Americans. In the capital the fellowship with other missionary families was a precious advantage. We celebrated Christmas, Thanksgiving, and birthday parties together. With the Bill Richardsons we even had Groundhog Day celebrations.

Another advantage of living in the state capital was the American school for our kids. Our kids went through the eighth grade in Brazilian schools and did well, but we wanted them in the American school to help them prepare for university in the States. A special bus stopped at our house by 7:15, then made the route of picking up other students, and arrived at the American school about 8:15. The school was situated on the eastern outskirts of the city. We had to get up at 5:45 for breakfast, have our daily devotionals (which included praying for the missionaries), and be ready for the bus. I prepared their lunches while Leona prepared breakfast. Usually sports practice, whether basketball, soccer, or volleyball, was after school. After their practice, a bus would bring them to the center of Belo; they would walk the 10 blocks, climb the steep street to get home, or wait in line for a crowded city bus. They usually preferred walking.

The Centennial Evangelism Campaign

Brazilian Baptists had great expectations for the evangelism campaign that would celebrate 100 years of Baptist existence from 1882 through 1982. In 1882 Southern Baptists started work in Brazil with William Buck and Anne Luther Bagby. A special evangelism tract called "Good News Brazil" (*Boas Novas Brasil*) was prepared for the occasion. This evangelism crusade involved Texas Baptist associations partnering with Brazilian state capitals. The Brazilian state conventions would supply Brazilian pastors for their churches in the interior areas. Tarrant County in Texas adopted Belo Horizonte. The main thrust of the campaign was that every Baptist should tell his or her salvation experience to one person every day.

Leona and I were visiting Nely Terrinha, a sick member. A friend arrived to buy some shirts from Nely. Nely was artistic and painted designs on T-shirts to sell. We used the *Boas Novas Brasil* tract and told our testimonies to the friend. She was touched and confessed that she needed to change her life. We gave her a tract and had prayer with her. On Wednesday night a week later she arrived at prayer meeting. I gave the church members the opportunity to tell how God had worked in their lives during the past week. That woman stood up and told how she had returned home from Nely's the week before and thought about her life. She lived a long way from our church. She couldn't find peace, so when she arrived home, she knelt beside her bed and poured out her heart to Jesus; He saved her. That night she was very happy. The next Sunday she brought her husband and two little boys. Not long after that, her mother died; she asked me to conduct her mother's funeral.

Another experience happened at this time in the office of the lawyer that administered the legal details for the building our church was renting. I was in his office because the church wanted to rent an empty apartment above us to expand our Sunday-school space. I discovered that lawyer Moacir had an interest in the professional Athletic Soccer Club that had its clubhouse in the Planalto neighborhood. Joao Leite was the goalkeeper for the professional Atletico Futebol Club (Athletic Soccer Club) Team. Joao had been converted and was baptized in First Baptist Church in Belo Horizonte; he became the first evangelical convert among the professional players in Brazil. I told the lawyer I knew Joao personally and that my sons were fans of the Athletic Soccer Club.

Mr. Moacir knew Joao Leite was a believer. He said: "The team has made a great change internally since John (Joao) has become a believer. A lot of arguing and disharmony was common in the club before but not any more."

This was my cue to say something. I asked him, "Would you like to know why?" Mr. Moacir said *yes*, so I gave my testimony that began with my salvation at 8-years old. When I finished, tears were streaming down his face. He said he would like to visit our church some day. Well, as often happens, Moacir didn't accept Jesus that day and didn't visit our church. I left him the "Good News Brazil" tract. One thing is for sure; he never will forget that moment when he, a man, was moved by the Holy Spirit to change his life but didn't! He also knew that John Leite was a changed man that had won two of his teammates to Christ. At the end of each game John also gave every opposing *goleiro* (goalkeeper) a Bible.

Although Joao Leite and his wife, Eliane, were busy people, they became our friends. The first few years when I was pastor in Planalto, Leona and I promoted youth banquets among some of the churches surrounding Planalto. We used the Baptist school cafeteria for the banquets. Three times we invited Joao Leite and his wife to be speakers for these banquets. His wife was captain of the women's national volleyball team and one year played for Brazil in the Olympics.

Sofia Mendes Pessoa

Sofia moved into her son's house in Planalto after a tragedy in her sister's life. Sofia had lived across the city near her sister who had a spiritist *terreiro* (backyard court) at her home. It was used for spiritist worship. These spiritist sessions usually were held every Friday night. A lot of drum music and singing weird songs accompanied the spiritist sessions. Sofia was the president of her sister's spiritist worship center.

The family was having a reunion picnic in another town. Some of the family members were swimming in a river. One of Sofia's nephews, the son of her sister that sponsored the spiritist center, disappeared in the water. Her sister and the whole group were in great panic; they wept hysterically and moaned in grief. After a while Sofia's sister, in desperation, said, "Jesus, if you are real, please bring my son's body to the top." Her son's body rose to the top of the water. This greatly impressed the mother. A few days later she was walking down her street and heard music from a Baptist church. She went in and listened and accepted Jesus as her Savior. She closed the spiritist worship center. Sofia also began seeking peace in her heart. She moved to live with her son and widowed daughter that lived close to Planalto Baptist Church.

To promote our revival we put information about it in the mailboxes of the homes in the neighborhood. Sofia received an invitation and sent her granddaughter to locate the church. She had been listening to a radio program and already had begun studying a Seventh-Day Adventist Bible course. Sofia was a very large woman. She had great difficulty walking because of arthritis in her knees. Her son brought her to church; at the door she asked a member whether she could attend. From that Sunday on she didn't miss a service; before long she decided that only Jesus could save her soul. She was in the new believers' class and preparing for baptism, but she had a problem: she hadn't been able to quit smoking. She had smoked since she was 16 and now was in her 60s. Brazilian churches didn't baptize candidates until they gave up smoking, drinking, or other vices. I didn't try to change this practice, because this was Baptist policy. I agreed because it helped people more quickly overcome their vices.

A group from the church went monthly to the woman's home and held a worship service. Her daughter was very polite and even prepared snacks but never stayed to worship with us. Because of his job her son was not home during the week.

Months went by; Sofia didn't have the power to quit smoking. Her son smoked, her daughter and possibly even the granddaughter smoked. On the weekends several family members visited; all of them smoked. They had literally a "smoke house". So for Sofia to quit in this home environment was difficult. One day she threw the cigarettes and matches down on her bed and sincerely cried aloud: "Lord, you see that I cannot give up smoking. I am helpless. Help me!" At that moment all desire to smoke left her.

In our rented building we didn't have a baptistery, so we used the swimming pool at Jehova and Yeda Araujo's home, which was close to the church. (This family's 5-year-old son was run over by a car.) The day that Sofia and others were baptized was a glorious day. Several of her family members were present to witness her baptism. Sofia had to be helped into the pool. A deacon helped me baptize her. Because her legs might give way when we raised her up out of the water, we had a chair to sit in for the baptism. After the baptism Leona took Sofia home; she said: "Oh, I feel so light, I just feel so light today!" This was the way she expressed her joy of being able, through baptism, to identify with Jesus and her new church. She also was very relieved for her victory over nicotine.

Praying, Seeking, Waiting

I sought to find the owners of the lots adjoining the lot we had bought for Planalto Church's future home. A banker had bought the adjoining lot for an investment; he wanted the equivalent of $12,000 cash. We had about $8,000, but inflation was more than 50 percent a month. Lots along the avenue on which we had bought were zoned for commercial use; however, some houses had been built illegally. Commercial buildings could build on 80 percent of the land, while houses could use only 60 percent of the lot for building. We faced the difficulty of getting permission to build a church. So we were praying, seeking, and waiting for the Lord to work out a way to buy the banker's lot.

God answered one prayer in another area with the arrival of John and Monica Hatton to our church. John was the son of missionaries Alvin and Katie Hatton. John had married Monica, a fine Brazilian Christian, and had moved to Belo. John was an artist and was employed by Bethany Press in Belo Horizonte. John accepted the leadership of the São Bernardo mission.

A New Preaching Point
Irani and her children from a neighborhood called SESC began attending Planalto regularly. Because of the great distance from Planalto we started a Bible study at her house. Her husband was not happy with an Evangelical group meeting in their home, so we had to find a different place. The name *SESC* is an abbreviation for a large business men's club-retreat hotel. We were able to rent a vacant store building and started a Sunday-afternoon service. This preaching point was to be the responsibility of the Planalto youth along with their leaders. Now we had four preaching points and missions.

Now Planalto Baptist Church had four preaching points and missions. However, Barro Preto Baptist Church, second-largest Baptist church in Belo, bought property and began a mission not far from the place in which our mission was renting in the store building. By the end of 1982 we united our SESC mission with its mission. Starting a mission close to ours really was a relief, because this group of people could take the Baptist work forward quicker than we could. Praise God for leading them to the SESC neighborhood.

Held Back for a Reason
The apostle Paul was not allowed to go to Bithynia because God had another plan for his ministry. In our lives this happened several

times. In the first part of July Leona awoke one Sunday morning to find she had the mumps. Saturday had been a very busy day with a birthday celebration in the home of Irani in SESC and then a G.A. program at Planalto Church. Leona had a backache but didn't dream she had something such as the mumps. We had no doubt about the disease she had, because she looked like a puffed-up toad frog and had difficulty swallowing. On Saturday she had had contact with many people. The question was: *Who would have the mumps next?* This also was occurring only a few days before we were to leave for the annual South Brazil mission meeting. So we sent Jonathan and Charlotte with Leo and Dorothy Weatherman with the understanding that we would depart when Leona was better.

Maybe God had a reason for us to miss part of the meeting. In a worship service at our church Deuzita, a young mother of two small children, had made a decision. She had been attending my new-convert class and was happy about her decision. For a long time she had suffered with severe headaches; now she had been taken to the hospital. Leona visited her on Friday and I visited on Saturday. Sunday Leona was in bed with the mumps, so I visited her alone. While I was present, she went into a coma. The relatives and friends present thought she had died. The nurse asked me to help take her three floors below to the intensive care ward.

Monday through Thursday I had visited with many of Deuzita's relatives and friends in the hospital waiting room. During those days I witnessed, read the Bible, and left literature with a large number of friends and relatives that were waiting. She had a brain tumor and had no hope of recovery. She was the only one among her family that had made a decision for the Lord. She had told some of them about her salvation experience and about our church, which she now called *my church*.

Deuzita died on Thursday; at 5 p.m. on Friday the funeral was held. The family and relatives, all Roman Catholic or spiritist, arranged for a Roman Catholic funeral. A large crowd attended the funeral. Our church stood by the family; before the priest arrived, I was asked to read some Scripture and pray. I gladly took the opportunity. After the priest finished, he didn't accompany the people to the burial site, so I had another opportunity to tell Deuzita's testimony of accepting Christ as her personal Savior.

Early Saturday Leona and I left for mission meeting. If I had not had the second gas tank, we couldn't have made the trip to mission meeting until Monday, because this was the period of time in which the gas stations were closed on Saturday and Sunday. We were sailing down the highway when I realized the tire had a problem. God blessed us, because I was able to stop at a popular rest stop that had natural water springs. A trucker was there filling his water jug and relaxing for a while. I started raising the car with the jack. Guess what? The jack broke! This was the third time I had a jack to break. I asked the trucker whether he had a jack I could use. Since the truck jack was too tall, I had to lift the back of the car up while Leona pushed the jack under the car axle. After the third time for a jack to break, I bought a hydraulic jack for a spare. Guess what? I never had another jack to break!

You may think that we had a lot of tire problems; we did. Once I was alone and stopped at a place that changed tires. The day was blazing hot; the man fixing flats was working in the sun. When I arrived, he was working on a "18-wheeler" truck tire. He was whamming the tire with a tire mallet that looked as though it was a sledgehammer but had a very hard rubber hammer instead of iron. He was trying to break the tire from the rim and was not succeeding. He was older and looked tired, so I volunteered to hit the tire a few times for him. He accepted with a smile. I raised the hammer high, carefully looked at my target, and with all my might whammed at the tire. Instead the mallet hit the rim and bounced wildly out of control. The head or thick rubber hammer hit the man on his shin; although the hammer was made of thick rubber, a blow from it would have hurt badly. Shocked, I looked at him with an apologetic gasp. As he stood there staring at me, I began apologizing. Then he smiled, pulled up his trouser leg, and showed me his wooden leg. The man just laughed!

Good Things Continue to Happen

The month of July is vacation month—actually time between school semesters. After our return to Belo from mission meeting, we had Vacation Bible Schools at Planalto Church and Santa Cruz mission. We received word that the other apartment above Planalto

Church was to be vacated. Maybe the occupants couldn't stand good gospel singing and preaching. Anyway, we rented that apartment, too. That gave us space for more than 200 people in Sunday school.

The last week of July after the state convention I formed a committee to plan the organization of the Minas Gerais Baptist Men. This committee also worked with me to prepare next year's program for the Baptist Men.

Paul and Pat Renfro, friends since Portales university days, for several years sent us $50 a year and the last 20 years sent us a $100 a month for the Lord's work. Through the years their contribution helped to buy three lots, helped build two buildings, supported a lay preacher for a while, and bought an electric organ for Planalto Church. During 30 years of our ministry their faithful giving made a big difference.

I was pleased with the progress Planalto Baptist Church made in 1980. We had 23 baptisms and 23 transfers of letters from other churches. We finished the year with 138 members and 276 enrolled in Sunday school; these statistics included the two missions but not the other two preaching points. The number enrolled in Sunday school showed potentiality for a great future. We raised our goal for monthly contributions to the equivalent of $1,322; in two months we had reached that goal. We bought a lot for the São Bernardo mission a few blocks from the slum area in which the mission had been meeting. Even though São Bernardo mission now had a lot, a long time passed before the mission could move away from the stinky, polluted creek. More than once every year that creek flooded. This is the location at which John Hatton was pastor.

Have You Ever Heard of Anything Such as This?

For several months four children from one family attended regularly. The three older ones had made decisions for Christ. The mother was a strong Roman Catholic; the father leaned toward Evangelicals. After we missed the kids for a couple of Sundays, Leona and I went to visit them. Their parents told us that the three older ones couldn't return because they no longer were doing their homework in the Sunday school quarterly; they wouldn't study during the week but waited until Sunday morning to prepare their lessons. The 8-year-old girl could continue going because she was doing her homework during the week. These parents believed their children were abusing their privilege to attend our Sunday school if the kids didn't prepare and take advantage of their opportunity. *Wow!* Have you ever heard of parents with this attitude? How many children or adults would we have in our Sunday schools today if all adults had this idea? After we visited the parents, they let the kids return, but I appreciated their thoughts about the value of using Sunday schools for real study.

Another Rain Experience

For several years missionary Mattie Lou Bible worked with young people/students in our state. She scheduled a Monday-night Bible study for the youth at our church in Planalto. One of those Monday nights I took Mattie Lou, Jonathan, Charlotte, and a Panamanian young man in the mission car. Belo Horizonte's streets went up or down—rarely on level ground; however the main boulevard out to the church curved through the valley. Sprinkles of rain had started falling when we left the church about 9 p.m. About halfway, some three miles from home, we were traveling up the boulevard facing water rushing down from hills on both sides. By now the rain was a downpour; water was a foot or more high. Cars around us began stalling. I had the accelerator mashed almost as far as it would go; the car was pushing uphill against the rushing water that carried trash from the streets. Amazingly that very morning, as I returned from taking someone to the airport, for the first time I noticed a break in the center divider of the boulevard. The break allowed cars to turn left, just before they reached the Belo Horizonte Hospital. I thought to myself: "If only I could get to that spot and turn left off this main boulevard, I could get to higher ground and away from so much water." I knew that if I went the usual route home, I wouldn't succeed, because a lake would be at the foot of the next hill.

We were scared, especially the boy from Panama. Up, up, up that long hill we crept, while cars were stalling around us. Never had I seen water a foot deep rushing down a street as was happening at that moment. The car was straining against the powerful, rushing, muddy water. I was praying, "Lord, just let me get to that place where I can turn left." By this time no other car was behind us. In the distance I could see only lights of cars that had drowned out. The street lights were out; the rain was pouring down so hard that the windshield wipers, as they swished back and forth, just left a fleeting glimpse of what was before us. I finally saw the distorted flow of water that indicated that a gap was in the concrete dividing the six-lane boulevard. I turned to the left; in a moment we were going up a hill by the Belo Horizonte Hospital. This street had a lot less water descending. When we arrived, Leona, worried about us, was at home in the dark. The electrical transformer beside the house blew out; it left that area in the dark. We never will forget the experience. All of us in the car knew God had answered our prayers.

The downtown river went way over its banks again; many people were left homeless. That filthy water flooded stores along the river. Terrible floods were predicted to occur again.

Paulo Soares' Conversion

Paulo Soares and Amelio Terrinho were drinking buddies. Paulo worked for Mannesman Steel, a German company. Paulo had 12 children; a sister-in-law also lived with them. This made a total of 15 in the home. The family was constantly embroiled with family problems. The Holy Spirit was working in Paulo's heart. One night, while he and Amelio were drinking, Paulo expressed his troubled heart.

Amelio said: "You know what I think you need to do; you need to go to my wife's church." This was a strange thing for Amelio to say, since he hardly ever went to church, although our whole family frequently was in their home.

One Monday night, as we held a committee meeting at church, in walked a tall, black man I never had seen before. He sat down on the back row; our small committee was in the front. I was facing the back, so I was the only one that saw him. I went to him and introduced myself. He told me that Amelio Terrinha had suggested that he should visit our church. He was passing by and saw the door was open, so he stepped inside.

We were about through with our meeting, so I gave my attention to Paulo. That night he accepted the Lord. He told me the problems that he was having with his teen-agers. His wife, Maria Jose, and his sister-in-law, Terezinha, were staunch Roman Catholics. He had bought a Bible. I told him to start reading it and praying for his kids and to invite them to visit our church but not to be pushy. The next Sunday Paulo brought two or three of the smaller children with him. He was very happy.

As was our custom, Leona and I visited Paulo and his family. Terezinha and some of the young people didn't enter the room in which we were; Maria Jose was openly displeased. But evidently they were surprised that an American white couple would be interested enough to visit them.

Paulo grew in the Lord and seldom missed a service. He was burdened for his family and continued to bring to church two or three of the smaller children. Then one day he asked us to eat Sunday dinner with them; we accepted. His wife might have been surprised that we would go. For special occasions even the poor people want to do something real special, such as buy Coca Cola, Pepsi Cola, or Guarana soft drinks. Of course not many of the family could sit around the table, because we were a family of four. This visit softened some of the youth in the family. Soon we were able to have a Bible study in their home; others were converted. Yet the wife, Maria Jose, and her sister Terezinha resisted openly; when we arrived they would greet us and then leave the room.

One day Maria Jose asked Leona why we didn't accept Mary, the mother of Jesus. Leona explained our position about Mary—that she was highly honored to be chosen by God to be the mother of Jesus, but she was just a woman and not mother of God. Leona also stated that Mary had other children, which Maria Jose didn't accept. Leona explained that to have children was no sin; after all, she was married. To have children didn't remove the honor of being chosen of God. We don't pray to her or worship her; the Bible says we are to bow to no one but to God. That didn't set well with her, as Maria Jose prayed to Mary and believed she had certain powers. Some years later, after Maria Jose and Terezinha accepted Jesus as their only Savior, she warmly apologized to Leona and admitted to us how mad she had been. Maria Jose and Terezinha both became very active in church. Before Terezinha died, several times we ate in the home.

The Highfill Family

In 1972 Don and Erma Highfill and kids Robert and Becky arrived in Brazil. They became a part of our Minas Gerais missionary family. After language study they moved to Uberlandia, the largest city in the west of Minas Gerais; it had more than 200,000 people. Uberaba, about 50 miles to the south, was the headquarters of Chico Xavier, the most famous spiritist medium who was born in Pedro Leopoldo (where we, with Araci, later started a church). Don served as the director of the Triangle Association. The Triangle Association covered a large area; the churches were few and far apart. Later Bryan and Brenda joined the family (born in Brazil). Don was musically talented; he played the piano and accordion and sang. Planting churches in this area was slow, but under Don and Erma's leadership great progress was made. Erma was involved in WMU, was G.A. leader, and later became the South Brazil mission prayer coordinator. For the last years of their ministry they moved into Belo but spent all their missionary years in Minas Gerais. With the Internet, she continues working in the U.S. as the Brazil prayer advocate, although the Highfills are retired.

Many years we saw the Highfill family only a few times a year—at the annual mission meeting and at our Minas Gerais mission retreat. Most of the roads were dirt; this made traveling slow. I had the opportunity to be at most of the annual Triangle Association meetings and pastors' yearly retreat at camp, where I fellowshiped with Don. At least twice the church the Highfills attended invited me to conduct a Bible study or revival. On those occasions Bryan informed me how many minutes I could preach (what he considered to be my allotted time) and threatened to stand up to let me know my time was up. He considered this his responsibility. Bryan didn't consider me a good Skip-Bo partner. We always looked forward to fellowship with the Highfills.

Erma made a name for herself as a great cook; one specialty we enjoyed was her Brazilian cheese bread. She also was known for her decorated cakes.

Chapter 19

Promise, Praise, Power, Pressure, Problems, Possibilities, and Progress

And let us not lose heart in doing good, for in due time we shall reap if we do not grow weary. So then, while we have opportunity, let us do good to all men, and especially those who are of the household of the faith (Gal. 6:9-10).

1981-1984
Introduction

"*But seek first His kingdom and His righteousness: and all these things shall be added to you. Therefore do not be anxious for tomorrow; for tomorrow will care for itself. Each day has enough trouble of its own*" (Mt. 6:33-34). These verses summarize the Beatitudes and many other instructions about how to live and glorify God. Pleasing Triune God has all the rewards Matthew 5 and 6 cite; however, verse 34 advises Christians about the ups and downs in kingdom service. "Each day has enough trouble of its own" alerts us not to be disturbed if everything is not an easy victory. Verse 34 stresses that Satan is present to provoke, tantalize, and try to wear us down. This chapter is packed with a variety of victories in kingdom living but also tells of days of trouble.

In December 1980 Leona went to the U.S. for Christmas and her parents' 50th wedding anniversary. She was thrilled to see Carl, who was in the middle of his sophomore year; likewise, Carl was thrilled to see her. At the end of January I met Leona at the airport in Belem, near the mouth of the Amazon River; we attended the Brazilian Baptist Convention. Some Brazilians feared that not more than 500 messengers would be at the convention because of the great distance for the people of the Southern states to attend, but more than 1,000 registered.

For the third year in a row Minas Gerais led in the organization of new churches. Minas organized 20 new churches in 1980. In 1981 two states, Minas Gerais and São Paulo, became financially self-sufficient from Southern Baptists' help. The Brazilian Foreign Mission Board had 69 missionaries in 13 countries.

Interest in Baptist Men's work was growing in Minas. My biggest disappointment was that some pastors laughed at the possibility of getting the men enthusiastic about mission work. The women were very supportive of my work with the men, but some pastors were obstacles. Sometimes, when I became discouraged, I asked the Lord: "Why, O Lord, do you want me to work in the two most difficult spiritual areas: stewardship and with men?" Stewardship is a difficult field, because people are more materialistic than spiritual and think that stewardship only involves money! Men's work is difficult because men (in general) are not as interested in committing themselves to Jesus as women are. After a day's work they aren't interested in any sort of meeting. Despite the difficulties, in early 1981 I attended two regional men's meetings in Minas, helped to organize two new societies, and had others scheduled. My calendar for the year already was pretty full with associational meetings, men's congresses, and the Royal Ambassador promotion. I had the blessing of finding a dynamic seminary student to lead the boys' work. I put Elmiro de Oliveira in charge of the Royal Ambassadors; this was a great relief for me.

Dr. Bill Richardson, director of the Minas Religious Educational Department, in the spring of 1981 started a second Bible institute at the Minas Gerais state camp. The camp is near the town Ravena, situated about 20 miles from Belo Horizonte. Since we had moved to Belo, we helped in this institute. Leona also taught a course at the seminary as well as some music students in our home.

Glory, Glory, Hallelujah
We finally bought the second lot for Planalto Baptist Church. We paid $16,000 for the lot; we borrowed $6,000 from two banks plus we

borrowed another $900 for the cost of the deed. We had to borrow the $6,000 at 6.6 percent interest that month, but they took the first three months of interest off the top. Everyone understands that this is done because the next month inflation may go up to 10 percent. For instance, we borrowed Cr$300,000 *cruzeiros* (Brazilian currency), but we only received Cr$245,000 because they held out Cr$65,000 in interest to begin with. We had only 11 months to pay interest on the Cr$245,000 plus Cr$20,000 a month on the principal. We were confident that God would provide. The inflation rate in Brazil later reached 110 percent: for instance Cr$81.000 was worth $1,322. I am not an accountant and had difficulty understanding and keeping up with the monetary system, which was mind-boggling!

I spent three afternoons at the city planning commissioner's office as I tried to get a permit to build a church in a commercial area. Some houses had been built illegally along this boulevard, so why the fuss about a church? Our dreams begin to be realized. We were under financial pressure for a while, but God always provided in an unimaginable way! To be able to buy a lot beside the lot we already owned was a victory through prayer. Now I envisioned owning a third lot. The owner of the vacant lot next to the second one was a Jewish woman living in California. I corresponded with her and found out that the lot was part of her inheritance; though she had no intention of returning to Brazil to live, she didn't want to sell her lot. Later I contacted her again and simply let her know that we would be interested in buying the lot if she decided to sell. About two years later she was in Brazil and called to let me know that if she ever decided to sell, the church could have the first option.

A problem arose with the lot we bought for the São Bernardo mission; a squatter had moved in. The squatter was confronted and promised to leave, but a lawyer advised him not to leave without receiving money, plus some extra, for the little house he had built. We paid Cr$160,000 to settle this problem. This was frustrating because some of our members didn't even own their houses; others for as long as 10 years had been adding to their houses as they had the money. Yet they put God first and gave sacrificially. Then we had to pay to get a squatter off a lot we had sacrificed to buy. Often I wished my friends and relatives could visit Brazil and see for themselves the mission work and sacrifice of the Christians.

Carl's Visit and Jonathan Leaves Our Nest

During Carl's first year in college the FMB started the policy of paying for a return trip for MK's during their college years. After his being away for two years, we were excited about Carl's visit. This was a real blessing for him and us as parents. The kids needed to return to their country, in which they were reared, to visit old friends and especially parents. Carl was like most other MK's; he was more Brazilian than American and longed to return to Brazil. A friend told us that Carl said after his return to college that he finally felt at home in the States. We were so thankful the FMB realized this need and provided funds for one return to Brazil.

The end of Carl's two-month stay, however, brought heartache: Jonathan would go back with him to begin his college studies at Hardin-Simmons University. We had been able to go to Hardin-Simmons with Carl, but we hadn't been back on the field long enough to accompany Jonathan and help him buy the things he needed. Big brother would have to help him with these.

These events caused me to reminisce. I remembered teaching them ping-pong, when I had to chase all the balls that went over the end of the ping-pong table. Oh, how patience was a necessity until they were so good at the game, most of the time they beat me. I remember the same thing with basketball. But chess was a different story. I had played a few games of chess, but almost from the start the boys both were ahead of me. One semester during furlough both had played on the Portales school's chess team. I couldn't beat either one. After Carl left for college, I challenged Jonathan to some games. Our chess board remained on his desk; when I passed through his bedroom on the way to my study during the day, I stopped to study my next move. When we returned to playing, I quickly and confidently moved, but he dodged me or put me on the run. We made only one or two moves a night, so I had a lot of time to plan my next move. Well, I always lost. But our father/son relationship became closer than before.

The Baptist State Board wanted all state workers to attend every annual associational meeting; we had 12 associations in the state.

Each associational meeting lasted at least three days. Being on the road a lot made time seem to fly by faster. I really didn't want this to happen, because Jonathan's departure was approaching too fast anyway.

Both boys are very tenderhearted. We noticed this when they were young. Jonathan never liked anyone yelling at him. We, as imperfect parents, under pressure to get him to mind us sometimes lost our tempers. We learned that if we talked calmly to Jonathan and explained why we had to discipline him, he broke down in tears and obeyed. Only one time did Jonathan rebel against going to church. Leona talked with him and asked whether his daddy, as pastor, had to be at church; his answer was *yes*. Did mom have to be at church? His answer was *yes*!

"Well, son, we cannot leave you home by yourself, so, yes, you have to go." After that he never questioned, "Why do I have to go?" Planalto church was so far from home that we couldn't return to pick up the kids, so when we went early to make visits before evening services, the kids had to go with us. I'm sure they would have preferred to be at home but I don't recall them ever complaining about going.

Jonathan and EABH (Escola Americana Belo Horizonte)

The American schools had a yearly sports tournament that was an exciting time. Since EABH was a small school, those that enjoyed sports, both boys and girls, usually played all three: volleyball, basketball, and soccer. The boys' basketball coach was rough on the guys and yelled at those on the bench for errors of those playing. His yelling upset Jonathan. In Jonathan's senior year the coach was angry with him for missing a practice to finish a research paper. The coach also was a classroom teacher; when Jonathan arrived in class, the coach chewed him out for missing practice. Jonathan already was upset at the way the coach yelled at the boys so much, so he just quit the team. The annual sports tournament was near; the teachers had planned a program and a banquet to raise money for their sports trip. The English teacher was in charge of a drama.

The day before the big event the students were helping decorate the gym for the program and also preparing food for the banquet. One of the teachers sent Jonathan to the main building to get something they needed. The school had a Brazilian family that lived on campus and that did handywork around the school; they were great friends to Jonathan. When Jonathan entered the main building, the Brazilian woman needed his help to do something. Jonathan didn't think her request would take long, so he helped her. When he returned to the gym, the teacher was very angry and wouldn't even allow him to explain his delay. In front of the group she yelled at him, so he walked off and said that he wouldn't participate in the program. The coach was mad because Jonathan had quit the team, so he and the school counselor decided Jonathan shouldn't even go to the tournament, although he was needed in soccer and volleyball. When the English teacher found out about the problem, he panicked, Jonathan was one of the key characters in a drama the group was to present for the parents. We knew the students had a program and banquet but nothing about Jonathan's part.

That afternoon Leona answered the phone and got an earful from a distraught school counselor. She wanted Leona to go to the school that very afternoon. She was raving about the fact that we had to do something with Jonathan. Of course Leona couldn't imagine what had happened. We were worried because the counselor talked like Jonathan had done a terrible thing. We just couldn't figure out why so much of an uproar erupted from the school counselor and teacher.

Leaving school that afternoon on the bus, the English teacher sat beside Jonathan; the two had a long discussion. Jonathan explained what happened; the teacher promised he would work things out with the others if he would promise to stay in the drama. Jonathan promised; the teacher smoothed things out. This teacher was very good and highly respected. When Jonathan arrived home, he explained to us what he had done but didn't mention anything about the program.

When we went to the program on Friday night, we understood the problem. Jonathan Richardson and Jonathan Tarry were the key characters to the success of the program. They did a wonderful presentation of a very comical play. We were amazed, because we thought Jonathan was quiet and mild. Jonathan went to the tournament and the sports award banquet.

Jonathan did well in soccer; he played most of the time as goalkeeper. The Belo team felt as though he should have been named to the all-star tournament team. He received the EABH honor of "most-improved player". Jonathan had several responsibilities at the American school. He was gifted with an ability to grasp his subjects quickly. He finished his homework quickly and then played games by himself while Carl and Charlotte worked until bedtime. He also was a blessing at church.

Because the school was small, the teachers had to double up on responsibilities; sometimes they did jobs they weren't qualified to do. One particular teacher was not too well-liked or qualified for his job. He used Copenhagen Snuff sent from the States because he couldn't buy it in Brazil. School regulation prohibited the use of tobacco at school; the students were unhappy with his habit of spitting into a clear jar during class. As he was cleaning the aquarium one afternoon, Jonathan found a can of his snuff on the bookshelf. He felt inspired to play a trick on the teacher, so he quickly stuffed it into his backpack. He brought the can home but had to be discreet so we didn't see him with it. A few squirts of "hot" pepper sauce (I mean HOT) around on the tobacco should spice it up a bit; then he decided maybe that wasn't enough, so he doused a little more. Next morning he arrived at school before the teacher, so he easily replaced the can at the place in which he found it. The class in the room at the time the teacher took a dip of the "hot" snuff soon spread the word around school that the teacher was very upset.

Sometime later Charlotte and a friend found another can on the science table. They decided to "help" the teacher "break the habit" by strategically removing the can from sight to a remote location. Months later they checked to see if their strategy worked and found the can in their hidden location; the tobacco was dried. They decided that IF the teacher had found the can, he was afraid it also had hot pepper.

JONATHAN TARRY
David's love for Jonathan always thrilled our hearts,
As Jonathan's love for David could not be torn apart.
So it is with you, Jonathan, as our second son.
More than David and Jonathan, we are closer to being one.

Words cannot express the depth of our pride and joy
When people cooed and ahh'ed about our second little boy.
You were so much fun to play with in every sort of way,
But trying to discipline you sometimes left us in dismay.

When you and Carl were in kindergarten in Brazil,
you were only 3.
I walked with you to school; you were as excited as could be.
However, after several blocks of walking, your little legs
became weary,
So I had to pick you up and much of the way carry.

The distance was so far, you wanted to be carried some
each day.
I said: "If you can't walk today, then tomorrow at home
you will stay".
Next day Carl, not wanting to leave little brother behind,
Begging cried: "Daddy, please let him go. I'll carry him,
I don't mind."

Jonathan, you have always had an amazing soft heart.
You have been considerate of others nearly from the start.
You have helped others as long as we can remember.
This is a Christian thing; continue doing it forever!

Once you brought some tadpoles from a water hole in the street.
With excitement in your eyes you said: "Mother, may I keep?"
Your mother was flabbergasted and wanted to shake her head
As she envisioned dreadful frogs living under your bed!

Once we were driving along the mighty Sweet River.
Your little quizzical mind was working with fervor.
Suddenly you said, "Daddy, where is the sweet in the river—
On the very bottom of the dirty red water?"

We always were proud of the grades you made in school
And even more proud that you observed the Golden Rule!

We are thankful missionary uncles and aunts influenced you
As living examples of what you should or should not do!

We are sorry we couldn't take you
to Hardin-Simmons University;
We trusted Carl could help you adapt to that institution.
Neither could we be present for your graduation celebration.
We trusted Uncle Pat and Aunt Doris would fill the gap
of our separation.

Jonathan, your mother and I prayed before and during your life
For God to choose the best young lady for your wife!
That life will be exciting, putting Jesus in first place,
And that you will win a victory in your spiritual race!

Dad and Mom

We had tried to prepare ourselves for an empty nest, but an empty nest was arriving sooner than we could believe. The day arrived for Carl and Jonathan to leave for the States. Our group of missionaries and school and church friends were at the airport to see them off. Inside we felt the excitement for Jonathan as he was entering a new phase of life, but we felt emptiness as well. We remembered a missionary colleague saying: "Be thankful your child is able to leave home and start out on his own. Not all parents can do that." Yes, we were thankful that God had blessed our three children with health. The separation is difficult to say the least, but we prayed that God would allow us to say "goodbye" without crying until later, for crying only makes the parting more difficult. God granted that desire.

All Brazil Mission 100-Year Celebration
In July 1981 a year before the actual centennial, all three Baptist Missions: Equatorial, North, and South, had one big meeting together to celebrate 100 years of Baptist work. Some of the missionaries we knew by name; others we had met at language school or at national conventions. A review of 100 years of Baptist work was presented in four 25-year segments. This lifetime event was a wonderful time to

376

reevaluate the blessings of God on the pioneer missionaries. The good times were mixed with some sad times of family deaths and persecution.

As we arrived in Belo after the great mission meeting, we went almost immediately to our Baptist state convention in Muriae in South Minas. The great event of this meeting for me was the men's meeting before the convention. For a year and a half I had been working to prepare for this day. We organized Baptist Men of Minas into an official entity of the state convention. I was pleased that we had 75 men and several pastors present for the event. Muriae is only about a four-hour drive from the beach, so we spent four days at the beach. We had to cut our vacation on the beach short because we had received a call from the FMB that two reporters from *The Commission* magazine were to arrive to visit with us.

Humbled and Honored

A photographer and writer from the FMB arrived in Brazil to make two special editions of *The Commission* for the 1982 centennial celebration of Baptist work. Don Rutledge, the photographer, and Eric Bridges, a new writer, arrived to spend a week with us. For most of a week I traveled with these two through the Sweet River Valley and visited places in which we had opened up new work. I took them to Virginopolis, Gonzaga, Governador Valadares, and other places I mentioned in the earlier chapters and told them many stories. Part of The Marvel of it All was our family's being selected to be featured in *The Commission* in the September 1982 issue. I felt honored to introduce and interpret for Eric's interview with Pastor Jose Alves Bittencourt, executive secretary of Minas Gerais, in the March 1982 *The Commission*. Also in the March issue was a story about our work and a picture of Socorro with her baby in Gonzaga.

Don and Eric were at Planalto Baptist Church in Belo for the Sunday services on August 3, my birthday. They saw how caring and loving Brazilians are when they celebrate birthdays. On that day each age group had something special for me. While he visited Planalto Church, Don found just the right face in Floriano Siqueira, a church member, for the cover on the February/March 1982 edition of *The Commission*. The next Wednesday Floriano had a stroke and remained in a coma for a month before he died.

Five Young People Die in a Lake

Marcia had been converted in Central Baptist Church on the other side of the city in which we began working in the Planalto mission. After we moved into the larger room of the mission, she started attending regularly; soon after that I baptized her. She was in her first year of university studies. Leona and I visited Marcia with her family; when I invited the family to visit our church, we were coolly told that Marcia, against their will, had made her choice. Because she was of age, she could attend, but we were not welcome if we were going to pressure any other family members to go to our church. Marcia's parents were Roman Catholic and were having some difficulty dealing with Marcia's becoming a "believer" and Baptist. Even so, Marcia secretly witnessed to her five sisters.

We were in Marcia's home occasionally and picked her up to take her to one of the missions; we had a good relationship with her parents as friends. About three years later, on a rainy late Monday afternoon, Marcia's 19-year-old sister, a neighbor girl, and three young men left a company party held in the residential area around the lake. They were in a small Fiat. The driver lost control of the car and flipped upside down into the lake. All five youths drowned.

This accident was a great shock to the Planalto neighborhood, because the girls were well-known. Early the next morning as soon as we received word, we went to Marcia's home. Arrangements were being made for the funeral of the two girls to be held together that same afternoon. Both families wanted me to have a part in the services before and after mass. Hundreds of people were present. The two girls were buried in a two-tier grave (one on top of the other) in the best cemetery of the city; both were in white caskets. When we arrived at the gravesite after the mass, a rock band was playing some worldly rock music that certainly was not appropriate for the occasion. Soon the band seemed to realize its music wasn't appreciated by the two grieving families; the members stopped playing their instruments. The priest, as usual, did not attend the graveside service, so I had a chance to bring a short message from the Bible. To say something appropriate to two distraught families that were spiritually lost was very difficult. But the words of the Bible passage I read were comforting and calming.

The burial was late Tuesday afternoon. At Wednesday-night prayer meeting, Marcia and Patricia, a younger sister, attended. Patricia accepted Christ as her Savior. Once before she had sneaked away from home to attend Vacation Bible School without her parents knowing, but this was the first time she had attended with her parents' permission. She didn't tell her parents that she had accepted Jesus. After the tragedy had waned, Patricia wasn't permitted to continue attending our services. A few days later we discovered the sneaky way the spiritists have to persuade people to become spiritist. We visited Marcia's family again; the other mother was present. We found them very distraught because a spiritist medium had called and said that the deceased daughters had contacted him with a message for the parents. The medium's question was: "Would the family be interested in visiting with him to hear what their daughter had to say?" This troubled them, but they weren't convinced the truth of the message. They asked us our opinion. We discovered that when an obituary is published in a newspaper, mediums follow up with a contact with the next in kin. Most Brazilians didn't have the money to publish an obituary. They used this tactic to make money and to try to win more converts to spiritism.

The Joe McCartney Family

God sent us some unexpected help in the family of Joe McCartney. Joe and Evelyn McCartney and their three children were from Ireland. The Bible confirms that Jesus is looking after His churches; He certainly was helping Planalto. The McCartneys were Baptists but were appointed by an interdenominational mission organization that sent them to Belo to work in the nondenominational seminary. They moved to the Planalto neighborhood and began attending our church. The oldest child, Michelle, was about 13. The three children were blonds, so they stood out in the congregation more than our children did, although Carl was blond. For about a year Joe taught the adult Sunday-school class occasionally, preached for me some when I was traveling, and held a special Bible study a few times. I saw that Joe was sound doctrinally and the whole family was an asset to our church.

Joe played the piano and accordion and could sing. A musical instrument was badly needed at the Jardim Guanabara mission. God had sent us a man that was not involved in church planting, but the Lord had sent him to the right place. Joe and his wife and the two smaller children began leading the work at the Jardim Guanabara mission. Michelle, a teen-ager, was very involved with the young people at Planalto Church. Joe and family helped us for one four-year term. When they returned from their year furlough, their mission organization no longer wanted them to participate with us because it said: "Baptists don't need your help".

1982—Hallelujah Night at Planalto

On March 14 we celebrated our last payment on the second lot in Planalto; now we could plan for a church building. I was still working with the city planning commission for a building permit. We were having the same problems that we had in Governador Valadares. The Belo Horizonte Planning Commission had no idea about Evangelical Sunday schools. Using the word *school* meant that all rooms had to be a standard size as they were in public or parochial schools. We had to make up another name that would satisfy the building commission. The good thing about the problem with the planning commission was that I met some high officials and had the chance to explain about Bible studies that went on in our Baptist churches. Many of the other Evangelical churches, including Baptists, had not received permits to construct their buildings, because the paper work and hassle took too much time. They built without permits. The city was cracking down on everything that was being built, so I felt as though we needed to go by the rules. A Baptist architect living in São Paulo drew the plans for a three-story building. He did not charge us. In June we began the excavation and structural part of our building. We put in the main pillars that would sustain the building and in a simplified way built only the ground floor .

Planalto and the Missions

Besides working around the state, I was still pastor of Planalto Baptist Church and her missions. As pastor I had the job of helping in time of death. I held a funeral for the mother of three members of our Santa Cruz mission. The Roman Catholic relatives also had planned the funeral, so, to our surprise, we participated in a double funeral. The priest went first with a two-hour mass; he spent much time putting down Evangelicals. Priests usually appeared, said a quick mass, and left. The deceased woman had made a decision at a home service I had led some months before. Just a few hours before she died, she reaffirmed that she stood firm in her decision and was sure of her salvation. I was surprised that the priest would waste his time lambasting us. One of the daughters would have interrupted him to protest if another missionary friend of the family had not restrained her. Later the priest privately admitted to that daughter that he didn't know anything about the Bible.

As pastor another ministry was performing weddings. At one wedding we waited an hour and a half for the bride to arrive; she was late because of a torrential rain storm. Brides are almost always at least 30-minutes late, but the storm delayed her arrival. The church was packed with people who waited patiently for her. If she had arrived on time, she wouldn't have been caught in the storm. The electricity went on and off during the storm, but we had a lantern to use if necessary. Because of the delay the new husband and wife missed their bus that night to leave Belo on their honeymoon. One other time in Governador Valadares Leona played the pump organ for an hour as she waited for the bride to arrive. From that experience Leona learned never to start playing until the bride arrived.

I think I know a little how Moses felt when the Lord challenged him to lead the people out of Egypt and into the Promise Land. We faced a seemingly impossible task. That was how on the surface our situation looked as we faced building without funds and buying property and building for three missions. Yet what we faced was a drop in the bucket compared to the multitude of neighborhoods to conquer. Therefore, when God opened the doors to begin a preaching point in another neighborhood and a church member was willing to lead, I as pastor couldn't say *no*. Therefore, again we had a neighborhood without a church in which three families of our church lived. I asked a man to visit them and show an interest in their spiritual lives. He held weekly services in one of their homes; a growing number began showing interest. Another member had a rent house in that area; he offered it for a meeting place. We didn't have even one bench to put in it but just a Bible stand to place on a small table. But that is how a new work gets started!

Beginning the Centennial Brazil/Texas Crusade

Texas associations partnered with the major Brazilian cities to send groups of people to hold evangelism services in the churches of those cities. Ron Boswell was furloughing in Fort Worth. He was asked to coordinate the Belo Horizonte crusade that was paired with Tarrant County in the Fort Worth area. The crusade was to last three years with a goal by the end of 1982 to double the number of churches in our area and reach the goal of a million members in Brazil. Belo was divided into regions: North, South, East, and West. In early 1981 the first group of 47 Texans arrived to have crusades in the western part of Belo. In chapter 20 Leona gives an interesting experience that she had in this crusade. All missionaries in Belo at the time were helping; most served as interpreters. Many interesting things happened during the week. The Richardsons, Mattie Lou Bible, and Cathryn Smith were on furlough and missed this campaign. During the day I was interim director of the Bible institute at the state camp, so I could help only at night.

One night I went with two of the Texans to a home in which about 80 people were gathered for a worship service. This was an outreach of Progresso Baptist Church in a neighborhood without a Baptist church. A young woman of the mother church stayed in the yard with the children; the rest of crowd crammed into the house. After the service a woman accepted Christ and wanted to tell her story. For two nights in a row she had had the same dream. She dreamed she was in a city totally inhabited by spiritists. She was frightened and tried to find a way out, but every way she turned, she was surrounded by a weird spiritist group. Finally a young man with fair skin appeared with a Bible in his hand and told her that the Bible had the answer to get her out of the terrible city. On Tuesday morning, after she dreamed the same dream the second time, she searched her house for an Evangelical tract to read but couldn't find one. She resolved that the next Sunday she would attend an Evangelical church. But that night she heard Evangelical music from a loudspeaker across the street. She was excited and thrilled. To her surprise the one that brought the message was a fair-skinned young man; he stood with a Bible in his hand. That day was her 43rd birthday. That night she accepted Christ and celebrated her physical birthday and her spiritual birthday together! God always amazes me how He puts things together in unusual ways.

About two months later, while I visited that church for a Brotherhood rally, I saw the same woman again. She told me: "Surely God was preparing me for something special in my life." She recently had a great test of her Christian faith. Lacking three days completing one month as a Christian, she said: "My oldest son was struck by a car and killed." With Jesus sustaining her she had a remarkable spiritual victory through those rough days and even composed a song to glorify Jesus for His spiritual help. A few days after the funeral she asked to sing at church the song she had composed, so she sang her first solo. As the woman was talking to me, her teen-age daughter was present. The woman joyfully presented to me her daughter, who recently had been saved. I asked about her husband. "Oh, he is here in the church now; this is the second time he has ever gone to church. Imagine", she continued, "before I was saved, I was taking three pills a day for nerves. I still was uncontrollable. Now I am off pills. God is near and real to me!"

Texas Crusade in Belo Horizonte—Northern Region

Later in 1981 the second group of Texans worked in the northern area of Belo Horizonte. This region is the place in which our church and missions were situated. Joe Vernon, a former pastor at Jackson Avenue Baptist Church of Lovington, had six people on his team. He was preacher for Planalto Church. While Joe Vernon was pastor at Jackson Avenue, he had led that church to send us $100 a month; this helped pay the rent for our missions. I had invited Joe to Brazil, so we were glad he was to work with us. Each mission of Planalto Church had two Texans working, while Joe Vernon and I worked the Planalto area. Leona and I as well as Charlotte on the weekend were interpreters. During the week we worked diligently, prayed earnestly, and visited many people. We had 21 members of a large family (adults and young people) in the area to make decisions during the Planalto campaign. If I could disciple them, that would be a big victory. After the crusade every week for two-and-one-half months I went to their home. These 21 all were living in a family compound in a lower-income area. Every time I left their house, I felt good about the studies, but in the end none of the people wanted to be baptized. I don't think some of them really were saved. This became the pattern I observed through the years—great numbers of people raising their hands and even going to the front at the end of a service during the partnership crusades. By far most of them were just taking a step toward God and not really making a decision for Christ. If we baptized 10 out of every 100 that raised their hands or filled out a card, we were doing good. Yet, I do not discount the value of planting seed. The results publicized in the U.S. state Baptist papers, however, were misleading for the number of actual converts was very small. A total of 650 decisions were recorded in the 18 churches and three missions that participated in the Northern Belo crusade. At least 90-95 percent of these decisions were just steps toward God.

Texas Crusade in Governador Valadares and Aimores
I didn't want Governador Valadares to be left out of the Texas crusade, because I had a deep interest in that city, so I contacted Bill McKinney of Natalia, TX. He was a pastor that had been to Aimores after the flood in Valadares and Aimores. Bill accepted and brought four other pastors with him; one was a Mexican pastor and a man from his church. We spent four days in Valadares and four days in Aimores. I had arranged an excellent interpreter for the Mexican pastor and his friend. Paul Popov was a descendant of the Latvians that had moved to Brazil after World War I. When he was young, he left Brazil with an older brother to live in the United States, in which he learned English. He was back in Brazil for a while; I asked him to interpret in the Valadares and Aimores Crusades. The two Mexican-Americans thought the Brazilians understood their Spanish well enough, so after a couple of days they dismissed Paul. The Mexicans really made a mistake, for the Brazilians didn't understand them that well.

After the crusade in Governador Valadares, Bill McKinney, a carpenter, and Lee Ewald stayed four more days at our house in Belo to build four pulpits for Planalto Church and her three missions.

We saw some examples of steps toward God that became real decisions. In 1979 after the flood in Aimores, the Texas disaster relief team held a home service with a couple; he was 83 and she was 76. That service prepared this duo in 1982 to make a real decision. Another interesting experience in the Aimores campaign was a visit that Bill McKinney and I had with a woman that made a decision the night the elderly couple made theirs. The day after her decision we stopped by to encourage her and talk to her mother. Her mother made a decision; then a neighbor woman arrived and wanted to know how to be saved. We were able to lead her to Christ; her expression was evidence of a salvation experience.

Near the end of 1982 the third group of Texans arrived. They worked in the southern region of Belo Horizonte. We do not have space here to describe all the experiences from these times.

Daddy Is Stricken with Cancer

My father didn't write often, but one day he wrote asking me to hurry home. He had prostate cancer and had to take radiation. I could tell he was concerned about his medical report. We hadn't planned to return to the States until Charlotte finished high school in May 1983, but I made plans to go home in August 1982 to be with him a month.

I was able to take him to his radiation treatments; we talked a lot. Daddy didn't confide much to his kids about his problems except to say he was lonely and wished some of his kids had stayed near him. He had stayed near his family and helped them out; however he had taken Mama a long way from her family. He wanted Helen or Margaret to live closer to him. Anyway, Daddy was a very remarkable man in the fact that he was honest and, after Mama died, kept us kids together until, one by one, we left home.

As I sat around the house with him, we sometimes talked about spiritual things, because I wanted to help him accept his situation and not be upset with God. After we all left home, Daddy didn't go to church much. He now was 77-years old; the doctor had given him about a year-and-a-half to live. He always had a garden and grew tomatoes, garlic, beans, squash, onions, and similar things. He canned tomatoes from his garden and canned fruits that he bought during season. His house—especially the kitchen—wasn't clean. Most of the time he cooked his own meals, but he did receive some "meals on wheels". Cleaning the house always was a challenge for Margaret, Helen, Joycie, or Leona when we went to visit him. When I was with him, I always did repair and paint jobs. Daddy always kept his car clean and the grass mowed. He took walks, but other than that he stayed close to home; he watched television and smoked his pipe. After most of us left home, he took up smoking to help him pass the time. His nervous condition didn't allow him to work regularly.

So in 1982 I spent a blessed month with my father; we talked some about the past, but Dad never shared much. He was distant in some ways; we never said anything about Mama. We prayed some together and he played his guitar some, yet I left with sadness in my heart. At every departure the most difficult part was Dad saying again and again, "I hate to see you go!"

I arrived back in Brazil just in time to attend the organization of Virginopolis Baptist Church. This is the town in which the city council made things difficult for Evangelicals; In chapter 11 I told about this. Another victory was having the military band playing for the organization of the church. Progress in favor of Evangelicals gradually was being made in Virginopolis. The first Evangelical church was a reality in Virginopolis!

1982 Final Centennial Celebration

The goal was to organize 10 churches simultaneously as part of the Baptists' centennial celebration in Belo Horizonte. First Baptist Church of Belo Horizonte was overflowing with people to celebrate only three churches being organized. Planalto was organizing its first daughter church: São Bernardo Mission. That was a great joy! The name was Planalto Second Baptist Church, but years later it changed the name to Nova Allianca Baptist Church.

The fourth and final group of 85 Texans forming 25 teams arrived in April to work in the central part of the city. This region held three days of combined evangelism services in a large gymnasium before starting revivals in 25 churches on Wednesday. The seed of the gospel was heavily planted. I was interpreter for the preacher in home visitation and evening services at Planalto Second Baptist Church, in the

São Bernardo neighborhood I mentioned in the previous paragraph. Leona interpreted for the group at First Baptist Planalto; Charlotte helped on the weekend. Three of our Texans were from First Baptist Church of Euless, TX. At Planalto we had a record attendance of 157 in Sunday School and 190 at the night service. The Brazilian Baptist Convention normally met in January, but in 1982 the Centennial Baptist Convention was moved to October 9-15 in Salvador, State of Bahia. Salvador was the place in which First Baptist Church in Brazil was organized in 1882 with two missionary couples and an ex-Roman Catholic priest. From that tiny beginning in 1882, 3,600 Baptist churches had been organized as a result of Southern Baptist sponsorship. During the centennial year 342 new churches were organized. São Paulo had 62 and Minas Gerais had 51. Yet one of the most thrilling things was that the Brazilian Baptist Convention supported 70 missionaries working in 14 countries.

The SESC Preaching Point

Irani and her children from a neighborhood called SESC began attending Planalto regularly. Because of the great distance from Planalto, in 1980 we started a Bible study at her house. Her husband was not happy with a group meeting in the couple's home, so we had to find a different place. The name *SESC* is an abbreviation for a large business men's club and retreat hotel. We were able to rent a vacant store building and started a Sunday-afternoon service. This preaching point was to be the responsibility of the Planalto young people with their leaders.

1983—Diminishing Activities

My father had taught me always to be doing something. If you see something to do, do it! I had tried to apply this to my life. A professor at seminary encouraged us to keep abreast with the community, city, and state wherever we lived. I needed to adapt to Brazil, city, county, and state. That required learning a vast vocabulary in the Portuguese language. After about 15 years I realized I was up against a brick wall as I tried to stay up with the world, especially both South America and North America. I quit subscribing to the *U.S. News and World Report*, *National Geographic*, and the local daily newspaper. The Royal

Ambassadors from First Baptist Church of Lovington had been sending the *Lovington Leader*, a daily paper. Although these newspapers always arrived by ship, still the news was new to us. I continued to receive the *Baptist New Mexican* and *California Baptist* weekly papers. In 1979 Milton Schmitt of First Baptist Church in Dallas had the *Baptist Standard* sent until I had this weekly paper stopped. I still had the weekly *O Jornal Batista*, the Brazilian Baptist Convention paper and the monthly state Baptist paper, and lots of mail and books to read. Aside from these we received *The Commission*, the monthly magazine from the FMB, and other magazines from the Southern Baptist Sunday School Board that were sent to us. I tried to keep up with some of this reading while I stood in lines at banks or other places. Each day I also kept a list of about 25 things I thought I needed to do. I was so busy, I had little time to read the Bible. I read enough to get my messages, but I didn't study the Bible.

I had no time for serious praying. I was drifting into a pattern of using my own strength to do a lot of things for the Lord. I am inserting this personal situation now as a prelude to things that will happen in my story. Another thing that took some time but was joyful was answering letters from the states. We received a great deal of correspondence from R.A.'s and G.A.'s as well as from the women's missionary circles. Some of these local organizations were named after us. We kept a notebook with name, address, age (of the boys and girls), and date of the letters. We replied to every person that wrote us. I finally began making form letters to send, especially to those who asked specific questions about our work. Throughout the years we received hundreds of these letters and cards from almost every state in the United States, Canada, a few from Africa, and other places. This correspondence was wonderful and refreshing to our hearts. My home church, First Baptist Church of Lovington, took the responsibility to send out 250-300 quarterly newsletters for us; this cost us nothing. We can never thank First Baptist of Lovington enough!

Six Months from an Empty Nest

We loved all of our children the same, but in January 1983 we had only six months before our nest would be totally empty. This was on our hearts like a heavy weight. We knew our boys had difficulty adapting to the United States culture. They were blessed, however, because First Baptist Church of Abilene, TX, had an adoption plan for missionary kids. A couple had adopted both Carl and Jonathan; our boys spoke highly of their watchcare over them. On holidays Carl and Jonathan could visit with their grandparents in Portales and Lovington and Uncle Pat and Aunt Doris and cousins in Roswell, NM. In a wonderful way God was answering our concerns about our boys! What would God do for Charlotte?

Charlotte had written for several university catalogs but strangely didn't receive many. Our eight-day vacation on Cabo Frio beach was to be the time for her to study those catalogs. For my leisure reading I took a year's supply of comic strips from the *Lovington Leader*. For two days the rain kept us from the beach, so we played games. Games had been less enjoyable since our family had dwindled to three people; what would life be like when just two of us had to live together? On January 25 when Charlotte had her 17th birthday, I wrote this poem about her.

CHARLOTTE'S 17TH BIRTHDAY
On this day 17 years ago
My heart was made so happy, you know,
That everywhere I went my face was beaming
Because a daughter had brought my life more meaning!

A daughter so cuddly, friendly, and happy—
You often did not want to take your nappy.
Sometimes you would confuse your day and night,
For your parents to sleep in the dark didn't seem right.

When you fell asleep, cuddled with your Minnie Bell mouse,
We felt as though we had an angel in the house.
But walking and climbing you became very curious
And meddling into things sometimes made us furious.

Learning together the English and Portuguese language,
Mixing them up you would always manage
To express yourself in an interesting way.

"A lua e pretty" is an example of what you'd say.

So 17 years have quickly gone.
You and Minnie Bell never have been alone.
That's why we have a Minnie Bell mouse candle on your cake.
It's for both you and Minnie Bell's departures' sake.

Through the years we've had joy and peace of mind.
We are sure you are the best daughter we could find.
Mother and I are very, very grateful
That God spared your life. We are extremely thankful.

Our wishes and prayers are very sincere.
We hope they always will ring in your ear.
Love Jesus Christ with all that your heart is able.
Serve Him daily and you will always be stable.

Now, happy birthday and many more to be.
Forgive Mom and Dad the mistakes we didn't see.
Thanks for being sweet, understanding, and giving.
That's why we believe you are the best daughter living.

Back to Normal Things

As we returned to Belo, Leona and I began the work on the Planalto Church directory. The seminary girl staying in our maid's quarters wasn't much help to us. Her Portuguese was worse than ours; she just didn't have the knack to be a secretary. I was hoping she could type the weekly church bulletin, but her typing was terrible. That was the day of stencils; corrections were difficult. Just after we returned from the beach, she fell and broke her arm, so I sent her home to get treatment. She didn't clean the house well either, so when she asked for time off, just when we were to have visitors, I had to tell her to find another place. This was always difficult; we wanted to help her because she was a pastor's daughter. The girls we helped usually were very helpful to us.

The Planalto Church secretary was a fine young woman. Lenora had a health problem that doctors in Rio de Janeiro or Belo could not diagnose. On Saturday I had a feeling that someone was going to die—and not one of the older people. Therefore, early Sunday morning I was not really surprised when we received the call that Lenora suddenly had died at 21 years of age. She was the granddaughter to the man I mentioned that was on the cover picture for *The Commission* magazine in September 1982. Lenora's death was a shock to the church, but I felt as though God had prepared me. Because her death occurred early Sunday, the church people heard about Lenora's death when they arrived for Sunday school. The church family could minister to the family; many spent the night at the church with the family and Lenora's body. She was buried early Monday morning.

Belo, with 2,500,000 people, had several cemeteries. One that we occasionally visited made me uneasy. Mostly middle class and poor people were buried in that cemetery. In the area in which the poor people were buried, the bones were dug up about every five years; this made room for new, poor occupants. More than once we were in the cemetery to bury someone when wheelbarrows of bones were being carted somewhere else.

Our Baptist Men's work was growing fast. My heart soared with joy by the result of the first evangelism-mission team from the Minas Gerais Baptist Men's state department. Returning from that trip the men bubbled with enthusiasm; as a result some men in local churches started to make trips on their own. Also 97 men attended our third state men's camp. I received commitments from three other Baptist church men's organizations to help three state missionaries in pioneer areas of Minas Gerais. The boys' camp in 1983 had 130 campers; every bunk bed was used.

Special Time with Our Only Daughter

Since we had only one daughter, we could say that she was our pride and joy among girls. We had participated in many of the sports events. We didn't schedule anything on Friday nights at our church or missions. Saturday afternoons were used for some of the school soccer games but not for volleyball or basketball. Leona was able to attend nearly all of Charlotte's school activities; I did my best to do the same. The American school had more extracurricular activities than did the Brazilian schools.

Charlotte had a good dose of stamina in her genes. She was slow but meticulous in what she did. Making the honor roll for her was a lot of work, but most of her semesters in high school she reached that goal. Her senior year she even took the International Baccalaureate Course in Portuguese; this made her more proficient in Portuguese, but she didn't need that credit in college. The course was worth college credit in most European schools. During her last two years Charlotte took home economics and loved those classes. She believed she would major in home economics in college. Her senior year in high school she wrote to schools that offered these courses; that put Hardin-Simmons out because it didn't offer home economics. She received catalogs from North Texas State, Mary Hardin-Baylor, New Mexico State, and University of New Mexico.

Charlotte's SAT score was very good, so we were assured she would get into a good college. Charlotte is only five-feet tall but very athletic. She was on the basketball, volleyball, and soccer teams. Usually a taller person plays goalie, but she was exceptional at stopping balls in her reach. Her coach praised her for her courage. She scared us because she had that courage. She was the best dribbler on the basketball team and the only one that could dribble left-handed nearly as good as with the right. The girls' coach was the superintendent of the school. During games he yelled and screamed at the girls; this embarrassed me, especially when our team played against the Brazilian teams. I was afraid that they would think all American coaches yelled angrily as he did.

One Saturday after a game Leona and I took two other girls home. They were crying because they had been yelled at so much. I felt very bad. Heavy rains had forced the cover off a manhole in the street; I was listening to them and didn't see the open hole. Both left wheels— the front and then the left back—hit the hole. From the loud noise I knew we had a problem! Stopping the car immediately I jumped out in the rain and saw that both tires were going down rapidly. On Saturday afternoons most commercial places were closed. I had only one spare. *What would I do with two flat tires?* I quickly opened the trunk of the car and grabbed the hammer out of the toolbox. After a quick analysis I began pounding the place in which the rim was bent on the back wheel, which was going down slower than the front tire. I remembered a similar situation with Leona and thanked God for giving me that thought. I got the rim bent back before the tire went down too much to drive on it. I changed the front tire with the spare; we were on our way. I later called the school superintendent about what he was doing to the girls, so he diminished the yelling and making many unnecessary comments.

Our girls played against one Brazilian club team made up of semi-professional women in their 20s. When Charlotte was a junior, the coach scheduled that team to play the girls three times. The first game the other team beat our girls about 80-10. The next time the score was about 60-20; the third time the score was 50-40. Playing against these woman prepared our girls for their tournament. In both Charlotte's junior and senior years the Belo American school girls' team won all of its tournament games in those three sports in the small American school tournaments and did well in the larger school tournaments. The boys didn't do so well. None of our three kids was the best on any team, but all of them won awards in sports events. During her senior year Charlotte lettered in volleyball, basketball, and soccer.

Charlotte was a blessing around home also. We gave the kids an allowance; they were responsible for certain chores. We helped them make choices on how to spend their money. We insisted that they learn how to save some of their money, so I opened bank accounts for them to learn how to control their money. This paid off, because while they were in college, we had no problem with them spending more money than they had.

Charlotte became interested in ventriloquism. She used my doll and soon was better than I. Members of our church and a few from other churches who found out about her talent invited her to perform at children's parties. She was active in our youth group at church and participated on weekend trips to other churches. She completed the Queen with a Scepter step in G.A.'s. This is one of the higher G.A. steps that requires learning Scriptures and actually doing mission projects.

After two years in college Jonathan returned to Brazil for the summer. Oh, how good to feel his embrace! He arrived in time for Charlotte's graduation and thus got to visit friends that still were teaching, working, or studying at EABH. We went to Governador Valadares and spent a few days where he could re-live some of the years of his childhood.

I was asked to write a poem for graduation day for the five senior girls leaving EABH (Escola Americana of Belo Horizonte—American School.) I wrote the following poem.

FACETS OF A BEAUTIFUL LIFE
Life is much like a diamond or other precious stone.
Carefully cut and polished each has value of its own.
Each facet adds a sparkle that cannot be left out.
For the stone to be appreciated, that's what life is all about!

The quality of a precious stone really determines its worth,
And in this sense each of you were equally precious at birth.
But the wholesome facets are those that bring out great admiration.
That makes a person's life wonderful to family, friends,
and our nation.

As you experience this very important graduation night,
New facets may need to be cut and polished to sparkle bright.
But most facets of life by now already have been made.
Your basic philosophy, spiritual concepts, and character are laid.

The next wholesome facet is basic for your character:
An optimistic outlook on life produces peace and laughter!
Peace with God and self, that should become your priority—
Carefully analyzing situations before following the majority!

The wholesome facet to give of self, more than to receive—
To help better the world and its problems relieve—
This facet is left out of more and more lives today.
The idea of living to serve is becoming an old-fashioned way.

Another facet is to be a good citizen in society—
Involving oneself in church, government and community!
To be responsible means to manage one's life and live right—

Obeying laws and helping those in an unfortunate plight.

The facet of moral integrity will sparkle even at night
And like flowers give fragrance for those without moral insight.
Although the forces are strong this facet to dirty and mar,
A stronger force, when permitted, will not allow a scar.

But evil from the deceiver destroyed your image a lot.
Then God sent His Son, Jesus, to undercut Satan's plot.
And salvation by grace through faith in Jesus brings new life again.
Then the spiritual facet is eternally cut; you are forgiven of sin.

The spiritual facet reflects God in you, my dear young ladies—
Opening up a whole new world with God when you are ready!
Facets flash joy, serenity, peace, worth, fulfillment, and more love,
Glimmering hope, satisfaction, and certainty in heaven above!

Facets, facets, glimmering and shimmering to bless the earth,
Fulfilling the hopes and dreams each parent had at your birth.
Twinkling and glowing brilliantly like stars in a cloudless night,
Your WHOLESOME VALUES will be beautiful
in God's eternal sight.

Now that you will leave home, what will you become?
Forget these facets of life as many others have done?
Or will you continue to hone and polish each facet with care
And become one of the world's jewels so precious and rare?

Joe Tarry, May 1983

Move to Apartment

Since Joe and I now had an empty nest, we didn't need the large house, so we decided to move to the vacant mission apartment before we left for furlough. While we were gone, Wade and Sherry Akins and family could move to the house when they finished language school.

Crammed into the nine weeks Jonathan was with us, we took a trip to the beach. We had a great time on the beach. Jonathan always enjoyed making sand castles. We bought fish and the largest shrimp we ever had seen and packed them in the ice chest to take home.

Jonathan enjoyed the annual South Brazil mission meeting. He affectionately was welcomed by his missionary aunts and uncles and their kids—in the missionary family considered to be cousins.

Joe and I had helped Jonathan move from an apartment to a house he bought in Dallas—now he helped us move to an apartment. We got everything moved into the apartment on Aluminum Street just before we went to the state convention in Montes Claros. The apartment had been vacant since missionaries Jack and Jean Young had moved to Rio de Janeiro. The apartment complex building had 50 family units with parking places in the garage underground. Our apartment had rights to two parking spaces. The lovely mission apartment was on the 10th floor. The front and back were almost solid windows; this allowed a wonderful breeze to pass through. We didn't have time to unpack things; we just set the beds up so we could sleep and plugged in all electrical appliances. We left the next day for Montes Claros. We enjoyed the convention and our visit with missionaries Jesse and Wilma Kidd.

We were gone about five days; when we arrived home and reached the 10th floor, a terrible smell greeted us. We soon discovered the source of the smell. The refrigerator was plugged in, but the electrical switch for that side of the kitchen was off. Opening the refrigerator freezer door almost knocked one backward because of the terrible smell. Several pounds of those huge shrimp, fish, chicken, and beef had ruined. As though it was a thick cloud the horrific smell spread into the apartment. You cannot imagine how bad this was. We quickly stuffed all the spoiled meat into plastic bags. Our next-door neighbor, Nancy, said she was worried about the smell and wondered what had died in our apartment. To kill the odor I used every suggestion given: coffee grounds, disinfectant, and baking soda. When we left for furlough, I left coffee grounds and baking soda inside the refrigerator and left the doors open. I jokingly told missionary Kathy Richardson to let me know when the smell was gone and we would return. We were so thankful to find that the smell ultimately went away.

Our Trip to the U.S. by Way of Venezuela

Missionaries Buck and Ila Mae Smith were friends from Portales and Dora, NM. They had invited us to stop in Venezuela to visit with them on one of our trips back to the U.S. We set up a visit; they met us in Caracas, but they lived in Maricaibo. We stayed in the mission guest house and had a wonderful visit. Leaving Caracas was hectic; the flight was delayed. We arrived in Miami about midnight and missed our flight from Miami to Dallas. We were taken to a hotel for the night. In our frustration we didn't realize that Leona's suitcase didn't arrive with us. Leona and I took a taxi back to the airport. Everything was closed; the only activity was that of the janitors who all were Cubans and didn't speak English. Later in Dallas Leona's piece of luggage caught up with us.

Furlough Events

For our furlough Hillcrest Baptist Church offered us the use of that church's old parsonage. This was God's timing, because we wanted to stay in Lovington since Daddy's illness with cancer was progressing. Hillcrest Baptist Church had a special place in my heart, because Daddy had had a part in its beginning.

About 1949 Pastor J.C. Quarles asked Daddy to be the song leader for a tent revival promoted by the Southeastern Association. The tent revival was the beginning of a mission that was three blocks from our house. Aunt Susie, a very good pianist, was asked to play the piano. Daddy gave a piano for the mission. From that revival Hillcrest Baptist Church had its beginning. J.C. Quarles was a converted oil-field roughneck. He had preached some in the country church near our home on the farm. Lovington was booming because of much oil drilling. Daddy built the first building that the little church had. Daddy remained song leader until the church had grown to a size requiring a better-trained song leader. Then Daddy returned to First Baptist Church.

The first big thing for us in the States was to get Charlotte enrolled at University of New Mexico. We went to orientation classes with her. Moving onto an immense complex campus with thousands of students was an enormous contrast for a girl that had graduated in a class of five girls and little more than 100 in the whole school. Leona and I were a little worried. We had known Tommy and Martha Donham since the first year I went to Eastern New Mexico University in Portales. Then they transferred to New Mexico State. After graduation he was employed by Sandia Laboratories in Albuquerque. They regularly corresponded with us and other missionaries; on every furlough we saw them. While Charlotte was in Albuquerque, they became her mom and dad; we couldn't have found a better couple. We visited Baptist Student Union with Charlotte. In the Baptist Student Union she found the spiritual strength to carry her day by day. At UNM we were able to get Charlotte into the only dormitory that wasn't coed. Coed dorm was cultural shock for us; things had changed since we were in college.

The Donhams were so good to Charlotte. Martha took Charlotte shopping and became a real friend to her; she gave her motherly advice. When Charlotte had to get everything out of the dorm, they allowed her to use their garage and left their car outside.

Two students from Lovington also were going to UNM, so they took Charlotte under their "wings" and provided her with transportation when she had to go somewhere. The first year they were in college, none of our kids had a car.

An Answer to Many Years of Prayer

For many years I had prayed that I would be with my father when he died. Now he was getting close to that inevitable occasion. Because we needed to be close to my father, Leona and I avoided taking many speaking engagements for the FMB. One semester Leona took two courses at the College of the Southwest, only 15 miles from Lovington.

We chose not to live with Daddy because he had his lifestyle of going to bed early and getting up at 4 or 5 a.m. When he arose, he turned the radio on loud, because he was hard of hearing. We did visit him a lot. He still drove his car around town and took his walk sometimes at 5 a.m. in the summertime. He also visited us often.

On January 1 he decided to enter the Lovington Care Center, as all of the family had been urging him to do. He parked his car in the front where he could see it all the time and occasionally went to town or visited us. On February 1 at just past midnight he called us. Leona answered the phone; he said he was packed and ready to leave. Leona sweetly said: "Mr. Tarry, don't you think the hour is early? Wait until morning; we will get you and your things." He accepted her suggestion. If I had answered the phone, he would have insisted that I go authorize his leaving immediately. Leona had a way with him that I didn't have. I am glad that Leona answered the phone.

About two weeks after Daddy returned to his house, he began to have hallucinations. One night he called me and said that the house was falling down on him. He used the biggest nails he could find to strengthen the nice door facings to keep them from falling. In February the temperature was very cold. Another night Dad called us; he was confused and frightened. He had crawled out a front bedroom window in his pajamas, but he couldn't get back into the house because the door was locked. He finally began to think rationally and climbed back through the window and called us. We went to comfort him; I got him back to bed. At about 3 he assured us that he was fine, so we started home. About halfway home the car motor died. Leona strained an arm trying to turn the steering wheel without the motor (no power steering) while I was pushing the car to get it out of the middle of the street. For months that caused her to have a severe tennis elbow. For a week I slept in the house with Daddy. I didn't know what I was going to do with him. He refused to return to the care center.

Then one night Daddy showed me that his left leg was severely swollen. The next morning I took him to his doctor, who told me that he was near the end. The doctor suggested we take him to the Lovington hospital. The doctor said he probably soon would go into a coma and suggested we just try to keep Daddy comfortable. Medically they could do nothing. The doctor said his father had a similar case of cancer.

We put him in the hospital; I notified my brothers and sisters. For two days Daddy was normal and then drifted into a coma. My sister Margaret and brother Bill (Esteen) were able to arrive while Daddy still was lucid. When Helen arrived from California, Daddy opened his eyes and talked to her a little. Then he returned to the coma again. My younger brother, Thomas (Skeeter), was living in Wyoming. He wanted badly to see Daddy still lucid but couldn't get there until late Thursday. When we told Daddy that Tommy (Skeeter) had arrived,

God gave Skeeter the pleasure of seeing Daddy open his eyes and show Skeeter that he was grateful to see him. God was so gracious and caring.

Someone was with Daddy day and night, but we were not very talkative. Each one of us was in our own world of memories. Once and a while we shared, but most of the time we were silent. Daddy never told us in words that he loved us. All of us missed that. He never bought us a birthday or Christmas present either. He did not buy himself much either—just necessary things. After Bill and I started working, we had a little money to buy small, cheap presents. One Christmas I bought Daddy a 10-cent tie clasp, but he never wore it.

I know Daddy loved us more than he expressed, because I know he didn't sleep well when we were not home at night. As a teen-ager I tried my best to slip into the house and go to bed without his hearing me, but I seldom succeeded. I remember the last whipping I got. I still had the splint on my broken foot. I was picked up by a friend and went to another boy's house to play games. I didn't return until 1 a.m. I couldn't see my dad waiting for me in the dark, but when I got close to the house, he started after me with his razor strap. I tried to beat him around the old washpot. When he caught me, I got a good thrashing. I was supposed to be in at 11. My dad had lost much needed sleep as he worried about me not returning home on time. So he did care, although he didn't say so.

In a way I got close to my dad as I worked for him. When he had a job in the country, he always hummed or sang his favorite hymns as we traveled to the work site and as he worked. One of his favorites was, "All the Way My Savior Leads Me". Daddy expected me to do as much as a man would. When we were pouring a large floor, I often had to shovel the gravel into the cement mixer. I then pushed the wheelbarrow running over with wet concrete. This work was a man's work. Although Dad did not praise me, other people did. The heavy work did help make me stocky and strong for football.

By midnight Thursday only three of us remained to spend the morning hours with him: a nephew, Kenny Livingston; Skeeter, and me. About 5:30 Skeeter and Kenny went to get some coffee. At 6 a.m. Daddy expired; I was the only one with him. God answered my prayer and allowed me to be with Daddy when he died.

400

Daddy's funeral was held at 2:30 Sunday afternoon, March 4, 1984. His old friend, Pastor J.C. Quarles, brought the message; Pastors Harry Pittam and Kelly McCarthick assisted. Pastor Quarles revealed that Daddy as a young man had received the call to preach and reported that he was sorry he had not obeyed. I already had suspected this. I think this was the reason our daddy wasn't able to find much joy and peace in life.

God's timing always is perfect; I could see that was true in my father's death. I had been concerned that we would have to return to Brazil before he died. Daddy's estate was settled quickly.

We were concerned about Mr. and Mrs. Isbell. For 15 years Irma had suffered from Parkinson's disease; Tony definitely had Alzheimer's disease. How would they be able to stay 10 miles from Portales on the farm? We received enough money to make a good down-payment on a house in Roswell; we thought Tony and Irma would be happy to be closer to Doris. We took them to see the house, but Tony seemed confused. Finally he pitifully said, "I don't know what I would do in town! I don't want to leave the farm!" We saw the anguish on his face, so we told them that they could continue to live on the farm. They were able to stay on the farm until the middle of 1988.

Charlotte Has a Scary Experience

Another part of our inheritance was Daddy's little Toyota Corolla. None of my siblings wanted the car. The Toyota was a stick-shift car; that was what Charlotte had trained on in Brazil. Charlotte didn't have a car, so we gave her the Corolla. I drove the car to Albuquerque; Leona, with her folks, followed me. Charlotte and Leona followed me to the west edge of Albuquerque to a location at which Charlotte could practice maneuvering the car for a few minutes. We left her alone to drive back; we would meet her at the Baptist Student Union. Those were scary moments for us. We were relieved when she arrived at the Baptist Student Union. Her BSU director promised to take some time with her driving around Albuquerque. When Charlotte first enrolled in school, I told her that whenever she went with her friends, to pay close attention and learn the streets of Albuquerque.

The next weekend after Charlotte had gotten her car we were in Roswell. Charlotte and her two friends from Lovington planned to meet us. The friends suggested Charlotte could get some experience by driving to Roswell; they would take the car on to Lovington, spend Saturday, and return to Roswell Sunday afternoon. So the group left for Roswell on Friday afternoon even though snow was falling. But the kids had made plans and would carry them out. Charlotte wanted to tell us goodbye in person. By the time they arrived at Clines Corners, where they left I-40, the road was icy. On the exit curve Charlotte slid into a steel reflection pole that helped stop the car before they slid in front of a big 18-wheeler truck. The car wasn't damaged, but they were scared. The boy said that if he had been driving, he probably would have hit the brakes and caused the car to slide worse—perhaps into the truck. This experience was scary for us, but we realized we had to leave Charlotte in God's hands just as we had the boys. Leona believed God was showing us that He was adequate to take care of Charlotte when we were in Brazil—just as He had when we were about 150 miles away.

From Roswell we went to Abilene, TX, for Carl's graduation from the university. We were proud of Carl, as parents are. He had majored in English, so he had to have a second language. Even though he knew Portuguese very well, he would have had to go to a university that offered Portuguese to take their test to give him the six-hours credit he needed. So, he decided to take a year of Spanish (six credit hours). His tutor in Spanish was MK Kathy Doyle from Costa Rica and Guatemala. Kathy later became Carl's wife. Now he was graduating but did not know what he would do. He thought of teaching on the university level. After graduation Carl did one semester on his master's degree and joined the Air Force.

During the last two weeks in the U.S. Leona and I saw God put together a number of good things for us. These blessings were by churches and God's choice people. We praise God for The Marvel of it All. One of the blessings was our visits with relatives in the Fort Worth/Dallas area.

Another blessing was a meeting with some members of Shady Oaks Baptist Church of Hurst that participated with us in the Texas centennial crusades in 1982 in Belo. Because of that encounter in

Brazil the church blessed us this last week in the States with a potluck supper and invited people who had met us during the crusade and some of the retired missionaries in the Fort Worth area. Carl and Jonathan were with us for this also.

Return to Brazil

The next day after the celebration at Shady Oaks Baptist Church, we left Dallas for Brazil. Returning to Brazil was a very solemn experience. On the plane Leona and I didn't talk much. At about noon we arrived at the new international airport of Belo Horizonte; this was our first time to land there. By American sizes the airport was small but was the nicest we had ever seen. Two missionary couples along with a group from our church met us there. The missionary drove our car for me so I could get accustomed again to the traffic. We were well aware that we were nearing Belo Horizonte 30 minutes after we left the airport, because the customary black smoke belched from the exhaust pipes of trucks and buses. The wild drivers sped past us; they dodged potholes in the pavement. We had to watch for the motorists that ran red lights or honked at the very second the traffic light changed. The cobblestone streets still were rough; hundreds of skyscrapers engulfed us.

I had forgotten how difficult driving was. Yes, we were back in Brazil in a car without power-steering, power brakes, automatic transmission or air-conditioning. Because she still was suffering from tendonitis, Leona wouldn't be able to drive the car for a while.

Apartment-living was going to be a new experience for us. We hadn't lived in an apartment since our first year in seminary in 1958.

Back to Work

We were blessed to see church members at Planalto and the missions again. We also enjoyed seeing the people at the state Baptist office and other places. We had nothing to hinder us from giving more time to the Lord's work.

July was one of the busiest months, as we always spent about eight days at annual mission meeting including a day going and returning. We received our 20-year service pin with the FMB; I was reminded that we had passed more than the halfway mark in our missionary career. Without a doubt we had entered the arena of being veteran missionaries. We could see several things that we could give all of our time to do; for instance, if we were to try to start a church in the area surrounding our apartment building, we had a territory of about 800,000 people to whom we could witness.

We were glad Planalto Church held a very good Vacation Bible School without our help. During our absence the church had proven itself able to have a big VBS without us; it had 130 enrolled.

A week after our South Brazil meeting, we spent four days at our state convention. In 1984 the state convention was at Mantena on the eastern side of the state. Mantena is in the Sweet River Valley area; we had visited there many times. The biggest problem was the narrow, dirt road from Governador Valadares to Mantena. That trip from Valadares to Mantena took four hours to drive about 110 miles. On the way to Mantena the dirt was terrible, but a very unusual thing happened during the dry season—rain fell. As we returned to Valadares after the convention, the road was muddy and slippery. I saw something I never had seen before or since. A pastor had a flat and didn't have a spare. He jacked his Volkswagen up, took the wheel off, stuffed the tire full of tall grass, and drove on into town.

The big event in August was our revival with former priest Anibal Pereira Reis. I wrote about him in chapter 2. By August 1984 he had published more than 40 books about many subjects about the Roman Catholic Church. Despite a lot of rain we had good crowds and had 30 people to accept Christ or show an interest in their spiritual lives. Our worship room was overflowing with at least 200 people present on the last night.

Anibal stayed with us; we had a wonderful time sharing spiritual thoughts. He showed us a lump on his neck and said the doctor wanted to take a biopsy of it. We were concerned. Sure enough; the lump was malignant; about a year later he died. We lost a dear friend; Brazil lost a powerful preacher.

Chapter 20

Safety Rules

(Leona's Story)

From our single women missionaries I learned various precautions for safety. Rule #1 was always to drive with the windows closed and doors locked. About 10 o'clock one night I was traveling home from a children's-home board meeting. Alfonso Pena is an eight-lane avenue and usually had cars in all lanes. I was in the center of the four-lane side going up and had to stop at a red light. I saw a group of kids on the center curbing that divided the lanes in the opposite direction. One boy started in my direction; the window was open about three inches. Many times I would give a pencil or something small to kids who approached me, but rarely did I give money, because I didn't want the kids buying drugs. That night the boy who walked near me didn't want anything but money, so I refused. I felt safe, because cars were stopped all around me; they also were waiting for the light. When the light changed, I took off with the rest of the cars. That scared me enough to make me remember always to travel with the windows closed.

One Sunday night I was returning home from church by traveling my usual 45-minute route. I arrived at the principal street going toward home; the light was red at the corner of Bahia and Alfonso Pena—a very busy intersection in the center of Belo. Several bars were situated along the narrow, one-way Bahia Street; at that hour of night one usually saw drunks staggering along. While I was stopped, a drunk walked to my closed window and wanted money. I told him *no;* he was angry and got in front of the car and started trying to get on the hood. The light turned green, but he didn't move for me to go. By now a long line of cars was behind me. What I didn't know was that the car immediately behind me was Joe's. He was watching all that was happening. Just as the man decided to allow me to pass, the light turned red again, so he backed off and yelled, "You can go now", but the light was red. He kept yelling for me to go and was frustrated that I didn't. Finally the light was green again; I went before he stepped back in front of the car. I wasn't afraid, because he was too drunk to hurt me as long as I stayed in the car.

Another night Joe and I were stopped at the same place I just mentioned; a young man demanded money. Joe refused; the man threatened to scratch the car with a nail. Joe told him to go ahead and scratch it, because the car already had scratches. This shocked the young man, so he didn't try to scratch the car. For some reason some people in the Santa Cruz neighborhood thought a great sport was to be the first to scratch a new car, so our car already had been initiated.

For exercise Joe and I walked in our neighborhood; to those we passed, we handed out tracts. To eat along the walk I even put a handful of pinion nuts from New Mexico. Our neighborhood was a quiet area, because most of the streets were not through-streets. Sometimes I would stop at the bakery or the vegetable market to buy milk, bread, or vegetables but never more than I wanted to carry home. In our area I never felt threatened, but one day I met a boy pushing his bicycle. When he got even with the place in which I was walking, I made the mistake of moving toward the wall instead of toward the street (Rule #2: walk near the street). He stopped with his bicycle pinning me to the wall. He wanted money. I explained that I was walking only for exercise and that I had no money to give him. He said he didn't want to hurt me, but he needed money. I said I was sorry but that I had none; he apologized and let me go. That day God protected me, but it was a warning that I never forgot.

Rule #3 was to avoid eye contact with others when I walked down the street but to be alert about those around. One Sunday evening a seminary student and I rode the bus home as we returned from church. As the passengers got off, a thief grabbed a woman's purse and ran. This scared me, because Joe was traveling and I was alone except for the seminary student. Had the thief taken my purse, I would have lost the house key and all money I had with me. The seminary student walked with me to get a taxi to go on home. A bus would have left me a block from home—not so far to walk, BUT I would have to cross the avenue on which street boys waited to ask for money from the stopped cars. During the day I would not have been afraid, but I didn't have the courage to walk alone at night. As the taxi driver neared our street, I pointed to the street kids and told him I was afraid of them. He said: "But for the grace of God, I would have been one of those."

Rule #4 was that when I was in the general public, I did not wear expensive jewelry or jewelry that even looked expensive. Because we lived in the heart of semi-precious stones, Joe has given me some nice rings, but I saved them to wear on special occasions or more private gatherings. We have known of even men being robbed for their wedding bands, so we learned to be more cautious. The first time a man called my attention to my wedding rings was in Governador Valadares. A man selling at the old market asked: "Are those real?" I was puzzled by his question, but I finally understood he was talking about the diamonds in my wedding rings. Years passed; Dario, a member of Planalto Church and a military man, had his wife, Zilar, ask me whether my diamond rings were real. Zilar was one of the women that sometimes went with us to visit; sometimes we visited in the slum area of São Bernardo not far from Planalto Church. When I confirmed that they were real, she told me of Dario's concern. He said that I not only was endangering my own life but also the lives of those that walked with me. Inside the slums sometimes only narrow walking paths instead of a street or normal sidewalks exist. The crime rate in the slums is high, but I never felt afraid of walking there during the day. I told Joe about Dario's concern; we decided to buy for me a simple gold band. I put my diamond rings in our house safe.

Our next-door neighbor was a tall English woman. She was walking down our quiet street to the apartment when a man appeared from behind and jerked the simple gold chain from around her neck. He apparently had experience to know just how to yank in a fashion to break the chain. It cut her neck but otherwise didn't hurt her; he was gone as quickly as he had appeared. I thank God that I never was hurt or robbed on the street.

Bus Trip to Rio de Janeiro

Only on rare occasions did I travel out of town alone; even then, Joe bought the tickets and saw that all was in order. On one occasion three of us women of the WMU were going together to a national WMU meeting in Rio. To get three women to decide which hour to travel was difficult, so by the time we three agreed, Joe could get tickets for us to ride only in the back of the bus next to the bathroom. We did OK, but Ruth didn't like sitting near the bathroom. Maria Bittencourt planned to stay in Rio to visit for a few days with her daughter. Ruth and I wanted to buy our return tickets as soon as we arrived; since we would be traveling on a holiday weekend, the buses would be loaded. Joe had warned me to be sure to get our tickets together. When we arrived at the ticket window, the only tickets available together were at the back of the bus; Ruth said we didn't want those places. She thought we should buy the seats across the aisle from each other toward the middle of the bus. She just knew that one of the others in the window seat wouldn't mind trading. So we bought the tickets.

After our meeting Ruth and I took a taxi to the bus station. About every hour of the day the bus stations in big cities in Brazil have hundreds of buses arriving or leaving. They would compare to our large airports. Each bus company has its location to load (and a different spot to unload) on the lower ground floor. The passengers leaving wait on the floor above; many seats are available as they wait for their bus. The ticket has a number of the departure gate of the bus; only near the departure hour is a person supposed to go through that gate and down the stairs. Since this was a holiday weekend, people were thick as ants on candy.

Ruth and I boarded our bus only to discover we both had a man seated next to us by the window. Neither man wanted to trade for the aisle seat. Ruth was worried about having to sit beside a man. I noticed, however, that she went to sleep even before the bus was out of the city of Rio. I was worried that I would fall asleep and that my head would fall on the shoulder of the man at my side. Through the straps of my purse I crisscrossed my arms and sat very stiff. I was afraid of going to sleep.

Finally I dozed off but was awakened by a person wanting to go to the back, but something was in the aisle. The person said: "Madam, did you drop something?" My arms still were crisscrossed with my purse. Even though I couldn't think of anything I would have dropped, in the dark aisle I put my hand down to see what was there. My hand caught the leg of the man across the aisle behind me. I was shocked! I guess the man woke up, because he moved his leg; the person was able to pass by. The more I thought of my having grasped the man's leg, the more tickled I got. That was a miserable trip back to Belo, but I learned my lesson. When two people are traveling together, ALWAYS buy seats together, even if those seats are near the bathroom.

Leona's Story of a Texas Crusade for Brazil's Centennial

The evangelistic crusade with the Texas people was building up to the centennial year of Baptist work in Brazil in 1982. This was an exciting time. In 1981 for house-to-house visitation I interpreted for Pastor Charles Clary from Tate Springs Baptist Church in Fort Worth. Each morning I picked up my group of Americans; we drove to Vista Alegre. This was a neighborhood of lower middle-class people and had some slum areas. Pastor Antonio de Freitas, a dynamic preacher, was our host pastor. Antonio was reared a Roman Catholic and had tattoos on both arms and hands. He along with two or three members from the church went with us to the homes. One afternoon a little earlier than usual we were walking back to the car to return to the hotel, because one of the women didn't feel well. A church member met us and explained that a 103-year-old woman had agreed to talk with our group; would we go? When I heard how old this person was, I believed we couldn't turn down the request. The two American women decided to wait in the car while we made the visit. When we entered the home, the first thing I saw was a wall-sized picture of the pope. He was visiting Brazil and a few days earlier had been in Belo. We were ushered into a very small bedroom that was big enough only for a twin bed and room for our group to stand. The Brazilian church member introduced us and explained the reason of our visit. The woman, Maria, was amazed that these Americans would travel so far just to tell others about Jesus. She felt honored that we would enter her humble home. Pastor Charles gave his testimony and I translated. Pastor Antonio explained that we were there to tell about Jesus and how to have His salvation. After I read the Scripture, I asked Maria whether she understood about salvation. She assured me that she did, so I asked her whether she wanted to invite Jesus into her heart. Without hesitation she said *yes*. I thought, *She doesn't understand my accented Portuguese; this is too easy,* so I reworded my question. Again she replied *yes*. I turned to Pastor Antonio, but he seemed confident that she had understood. I prayed; then she prayed. Tears were running down her cheeks.

We all rejoiced that God had given her this opportunity to hear the simple plan of salvation and to make her decision. After the service that night one of the neighbors met us to tell us that after we left that afternoon, Maria had to be taken to the hospital. Before she met her Maker, she never was able to go to church to make her decision public. But we believe that surely we will meet her in heaven. *What if we had waited until the next day?*

Translator in Rio

The last week in July 1984 I had a ticket to go by bus to Rio de Janeiro to translate for volunteers in an evangelism crusade. Missionary Bill Mosley called on Saturday and asked whether I could help in Rio, because they were short of translators. I agreed to go.

Sunday afternoon we had been in Planalto visiting and had stopped in at a "snack bar" to get a bite to eat before church services. We each ate a popular Brazilian snack—a *pastel*—a fried pie of chicken. The one I ate was spoiled; before I got home I had a bad stomachache. I immediately mixed up the salt-sugar medication we used for upset stomachs. We acquired the recipe from a missionary and found it to be very effective: to one quart of pure water add eight teaspoons of sugar and one teaspoon of salt. By the time I was to leave on the bus, my stomach was better. I took a jar of the mixture with me to drink along the way. God blessed and my stomach didn't hinder the work in Rio.

Visit to Paraguay

The summer of 1985 Jonathan and a group from his college went on an archaeological dig in Capernaum. Carl had joined the Air Force (his dream) after he worked a semester on a master's degree at Hardin-Simmons. He and Kathy Doyle, a missionary kid from Costa Rica and Guatemala, were engaged. I grew up with Kathy's parents, Don and Pat (Sloan) Doyle.

In 1985 Charlotte accepted her FMB-paid MK trip back from college to Brazil. We planned a trip to visit Paraguay. We had a direct bus from Belo to Iguacu Falls, at which missionaries Linda and Ken Watkins met us. We had been in Golden Gate Baptist Seminary with the Watkinses; they had invited us to visit them in Puerto Presidente Stroessner, Paraguay. This city is just across the river from Iguacu Falls. Earlier we wanted to go into Paraguay with the boys but couldn't because of the Brazilian government restrictions. Those restrictions had been lifted. We had a wonderful visit. Linda played her harp, an instrument popular there. They took us to see the new, huge hydroelectric dam called *Itaipu* on the Paraguay River.

Ken took us to the street market in which many Brazilians bought items to take back to sell in cities in Brazil. The Brazilian government knew this contraband was occurring; they were trying to bring it under control by limiting to two items of a kind to be brought into Brazil. We bought numerous items for souvenirs, but we did not bring more than our limit. I have a collection of dolls from various places, so I had to buy a Paraguayan doll.

Ken took us back across the bridge to get our bus at Iguacu Falls. When we arrived, the bus station was crowded. The people had many bags; some people had new leather bags such as one we bought. Confusion seemed to rule as people were trying to get other passengers to trade off extra items to put in their suitcases. Once the bus arrived in São Paulo, they would trade back. The Brazilians had bought several of the same items such as jeans, makeup kits, watches, and hairbrushes—all to re-sell in Brazil on the black market. Before the Brazilians boarded the bus, they would mix up their buys so no one had more than his or her limit of items. One man asked Charlotte and me whether we would put two pair of jeans in our suitcases. Joe was horrified that we accepted. In accepting I really wasn't thinking clearly.

After everyone was on the bus, Joe was explaining to me how

they even could have put drugs in the pockets of the jeans. Then I began to worry for Charlotte and me. *What could I do now since the suitcases already were loaded?* I just worried along with Joe.

About 30 minutes out of Iguacu the bus was stopped at a police checkpoint. A man got on the bus and explained that everyone would be getting off; we were to take whatever we wanted from inside and they would confiscate what was left. Two people at a time were called to get out. They had to identify their luggage and open it for the officials; they also were frisked by a police officer. A truck was backed up close by; the officials were removing items from the suitcases and bags and putting them into the truck. Finally only one other couple and we three Americans were left on the bus. We were expecting to be called to get off the bus, but we weren't. We marveled that we didn't have to descend. I was able to quit worrying about the jeans. Thank you, God!

Finally after an hour, the officials were satisfied and allowed the people to reload the bus. The people were angry; even though the hour was quite late, they wouldn't allow the driver to turn the inside lights off. As we traveled, no one wanted to sleep. The people in the group talked about how many things they were able to hide on themselves, even though they were frisked. Joe was sitting behind us; the man that sat beside him told him that he had gone to the bus garage earlier and, with the driver's permission, hidden his most valuable buy (small electrical stereos) in an area by the motor of the bus. No doubt he paid the driver to allow him to do that.

I have a very good friend that traveled to Paraguay regularly to buy items to bring back to sell. She shared a few incidents with me about her travels. I began to understand a little of the group's system. My friend knew many of the people on the days that she traveled and knew those she could trust. I assume she did some trading as these folks had done.

The bus traveled about another two hours; then the motor died. We were stranded out in the middle of nowhere with a group of angry people. Finally another bus arrived; everything had to be transferred to the new bus and the people settled down again. The passenger sitting by Joe had to get his valuables out the motor area of the stricken bus.

A group in the back of the bus had a brilliant idea as to how they could get a return on the money they had lost. Someone suggested the license-plate number of the crippled bus along with the license number of the truck used to collect the items. That should give them a lucky number, so they formed a lottery pool. Then the people in the front wanted to join the pool, but those in the back didn't want to enlarge the pool. Joe thought the idea was ridiculous. How could a license plate number of a broken down bus be "lucky"? This just shows how spiritually depraved people grasp at crazy ideas to recover their losses. When we approached São Paulo, various ones requested to get off the bus at the edge of the city. That meant the driver had to descend to get that person's luggage. Numerous people did this; this further delayed the arrival of our already late bus. We decided they still were afraid that the officials might be waiting to go through their baggage again at the bus station, because we later saw some of them at the station in São Paulo waiting for their connecting bus. Our bus from São Paulo to Belo was calm; on most of the nine-hour trip home we were tired enough to sleep.

Time passed too quickly; before we realized it, the day arrived for Charlotte to leave. We took Charlotte to the Belo International Airport to get her flight back to the States. She gave her passport and ticket to the ticket agent; he looked at them and said: "You need signed permission to travel alone." I'm sure the look of surprise was on our faces.

She answered: "But sir, I traveled alone to get here."

He looked again at her passport and saw the date of birth: "Oh, excuse me. You look so young." Today she would appreciate those words, but at that time she didn't appreciate it so much; after all, she was 20.

Job as Joe's Secretary

In 1985 Joe wrote in Portuguese the first book on stewardship. On an IBM typewriter I typed the first two books. That was very difficult; I wasn't happy about doing more of this. For the third book Joe paid a seminary student to type the manuscript, but her typing and Portuguese were worse than mine. A Canadian missionary could print the book at a good price, but every page had to be just as we wanted it in the book; no correction ink could be used. Finally our new missionaries, Ken Richardson and Jimmy Joseph, insisted that we buy a computer if Joe was serious about writing. Computers were very difficult to find and very expensive. But they insisted that we at least see about buying one. We contacted a colleague in Rio about getting a computer. She told us about a man that would put together a computer for us; this was illegal, but that was the only way to get one. In 1987 we got the computer; Jimmy and Ken were faithful to their promise to get it set up and going for us. Ken was my teacher. Joe would put his writing on the computer and I would correct it. He had a committee of three Brazilians to read the manuscript and to make corrections and suggestions. I then made the corrections they suggested; doing this was much easier on the computer. I jokingly tell people that the computer saved our marriage; we are thankful for Ken's insistence.

Miraculous Sale of My First Chevette

About 1984 I was so involved in many things and Joe was traveling so much in the mission car that he believed I needed my own car. He bought a nice-looking, well-used alcohol Chevette. This model was in the early years of making cars that were alcohol-fueled cars. These cars had a small, quart-size container of gasoline near the carburetor; in colder weather this helped start the motor. I enjoyed the car; it served well as long as it stopped on more-or-less level ground. The Santa Cruz mission was on a steep hill; every time I parked in front and headed downhill, the motor would flood. If I parked headed uphill, the motor would start, but to start going uphill was difficult. So I parked on the street below the church and walked up to the church. Finally Joe decided to sell the car and buy another one, but knowing the problem he didn't feel comfortable selling it to a friend.

One Sunday morning Joe drove my car to Barro Preto Baptist Church for a service. This church was in a nice neighborhood near downtown Belo. After the service a man was looking at the car. The man said: "Nice looking car; would you consider selling it?"

Joe said: "This is my wife's car, so I will have to consult her about selling it." Joe really was eager to sell, but the offer took him by surprise! Being honest Joe told him about the problem with the car. The man told Joe that he lived in a high-rise building across the street. He said he previously had a car like ours and understood the problem.

414

From his apartment he saw our car and wanted to buy it.

The man gave Joe his business card; Joe agreed to call him with our answer. *Wow!* We believed this was an answer to our prayers. We certainly didn't take long to make our decision and to call the man back.

Joe found a pretty golden metallic Chevette car—a newer model. This car also ran on alcohol but never gave the problem the older one did. We think the newer models were better adapted to running on alcohol. This car was very simple but was easy to drive. A person in a group of American volunteers riding with me asked me to turn on the air-conditioner. I turned on the fan; he was shocked. *What, no air-conditioner?* Air-conditioners still were a luxury; very few cars had them. Certainly the missionaries' cars did not.

We bought for the mission a very nice Chevrolet Monza car; we bought it from our next-door neighbor's sister. The FMB was in a financial crisis; no money for new cars was available. This car also was an alcoholic. Our neighbor had died; the older sister didn't drive. The price was very good; we knew it was a good buy. That was a heavier car and very firm on the highway. The alcohol was supposed to be cheaper, since this product was made in Brazil from sugar cane. But that didn't turn out to be true; the gasoline also gave better mileage per gallon. Gasoline was more expensive because it had to be imported; even so, it was mixed with alcohol. We used the Monza car as a mission car until the transportation chairperson finally told Joe he needed to get a new car. The car was still in good condition but had many miles from being driven all over the state of Minas. As our personal car we bought the Monza from the South Brazil mission and sold the golden Chevette. We kept the Monza until we retired.

Grandson #1

Kathy and Carl had a son named Andrew; he was born in September 1990 at Travis Air Force Base Hospital in California. We didn't get to see him until 1992 when he was almost 2. By then he was walking and talking. Carl and Kathy and the two kids visited us in Roswell. Carl had to report for duty at Scott Air Force Base in Illinois, but Kathy and the kids stayed with us in Roswell. Charlotte was getting married in August; Kathy was attendant and Michelle was flower girl. We made dresses for Kathy and Michelle to wear in the wedding. Andrew was enchanted by horses; since Uncle Pat and Aunt Doris Bowen had horses, he had an opportunity to pet a real horse. He called me *MiMi*; since Doris had a horse, she was *MiMi HaHa*. At a hobby shop I bought a cute wooden rocking horse. As a present from his MiMi I painted it and put Andrew's name on it.

Experiences with Doris

In 1991 Doris visited us. We met her in Rio de Janeiro and saw many of the sites; however, because of strikes of national park employes, Sugar Loaf and Corcovado were closed. This was disappointing, because these two sites are the most popular ones. We could see them from a distance, but we missed climbing Corcovado to see the huge statute of Christ the Redeemer. We drove to a high lookout point at which we had a breathtaking view. Doris got her feet wet at beautiful Copacabana Beach. This was midwinter (June 12); the water was too cold for swimmers or even for wading.

We drove up the coastline from Rio to Cabo Frio—a beautiful beach with white sand. The ocean always was crystal clear; we walked out into water until it was up to our chins and still saw our red toenails. The beach-club apartments are about a mile from the beach in a slum area; this surprised Doris. The street to the apartments was dirt and full of chuckholes that Joe tried to dodge. I loved this beach because of the beauty. Around the cove was another nice village with a beautiful Baptist church. That week Wayne Bristol from Oklahoma, a graduate of Wayland Baptist University in Plainview, TX, was preaching. We decided to attend that night. The sanctuary was full with about 700 people.

On our way back to Belo Horizonte we bought a stalk of "golden" bananas. The bananas are small, about two-inches long, but very rich. These bananas get their name from their "golden" color. Because they are small, you can eat too many before you realize it. You then get a stomachache. Joe told Doris, "Be careful; don't eat too many." Sure enough, she overdid it.

A group from North Carolina arrived to mount the prefabricated chapel in Diamantina in north Minas. Joe and I were scheduled to help as translators for the group; this gave Doris the opportunity to see an old, traditional, historic city. The first hurdle in Diamantina to have an Evangelical church was obtaining property. The Baptists bought an old house that had a larger back yard than some lots did. The old home could not be destroyed—or replaced. A second obstacle was getting a permit to mount a prefabricated building in the downtown area. The law wouldn't allow any building that didn't have an antique front. The city officials finally approved putting the prefabricated chapel on the back of the property behind the old house that had a genuine façade such as the 200-year-old houses all around did. The old house in front served as a parsonage.

Diamantina got the name because of the diamonds found in the area. A few miles out of town a group of *garimpeiros*—men that look or dig for precious stones—allowed us to watch them pan for diamonds. The men used large "gold" pans (funnel-shaped) to shift through the pebbles and look for diamonds in the riverbed. The water had been re-routed to allow them to work the ponds that were scattered on the now nearly dry riverbed. The men worked, filled their pans with pebbles and water, and then sifted this around and around until most of the water whirled out. If gold or diamonds are in the pebbles, their weight works them to the bottom of the pan. At a certain point the *garimpeiro* turns the pan upside down on top of black pebbles; diamonds or gold would have shown up easily. We were disappointed the men didn't find anything. Normally visitors are not welcomed to watch, but the *garimpeiros* were gracious and (for a tip) were willing to give us a show. Also the Brazilian woman guide was the wife of a well-known man in the city and had pre-arranged our visit.

A pile of gravel had been dumped in the parking lot of the hotel in which we were staying. All the construction team members spent their spare time looking for a diamond in the pile. Of course they didn't find anything of value.

Charlotte Arrives

Charlotte arrived in Belo for a visit just in time for mission meeting. We picked her up at the airport on the way to the annual mission meeting at Aguas de Lindoia, São Paulo. Aguas de Lindoia is a beautiful tourist place and is known for its good drinking water.

417

After mission meeting we headed to Governador Valadares to start work with the Dwight Lowrie-Wayne Jenkins team of more than 100 from the States. The group was divided into teams: some were for construction, some for street witnessing, some were for medical help, and others were for home visitation. On Saturday each team was introduced to the pastor of the church in which that team would help. The work started on Sunday and went through the next Sunday night. Charlotte helped as a translator with a medical team. Doris and I worked with a medical team plus bought and delivered medicine to the clinics. The day started with breakfast at the hotel; then at about 8:30 each team was picked up by a group from its church. The sponsoring church sometimes prepared the noon meal; after a short rest period work resumed. In our case that meant seeing more patients at the clinic. The home visitors started with their schedule of homes. About 5 each team was taken back to the hotel to refresh; then teams would return to the night services at the churches. If the distance back to the hotel was too far, the church also provided an evening lunch either before or after the worship service at about 9:30. By the time we returned to the hotel, we were exhausted but excited about the victories of the day. By the end of the week lasting friendships were formed between the Americans and Brazilians.

Visit to Ouro Preto

We took Doris and Charlotte to visit Ouro Preto, the first capital of Minas Gerais and a place a visitor to Brazil would not want to miss. This is one of the most important and popular historical cities and is known for the 13 Roman Catholic churches there. This old city was built on the mountains; the narrow one-way streets are steep. Much of the sightseeing is done by walking. The first insurrection for independence from Portugal was at Ouro Preto. The leader of the insurrection, Tiradentes—*tira* (remove) *dentes* (teeth) is his nickname because he was a dentist by trade—is buried in the old museum. Along with other interesting artifacts the jail in which the insurrectionists were kept is in the museum. However, Antonio Francisco Lisboa, the *Aleijadinho* (meaning "little cripple"), made the city famous with his artistic designs. He had leprosy and in his later years had to be carried to his place of work. The baroque style of architec-

418

ture has been preserved, as has that of Diamantina. One of the churches is said to be the richest in Brazil because of the massive amount of gold ornate overlay decorations. Before Brazil's independence all gold had to be sent to Portugal except what was used in churches. One pays to enter these historical relics and must be dressed appropriately—not in shorts!

A school of mines, in which students learn about the many precious and semiprecious stones and how to cut them, is situated on the main plaza. Walking down the street we were overwhelmed by students and men trying to sell their cut stones. At the same time they all were sticking out their arms at us. They knew we were Americans, so we surely had money, they thought. This area also is known for soapstone products. Many ornate statues and many other decorative items carved from soapstone are sold at a reasonable price. A museum of gemstones is at the school.

Back in Belo Horizonte

Belo had a population of more than three-million people and many cars. We lived just off the main avenue which has four lanes on either side of a cement divider. As you drive, you use turning signals, but when you are near a place at which you have to turn and you aren't in the correct lane, you have to use other measures when you can. Doris and I were headed down the avenue; I was in a center lane and needed to turn right, so I asked Doris to stick her arm out the window and wave her hand to give a signal to the cars behind that I needed to turn.

She asked: "What?"

I said: "Stick your arm out the window and wave your hand up and down." Doris couldn't believe her ears, but she obeyed. The cars behind allowed us in; we made our right turn and continued on our way.

One interesting street that we like to take our guests to see is "Peanut Street". This is a short street about a mile farther up the mountain from our apartment. Usually one or more cars are in the process of doing the experiment that we took Doris to see. I stopped the car, turned off the engine, put it in neutral gear, and we waited. (Our cars were still stick-shift.) Gradually the car started to roll up the street. Then we turned around; the car started backing up the hill. This is a mystery; various people have theories of how this happens.

Our wonderful time together ended all too soon. We took Doris to the Belo airport so she could return home.

Anna Pacheco

When we first met her, Anna Pacheco was about 50-years old. She started attending our Planalto Church even though she lived near the center of the San Bernardo neighborhood, about a 30-minute walk for an average person. Anna appeared to be a leper, but when she was small, she pulled a big pan of boiling water off the stove onto herself. Her face was disfigured; half of her fingers and toes were missing. Anna lived on a disablement pension of about $30 a month from the government. Two characteristics about Anna's Christian life were as noticeable as was a full moon shining on an ocean. She was among the first to arrive at the church, although she walked with difficulty. The second thing was that the first Sunday after she received her government check, she always brought her tithe faithfully.

Soon after she visited the church, Joe and I visited her. Her house was in the slum area; in fact, most of São Bernardo was a large slum area. A slum area has very narrow streets, with houses crammed close to each other. Many of them are made of scrap wood and cardboard; many have dirt floors. Where cars cannot drive, a narrow path leads to the homes. Sewer and wash water run in a gully along the street or path down to the river; sometimes the houses have no electricity. Anna cared for a mentally challenged nephew. We saw that Anna really needed help. We didn't discourage her from tithing, for she gave her tithe with consistency and with joy. We asked the church to put her on the list of needy members and friends; this basically meant that every month she would receive a basket of basic food supplies. This helped her a lot.

One year Anna went to the big city of São Paulo, the capital of the state of São Paulo, to visit family. At that time São Paulo had about 13-million people She was hit by a car and had many broken bones. She spent months in recovery! Finally she returned to Belo. She had even more difficulty walking, but she consistently arrived at church early. Now she was practically deaf from the injuries in the accident.

420

Even though she hardly could hear the lesson or the message, she was worshiping God. She was one of the greatest examples of a Christian I ever met—a real inspiration to us. Praise God for Anna Pacheco!

Preschool Class

When Planalto Church was preparing to build, I asked the building committee to remember the preschool class (for babies). One day I was walking downtown and passed a store with its display of bathroom fixtures sitting on the sidewalk. I saw a child-sized commode. I was so excited! As soon as I returned home, I told Joe; we returned with the car and bought the commode. The mothers were very happy about the interest we had in the little ones, since few had a concept of how much a small child can learn when taught on his or her level. We had a very good, organized class. By now the Brazilian Baptist Sunday School Board published literature for this age group. Our room was small, about nine-feet-by-15-feet, plus its own bathroom with the little commode and sink, but we were proud of it. At times we had 16 present (birth through 3-years of age) and three helpers. In the States this kind of ratio never would exist.

We had wooden blocks, a little stove and table, and even a stairs/rocking boat, but most all the other materials—the puzzles, books, and games—were homemade. The parents were very cooperative in taking care of the supplies. We had the elected teachers to teach during the Sunday-school period and then a schedule of volunteers along with one of the elected teachers to help during the worship period. That way the burden was shared; no one missed many worship services. Since the night services were better-attended than the morning services were, the little ones' classroom was scheduled to be open also.

Once or twice a year we planned a special outing with the little ones (along with their parents). One favorite spot for a picnic was the city zoo. One year we saw a baby elephant playing with its mom.

From time to time a parent would admit the desire to stay home from church, but the parent's little one would cry to go, so that encouraged her to bring him. Jesus said, *"Permit the children to come to Me; do not hinder them; for the kingdom of God belongs to such as these"* (Mark 10:14). We were thrilled to see the parents attend church because the little children didn't want to miss.

Leo and Dorothy Weatherman first were our Minas State Camp directors but had moved to work with prefabricated chapels in the State of Rio de Janeiro. Joe went to a national meeting at the Rio state camp; I stayed with Dorothy. Dorothy was a very good seamstress and enjoyed sewing. She had a new doll pattern and suggested we make a doll for our class. We made the doll, painted the face, put yarn for hair, and even made clothes. The doll was a success and was loved by the children in my Sunday-school class. Since many women knew how to sew, I used this doll to show the churches how they, too, could make dolls for their church.

Bible Drill

Every year the associational children's leaders planned an annual children's rally at the Baptist school. The rally included a Bible-drill contest. The leader of the group asked whether I would be in charge of the Bible drill. I prepared the Scriptures on the same plan I had known in the States. Then the youth leader requested I do the same for the associational youth rally. I sent all the churches the Scriptures the kids were to memorize and the regulations for the drill. I did this for two years. We had about 15 churches to participate in the youth drill. I realized this was too many for everyone at once, so the second year we had the drill in each of the five regions of Belo Horizonte. At the annual youth rally two winners of each region participated in the final drill. I was proud of the kids for their work and participation. When we were gone for furlough, the new youth leaders discarded the Bible-drill program. I was very disappointed.

Associational Preschool Work

Missionary Janis Sumerlin, state religious-education director, promoted studies for leadership of each age group. She requested that I be in charge of the preschool area (birth-3 years). Each quarter she promoted in the Central Baptist Association a "preview study" of the new literature for the next quarter. I studied the preschool (0-3 years and 4-5 years) literature to present to the women that attended from the 100 churches. Teachers' aides were available. At first the materials were in black and white and had to be colored, but later they were produced in color. These had to be cut and made into books, puzzles, or "toys" for teaching. Since teaching babies was a new concept, so was the concept that "playing" was teaching.

A few times we were invited to conduct a clinic in one of the associations of the state. I also took advantage of Joe's travels and took my box of "toys" and teaching aids to show the churches how to use them. I wanted to show how the parents could reach young parents by reaching their children.

I am amazed at how quickly the idea of nursery schools spread, as more and more mothers began working outside the home. In nearly every neighborhood nursery schools popped up. Maybe the public picked up on the idea from the Baptists?

Edna—Adopted Brazilian Daughter

The Central Association held quarterly teacher-training sessions that lasted about two-and-a-half to three hours. Edna attended my group for preschool teachers. After the preview study Edna would stay and help me put my materials in the boxes. She was about 20-years old and was interested in working with preschool children. Edna was very helpful and was like a spong—absorbing all she could. After two or three studies she offered to help prepare the materials for the preview studies. Our friendship grew; one day she called to invite Joe and me to eat Sunday dinner with her and her friend, Leomar. At that time she was living with Leomar; Leomar was a good friend to Janis Sumerlin. We had a good time visiting and eating. At the preview study for April-June we presented some suggestions for gifts the children could make for Mother's Day. For me Edna had made a large card with stickers, stamps, and written sayings. One of the sayings was: "You are the mom I have always dreamed of having." That really touched my heart deeply; from that time on, our friendship grew. So Edna became our "adopted" Brazilian daughter.

Edna's mom died when Edna was born, so she never knew her. As time passed, her dad remarried, but the new "mom" never accepted Edna. When Edna was about 8-years old, her dad allowed her to live with and work for a family in their village. This meant washing the dishes, watching a smaller child, and performing many other house chores. From then on Edna worked and went to school; the fact that they allowed her to study was a blessing. As a child she never knew what playing was like.

When she was about 15, the family for whom she worked decided to move to Belo Horizonte and asked her dad to allow Edna to move with them. Her father finally agreed, so she went to the large city. After some months in Belo the family decided it no longer needed her, so the woman found another family with whom she could live and work. Their moving really hurt Edna's feelings deeply, but she transferred to her new home. In this move the Lord clearly was at work, because the new family was Christian and took her to church for the first time. Edna loved the church; before long she accepted Jesus. In that church she met Leomar; they became good friends. Their friendship grew; Leomar could see that Edna had leadership traits. She helped Leomar in the children's class; that is why Edna attended the associational preview study. Leomar also invited her to live with her.

The government housing was scheduled to build some new houses for people on low incomes. Three friends put in a bid for a low-income house. They had agreed that if one of their names was drawn, that one would pass the house on to Edna. With God's blessings one of her three friends' names was drawn, so Edna had a new house. From her salary at the Minas Baptist Seminary Edna was able to make the monthly payments. Various friends helped financially to get the house finished in a fashion suitable for her to live. Edna also cleaned house for a pastor and his wife.

An aunt of Edna's was very sick from Chagas, a disease transmitted by a beetle that is common in Minas Gerais. Not long before the aunt died, Edna visited her; the aunt made Edna promise to get the blood exam to see if she, too, had the disease. When Edna got the results, they showed positive. Our mutual friend, Dr. Carlos Leite, didn't have confidence in the laboratory results, so he paid for Edna to have the test taken in a different laboratory. The test results still were positive. Oh, what a sad day! She took some treatments; the disease seems to be under control. We do not know what the future holds—maybe many years and maybe not. Like so many other Brazilian children she had such a simple background, but she has blossomed into a beautiful woman and a servant for God.

We prayed that Edna would meet a good Christian man to marry so she could have the happy home that as a child she never had. God answered the prayers of many friends; in 2004 Edna married a wonderful Christian man. At the time of this writing they live in Manaus and have a precious 5-year-old daughter that calls us "*Vovos Americanos*" (American grandparents). She has truly blessed our lives. We pray that God will give her many happy years.

A Drunk Thanksgiving Turkey

Most missionaries considered their colleagues to be family. Missionary children considered the adult missionaries as uncles and aunts. This is why in this book we want you to meet other missionaries. We enjoyed visiting with Jesse and Wilma Kidd. They lived in Montes Claros, the *Sertao* (interior, back-country) northern region of Minas Gerais. We usually visited them when we were to participate in some type of mission work, but one year Leona and I visited them for the American Thanksgiving celebration. The wild turkey meat always was very tough. We never bought one, but a few times one was given to us. By 1985 we could buy nice butterball turkeys in the supermarkets in Belo but not in Montes Claros, so Jesse had bought a turkey from a rancher. When we arrived, the turkey was tied to the clothesline with a long, strong cord that allowed the bird to walk in the yard. The turkey was accustomed to sleeping in a tree, so at dusk he tried to fly up on a shed to roost. The cord was too short, so he kept falling. When Jesse arrived home from church, he lengthened the cord so the turkey could roost on the shed.

The next day Jesse and Wilma planned to kill and prepare the turkey. Jesse had been told he could give the turkey some beer before he killed him; this would relax the turkey so the meat wouldn't be so tough. We also had heard that Ronny Boswell several years before had done this in Belo Horizonte, but we never tried this. Jesse didn't like the idea of buying beer, but he decided to go across the street to the bar and buy some; he just didn't know how much to purchase. He told the neighbor (bartender) why he needed some beer; the man gave him a glass of beer. Wilma, Joe, and I gathered around to help while Jesse forced the turkey's beak open and poured beer into his mouth. First the turkey began blinking his eyes fast. Joe loosened his grip on him as the bird began to relax; the turkey started staggering backward. He wanted to go forward, but each step was backward. He finally collapsed on the ground. The moral to this story is that once a person indulges in an alcoholic drink, he stops advancing forward. We don't know whether the meat was tenderized. We had bought a butterball turkey in Belo Horizonte. Wilma cooked it and gave the "wild" turkey to a pastor's family. The pastor recently had died.

Jesse was the director of missions and supervised the planting of many churches in Montes Claros and the north region. In just a 10-year period their accomplishments in that area were great. The mayor of Montes Claros gave Jesse an "honorable citizen award". This was an award that foreigners rarely receive. The government had poured a lot of money into making Montes Claros a large city of more than 300,000 citizens.

In World War II Jesse had been a combat soldier. Wilma shared with me that Jesse still had terrible nightmares about his war experiences in Burma and China. Fifty years had passed since the war; Jesse hadn't shared these experiences with anyone. I told Joe about Jesse's situation. Our friendship with Jesse and Wilma was more like that of brother and sister. In 1987 Joe decided to talk to Jesse and try to get him to unload some of the burden that he silently still carried. This seemed to help Jesse; he shared three short incidents that will make all Christians and especially Baptists proud of World War II veterans.

Because he had been drafted into the army, Jesse had been mad at God. His plans for life were interrupted. The soldiers' long train ride through India took them to Lido, at which point they boarded trucks to Burma. Then his unit ended up in a jungle and prepared to retake the Burma Road from the Japanese. Chinese forces that had been cut off from China had trained for jungle combat while they were in India. These Chinese soldiers would be guides for the American soldiers. Near the combat zone the platoon officer had given them the order to throw away every unnecessary item, no matter how small, because during the next months walking would be extremely difficult. Jesse looked at his little New Testament and contemplated throwing it away. He had become cold and indifferent about the gospel. At this point I will take Jesse's own words from Jesse and Wilma's book, *The Kidds of Brazil.*

426

A Chinese soldier rushed up to me and said: "Soldier, don't throw that away. You are going to need it!" Completely surprised I replied, "How do you happen to speak English and what do you know about this New Testament?" "I attended a high school in Chungking run by Baptist missionaries from your country. I know about that book; keep it." I put it in my pocket. He was right; I found out I did need it.

For several months our army units slowly moved through the jungle. Our final thrust to open the road cost many lives. A fellow soldier next to me was mortally wounded; my clothing was stained with his blood. After days of tense fighting we had a lull. I decided to slip away to a nearby stream. Maybe I could bathe and wash the blood out of my clothes. But I met an army chaplain standing squarely in my path. "Where are you going?" I told him my intentions and he told me to return to my platoon. I started past him, but he ordered me to follow him. He led me to a burial detail at work. I went to work helping to bury the bodies of fellow soldiers. We wrapped them in their G.I. blankets and buried them near the Burma Road. As we worked, enemy shells rained along the stream where I had hoped to bathe.

Once the road was opened, we were sent on to China. We were flown over the "hump" to the Chinese city of Kunming. We were there for only a few weeks. The 475th infantry was broken up into training detachments. China had decreed that foreign soldiers would not fight for them, but we could train them.

Our military unit was now in the heart of China. Japan was determined to have China's heart and made an all-out attack. We were too far from our main source of supplies. We had to evacuate! Our officers told us that the march would be long with no stops. If anyone dropped by the wayside, they would be left. If they fell into enemy hands, they would be tortured and executed without mercy.

About mid-afternoon I was sick with dysentery so severe that I could not go on. I crept into some thick bushes in an effort to hide and I must have passed out. Later someone awakened me. I realized it was a very old Chinese man. I couldn't understand him, but he motioned for me to get up and follow him. He had a severe curvature of the spine and walked with a long, wooden staff.

I couldn't manage alone, so he took me by the hand and pulled me up. He had me take hold of his staff with him and as he picked up my

427

heavy pack, slowly we started walking. Darkness had settled when we finally reached the old, ancestral temple where my companions were camped. I offered to pay my rescuer for his kindness, but he would not receive the money I held out to him. Remembering some hard chocolate bars that were part of my food ration, I opened my pack to give them to him. When I turned back to my rescuer, he was gone. I remember him now when I read Psalm 34:7. When we think of angels we envision blinding light, heavenly beings, and unearthly creatures. This time the angel of the Lord was an old, Chinese man with a curvature of the spine and who walked with a staff.

Joe was happy that he could help his missionary brother open up and share about his war experiences.

Trip to Salvador, Bahia

With the Minas Gerais Baptist group we traveled to the national Baptist convention in Salvador, Bahia. This was about an 18-hour trip. We stayed in the same hotel as the group did. Too often the Brazilians put Americans on a higher plane than themselves; they think we are too good to go with them and stay in the same hotels. Since Salvador is a tourist city, during vacation time vacancy in its hotels is more difficult to find. Somehow a mistake was made in the reservations; two daughters of our bus coordinator didn't have a place to stay. Our room had two twin beds plus the double bed. We asked that the two small beds be removed because the room was so crowded. When word reached the bus captain that we had two extra beds, he asked whether we would be willing to allow the two sisters to sleep in our room with us. We felt a little awkward but agreed; the two extra beds were brought back. The stay in this hotel was very different.

The only time in our 35 years in Brazil that as Americans we felt "mistreated" was in that hotel. The first day when we arrived, we had four towels—one each; the next day we had three towels; the next day two and finally only one towel for the four of us. Since each day we left early and didn't return until late, we never had the opportunity to talk with the cleaning people; the person at the desk didn't have a key to the supply room. The day we had only one towel was on Sunday; that day we didn't leave the hotel as early. As soon as we realized about the lack of towels, we told the manager. He said he couldn't do anything because he didn't have the key to the supply room. The girls got the word out; soon various members of our Baptist group brought towels to us. No one else in the Minas group had a problem of a towel shortage.

Each day in our two buses our group traveled to and from the convention center. Outside the convention center one could buy quick foods. A couple of times we bought hot dogs from a stand maintained by a father and his 10-year-old son. The hot dogs served as our evening meal. The boy's hands didn't look as though they had been washed all day. One afternoon I went to their stand; the father was gone, but the boy greeted me very cheerfully and wanted to serve me. I told him I wanted a hot dog; being careful not to touch the food he quickly proceeded to prepare one for me. Our colleagues on the bus were horrified that I had allowed the boy to prepare the hot dog, since he had such dirty hands. I assured them the boy had been careful not to touch the food. A Brazilian hot dog's only similarity to an American hot dog is that it contains a wiener. The homemade tomato relish, corn, and occasionally English peas with the wiener and bun make quite a good meal. I enjoyed my meal; God took care of me.

Chapter 21

Rooted and Grounded in Love

That He would grant you, according to the riches of His glory, to be strengthened with power through His Spirit in the inner man; so that Christ may dwell in your hearts through faith; and that you, being rooted and grounded in love, may be able to comprehend with all saints what is the breadth and length and height and depth, and to know the love of Christ which surpasses knowledge, that you may be filled up to all the fullness of God (Eph. 3:16-19).

1985-1989
The Serra Verde Preaching Point

While we were in the States, Geraldo had started attending our church in Planalto. When he was young, Geraldo had made a decision but had drifted from the Lord. He and his family were living in the Serra Verde neighborhood, a large housing complex for low- and medium-income families. About 8,000 people already lived in this government-built housing complex; the area had space to build more apartment buildings. With Geraldo and Deusa's consent, in their small living room we started a Sunday-afternoon Bible study. Deusa was a Roman Catholic, but she was cooperative with this idea. Leona taught the children in a bedroom while the adults' Bible study was in the living room. This was the beginning of what became a thriving church.

Starting Construction for First Baptist Church Planalto

Planalto mission had grown from one tiny garage to one small storeroom and then to a larger store room on the ground floor. We finally were able to rent the two apartments on the second floor and to use them for Sunday-school space. God had blessed us! The mission had been organized into a church. We bought two above-average lots and finally were able to start moving dirt for the construction of the building. We had many truckloads of dirt moved as the hillside was cut away to make the first floor level with the street in front. God was with us; we didn't have to pay much to have the dirt moved, because the city needed the dirt to fill in lower places somewhere. A thick, 14-foot-high retaining wall had to be built to keep the embankment from eroding before we started building. Guess what we built next? Exactly where the baptistery would be in the temporary building, we built the baptistery with a dressing room on each side. For several months we had baptisms in the open before we were able to build the temporary building. Having baptisms in the open created some curiosity for people passing in front of our property. Many people never had seen a water baptism. We put in place some of the major pilings to be used by the temporary building and later by the final building. A Baptist architect drew for us a free blueprint for a three-story building.

Patience Is Necessary to Be a Missions-Minded Church

If we had not shared our financial blessings with others that also had needs, we could have begun building Planalto Church earlier. We had bought a lot and built a small building for Nova Alianca Baptist Church and rented places for SESC, Jardim Guanabara, and Santa Cruz missions. Finally we were able to buy property with a small house for Santa Cruz, even though that was to be temporary.

The Santa Cruz property was on a steep hill, so from lots above, the rainwater descended with force. It passed through our lot and moved on down through a drain in the wall to the neighbors below. The wall was made of mud bricks and was plastered. This hole in the wall had to be kept clear, or the water would pile up. During a very hard rain the drain was too small and became stopped up with trash; this caused the wall to fall on the adobe two-room house next door. When the wall fell, the 96-year-old man and his son, who took care of him, had just moved from the front room to the kitchen. The fallen wall smashed in the front part of the little house. A few days later the old gentleman died of natural causes. God had blessed us in that the old man and son had moved into their kitchen, so they weren't injured. This little house was behind another son's house that was well-constructed. The family didn't like having a church next door to them. One of the sons said: "If my father had been killed by the wall, I would kill every member of the congregation, one by one." We rebuilt the wall to be much stronger, rebuilt the front room, and bought two beds, mattresses, and bedding to compensate for the neighbor's loss. In kindness and Christian love to some extent we gradually made friends with the neighbors. When houses are built on hills, those above are responsible for those below. We had bought that property not because the location was good, but because we needed to get more space than a rented building could offer.

The flooding in 1985 was much like that of 1979. Governador Valadares and other cities again were flooded, but the flooding was not quite as bad as it had been in 1979. Jordelina, one of our members in Planalto, lost her little shack. The city developed a new neighborhood more distant from our church and gave a small lot to those that had lost their homes. Planalto Church voted to help Jordelina build a little house on her lot in the new neighborhood.

We helped pay seminary expenses for two seminary students who worked with Planalto Baptist Church. At one time we had six seminary students that helped in the missions we were sponsoring. Five of these six seminary students finished seminary. Money received from Paul and Pat Renfro and Jackson Avenue Baptist Church of Lovington assisted with these expenses.

Writing Three Stewardship Books

I believed the Lord was leading me to write something different to promote stewardship. Brazilians enjoyed poetry; some of them could dramatically recite long biblical passages as well as long spiritual poetical dissertations. For the book I wrote some poems and drew some illustrations that would point out stewardship truths. I wrote these poems to make a break between explanations of biblical aspects about stewardship. These two books were entitled *The Enriched Christian Life* and *Knowing the Mind of Christ*. A third book was a teacher's guide. I wrote a musical course for Johnnie the Baptist, my ventriloquist doll, to teach people. The chorus was a success! The words translated into English take away the rhyme of Portuguese, but this is the message.

432

I am a steward for Jesus!
He merits all I can be!
My tithe, time, talents, and things—
My testimony to Him I bring.
Glory to Jesus my Savior and Lord—
Because in Him I am who I am!
I am a steward for Jesus!
And I'm happy in all His blessings!

Giving Up Loved Ones with a Sweet Spirit

As pastor of a church that had missions, I faced many burdensome responsibilities. Funerals are a part of life. Already I have told about some experiences I had with funerals, but I wanted to share a few others because of some unique situations I encountered. In 1984 a police officer named Carlito and his wife, Sueli, attended our church and accepted Christ. Their intense interest in their spiritual lives mostly was because his mother and an infant son died a few days apart from each other. Afterward Carlito and Sueli were extremely enthusiastic in their new life with our Lord Jesus Christ. In time God blessed them with another healthy and happy baby boy. For our Christmas program this child was used as our "baby Jesus" in the manger. In February 1985 this sweet little boy contracted meningitis and died a few days later. After the funeral message Carlito wanted to say something. He said that before the child was born, the father had dedicated this son to the Lord. Carlito had hoped that God would call the boy to preach the gospel. The father said he believed God had allowed his baby boy, as baby Jesus in the manger, to "preach", because several family members attended that program. This represented their first time ever to be in an Evangelical church. Carlito told how he had written a special song to the boy. Each evening when the dad arrived home from work, he sang the song to his infant son. The baby would smile and listen to his father. Then for everyone at the funeral Carlito and Sueli sang the song. This was impressive but very sad, yet this was a victorious service for the two young Christians. After that, one of Sueli's brothers and his wife made a decision for Christ; some of the other family members showed interest in their own spiritual lives.

Carnival in Brazil

Can a book about living in Brazil be a book without something about Carnival? After all, Mardi Gras in the U.S. doesn't make America be America, but Brazil is known best for two things: soccer and Carnival. From all over the world people travel to watch the Carnival parades in the major cities of Brazil, with Rio de Janeiro as the favorite. Nominal Roman Catholics and spiritists participate in the parades and clubs, in which everyone wears costumes. The "samba", a mixture of African and Brazilian Indian dances, sets the style for the parades. Professional designers, both for costumes and floats, work all year preparing for the parades. The largest samba schools put on dazzling shows in hopes of winning the first-place prize. The floats, which are fantastic to behold, have a theme. The floats in the Rose Bowl or Macy's parades are no more spectacular than are Brazilian Carnival floats.

Some of the samba schools that perform between the floats have thousands of participants. Each samba school has a uniform; during the four-and-half days of Carnival celebration students perform only one time. Each group has a singer who leads; the performers repeat the phrases. A variety of drums beat the rhythm for the dances. All of the songs are similar, but each has a little different message. Most of the women wear beautiful, long dresses, but as years have passed, half-nude women and women wearing only a string appear on some floats. The men usually have on glistening satin tight pants and shirts and sometimes a hat. Some spend most of a year's salary for the costumes. For a whole week the parades and club parties go on from about 8 p.m. until daylight. During Carnival commerce practically shuts down.

In Portuguese the word *carne* means meat or flesh. Carnival week truly is a week of licentious or sinful celebration. The idea is to let go and satisfy the flesh that has been confined within the moral system (that has little influence all year long anyway), but at this time of year satisfying the flesh is openly permitted and expected. Many Roman Catholic priests approve of this, but some don't. A king (called *Momo*) and his queen are chosen to reign over the celebration. The dancing is nothing more than twisting, turning, and prancing in frenetic movements. The idea is to forget all problems, worries, and difficulties in normal life. During those days Brazilians live in a fantasy world. Crime, rape, homicides, and automobile accidents rise sharply; this floods the hospitals with injured people. Evangelical Christians use this time to go on retreats at camps or to have special church activities. This festival always is in late January or early February; it ends on Ash Wednesday before the 40 days of Lent. On Ash Wednesday Roman Catholics go to their local churches and have ash put on their foreheads; this represents an act of repentance for their licentious living during Carnival week. The next 40 days is a period of fasting and repenting until Easter; this fasting amounts to giving up red meat and maybe something else. During those 40 days the price of fish increases. One of Brazil's greatest contemporary poets, Carlos Drummond de Andrade, said: "The people of Brazil get drunk with illusions through soccer and carnival. These are the two great sources of the people's dreams." Southern Baptists and other Evangelicals, however, have better dreams for Brazil, an immensely beautiful country.

A Dream Suddenly Happens!

One Sunday after we conducted Bible study at Geraldo's apartment, I asked him whether he had thought about ever having a church in that huge Serra Verde apartment complex, which at that time had 1,140 apartments and plans to build more. I asked this question without having any idea how that would be possible, because no lots had been set aside for Evangelical churches. A few days later he called and told me that two lots set aside for commercial buildings were for sale in the area. Only three or four stores had been built in this section of the apartment complex.

I immediately called Elon Braga, a deacon at First Baptist Church and a city councilmember. One of the lawyers for the city that worked in the area of apartment establishments in Belo Horizonte was a Presbyterian. God was working! This Presbyterian lawyer was able to get a clearance for those lots to be used for a church. For those lots Leona and I made the down-payment and the monthly payments. God does great things and often uses human servants to bring great victories for His name. This definitely was an act of God using His servants to open the door for us to buy those two lots. After all, the Roman Catholic Church already had been given six lots on the back side of that huge block, which originally had been zoned for commerce. A Brazilian custom was to give Roman Catholics property for their churches in every village, town, and neighborhood.

Back to State Responsibilities

In January 1985, after five years of developing the Baptist Men's work, I was able to find a very capable Brazilian man, Josue Marcus, to lead the Baptist Men's work. Josue Marcus had retired early from the transit department; I was very happy to turn the responsibility over to him. The men's congress in July was better than we had had before. I was sure that the Baptist Men's work in our state was on its way to great things. I returned to the state stewardship department.

Our revival at Planalto Church was the best ever. For an outdoor revival we were able to get permission to block off the street in front of the building in which we met and to put the pews in the street. A Jesus film was shown each night; this outdoor meeting attracted many curious people that normally walked by the church. Wade Akins, our state urban and mass evangelism director, led the revival. We had the highest attendance ever. Most of those making decisions were children.

Ten years had passed since we had visited Virginopolis Church that we started while we were in Valadares. In chapter 11 you read about opening Virginopolis for Christ. This was the city in which the Roman Catholic priest and the town council would not allow Evangelical Christians to buy land or building material to build a house. The church still was struggling, but our singing, preaching, and chalk talks made an impression on a few more people in the town. Later we received word that several of those that attended the revival now were attending regularly. We also learned that a Presbyterian medical doctor and his wife had moved to Virginopolis and were attending the Baptist church.

Carl and Kathy's Wedding

In July we returned to the States for Carl's wedding on August 7, 1985. Because Kathy's folks, Don and Pat Slone Doyle, were missionaries in Guatemala and we were in Brazil, the family decided the best place for the wedding would be near Pat's sister in Dickinson,

TX, so she could help get things together. Because of the distance, none of our family could attend, but we were looking forward to seeing Kathy's two grandmothers who lived nearby. We knew both of them personally. However, just days before the wedding, both Grandmothers Doyle and Slone became ill; soon after the wedding both died.

A Word of Thanks for Southern Baptist Support

After the fourth night of a Christian growth and stewardship revival at the Santa Cruz mission, a little boy said to our seminary pastor's wife: "Poor, Poor, Pastor Joe. He must get tired driving to the United States and back every night to tell us about Jesus." Some children have unique perceptions!

I am thankful we had a mission car and a house. We had money for gasoline; this usually averaged from $2 to $2.50 a gallon, while Americans back home were paying 75 cents. The Southern Baptist Convention paid most of our medical and dental needs. We always felt loved and respected. Because of the Southern Baptist Cooperative Program and the Lottie Moon Foreign Mission Offering every December, we didn't have to visit churches and beg for financial support. When we visited churches and did our deputation work, we thanked them for their financial support, but we didn't ask them for anything except prayer. We were very grateful and rejoiced that God led Southern Baptists to provide so well for His missionaries.

Moving into Our New Building

Near the end of 1985, Planalto Church moved into its own building. Nearly nine years had passed since this church had started as a mission. In the new building Leona made sure the children had a nice place in which they could learn about Jesus. The worship area was not much larger than in the church's previous location, but this property was ours. The auditorium seated 200 people. All of the building actually was temporary, but some of the structural work was for a building that eventually would have three floors. Now we could press on to building something for the Serra Verde mission.

Extra Blessing for Serra Verde

One day I received a telephone call and heard the excited voice of Geraldo Silva. He said, "Pastor! Pastor! Another lot is for sale next to ours at Serra Verde. Another church is looking at it. We must buy this property!" I immediately called the company that was responsible for selling the lot. This company knew me well, because every month I was making payments on the other two lots. I told the company that we wanted to buy the lot that was for sell. Since we had gone through all necessary paperwork to get approval to buy the first two lots, these people agreed to sell to us immediately. *Wow!* Now we probably had the largest piece of property of any church in the whole city. The church could have a large worship area as well as an educational area, a medical clinic, a kindergarten, and other things. Oh, how good God had been for us to acquire space in an apartment complex! This was rare!

We started a foundation for a two-story building. The priest saw the construction; to view what was going on he crawled through the fence that separated our properties. Hildo Ribeiro, a member of our Planalto Church, was the constructor. The priest asked him: "How did you get property in front of ours?" Hildo didn't know how to answer him. I told Hildo he should have said that we paid for ours and they didn't. The Roman Catholics really got busy building their church, which up to that point only was a shed. To God be all the glory for great things He had done for us at the Serra Verde apartment complex and at our church.

An Unbelievable Disappointment

To keep someone from squatting on the land we had put a barb-wire fence around the San Bernardo lot. For about a year nearly every week I went to the abstract office in downtown Belo Horizonte to get our deed. To get to that office I had to walk up a steep hill. More than 30 times I went to get the final document—unbelieveable! Every time the people there promised that by the next week, it would be ready. Finally our furlough time arrived; the document still was not ready. I left the responsibility for Laisete to pick up the deed. When we returned from furlough, Laisete gave me the deed, but I didn't check to see whether the "warranty deed" was included. One day as Laisete passed by the property, someone was putting building materials on the lot. When Laisete called me, I hastily went to the site; the man showed me his deed to the property. The owner had sold the lot twice; we didn't have the warranty deed, so we lost the lot. The lot was in a good location on level ground. Out of dozens that I had a part in buying for our missions and other churches, that was the only lot that we lost. Later another pastor led the mission to buy two lots in the heart of the San Bernardo neighborhood slum. When the San Bernardo mission was organized, we had a day of rejoicing. The name was changed from Planalto Second Baptist Church to New Alliance Baptist Church.

Fruit of Southern Baptist and Brazilian Baptist Labor

I remember that after the first national evangelism campaign in 1965, pastors in the Sweet River Valley begged God to call out young people to take the gospel to all of Brazil and to the whole world. By 1986 we had an unusual problem: how were the Baptists going to give financial help to so many young people that were surrendering to preach, teach, and take the gospel to the lost? The Brazilian Baptist Convention supported (with SBC help) three seminaries, two training schools for women, a Foreign Mission Board, and a Home Mission Board. Most states had seminaries and Bible schools. About 4,000 students in these schools were preparing for full-time ministry. The Brazilian Baptist Convention had about 4,000 churches and nearly that many missions. The Brazilian Foreign Mission Board had 116 missionaries in 16 countries and two territories. The Home Mission Board had 392 missionaries that worked in Brazil. All that the SBC had envisioned through its missionaries in Brazil was being fulfilled. However, only about a fourth of the counties in Brazil had been touched by the gospel.

Some Personal Activities

The rains had caused so much damage to the little house we were using for classrooms at the Santa Cruz mission that we had to tear it down except for one little room. We already had built a small worship hall; we needed to build five classrooms for groups that had been meeting in the house.

From the strategic properties fund we were blessed to receive $800 to help build some more at the Serra Verde mission.

Since I had been having very good responses teaching the first book I had written on stewardship, I asked the state board whether I could change the name of the stewardship department to Christian Growth and Stewardship. In the books I stressed loving God, the Father, and Jesus, the Savior and Lord, as a reason for freely giving time, talents, tithe, and things. The attendance in the stewardship rallies picked up a lot. The invitations for those studies were so many, I couldn't give as much time to the church and missions. We were working to get Planalto Church ready for supporting a pastor.

A Change in Christian Growth and Stewardship Revivals

At evening services the stewardship revivals (rallies) had consisted of using John the Steward, the doll, my trumpet, chalk talks, and about two hours of Bible study. But each time I returned home exhausted. Attendance at these events pleased me very much. For example, at Capitao Eneas in northern Minas Gerais we had an average attendance of 91; this was in a church of 110 members. The rally was Thursday through Sunday night. I was thrilled that most of the churches gave me Sunday school and the evening Training Union hour as well as the worship hours in which I could present. This made at least seven hours of teaching the Bible in five meetings. On Thursday through Saturday audiences had no problem if I used two or three hours. At Capitao Eneas church members in high school insisted on skipping school; all of them studied at night. I did not approve of this, but I was happy they were putting their spiritual needs above educational needs.

Two weeks later I had a revival at Barra Mansa in the State of Rio de Janeiro. I decided I would test the people as to whether my "show" was getting the attendance results or whether the Bible teaching would hold their interest. I did not take my trumpet or the chalk-talk equipment.

Barra Mansa is in the mountains; in March 1987 the fall season was beginning. A cold spell hit the area; the weather was so unusually severe that after we arrived at the hotel, Leona and I went to bed just so we could stay warm until the evening service started. No homes, churches, or hotels had heating systems. I wondered how many people would show up for the services that night. Amazingly, the house was packed! We had a wonderful revival—attendance in each service averaged 180. The people were highly attentive to the teaching messages; what was most impressive, the young people seemed to love studying the Bible. From that day on for the next 11 years, John the Baptist Steward and I represented the whole program—no trumpet or chalk talks anymore!

Central Baptist Church of Barra Mansa had only one lot. It had built a two-story building, with the top floor being the worship area, but under the leadership of Pastor Gerson Januario, whom I knew when he was a teen-ager in Governador Valadares, the church was overflowing. This church had six missions and a radio program. At the local college Gerson taught Portuguese. A month after we held the revival, Pastor Gerson wrote and said that in just one month the church's tithes and offerings had doubled. About three years later I returned and encouraged the people to pray about buying a vacant lot behind and beside them. They had tried to do that, but both owners were antagonistic toward Baptists. After I finished the second conference, their giving increased again. In 1998 I returned one more time; by this time the church had bought both lots. Oh, how God honors persistent prayer! By that time I had written seven other books; many members in that church had all of the books. I was blessed to work in that church.

Leona's Parents in Surprisingly Bad Health

For two days a week a cousin in Portales had been helping Leona's parents, Tony and Irma Isbell, but she never had written about how bad the Isbells' health had become. We received a letter from Evelyn, the wife of Leona's brother Wayne; she encouraged us not to delay our return, because she was afraid Tony might not know us. We changed our plans and decided to leave earlier. In November we left Brazil to spend an eight-month furlough on the farm with the Isbells.

We were surprised at how in the last two years their health had failed. They were living in fear! Irma thought little people were living in their attic. The medicine she took for Parkinson's disease was causing her to have hallucinations; because Tony had Alzheimer's disease, his memory was much worse. Most of the time at night he didn't know he was in his own house; he always wanted Irma to take him home. For Leona and me this was very sad. For me they had been the perfect mother- and father-in-law.

We had Christmas on the farm; all of Tony and Irma's children were present. When I finished the Christmas devotional, I asked Tony whether he had anything to say to us. God gave Tony the stability in mind and tongue to admonish his children to stay on the right path— the way, truth, and life that only Jesus could provide. Those were his last good, intelligible words. As long as possible, we kept him on the farm. As Alzheimer's patients do, at night he became very confused. Irma couldn't get him to do anything, but he responded better for me. At bedtime I would take him to the bedroom and help him get dressed and into bed. Sometimes he would say: "Someone has torn up my bed; I'm going to have to make it up." If I couldn't convince him that all was fine, he then would begin stripping the bedding.

Leona and I began looking at rest homes. We registered Tony in ones in Clovis and Portales. Then in January the Roosevelt Care Center in Portales called and said it had a vacancy; did we want it? This call was not expected so soon. After we talked with the siblings, we decided we best take it, because when Tony got worse, we might not be able to find a vacancy in Portales. That was a very difficult decision; Irma and Leona cried many tears, yet they both knew we had no choice. At least Tony was in a wing of the Roosevelt General Hospital in Portales. Daily Leona went there to feed him the noon meal. He was going down pretty fast; after he wandered into the hospital area one night, he had to be restrained. As he wandered and became lost, Tony happened to encounter his doctor and asked for help. Irma improved because she was able to sleep at night. But still the regulation of her medicine was difficult; she continued to have horrible hallucinations. When we could get away for a day or two, she would travel with us. But before we returned to Brazil, plans had to be made to move Tony.

A nephew, Ron Bowen, became the administrator for a new care center in Roswell; the center had an Alzheimer's unit. That was an answer to prayer and would be the logical place for Tony to go. Doris, Tony and Irma's oldest daughter, lived in Roswell. Doris found an apartment near her house for Irma; Ron had offered to live with her.

Our next project was attending Charlotte's graduation from University of New Mexico, from which she had obtained a degree in community health education. Soon after graduation Jonathan and Charlotte went with us to England to visit Carl and Kathy. We had a wonderful five weeks of sightseeing and visiting. Jonathan stayed three weeks and then returned to work. The experience of seeing the stone walls of the castles helped us visualize the biblical stories of the walled cities.

After we left England, we returned to the farm and in our spare time cleaned it up. I sold the old junk machinery; Leona and I had new windows put in the house, had a new roof put on the workshop-well house, and had it and the house re-stucco painted. The farm was spic and span to the point that I could run a lawnmower over the whole area and not hit a single bolt or nut. We got the place in excellent condition so it could be sold.

Thinking Tony would pass away soon, we asked for an extension of time for our return. After the two-week extension was up, we decided that to sit around waiting for someone to die wasn't the proper thing to do, so we decided to go back to Brazil. The last time we went in to see Tony, the emaciating power of the disease made him hardly recognizable. He knew only that we were family. In several weeks he had not talked but mainly uttered words that had no connection. I asked him whether he would like for me to pray and read the Scripture. Very clearly he said: "That would be a good idea." To hear him plainly speak that one sentence was God's gift to us. We had a difficult time saying goodbye, because we knew we would not see Tony again on this earth. Yet we felt a peace in knowing that God's timing is not ours and that God was in control. God gave us the strength to say goodbye. We were thankful for the months we had shared together.

Less than two months after we returned to Brazil, Tony died. Charlotte and Jonathan were able to attend the funeral. Jonathan had finished college and was working for Rockwell Corporation in Dallas. At the University of NM Charlotte was working on a masters degree in community health education. Carl and Kathy were in England and had given us our first grandchild, Michelle Nicole, a cute little blonde-haired baby.

The Blessed Discovery of a Long-Time Physical Ailment
All of my life I had felt something strange going on in my body. One time in particular while I participated in a fifth-grade class spelling bee, I had a strange, unexplainable feeling. I felt faint and had a strange sensation in my elbows. This occurred many times after that.

In my sophomore year of college I began to push myself to make excellent grades. Three hours a day I worked as a janitor at the university. I was active in the Baptist Student Union; each year I held an elected position. I had dropped band and orchestra because they took up too much time. Because I love music, I replaced those with university choir and men's glee club. Wednesday night was given to National Guard duty. I had difficulty concentrating on the academic materials, so I stayed up long hours. My trouble sleeping and headaches were symptoms of my problem. What did I do to perk myself up? I ate candy bars or cookies to give me more energy, because most of the time I also felt exhausted.

During my junior year my health problem became worse. Big knots grew under my armpits. My chest felt as though the muscles were pulling away from the bones. I prayed, "What is happening to me, God? I have surrendered my life to YOU. I am preparing to go to the mission field." I had a definite call to missions! I couldn't understand what was going on. I had no idea that I had hypoglycemia and that I was creating a stressful situation by eating sweets, since I loved sweets so much.

During the summer after my junior year I went to Jamaica as a BSU missionary. Because I wasn't under so much stress, I got better, but still I had no idea what was wrong.

After I resumed my studies, I soon had the same symptoms big-time! Yet I didn't diminish any activities. When I was a junior, a state BSU position was added to my activities; when I was a senior, another was added. Occasionally on weekends I went on Life Service Band trips with a group; occasionally I preached at a church that was without a pastor. My grades were good; I usually made the honor roll. No one knew what was going on inside me, because I covered up my condition. The excruciating pain almost was more than I could bear. On television I couldn't watch anything that was violent. I didn't think I was suicidal, but I knew that was a possibility. I went to a well-known Portales doctor; he said I was a good specimen of a perfect body. Yet he said I should give up my goal as a minister. This was impossible, because I knew God had called me. I also suspected that if I went to a psychiatrist, the FMB wouldn't appoint me. One night I fell on my knees and poured out my problem to God. He said to me, "Joe, you are your own problem. You are striving too diligently to achieve." This helped some, but why couldn't God have said, "Joe you have hypoglycemia"?

By the time I was 40, I knew sugar was my enemy, but diabetes never showed up on my blood tests. Grandmother Tarry had died from complications of diabetes. She lost her toes, then a foot, and finally one leg up to her knee, but at that time no one else in my family had diabetes. In about 1980, one morning after I ate pancakes I felt so bad that I went to the Evangelical Hospital and had a blood test. No diabetes, yet I knew sugar was a problem. But I just couldn't stop eating sweets, if that wasn't my problem. I was depressed.

In 1983 we were visiting my brother Bill and his wife, Muriel, in Silver City, NM. While they were at work, Leona picked up a medical book Muriel was reading. The book happened to open to the subject of hypoglycemia. (I believe her picking up this book was God's guiding.) Leona read a page and exclaimed: "Joe! This sounds like your problem!" I read the symptoms and could identify with nearly all of them. But hypoglycemia never had shown up on my medical exams. For our furlough physicals we went to the Cooper Clinic in Dallas. I was sure the doctors would discover I had hypoglycemia and that they would tell me what to do. As the doctor reviewed with me my health exams, he still didn't mention hypoglycemia. I asked him whether hypoglycemia showed up. He asked: "Do you think you have hypoglycemia?" I said, "I think I do." "You didn't ask for that exam, so it wasn't taken," he said. He gave me a brochure and told me to follow the diet. After I read the diet, I was disappointed, because if I had to follow that particular diet, life hardly would be worth living.

Earlier Leona's younger sister, Connie, was discovered to have hypoglycemia. Her older sister Doris found a book about the subject and asked Connie to read it. While I was on furlough, I read the book,

Exhaustion—Causes and Treatment, that Dr. Sam Roberts wrote in 1967. The book was about stress, but nearly half of the book was on hypoglycemia. In those days very few people knew about or believed in hypoglycemia. Even today I am amazed how many don't believe it exists. In earlier years this was called *chemical imbalance*. Dr. Roberts said that doctors don't check for hypoglycemia and that the sufferer has to ask for a "glucose-tolerance test". He also said that hypoglycemia is one of the major causes for suicide. If a person has a sudden change in attitude or actions or experiences loss of interest, that person should be checked for hypoglycemia, because these symptoms indicate low blood-sugar. The author of the book said that probably more people have hypoglycemia than diabetes. He even said that when a husband and wife have a problem in their relationship, or if one of them has experienced some type of sudden change, both of them should have the glucose-tolerance test, because one of them may have hypoglycemia.

This book had the evidence I sought. After we returned to Brazil, I went to the Evangelical Hospital and asked for the test. Sure enough, the personnel there confirmed that I had hypoglycemia. By cutting down on sugar I felt almost as though I was a new man. I tell this because I hope my story will help others. I have helped several people in Brazil. I am amazed that this test is not a requirement for physical exams just as diabetes is, because this disease really is confusing and devastating. When someone knows that a problem exists, but doctors say the person needs to go to a psychiatrist, this is incompetence on the part of the medical personnel.

Am I Going Blind?

For some time I had been having eye trouble. Across my vision I began to see spots and clouds floating back and forth. *What was going on?* Irma also was having trouble with her eyes, so we made an appointment with an Albuquerque doctor that diagnosed both of us with macular degeneration. He told us to take vision pills. He didn't explain to me the situation well enough for me to get a clear picture of what I was facing.

446

Back to Brazil

In early September 1988 our airplane nudged up close to the accordion-type walkway as it rolled to a complete stop. We had reached the international airport of Belo Horizonte, our Brazilian home. This was early spring in Brazil, so the sun was warm, the air crispy, and the sky at the airport blue, but 18 miles from the airport smog hovered over the city. On the way to the apartment, the near fender-benders and noise of the city shocked our ears that had become accustomed to the sweet, almost complete silence of the country life on the farm that for the last eight months we had experienced. Soon we were standing on the 10th-floor apartment veranda. We were surrounded by tall buildings and the noise of automobiles, sirens, and all that goes with a city of three-million people.

During the first days after we returned from the States, several things such as reactivating our bank account had to be done immediately. When no bank-account activity is shown for several months, the account is closed until another deposit is made. My impression was that I always chose the busiest bank in town in which to do our banking. After I waited for more than an hour to reactivate my account, I had to go to two other banks to pay bills that only could be paid in those banks, I impatiently waited at each one. My day was gone! After weaving and dodging people as I made my way to the bus stop, I caught an overcrowded bus for home. Buses and trucks belched out black smoke, horns honked, and when the light turned green, motors roared. By the time I arrived at our apartment, I was almost gasping for clean air. I decided that when we retired, if I didn't die of lung problems first, I wanted to live in a small, quiet town.

A Description of the Santa Cruz Mission

The next night, after we arrived on Thursday, we went to the Santa Cruz mission. It was unprofessionally built and had rafters open to the public eye. The gray, cheap, corrugated, asbestos-like roofing was not a pleasant thing to see. The clothes and shoes of the worshippers painted a picture of different financial conditions than those to which we had encountered while we were in the States. The untrained voices of those singing hymns, however, shattered the cool night air in melodious joy of sincere worship. The night breeze took the joy produced by those voices and carried it through the open windows, where it mingled with voices of children playing in the street, dogs barking, and the chants and drumbeats of a spiritist group from a back yard on the corner. The benches soon became noticeably hard as we listened to the people share their joys, sorrows, and concerns. Their needs were the same as those of people all over the world, but their needs often were more severe than those of their Christian brothers and sisters in the United States. I was ashamed that I even noticed the hard benches.

Leona had left Planalto Baptist Church in late 1986, several months before I did, to help the Santa Cruz mission. So I visited with Leona to see how things were going at Santa Cruz. As one entered the front gate, a spiritist family lived on a steep hill above us on our right. Sometimes these people threw trash down on our property. On Sunday mornings the family on our left did everything possible to disrupt our services. The adult children and grandchildren visited the parents. Yelling and screaming, they played in the back yard. Our windows were about four feet from their wall. We had to open the windows for fresh air, because for several years we didn't have ceiling fans. Their dogs barked and they all talked loud, so to enjoy the worship service we had to ignore the noise.

With every heavy rain, water rushed like a waterfall down from above. For years the building was flooded two or three times a year. I lamented that we had bought the property, but the price was what we could afford. We had built only a temporary structure, because in the near future we planned to move. I no longer was pastor at Planalto and hoped that soon the rest of my missionary career would be free to conduct Christian growth and stewardship revivals.

The next Saturday I took Leona to Serra Verde Baptist Mission with me. We planned that two people would be baptized as we dedicated the mission's baptistery. While Leona and I had been away, a seminary student had been responsible for the services, but I still was considered pastor. Two neighboring Baptist churches also were present, so inside and outside we had more than 200 attending.

My Eyesight Worsens
By the time we returned to Brazil, my sight was worse. I had dif-

ficulty reading my Bible, identifying street signs unless the letters were large, or recognizing people at the back of the church or at any longer distance. At night the car lights looked as though they were two big stars approaching me. About two miles up the mountain from our apartment Belo Horizonte had one of the best eye clinics in South America. I had an appointment with a doctor at the clinic; he gave me a prescription for special capsules made for me. One ingredient was selenium. I really was afraid I was going to lose my sight. I took those big green capsules of a special mixture; gradually the dozens of black dots and floating clouds began to diminish. Again God was gracious to me!

Later, when I was back at the eye clinic, an American couple was leaving the doctor's office. I saw that this husband and wife were in distress. I introduced myself and discovered they were Larry and Dana Stucky from São Luiz, Maranhao, a city far to the north of us. They were Baptist missionaries of another group but were friends of our SBC missionaries. In fact at that moment their children were with our SBC colleagues. I asked what their problem was. Early the day before Larry had awakened with a severe pain in one eye and loss of vision. An eye doctor in São Luiz told him to get to Belo Horizonte as fast as possible, so they caught the first plane to Belo. The doctor in Belo had told them that his problem was a severe separation of the retina and that something had to be done quickly. This threw them into a dilemma: they could fly to the States, where they were sure medical connections could be made, or they could stay in Belo Horizonte and have the surgery. God would have to work miracles, however, if they were to go to the States. I invited them to our house. They had left their city with hardly anything except their documents and some cash. If they stayed in Belo, Larry would have to stay a week or two in recovery. We assured them that if he had the surgery in Belo, they were welcome to stay with us.

Dana got on the phone (by now we had a satellite-dish phone system) to the States and worked things out to have the surgery in the U.S. if they could get out of Belo that night. We began praying that things would work out; they did. The Stuckys were able to get a flight out of Belo to Rio and on to the States the next day; a surgeon was waiting for him there. Later they wrote us a nice letter that also told us they were transferring to work in Albania. God certainly looks after His servants, although He allows trying circumstances!

As for my eyes, after two years the medicine had done all it could do for me. For the next 16 years the problem was stabilized, but eye strain still bothers me a lot.

Double Tragedy for the Pastor and Family

I drove out to check on New Alliance Baptist Church in the San Bernardo slums under the leadership of its first full-time pastor. This had been the first mission of Planalto Church. I saw the new small, temporary building. One of the pastor's sons had been hit by a bus. As the bus skidded to a stop, the front wheel pushed the boy along the pavement. The miracle was that the boy wasn't run over, but he had several broken bones and bad pavement burns. On Friday a week later a younger son pulled a pot of hot beans off the stove and burned himself severely. The pastor lived in a small, crowded house on the far south side of the city. The next day I visited the pastor and his sons in the hospital; my heart was warmed with compassion for the pastor's Christian faith. I also felt very good because he was wearing the shoes and suit that I had given him before we went on furlough.

We didn't have to pinch ourselves to know for sure we were back in Brazil. The wonderful part, however, was the joy that so many dear brothers and sisters in Christ showed in phone calls, visits, and hugs; they showed how much they missed us. Sunday night at church Leona put her keyboard on her lap so the little children could sit near her on the bench on which she normally put the keyboard. Despite leaving Tony near death as he lay in a care center, leaving Leona's mother, who needed us, and saying goodbye to our children, we both agreed that Brazil was the place in which God wanted us most

Did Paul Approve the Tongues Spoken in Corinth?

Because of the great confusion that charismatics had caused in Brazil and especially in our state, I felt compelled to write about this issue. In 1987, writing in Portuguese, I completed the book *Did Paul Approve the Tongues Spoken in Corinth?*; I finished it in time for our state convention. Pastors and laypeople received it well.

A Refreshing Burst of Spiritual Growth

Since 1982 I had been concerned about my spiritual life. I didn't doubt my salvation and that God was blessing me, yet I knew I was missing out on much that God had for me. In all of the spiritual-growth revivals I had held, I felt close to God. Yet as I returned home from these times with God, I had a "letdown" and knew some changes needed to be made. For instance when I was not in a revival, my thoughts weren't under the control of the Holy Spirit. I read the Bible some, but I didn't really study it. My prayer life was minimal. Although I prayed some while I drove long distances, at home my prayers usually were hurried. For six years I had been asking God to help me get out of the rut.

On a Friday in November 1988 Leona went to a WMU camp. On Saturday morning I went to my knees in prayer. After I prayed a while, I said, "O God, I am tired of living like I am. I want more of You; I must have more of You. Help me!" A wonderful, precious wave of the presence of God the Father, Savior, and Holy Spirit swept through me from head to toe. This was what I needed and desired. I was overwhelmed by the presence of the living God in an undeniable "takeover" of my whole being. At this time the Lord also gave me the general themes for nine more books to write. That was amazing and beyond my comprehension.

After I got up from my knees, I contemplated this experience and remembered what He had said to me when he spoke to me about a year before we left Governador Valadares in 1975. When that occurred, I had just turned onto the Rio-Bahia Highway on a journey north of Governador Valadares. Out of the blue, God spoke to me and said: "Joe, if your ministry ever goes beyond the present stage, this will happen through writing and in the latter days of your ministry." When I wrote the books on stewardship or tongues, I hadn't remembered this. But now, this revelation was overwhelming.

The results of that wonderful encounter with the Lord changed my prayer life, preaching, and Bible study. For several years I had been taking prescription sleeping pills. I often dreamed amazing things about God and about Him saying things to me. These dreams were so vivid and profound that I thought I could remember them forever, so I didn't get up and write anything down. The next morning I

451

could remember the blessed experience but nothing that was said. Precious things were lost.

After that Saturday-morning experience, when I awoke at 2, 3, or 4 a.m., I went to our living room and prayed. I didn't take another sleeping pill. As I progressed in writing the books, during those prayer sessions with God a lot of the material was given to me. All day long I had Bible passages I pondered in preparation for the next pages of the books, so day and night my mind was on spiritual things. The fact that the first things on my mind at night when I awoke were spiritual things and continued this way during the day became my joy! The moment I finished with something that was secular, my mind returned to spiritual matters. I started beginning my day with God along the outline, "Daily Preparation for Walking with God", that appears at the end of this book.

I had hundreds of sermons in written in Portuguese. I hadn't been able to preach without following a sermon guide. From this point on I was able to preach from the text without first writing my sermons out. My preaching became expository sermons that followed the text word for word. I had freedom to preach biblical texts without having to follow a three-point sermon.

After that wonderful experience, Bible study was the most delightful thing for me. The Holy Spirit oriented me to begin writing from the Book of Genesis; in this way I carefully studied the whole Bible word for word.

When I told Leona about the books that I believed God wanted me to write, she was not a happy person. Leona couldn't face nine more books of refining manuscripts on a typewriter. She wanted to be a part of my life, but the old-fashioned way took too long and was too tedious. The timing for this event was perfect. I think the Lord used Ken Richardson and Jimmy Joseph, two newer missionary colleagues, to help us. In chapter 20 under "Job as Joe's Secretary" Leona gives her account of this.

I asked our State Board to appoint a committee to read the manuscript of the first book in the series. After the committee of two pastors and one layperson had read the first book, they selected the title: *Revival: The Eternal Purpose of God*. The general theme of all the books is "the difficulty God has in maintaining a spiritual people".

452

The first book is about the difficulty God had in maintaining a spiritual people in the Old Testament period. The second book was the same theme but covered the New Testament period. The third has the same theme from the second century through the Reformation: its title would be *The Gates of Hell Shall Not Prevail*. The fourth book has the same theme for the 18th and 19th centuries: *Destruction of Faith in the Bible*. The fifth book covers the 20th century and is entitled *The Deceit of the Ecumenical and Charismatic Movement*. The sixth book, *The Stupidity of Struggling With God*, is on brokenness. The seventh book is about the same subject and has the subtitle: *Take My Yoke upon You*. The eighth book covers the area of stewardship and has the subtitle *Your Treasure and Your Heart*; the ninth book is about the true individual revival and is called *In the World but Not of the World*.

Santa Cruz and Jardim Guanabara Missions

After 11 years as a preaching point and mission, Santa Cruz Baptist Mission in December 1988 organized into a church with only 27 members. The Santa Cruz mission had been the most difficult work of all the missions. This mission was right in the heart of a traditional Catholic area dotted with spiritist home centers.

Tupi Baptist Church bought a lot in a good location in Jardim Guanabara neighborhood, so our mission joined this one as I had told the people we would. We furnished them with building supplies left over from constructing the Planalto building, some benches, and a pulpit. When Planalto Church organized the Santa Cruz mission, we were left with only Serra Verde Baptist Mission. Serra Verde had the most ideal situation of all the churches we had started, since it was in the center of a large apartment complex that had both lower- and lower-middle-income-class apartments. About 8,000 people surrounded the Serra Verde mission. Only a few already were Baptists. The pastor and members had as their neighbors a "gold mine of souls".

The Tract Ministry

Handing out tracts is something anyone can do. Missionary Kent Faris, who worked in the State of Espirito Santo, is the most dynamic man I have ever known in how he uses tracts. His vibrancy about the value of tracts rubbed off on us. I also wrote three or four tracts of my own and stamped our address on them. In thinking about tracts, one day I remembered a little rhyme that I learned when I was a kid: "Barber, barber, shave a pig. How many hairs will make a wig? Four and twenty, that's enough. Give that barber a pinch of snuff!" I thought to myself, "How many tracts is enough? To win a soul is very tough." The point is, only a few tracts handed out immediately produces saved souls, but gospel seeds are planted in many hearts, regardless of known results. The fact is, we never know, but I was delightfully surprised after our trip to Fortaleza on the north coast of Brazil. In January 1989 Leona and I attended the Brazilian Baptist Convention in Fortaleza. A man had torn off the back part of the tract we had given him and sent it to us. On it was written this sentence: "I want to be with Jesus eternally." That made my day! Another example was from a youth to whom I had given a tract when I was in downtown Belo Horizonte. He called and wanted a Bible, so I met him at our apartment. I gave him the Bible and found out he already was attending a Baptist church in the city. I had the opportunity to encourage him in his walk with Christ.

We gave out tracts everywhere and still do. On our exercise walks on the streets around our neighborhood Leona often took one side of the street and I the other as we handed out tracts. Seldom in this populated area with high-rise apartments all around us did we meet the same people. We also put tracts in the mailboxes in the fence walls of the few houses that were left in the area. Only one time did a man get mad at me. In front of his friends who were drinking beer at a sidewalk table in front of a bar, he cursed me out. He was furious. After that, every time he saw me, he made a scene in front of the bar. I prayed for him. One day after I had not seen him for awhile, I asked about him; he had died. Another man had entered hell!

100 Years of Baptist Work in Minas Gerais

Minas Gerais still is the second most-populated state in Brazil. The first Baptist work begun in Minas Gerais was by missionary Charles Daniel in 1889, in Juiz de Fora, the second-largest city in Minas situated near the state of Rio de Janeiro. Big plans were made for the centennial celebration in Juiz de Fora, even though that first church Daniel started had died. Actually the oldest continuous church is in the city of Ipanema in the Sweet River Valley, so on numerous occasions I visited that church. Ipanema Baptist Church is a good church and had made a big impact on our state. In fact our first Brazilian state executive secretary, Jose Alves da Silva Bittencourt, was from that church. During our time of service in Minas Gerais, the SBC missionaries that served in Juiz de Fora were Billy and Lee Ann Gilmore and Frank and Doris Hickman.

In 1989 another change had taken place in our state work. Pastor Bittencourt retired as our state secretary; Pastor Aloizio Penido Bertho took his place. Pastor Bittencourt and I had led 88 percent of the churches in the state to giving regularly to the Cooperative Program. This by far was the best in the Brazilian Baptist Convention. We had more than 450 churches but still had more than 400 counties out of 723 without Baptist work. So after 100 years the task of planting churches all over our state still was very large. Baptists of Minas Gerais made big plans for the decade of the '90s. Evangelism and stewardship were big parts of the Plan for the Nineties.

Summary of Lowrie and Jenkins Partnership Teams

I have spoken about the partnership teams from Tarrant County, TX, that worked in our state for the centennial celebration of Baptist work in Brazil. In 1987 the FMB asked Leona and me to work with a team that wanted to go to Teofoli Otoni, Minas Gerais. Leona and I met the team at Teofoli Otoni, a very familiar "gemstone" city north of us on the Rio-Bahia Highway. This was a good experience. In 1988 this team wanted to go to Governador Valadares after I had suggested that it would be a good place for a larger group to work. Their two coordinators were Wayne Jenkins from Louisiana and Dwight Lowrie from Texarkana, TX. In 1988 they brought 70 people to work in 17 churches in evangelism, dentistry, doctors and nurses for medical clinics, and a street-evangelism team. The work covered a full week; hundreds of people were led to take steps toward God.

They fell in love with the city so much that for the next four years they returned to Governador Valadares. Then they went to Juiz de Fora for four years, back to Governador Valadares again for six years, and were there when we retired in 1999. After 2003 they went to São Paulo two or three years and for the last three or four years have been going to Belo Horizonte. The number of participants grew until one year they had 201 participants. Thousands of people have heard the gospel; thousands have had Americans visit them in their homes. The majority of these people only made steps toward God, but planting seed is important for a spiritual harvesting. We are sure the Holy Spirit continues to work; the work of partnership missions is important. The Lowrie-Jenkins crusades always were worked into our schedule in July between the annual missionary meeting and the Minas State Convention. July was crammed full of activities for us. For 14 years we worked with these two great men and their teams.

Baptist Work in Mariana and Ouro Preto

Mariana
Mariana is the first town established in Minas Gerais. Mariana is situated about five miles from Ouro Preto. Settlers found gold in the area; this brought a gold rush to those steep hills and mountains. In these two extremely Roman Catholic cities, closed to Evangelical churches, Brazilian Baptists had goals to plant a church.

When we lived in Governador Valadares, our family visited Mariana for historical purposes. This was Minas Gerais history not only for Leona and me but also for our kids studying in a Brazilian school. Behind the cathedral in Mariana is a museum loaded with Roman Catholic paraphernalia that is related to the history of the cathedral. The guide asked us whether we would like to go under the museum to see the tombs in which the bishops and archbishops were buried. Sure, why not?

We descended the stairs into a dungeon-like room in which the walls were almost full of square, marble-cut stones that closed the tombs in which the bishops and archbishops' bodies were laid. On the marble lids the occupants' names were engraved. An indention in the wall to the left of the entrance door had a small, raised area with many candles blazing. I was curious about the reason for the candles glowing in a place in which bishops and archbishops had been dead for a long time. He told me that the candles were lit to help the souls of those entombed to enter eternal bliss. Frequently priests went there to pray for the departed souls of the bishops and archbishops. This was the opportunity for us to give our experience of certainty in salvation before we died.

I asked, "Are you telling me that these bishops and archbishops didn't know if they would ever be with God in eternity?" The guide said, "*Sim, senhor*" (yes)! Then we told the guide about the certainty we had about where we were going when we died. We mentioned verses such as John 3:16; 3:36; 5:24, and others. After the museum we visited an old gold mine at the edge of Mariana. We rode in an old gold-mine cart, now energized by electricity, down into the gold mine.

About 30 years would pass before Baptists were able to organize a church on the outskirts of Mariana. I was present for that event and twice returned to lead the people in stewardship and Christian-growth studies.

Ouro Preto
Ouro Preto is much larger and is a better-known city than is Mariana, for it was the first capital of Minas Gerais. About 1993 a Baptist pastor bought a house and a vacant lot on the main cobble-stone street that entered the city. In his house he began a preaching point. His property, like most in Our Preto, was on a very steep hill-side. He built a sturdy foundation and two rooms at the bottom. Later he dug into the hillside and built four rooms—two small rooms on new ground and the other two on top of two rooms underneath. For the third story he dug out more of the hillside for larger space and built over the rooms underneath. The fourth story was street-level. On this floor he built a room large enough to seat about 100-120 people. The city officials realized what he was doing and therefore wouldn't give him a permit to occupy the building. Until the permit was granted, the church group had to meet in the rooms below. The front of the building had to look like other old buildings of the 1700s. He received threats that he would lose his property. For two or three years court processes were against him, but he remained faithful. He and his family were persecuted. Three times during this long struggle to establish a legitimate Baptist church in Ouro Preto I spent four days with him and his family. My part was to encourage them through Bible studies,

but I believe they inspired me more than I inspired them. Through people there, the Holy Spirit was doing a great work in Ouro Preto. In 2002 this pastor wrote a book of his challenges, persecutions, and suffering.

Wrapping Up 1989

In September and October I had six revivals; when possible I had a special meeting with the pastors in the area in which I was preaching. We discussed the plans the state board had for the 1990s—the beginning of a crucial decade. Before the end of the year I made other trips to meet with the rest of the pastors of the 13 associations that we had at the time.

Leona went on several of these trips and promoted Sunday schools for preschool-age children . Most of the churches still had the "babysitting" mentality about these children. Leona had developed a great heart for the children while they were innocent. Much of the time they would cooperate better than older children, youth, and even adults would.

We went to the States for Christmas to see Leona's mother and our children. Carl and Kathy had moved from England to Travis Air Force Base in California but brought our first grandchild, Michelle, to New Mexico to see us—or for us to see her!

Chapter 22

Striving to Be a Blessing in Brazil

Therefore, be sure that it is those who are of faith who are sons of Abraham. And the Scripture, foreseeing that God would justify the Gentiles by faith, preached the gospel before to Abraham, saying, "ALL THE NATIONS SHALL BE BLESSED BY YOU" (Gal. 3:7-8).

Gentiles represent the grafted shoot into the children of Israel that has become responsible for taking the Good News to all nations!

1990-1994
Introduction

In 1990 we arrived in Belo Horizonte in time to get into the hustle for the Brazilian Baptist Convention to be held the last week of January in our beautiful city. We both had been on committees in preparation for this great event. I had worked on the Spiritual Preparation Committee; Leona had worked on the preparations for the WMU's meeting the day before the convention. I also had the blessing to be the guest speaker for the Baptist Men's congress that met a day before the convention. I think I was the first pastor to have that honor. for the laymen had plenty of qualified men speakers. I had organized the Baptist Men of Minas Gerais and had worked with them for five years. The national men's congress, the pastor's conference, and WMU all met the same day before the convention.

The greatest thing happening in April was the statewide spiritual awakening conference lead by Sammy Tippit. Sammy was a good friend of Wade Akins, our state evangelism director. While Sammy was pastor of an international Baptist church in Germany during the days of the communist regime, he crossed the border and worked with

Romanian Baptists. This was before the Iron Curtain fell. He had several scrapes with the communist regime. Later he organized his own evangelistic association.

My goal for 1990 was to attend all of the 18 associational annual meetings. By July I had time to hold only two revivals and two stewardship clinics, although I had 35 invitations from individual churches. The evangelism department and the state executive secretary took the larger spiritual-growth conferences and promoted the emphasis of the 1990-2000 decade.

The seminary student that Planalto Church had invited for the Serra Verde mission didn't work out, so I reassumed the work there. When I couldn't be present, I used someone from Planalto Church or the mission to fill in to preach.

The Adoption of a Boy by Consent

I held a revival in First Baptist Church of Mantena on the eastern edge of Minas Gerais. Later I received a letter from 10-year-old Fernando Lucas Benfica, who lived across the street from First Baptist Church in Mantena. His father had died and his mother was a schoolteacher. He had heard about the hundreds of kids that were under the Christian Children's Fund in Governador Valadares. The children had adoptive parents in the United States that sent them money monthly and gifts on special occasions. He wanted an American father too, but he didn't qualify under the Christian Children's Fund. He wanted to know whether I could arrange an American father for him. I couldn't think of anyone; three or four months passed. Leona and I were in that area again, so we visited him and his mother. His mother was having health problems; her job paid very little. She explained why he wanted an American father. I didn't promise anything, but in my prayers I remembered him and wrote to him occasionally.

I sent him a little money for Christmas and his birthday. I sent him a copy of the two stewardship books that I had written, even though I knew that a 10-year-old boy probably wouldn't be able to understand much except the illustrations. He wrote me occasionally; each time he thanked me for something I had sent. I was impressed. I didn't know whether his mother was helping him write the letters.

As the years went by, every year I sent him a new book as they arrived from the publisher. He began asking me about certain things he had seen in the books. I knew from his questions that he not only was reading them, but he also was studying them. He was very active in his church. This first contact with him was made about 1993. By the time he was in his last year in high school, he was the evangelism leader for his church of about 800 members. After he graduated from high school (the Brazilian school system is only 11 years), he was the evangelism leader in the association. He now is in seminary and has been overloaded with requests for his help in churches and the association.

He has been a blessing to us; we are proud he adopted us. He does need prayer. The trauma of the unexpected death of his mother in 2005 may be the cause of his bipolar situation, discovered in 2007. He does well as long as he takes his medicine.

Prefabricated Chapel Program
Missionary Marshall Flournoy designed a plan for a wooden A-frame chapel that cost about $6,000. To design the chapels he used the experience he had with his father's construction company. The wooden chapels were nice and seemed practical, so the Brazilian Baptist Sunday School Board accepted the chapels as a project and in the State of Rio de Janeiro built a shop for their construction. However, with so much rain over most of Brazil, the problem was decay of the outside wood of the building if it was not kept painted.

After the pieces were cut and painted with the base coat, they were delivered by truck to the construction site. Missionary Leo Weatherman and his wife, Dorothy, left Minas Gerais to work with the building and mounting of these chapels. Churches in the U.S. paid for most of these prefabricated chapels and also sent crews to help put them together on the site. Dozens of the wooden chapels were constructed and mounted in various states in Brazil. Leona and I helped by being "gofers" and translators for three construction teams. After I watched the mounting of two of these buildings, I believed we could build a chapel of concrete blocks just as inexpensively. I believed they would last many more years without as much yearly upkeep. I based my theory on my previous church-building projects.

Concrete-Block Chapels

Unexpectedly a church in Missouri contacted missionary Wade Akins about arranging a place in which to build a chapel. The Missouri men had been building chapels in Manaus on the Amazon, but Manaus didn't have a request in 1990; that left the Missouri team without a place in which to work in Brazil. Wade contacted me; I suggested New Alliance Baptist Church (formerly Second Planalto Baptist Church) in the São Bernardo neighborhood. We didn't have much time to get ready. I ask the bricklayer Hildo Ribeiro from Planalto Baptist Church to get the foundation and concrete floor ready. I had the foundation made sufficient for a two-story building, because I knew these people wouldn't be able to buy more land to accommodate future growth. The dirt street entering the São Bernardo slum area was so narrow that a truck with building materials had difficulty passing without scraping a house or the high concrete wall of the old airport. Cars even had trouble going down that street when people were sitting in front of their houses. Sometimes I was afraid I would run over their feet or hit a child that might dart out of a house in front of the car. During the rainy season the neighborhood was a sloppy mess. But these people needed the gospel; I was glad that the location of the church was in the heart of the neighborhood.

A team of seven men and three women arrived from Missouri; we went to the work site. The foundation and floor were ready, but some problems appeared. I had bought large, concrete building blocks shaped like the pumice blocks in the States. The Americans had laid small mud brick in Manaus. I had hired a few Brazilian men to mix the mud for the bricklayers and to help pour concrete into the columns. I had ordered tall, curved-top, church-style window frames made of steel. This crew had made its chapels in Manaus with square, wooden window frames. How to lay brick over these curved windows at the top puzzled them, but with the Brazilian men we resolved the problem. Another problem was the extra hard wood I bought. I had asked the lumberyard men for a special grade of wood for trusses, but they sent us a heavier and harder wood than I had requested. This slowed the crew down, because the wood was so hard that extra work was required to drill holes for the screws. Some bits broke; finding extras was difficult. The rainy, cold weather dampened their spirits.

Leo and Dorothy Weatherman had some extra time between building wooden chapels, so we invited them to Belo to help us.

The three American women had brought materials for a Vacation Bible School for morning and afternoon, with Dorothy and Leona as their interpreters and helpers. The children were difficult to control. VBS was held in the open air in the street with just the pews from the church in front of the church building. The leaders had more children than they could control for good teaching, but the goal for attendance was more than reached.

By the end of the third day the walls were finished, but we didn't have time to pour the concrete columns to stabilize the walls. These columns were spaced in the walls between the windows and at the corners. The columns along with the concrete band on top of the walls would strengthen the building.

That night we had a storm, so I didn't sleep much for fear the walls might fall. The next day we rejoiced when we saw that the walls still were standing. That day the first job was to pour the concrete for the columns. Once that was done, I could relax.

One of the Brazilian men I hired lived nearby and arrived the first cool winter day for work without shoes and wearing a thin shirt. One of the American men gave him clothes and a pair of shoes. We assumed that the men had eaten breakfast before they arrived, even though most of them ate only a piece of crusty French bread and drank a cup of coffee. With the help of some Brazilian women Leona and Dorothy were in charge of preparing the noon meals.

When the men had finished making the trusses for the roof, the trusses were much heavier than we had expected. We had a wooden, 10-foot-high scaffold made on which the men could stand and balance the trusses as each truss was anchored in place. About six men were on the scaffold to put the trusses in place and to hold them until they were secured. The Brazilian mentioned above, without shoes and thin shirt, positioned himself on the scaffold to help put the truss in place. The American nearest him saw that he was fainting! The American was in a dilemma: grab the Brazilian to keep him from falling off the scaffold or hold the truss. He grabbed the man and kept him from falling onto the concrete floor; the others managed to stabilize the truss. *Wow! What a scary moment!* I took the man to a doctor; the doctor said his problem was lack of nourishment. The men took up an offering to make sure the man and his family had something to eat. Seeing the needs helped the Americans compassionately bond with the Brazilians. The American team members felt the hand of God on them; this changed their attitudes from that of gloom to joy. The teams, American and Brazilian, working together got the roof on and the windows installed. By the end of the week the men didn't get the stucco done as they had hoped.

Wade Akins had arranged to use the community soccer field to show the Jesus film and to preach on Saturday night. Wade often preached and showed the Jesus films on the streets, so he had his pick-up truck fixed for mounting a screen and powerful loudspeakers on top of his truck. We were in our car following Wade. When the kids of the community saw the truck arriving, they started running after him and tried to climb onto the moving truck. The kids were too numerous to count. We were afraid someone would fall and be run over. Likewise, because of the kids, we barely could follow Wade. As soon as we stopped, the kids were all over the car; a few climbed all over the truck.

Wade was accustomed to street ministry; every few yards he used adults to hold a cord to keep the crowd away from the movie projector. Wade and his helpers were the only ones inside the roped-off area. The crowd was difficult to organize and almost too noisy to hear the film. However, the objective was achieved; through the film and Wade's message many heard the gospel. To those that made decisions Wade gave a New Testament.

On Sunday everyone gathered for the new building dedication. The churchy-looking building would be a good witness for that neighborhood.

At this same time Wade was working on a plan for building chapels throughout Minas Gerais and even spreading over all Brazil. Earlier on a furlough Wade met businessman Gary Taylor and explained this plan. Gary was interested in helping and arrived in Belo Horizonte on Friday in time to see firsthand the last of the work on the chapel in São Bernardo.

Wade asked me to meet Gary at Wade's home on Monday and to show him the expenses of the chapel that we had just built in São

Bernardo. I still had money with the $5,000 the Missouri church had given to stucco the outside and plaster the inside. But we wouldn't have money to build any pews or pulpit, because we had made a foundation for a two-story building and put in nice, tall metal windows. Gary Taylor designed a chapel and estimated a cost of about $6,000 for chapels that included building pews and pulpit. His plans included every nail, screw, and bolt. He planned to buy materials all at the same time for several chapels; doing this would reduce the price of the buildings. The building would be built, painted inside and out, with pews and pulpit installed—all completed in six days. This became the standard for chapels. For a few months Gary, his wife, Liza, and their two little children moved to Brazil to help get things going well. In 10 years (from 1990-2000), under the leadership of Wade Akins' coordination, crews (American and some Brazilians hired to mix the mud and help stucco or plaster the buildings) constructed more than 100 of these chapels in Brazil; most of them were in Minas Gerais. Wade always ended the week of construction with a dedication of the chapel building and Saturday and Sunday evangelistic services. The Brazilians always were amazed that the chapel could be built so quickly. The foundation had to be ready when the crews arrived, but the rest of the work was done in a week.

Another Accident at Santa Cruz Church

Earlier we told about the wall falling on the neighbor's little house at Santa Cruz Baptist Church. Sometime later Ronnie and Rose Mackey moved to Belo for three or four years for him to be foreman of the chapel construction for Wade Akins. In a lull in chapel building Ronnie Mackey offered to put a new roof on Santa Cruz Church. Missionary kids were on summer vacation, so Ronnie invited four MK (missionary kid) teen-agers from Rio to help him put on the roof. Ronnie climbed a ladder up to the edge of the roof to analyze the situation. Ronnie was extremely careful at building sites, but he didn't calculate how brittle the old roofing was and put too much weight on the edge of the roof. The roofing broke; this caused one of Ronnie's arms to fall. It caught a big nail on the end of a truss. The nail tore a deep gash in his upper arm. Ronnie didn't fall, but he began bleeding profusely. I took him to the nearest hospital emergency room. To my surprise in the lobby we met our elderly (94-years-old) emeritus missionary Arnol Harrington; he was checking into the hospital. Ronnie received immediate attention because of the bleeding. The doctor stopped the bleeding and sewed up the gash in Ronnie's arm. I thought this would be the end of the roofing project at our church, but Ronnie insisted on returning to the worksite. I know he must have been in a lot of pain, but he worked almost as though nothing had happened. Again, praise God for His tough volunteer servants.

Joseph Arnol Harrington
Missionary Joseph Arnol Harrington had been director of the Baptist school; for many years both Edna and Arnol worked in the school. After he retired from the school, Arnol was instrumental in buying the property for the state camp in 1966 and planned the buildings. After retirement they decided to stay in Brazil because they didn't have family in the States. Arnol had only one living nephew. Edna was an orphan and had no known living relatives. Before she died in 1980 Edna was sick for a while. By recording her favorite hymns Edna blessed Brazilian Evangelicals with her beautiful voice. We have an album of her recordings; they include her favorite number "Meu Brasil" (My Brazil).

During the last few years of his life I became Bro. Harrington's barber. After Mrs. Harrington's death he was able to continue living in his home with a Brazilian adopted daughter who was a widow.

A few days after I saw him in the hospital lobby, Brother Harrington passed away. Leona and I had gone to the Minas Baptist State Convention in a city about two hours out of Belo. We received a call informing us that Brother Harrington had died. I was the executor of his will, so we left immediately for Belo. One of his dearest friends, Professor Armindo, director of the Baptist school, went with us to identify him and sign the release from the hospital. That night we selected the casket and made arrangements for the funeral. At least in Belo, offices for acquiring death certificates and places to buy caskets stay open all the time. At about 2 a.m. we finished these activities. The next day Arnol was laid to rest in Belo Horizonte's best cemetery in the same lot with his beloved Edna.

A Bloody Mess

We always prayed before we traveled on a short or long trip. Perhaps the worst of the highways were the Rio-Bahia and Belo-Valadares highways. The Rio-Bahia was heavily traveled with buses and trucks. In the early years both highways were narrow, but the Belo-Valadares highway had more mountains and dangerous curves with drop-offs. Usually as we both went and returned, we saw three to five accidents on the Belo-Valadares highway. Leona claimed that she sent her guardian angel with me when I traveled by myself. The interesting thing about these accidents was trying to figure out how they happened.

The most curious accident I ever saw, however, occurred one time when I was alone. I arrived at a curve that allowed me to see four cars stuck into the mountainside above the highway in the distance. As I completed curve after curve, for short distances I would lose sight of the amazing situation; then the scene was visible again—four cars stuck into the side of the embankment. *Was I having an illusion? How could this be?* As I approached closer and closer, without a doubt I was not seeing an illusion. As I arrived on the scene, I saw the transport truck lying on its side on a curve; it was precariously near the edge of a deep abyss to the bottom of the canyon below. The truck had been carrying four cars on the top level of the transport trailer. When the driver couldn't make the curve, the four cars were thrown with such force that the chains holding the cars broke. This threw the vehicles into the side of the mountain. The tops were crushed into the soggy embankment about eight feet above the ground; the cars were stuck into the mountain. Those four small cars, varied in colors, left a mental picture that I haven't forgotten.

The amazing thing about so many accidents is that we were needed to assist the police in only two situations. Both times occurred when we lived in Governador Valadares in the early years of our ministry. The worst was when we were traveling from Governador Valadares to the beach near Vitoria, Espirito Santo. The high, rugged mountain range that runs north and south through Espirito Santo and Rio de Janeiro State is beautiful. The mountain descends rapidly to the coast. Many from Minas go to Espirito Santo to its beaches. Soon after we had begun our descent, we met a car that had been traveling

467

up the mountain but suddenly had made a 90-degree turn. Headon it slammed into the rock embankment. The driver must have been trying to miss something.

Three adults and three children were in the car. The steering wheel was bent by the driver's chest as he was thrown forward. He was in great pain and asked God to take his life right then. Two women also were in the front seat. The driver's wife had a kneecap that was visibly torn loose; her face was bloody. The back seat was a bloody mess. I guess the two women had hit each other violently in the accident. One boy about 12 had a dislocated jaw; one had a broken arm, and all were bleeding. The two doors were jammed. The driver was screaming, "I want to die, I want to die". I quickly began telling him the plan of salvation; he listened. The reason he wanted to die was that two of those kids were nephews; he was responsible for them. Soon other cars stopped to help.

The police finally arrived in a little Volkswagen and an ambulance. The officers were able to get the car doors open. The driver and his wife were put in the ambulance because they were in a more serious condition. We had the big Veraneio Chevrolet, so the police asked whether we would take the three badly injured kids to the hospital. Our kids were small, so all five of us managed to sit in the front seat and put the three injured kids on the back seat. The police car took the other adult; we were to follow the officer. He headed down the mountain so fast that I couldn't keep up with him. The kids in our car were crying and groaning. They were a bloody mess. When we arrived at the police checkpoint at the entrance of Vitoria, the police officer guide stopped us. He had decided to have another police car take the children because we wouldn't be able to follow him in the traffic to the hospital; we didn't know the way. The officers transferred the three kids to another Volkswagen.

Another time we were about 50 miles from Governador Valadares when we arrived at a place in which a headon collision had happened. An elderly man and his wife from Governador Valadares had been killed. The police requested that we inform a son and family in Valadares about the death of his father and mother. We didn't know the family, but we agreed to take the message. As soon as we arrived in Valadares, we went to their house to inform the son and family about the deaths.

Blessed to Be Alive

During the more than three decades we were in Brazil, many times I reflected on narrow escapes that I had in my past. The many narrow escapes in Brazil reminded me that several times before I ever reached Brazil, I had been spared. I don't use the word *lucky* to be alive, because *luck* implies that God wasn't looking over me. Young people do stupid things; several times I risked my life. Usually I was with friends.

1. When I was a small child, I had a severe case of pneumonia. The doctor didn't expect me to live.

2. When I was 16, I was thrown out of the back of a pickup truck and landed on my head.

3. When I was 19, I was run over by a Chevrolet Suburban while I worked on an oil-exploration crew. I was fortunate that the vehicle ran over my legs and not the upper part of my body.

4. As I worked for the same Amarada Petroleum Company, a rattlesnake almost bit me while I was on the survey crew. Later I descended the truck to pick up some geophone instruments (*jugs* in seismograph language); a rattlesnake was among the jugs. He could have bitten me on my arm or the face if I had not seen him the split second before he struck at me.

5. Playing a game of ditch-um at night, a friend and I, riding in his pickup, were trying to lose another car of boys. The game was to outrun or outsmart the driver in the other car. This time we went around the south end of Lovington on a dirt road, took the Hobbs highway on which we could pick up speed, and turned left about one mile out of town onto a dirt road. My friend turned off the pickup lights and left the road, to not kick up dust. He was driving about 50 yards parallel to the dirt road and was driving across the pasture about 20 miles an hour. I had read an article about a new garbage dump out that way; suddenly I decided that it must be at the end of that road. I screamed for the friend to stop. When we did, we almost were at the edge of the gravel pit.

6. When I was a freshman in college, some of us in the dorm became close friends. For a while I tried to win their friendship so I

could invite them to the Baptist Student Union and church services. I played some poker and canasta with them. One night seven of us went out driving; on that drive we also stole a few watermelons. On the way home we had to cross the train track that ran almost through the middle of Portales. Four boys were in the back seat and three in the front in a 1951 Ford car. The driver was Emil Wagner, a classmate from Lovington. I heard a rumbling noise, but noise from the radio and our talking was so loud that no one paid attention. When the front of the car was on the track, someone on the right side screamed, "Train!" Emil pushed the accelerator to the floor; the car jumped and jerked, but because it was in third gear, it didn't move much. My instant thought was that the car motor might die and we would be left on the track. When someone again yelled, "Train", I looked to my right and could see the nose of the engine and part of the two white lines crossing to make an X. The nose of the train as though it was almost against the window. I thought that was the end for me! The train barely missed us. I vividly can remember seeing one of the guys, an atheist, turn as white as a sheet. For several minutes after we were off the track, he just stared straight ahead without moving or saying anything.

The Joy of Working with Brazilians

Brazilians in general have appreciated American missionaries. A few pastors believed that Americans had been in Brazil long enough, but by far the majority showed a depth of respect for us, even as we struggled to speak the language. The generations before us, our generation, and the one right after us took great interest in the national and state conventions. Most of the last missionaries that arrived just before we retired seemed not to have an interest in the state and national conventions. Brazilians began asking: *Why?* At their meetings they asked: *Where are the new American missionaries?* Before, state and national convention committees and boards had missionaries helping, but the new missionaries didn't seem interested. The truth is that the FMB, now called the International Mission Board (IMB), did not want missionaries to get involved with the national and state leadership. Music missionaries, seminary professors, and religious-education missionaries all were to become church planters. About

1995 everything began changing.

The truth is that Brazilian Baptists, especially in the States of Rio de Janeiro, São Paulo, and Espirito Santo, had advanced spiritually. All the coastline states received the gospel first. Brazil, being the size of the continental U.S., has many remote areas and still is a vast mission field. Minas Gerais, the size of Texas and close to equal in population, probably does not have more than 100,000 Brazilian Baptist Convention church members. The Brazilian Baptist Convention is the largest Baptist group and was started by Southern Baptist missionaries. All Brazil has close to one million members. Yet half of the cities, towns, and villages in Minas Gerais do not have a Brazilian Baptist witness. However, at the time this book is being written, the IMB is pulling out its church planters except for "people groups" such as the Roma people, known as Gypsies, Japanese people, and others "unreached".

From the early 1880's until mid 1990's missionaries working with Brazilians on the state and national level were presented as being spiritual leaders that were partners with them throughout that great land. God has been preparing outstanding Brazilian leaders that are equal or more than equal to missionaries. However, the field is still ripe for harvesting bountifully; therefore, U.S. missionaries are still needed.

Leona and I have been wonderfully blessed by Brazilians who were both uneducated and educated. Some of those that made the greatest impression on our lives practically had nothing in material goods or even a high-school education. My mind turns to Deacon Tertuliano of Fifth Baptist Church in Governador Valadares. He was as black as any man on earth and had had little formal education, but he and his wife were examples of happy Christians. He was beyond middle age and had graying hair and a lot of kids. He had his heart in the Lord's work. He was a good witness in the Santa Rita neighborhood and always had someone he wanted me to visit with him. He had a sweet spirit, did not ask for more than the minimum things in life, and was extremely grateful to have a shelter over his head and something to eat on the table. His life was reflected by most of his children that took their Christianity seriously.

I also think of a Fifth Baptist Church member whom I loved very much. Antonio was tall, a loving husband of a dedicated wife, and

471

father of five or six children. I can say that his spirit combined with mine for the Lord's work; I loved him as a brother. One day while he was working in what would be the basement of a 12-story building for the Bank of Brazil, an older man was told to go down and work in a shaft for an elevator. Antonio insisted on taking the place of the older gentleman. The area caved in; Antonio was killed. We have no way to understand these things. I lost a brother. We are thankful God called us to go to Brazil and for Southern Baptists supporting us for more than 36 years. These are just two out of hundreds in and beyond the boundary of Minas Gerais with whom I served in some way.

Brazil has great men among the academically trained; mainly this has occurred because of American seminary professors. American missionary professors still are requested to help train Brazilian students.

Most missionaries that worked for state or national entities in Brazil also were church planters. For instance during the last 25 years of our time in Brazil, Joe Tarry was not categorized as a *church planter*. I was categorized as *state stewardship director* or *state Baptist men's leader* because I did what Brazilian Baptists requested and needed. However, from reading this book you can see that "church planting" was our passion. Dr. Bill Richardson was the religious-education director for Minas Gerais. but he started several churches while in Brazil. All of the missionaries had "missions" on their hearts!

1991

Our pace of work did not slow down, but the great difference for me at this point was that I was not doing anything on my own. The Holy Spirit was in control. I began each day with God; He put things in place. Disappointments still happened, however! I believed the Lord was leading to challenge the state to produce 300 spiritual warriors. This idea was derived from Gideon and God's 300 warriors. These "warriors" daily were to pray for a spiritual awakening in Minas. I didn't get 300 warriors, but I corresponded regularly with those that embraced the idea; they sent me stories that were refreshing their lives. Those that participated were blessed.

Starting Prudente de Morais Mission

I first mentioned Laisete Ribeiro da Silva as I wrote about Governador Valadares. He later started the Santa Cruz mission in Belo, was pastor of Planalto Baptist Church while we were in the States in 1979, and later was pastor of Second Baptist Planalto. To me Laisete was like a "son-in-the-faith" as Timothy was to Paul. He was very talented in cutting precious stones and in cutting all types of animals out of stone. The mayor of the town of Prudente de Morais invited Laisete and Genilda to his town because he wanted the young people to learn a vocation. He wanted Laisete to set up the lapidary shop and teach the kids those skills. After the mayor had moved them and put them in a nice house, the plan crumbled. I guess the city council had second thoughts or just would not cooperate with the mayor. Laisete had no place to go, so he bought a two-room, low-income house. He bought it in bad condition and at a cheap price. I thought, *Maybe God wants a preaching point in Prudente de Morais.*

Laisete located another low-income house with four small rooms for sale. It was four blocks from his and had a wall around the lot. He called me; those selling the property wanted the equivalent of $2,500 dollars for it. The city of Prudente de Morais didn't want to sell the property to a church, but God worked in our favor. I bought the property and put it in the name of First Baptist Church of Santa Cruz Neighborhood, in which Leona and I were members. I began paying Laisete a salary from the $100 a month that the Renfros were sending us. Prudente de Moraes turned out to be a difficult field also.

I again was pastor at Santa Cruz Baptist Church. I had been grooming Luis Paulo Terrinho from Planalto Baptist Church for the pastorate of Santa Cruz Baptist Church. I had hoped he would do this on graduation from seminary, but he accepted a larger church at the edge of Belo Horizonte. I could not blame him, but I was disappointed because I didn't want to be a pastor for the rest of my missionary career.

Araci Maria de Jesus

When she was about 30-years old, Araci was converted in the Santa Cruz mission. She quickly grew spiritually and was very devoted. She lived with her mother and cared for a niece, Ivanete. Ivanete's mother was Araci's sister; when she married, the niece remained with Araci. About four years after she became a Christian, Araci had a very serious circulation problem in her legs. For months she walked with great difficulty and had a lot of pain in her legs. The doctors didn't know the solution, but the church people prayed. Prayer and patience prevailed; God healed her to the point in which she could walk. She wanted to go to seminary, so Planalto Baptist Church helped pay her way through seminary. She worked for a company that made telephones. One Monday morning she arrived at work and on the door found a note stating that the business was closed. All the workers had left work Friday as usual and did not know that they had just spent their last day working for the company. The workers never received their month's salary or the amount usually given when employees are released. The telephone company claimed bankruptcy, but the truth was that the five owners had a dispute and couldn't reach an agreement. Before a suit could be brought against the men, they passed on to other relatives all their assets.

Araci's mother lived on a small pension, but that wasn't enough to support the family of three. One day the Holy Spirit gave me an idea. Since Leona needed help in the house, I decided to pay Araci a monthly amount to work at the house once a week and also at Santa Cruz Baptist Church. She could give the rest of her time serving the Lord in the manner in which the Lord laid on her heart. The family remained in the Santa Cruz neighborhood until the mother of Ivanete provided a small, three-room house for them on their property in a neighborhood some distance from Santa Cruz. Until we retired, Araci helped us at home.

Araci was the only Christian in her family, but she took Ivanete to church and had an influence on her becoming a Christian. One of the several outstanding things about Araci was punctuality. Although she had to ride a bus a long distance and buses didn't run as regularly on Sundays, she always was at church before 9 a.m.

In every way Araci was a great blessing. She served as church treasurer, church visitor, counselor, and in other ministries. She seemed to have a gift for solving many types of problems. After many years of Araci's witnessing to her, Araci's mother finally accepted God as her only savior and gave up her traditional religion.

Praise to the Lord of the Harvesters

From what I am writing, you may think that missionaries do all the work, but not so! As I write about what has happened in our lives, we know that we did very little. We were just in a leadership position, but people that God added to His circle of saints through us were involved in the results of our ministry. I cannot begin to tell you about all the hundreds of people that affected our lives by being joyful followers of the Lord Jesus Christ. They blessed our ministry while we at the same time blessed their ministries. By or through the Holy Spirit in all of us we were united by the bonds of love for Christ and were able to break down barriers that Satan put in the way. No missionary couple does all of the work. The bond of love and service together with our Brazilian brothers and sisters never can be adequately described on paper. Thank you again, Southern Baptists, for supporting us financially and in prayer so we could experience such a profound Marvel of it All.

1992

Leona had made some progress in creating an interest in the churches to provide, by introducing the concept of interest centers, teaching for the little children. This was the weakest part of the church-training area, so she was happy to see some signs of change. She had had her hands full, since she was treasurer for the Central Association WMU (l06 churches) and also for our state mission station. She was available to help Maria Bittencourt at the state WMU office when Leona was needed. Leona now had been on the state Baptist children's home board for at least 12 years; this demanded her time for one monthly meeting and occasional visits to the home. But most of her time was spent serving the Lord at the church in the Santa Cruz neighborhood.

The most exciting point for me was the 24 stewardship and Christian-growth revivals I held in the previous three years. All but one church had increased its giving from one-fourth, one-half, or doubled contributions from what it had been giving the month before the revival. Some people were saved in these revivals also.

Furlough and Wedding 1992

We were staying in our house we had bought in 1984 in Roswell. Leona's mother lived with us and was a joy to us. Most of the time Irma traveled with us. Considering she had Parkinson's disease, she was healthy. We had been in Brazil long enough for a seven-month furlough.

Charlotte moved to Fort Worth and since 1990 had been at Southwestern Seminary. She met Jim Whitley in seminary library. So one of the major events of this furlough was their wedding on August 8, 1992. Retired Brazilian missionary aunts in the Fort Worth area gave Charlotte a wedding shower, so Irma, Kathy, Andrew, and Leona drove to Fort Worth for the shower and to shop for a wedding gown. During this time Irma stayed with son Alton in Cleburne. He had a nice garden with some vegetables ready for picking. He told Irma to wait until he ran an errand and then they would go together to the garden. She thought Alton was taking too long, so decided she could at least start picking blackeyed peas. The ground was muddy, so she put on Alton's boots and crawled through the barbed-wire fence to the garden. She slid down in the mud, lost one boot, and couldn't get back up. All she could do was wait for Alton. The blazing sun in July plus fire ants caught her off-guard. No one knew how long she waited but long enough to get a very bad sunburn. Alton washed her with ice water and put aloe vera oil on her face, arms, and legs. When Leona arrived that afternoon to get her, her mother was red as a beet. Leona bathed her and helped her change clothes. The next day Leona, Kathy, Andrew, and Irma drove back to New Mexico. They had a bowl of ice water to wet Irma's skin – they were afraid of a sun stroke. God blessed and they made it fine. When Doris met them at the car in Roswell, Doris said: "Mother, what in the world happened to you?" Irma, in a joking manner replied: "Don't get close; it might be contagious."

The wedding was in Rosen Heights Baptist Church in Fort Worth. Since I walked Charlotte down the aisle, Jesse Kidd helped with the service. Wilma Kidd participated with the music. The wedding was lovely. Most all our families were able to attend.

1993
Impressive Differences Between Brazil and U.S.

As always our return to Brazil caused some comparisons to what we had seen in the States. After we were in some churches in the States that held 200, 500, and up to 1,500 people, I stepped off the distance from the entrance of our worship area to the pulpit in our Santa Cruz Baptist Church building; the distance was only eight yards. The worship area was only six-yards wide and had only one window on each side. The noise from our neighbors next door on the lower side still was distracting. The worst part was the house on the lower side. The residents were in the middle of cooking their Sunday noon meal by 10 o'clock just as we began our worship service. Church members who had only coffee and a piece of bread for breakfast surely could feel hunger pains after smelling the aroma of meat cooking on coals. The hard benches were a reminder that we were back in Brazil. However, we were excited to be home among people that overwhelmed us with hugs and hugs and hugs.

Gold Teeth and Gold Fillings

Always a phenomenon was going on among Pentecostal and charismatic groups; this time when we returned from furlough, the mystery miracle was gold teeth and gold fillings that God was supposedly bestowing on certain spiritually privileged people. At the same time some Roman Catholic priests had begun their healing programs. Along with these, amazing men with strange powers were busy among the spiritists. The atmosphere among these groups was as if everyone was competing with each other to see in which group God would do something different first. The Pentecostals and charismatics were making the headlines. Despite all those who claimed to be healed, the long lines of people that got up at 2 or 3 a.m. to stand in lines for hours seeking health treatment provided by the government had not diminished.

When we returned to Brazil, some charismatics were claiming they had received a special blessing from God; they were miraculously blessed with a gold filling or teeth. When the charismatics began getting gold teeth, Father of Saints Firmino Salles de Lima Albuquerque explained the phenomenon to a newspaper in Goiania,

477

capital of the State of Goias. I have translated and summarized his article to give you an idea of what some spiritists believe. The highest mediums among spiritists are called "Fathers of Saints" and "Mothers of Saints". He said the same phenomenon appeared first to Mother of Saints Guilhermina de Moraes Rocha in Salvador, State of Bahia, in January 1985. At that time she told a reporter of the *Afternoon Journal* about the incident and said the great god of spiritism, Oxala, had performed the miracle. Three days later in Feira de Santana, a nearby city, Father of Saints Ze Gomida received two complete gold teeth.

Soon after the public recognition above was claimed, a Brazilian spiritist author from Bahia wrote a book, *The Phenomenon of the Spiritual World*. He said the spiritual guides say that the news about these gold caps, fillings, or gold teeth were appearing among spiritists and that the news should not be spread around. The good spirits affirm that the strong man Oxala, the Great Maitreya of the New Age, will give an important notice near the year 2000; soon afterward we will be in the Aquarius Era. Until then the faithful ones of various religions will be graced with the phenomenon in a mysterious way—those who are anxious to merit the divine gifts of miracles. We are talking about the preparation for the kingdom of the Great Being that will dominate the worlds with one religion. This phenomenon is the fulfillment of Jesus' words: *"For false Christs and false prophets will arise and will show great signs and wonders . . .."* (They omitted the rest of the verse: *"so as to mislead, if possible, even the elect"* and added *"and marvels in the Last days"* (Mt. 24:24). They said that the "the Last days" refers to the "Era of Aquarius". This is a mixture of spiritist and New Age, but the Umbanda spiritists said these signs meant that the order of Oxala (African spiritist king) was to spread.

When spiritists or New Age people claimed they received the gold teeth first, then for the Christians, the gold-tooth hysteria should mean that the phenomenon actually was from Satan. Yet, the charismatics, Pentecostals, or Roman Catholics were not turned off by the claims that spiritists received the gold teeth first. They stuck to their claim that by the "gold-tooth" phenomenon, God was working in them! Our family dentist told me that for a while, dentists were using a material that looked as though it was gold. Even if spiritists were receiving gold teeth at all is a sign that Satan is at work. This was the pattern among the groups of Evangelicals that were (as also were most Roman Catholics) always seeking signs to prove that God was doing great things through them. For years now the pattern has been for signs to change regularly from one new thing to another. The apostle Paul said: *For indeed Jews ask for signs, and Greeks search for wisdom; but we preach Christ crucified, to Jews a stumbling block, and to Gentiles foolishness, but to those who are the called, both Jews and Greeks, Christ the power of God and the wisdom of God. Because the foolishness of God is wiser than men, and the weakness of God is stronger than men* (1 Cor. 1:22-25).

A Horror Story of Becoming a Mother of Saints

I had the opportunity to talk with some converted mediums. I will tell how they get the title "Mother" or "Father of Saints", for this is a curious part of demon worship. I already have told about Sofia, a president of a spiritist group. While we were at Planalto Baptist Church, another Christian woman that had been a medium moved to live with her daughter. For a while she worshiped with us. Dalila Figuerido Ciciliano gave a graphic explanation of the rituals necessary for becoming a Mother of Saints. I taped the conversation and have translated it here.

Dalila Figuerido Cicliano considered herself a Catholic spiritist who became more interested in spiritism because of her daughter that didn't have good health. She described her preparation for this high rank of medium. She attended both the Umbanda Center and Roman Catholic Church, as many other Catholics did. Neither the Roman Catholic Church nor Umbanda spiritism was helping her daughter, so she believed she needed a stronger force. She understood that Candomble (another branch of African spiritism) offered what she needed. The Candomble medium suggested she should become a Mother of Saints. She was given a tea made from grape leaves and a necklace with special power from Angola and was told to return in seven days. Her daughter had been scheduled for surgery, but her health improved. She didn't have the surgery; her whole life seemed to be better.

That same month a big party was held at the Candomble medi-

479

um's house. At that party a famous medium from the State of Bahia insisted that Dalila needed to be more involved. He was very smart and in the sessions spoke in African languages. Dalila enjoyed the party and session and thus fell for the Candomble branch of spiritism. She decided to become a Mother of Saints.

For seven days she was put in a room in which she was to rest and meditate. She was given a rock that represented a deity to worship. This was the first step and, since she had a job as a nurse and also had a small daughter, she could go no further than an *Abia* (helper) at this point. This was her initial step of separating herself to become one of the "Order of Satan". For most of the next five years she was sick. From that point of preparing, 14 years passed; she became so sick that she asked for three months off from work.

During this time her "Father of Saints" said time had arrived for her to become a Mother of Saints. She actually reached the goal of "Mother of Saints". For sanctification she was put in a room called a *rancor*; she was there along with other candidates. The ritual carried out was from the country of Angola. Blood from goats was used for the women becoming a Daughter of Saints, the second step to becoming a Mother of Saints. Her head was shaved; a mixture of goat, pigeon, and chicken blood, wine, and a liquid brewed from special types of leaves was poured over her head. She also had to drink some of this. She then was covered with chicken feathers that the blood caused to stick to her body. She remained in this situation for 24 hours before a Mother of Saints gave her a bath. She remained in seclusion for seven days.

After three months she was given a necklace according to the color of diet she was to receive. The necklace was called an *orixa*. During this time of seclusion she was given a daily bath at 4 a.m. and 6 p.m.; the bath consisted of a liquid brewed from various types of leaves and herbs. She couldn't see her family or go outside because those in charge of her ritual believed sunlight or the cool night air was harmful. Dalila explained that the ritual was like a prison! After three months of this type of prison, away from family and a normal life, a sanctification party was given. She had to drink blood again. During the 14 years of the process to become a "Mother of Saints", her life was saturated with sadness; her temper and incontrollable tongue were getting worse. Her husband had agreed to her being a Mother of Saints; during her purification period friends took care of her daughter.

The spirit that she was given to make contact as a medium was an Angolan cow herdsman. She never talked to other spirits. When he entered into her during a session, the aftereffects made her worse. She fussed with her husband and with others. She and her husband had bought a small farm in which they dedicated to her work. Soon many people sought her help. They brought all types of problems to her; these problems included whether or not a man should kill his wife and were problems of marriage, love, finances, and every other type of issue. To some extent witchcraft was used. In Candomble, according to Dalila, one of the favorite types of sorcery is the collection of 21 African seashells of different sizes (none large). The shells are thrown on the ground, floor, or table. According to how they fell, a medium or sorcerer made the predictions. When Dalila was a child, a medium gave Dalila her first set of these shells. The first time she used the shells, she didn't have instructions on how to read them, but she knew they existed. She was afraid she might not have anything to say, but she said the devil gives a person something to say and the seeker believes, no matter what the outcome. This is called the game of *busios,* or the game of conch seashells.

I asked Dalila how she felt when she sought the "spirit" of the old African cow herdsman. She said that a verbal description was inadequate for her to use to express all she felt, but at first heavy palpitations of the heart occurred. She felt very strong and definite heart movements, as though the heart was being hit by something. Then her body felt cold even on very hot days; her legs were weak. While she was in the trance, possessed by the demon cow herdsman, she lost consciousness of what was taking place. The demon actually spoke through her; she didn't know what he told the person seeking help from the spirit world. When a session was to be held, people brought a lot of beer, bread, and other things to eat, because the "cow herdsman" liked to eat. She ate for him but did not know or realize she was eating. The evil spirit using her liked hot beer; she, in her normal self, liked cold beer. A Mother of Saints has a "Daughter of Saints" as her helper. The Daughter of Saints that helped Dalila heated the beer until

481

it was very hot. Dalila drank this without burning her lips, mouth, or throat. She didn't know how she hadn't suffered from the hot beer, except that an evil phenomenon causes people to do strange things without having a physical effect. Such a mystery helps people believe in evil. They see things happen—even many beneficial things—that to them are proof. She always detested cigars; the smell to her was horrible. Yet in these sessions she smoked cigars or a pipe as all other mediums did. Also mediums have helpers who are sworn to protect the mediums if someone should seek to harm them after not accepting counsel.

The old black cow herdsman finally was the ruin of what Dalila had in the way of happiness. She quarreled even more with her husband. Her Daughter of Saints told her things she didn't know were happening. In her trances the spirit speaking through her quarreled and had terrible arguments with her husband. These arguments along with the times of special separation required for a Mother of Saints, when she couldn't sleep with her husband, caused her husband to find other women to satisfy him. When she found out about this, she was crushed, for she loved her husband. Her husband left her and never sought to find out about her.

Life became so frustrating, agitated, and disruptive that one day she went to her yard and broke into tears. For some reason she looked up to the sky and said, "Where are You, Lord"? Some Assembly of God people lived next door. For 11 years she had heard them making a lot of noise, but she didn't know they were praying for her. She had a Presbyterian sister that lived nearby, so she went to see this sister one more time before Dalila committed suicide. However, the sister persuaded her to go to a worship service; Dalila enjoyed it. Then she became ill. Spiritist people kept seeking her help, but she was the one that needed help. She planned one last party for her clients; during this party they would go into the nearby forest, kill animals, dance to the music of African drums and other instruments, and for hours on hours drink cases of beer; then she planned either to kill herself or to change. However, she was too ill to go to the party.

A short time later she invited the Presbyterian pastor, her sister, and her Assembly of God neighbors to carry all of the idols, fetishes, and every sign of Candomble into the yard and destroy them. She made her decision for Christ and found peace at last. Her daughter, with whom she was living, told me that her mother truly had made a 100-percent change in her life. I was hoping to win her daughter also, but soon after our conversation, I left Planalto Church and Dalila moved somewhere else.

Chapter 23

God Proven Always to Be Faithful
1994-1996

For I am convinced that neither death, nor life, nor angels, nor principalities, nor things present, nor things to come, nor powers, nor height, nor depth, nor any other created thing, shall be able to separate us from the love of God, which is in Christ Jesus our Lord (Rom. 8:38-39).

Introduction

The last years in Brazil turned out the most enjoyable of all. I enjoyed going to the churches and visiting with the pastors and their families. Many times I stayed in their homes—sometimes in pretty humble situations. Sometimes for lack of space for guests I slept in the same room with their children. But they put up with me; I cherish those wonderful times in their homes. Other times I stayed in a hotel or boarding house. I didn't turn on the television. Those were the times in which I dedicated myself to go deeper into God's Word and work on the newest book that I had started.

1994

Brazil was changing. When we arrived in Brazil, country and village life was much like that of the United States during the 1920s and 1930s. People in the country didn't lock their doors. But in the large cities, the people had bars on their windows and doors and covered the top of their eight-foot walls surrounding their property with broken glass to keep thieves out, but this did not happen in the country. Battery radios were available so people could get a vague idea of the troubled world in distant places. For years without any worry of harm to me I gave rides to people who walked on the roads. But by 1994 I was very cautious. By this time my most frequent passengers were police officers. Often, when I stopped at a service station/restaurant, a police officer was seeking a ride into Belo Horizonte. Usually he was to appear at a trial for a person that he had apprehended; thus the case was incomplete unless the officer who arrested the defendant testified in court. I had the opportunity to witness to the officer; sometimes the officer was an Evangelical Christian. As we traveled, these men talked; this helped me stay awake. I often gave a ride to a member of the church in which I had held a conference; this usually was someone that needed to go to Belo for medical reason. But by 1994 I no longer gave rides to strangers who along the road thumbed rides.

The last years were so busy, we weren't as faithful to write the quarterly newsletters or correspond as regularly with our families. We could claim that old age was creeping up on us.

1995

Santa Cruz Baptist Church called a young seminary student as pastor, so I was able to give up the interim pastorate there. Our hopes were high for the young pastor.

We had been able to stay on schedule publishing one book a year. I had been selling the books mostly at our national and state conventions and to the churches in which I held revivals. By 1995 I needed to print the second edition of the books on stewardship and tongues as well as the first and second books in the Revival Series.

Because of the books, especially *Did Paul Approve of the Tongues Spoken in Corinth?*, I was invited to lead a seminar for the state workers in the new state of Tocantins. The huge state of Mato Grosso had been divided into two states: the northern part became Tocantins; the southern part was named Mato Grosso do Sul. Missionary Ben Hope met me at the airport of the capital city; we flew in the mission airplane that he had been using for many years. We landed at a town near the state camp. The pastors and state missionaries met at their new state camp, which was very rustic. Most of the campers slept in hammocks they had brought from home. The hammock hooks were scattered around the rooms, so one would just chose a spot to hang the hammock. In various places in the north area of Brazil the hammock was common, but that wasn't true in Minas and further south. Men and women bathed in the river at separate scheduled times. The toilets were "outhouses". Everything was very rustic, but I enjoyed the experience very much!

Another Brazil National Stewardship Campaign

Missionary Craige Steele was named to lead Brazil in the second National Stewardship Campaign for 1998. Craige asked me to be responsible for promoting the campaign in the States of São Paulo, Rio de Janeiro, Espirito Santo, Minas Gerais, and Brasilia. The first thing was to meet with the executive secretary of each state and go over the suggested plans. The plans were good, but my experience had been that the states would accept only the material they wanted. The follow-up meetings were to energize the conventions; this I tried to do at the pastors' retreats and state conventions. After that I just trusted the states to carry out the campaign.

A Chapel for Prudente de Morais

Pastor Laisete and Genilda worked diligently to get a preaching point started in Prudente de Morais. In the beginning they invited people to worship with them in their home. Few people participated in their home worship. Finally a corner lot with a small house was bought. Laisete took out the partition between the small living room and kitchen/dining room to make room to crowd in about 30 people. One bedroom was used for the children's class. God was so good. The walls were bulging with people, but we had no funds to build.

I had been longing for the day in which I could get a group of Brazilians to build a chapel in one week as the Americans had been doing. One day Wade Akins called to tell me that a U.S. church had raised the money for a chapel, but it couldn't furnish the work crew for the job. Did I have any suggestions? I gladly responded, "I can get a Brazilian crew together." The exact space necessary to build a chapel existed behind the house in Prudente de Morais by turning the front of the chapel to the side street. The money to lay the foundation and floor was sent to me; I turned it over to Laisete; the work began.

Laisete did a good job directing and helping prepare the lot by filling in dirt at the back of the building and pouring the foundation and floor. I acquired volunteers from Baptist Men's organizations to do the building. They were from Governador Valadares, Belo Horizonte, and Divinopolis. The only Americans helping were Ronnie Mackey, Leona, and me. For most of the 10 years the chapel building was going strong, Ronnie and his wife, Rose, lived in Belo Horizonte. He had moved to Brazil to work with Wade Akins. He was responsible for helping buy the materials, getting building materials to the sites, and then supervising one of the crews. Sometimes two or three chapel buildings were built at the same time.

This was the first time Ronnie had been in charge of a Brazilian crew. Leona and I became emotional when we saw that hanging in front of the work site Laisete had a big banner that thanked us for our help and the Americans for providing the funds for the chapel. We finished within the scheduled five days. That included painting the building inside and out, having a sign painted on the front, and building the pews and pulpit. Leona and Genilda prepared the meals. The situation of Brazilian men building this chapel was the beginning of a dream that I hoped would help launch the Baptist Men of Brazil to start building chapels and also leading disaster-relief teams. Workdays began with a devotional and prayer by one of the workers. All in all the Brazilian men were proud to have the opportunity of building a chapel in five days.

Arraial do Cabo

Since the 1970s our family tried to have a week vacation at the beach either at Cabo Frio or Rio das Ostras in the State of Rio de Janeiro. The beaches in that area are clean and beautiful. The sand is as white as that of White Sands, NM. You can stand in water up to your chest and still see your feet. Arraial do Cabo is a town on a peninsula that reaches out into the Atlantic Ocean. A salt company captures ocean water in acre plots of land. The water evaporates and leaves the salt. The salt is collected and purified into table salt. The pastor at First Baptist Church of Arraial do Cabo was from Valadares. In fact as an adolescent he visited our home because he wanted to learn English; sometimes he went with me to youth meetings. Washington had finished seminary, written a book, and now was pastor of the prosperous Arraial do Cabo Baptist Church. Washington also spoke very good English.

Washington invited us to conduct a revival. We had a great response and wonderful fellowship with the church members. One day a member of the church invited us for a ride in one of his fishing boats. We sailed along the Atlantic Ocean edge in which few people got to visit. The fisherman/boat pilot anchored in one inlet so we could get into the water for a swim. The water was very calm and so crystal clear that we could see many large sand dollars lying on the sand in the water. This was a gold mine of sand dollars in perfect condition. We were able to gather several to take home. Going on farther north the fisherman stopped the engine and let the boat drift into a cave in which we could see a school of "Portuguese man-of-war" sea life; it was beautifully arrayed in pink. The water was so clear that we could see layers of this sea life moving slowly around in its habitat. He explained that you could touch the top of the "balloon", but you certainly didn't want to let the tentacles touch you. Brazil contains many of the wonders of God's creation; we were privileged to see things that even most Brazilians don't get to see. Words cannot describe the beauty that we saw. All of these blessings enrich our days on earth.

Another Unexpected Blessing

Only in heaven will we meet all of those whom we had the opportunity to help during our lifetime. One day in 1996 a man enthusiastically approached me at a men's meeting and with elation embraced me as an old friend. This man took me by surprise. He wanted to know whether I remembered him. He had to help me remember him by telling me his story. Fifteen years earlier with his brother-in-law he had visited Santa Cruz Church. He was a firm Roman Catholic and was not interested in the gospel, but he was impressed as to why an American would move to Brazil, live under more difficult circumstances, learn another language, and spend his life trying to help Brazilians. The Holy Spirit touched his life; he made his decision at the end of the service.

To help me remember him for sure, he reminded me that after that service, when I was shaking hands with those leaving, he took my hand and kissed it as he would have done with a Roman Catholic priest. He had done that in gratitude, but I gently reprimanded him for doing that and showed him in the Bible that I was a mere man. Yes, I remembered that incident. He then introduced me to his brother that he had won to the Lord. I was uplifted!

Strange Things Happening While I Write

To understand this topic heading I will give you the story behind the topic of the fifth book in Portuguese in the series on Spirituality, God's Purpose for Humanity. The title of the book is *The Deceit of the Ecumenical and Charismatic Movement*. This will be polemical; therefore, the book required a lot of study of extra material, prayer, and thought. In the next few years I hope to have this book and the other books I wrote in Portuguese written in English.

In chapter 9 of this book I tell about the beginnings of the charismatic movement in Brazil. In 1969 we received a cassette tape from the "World Tape Outreach Organization"; the tape was on faith the size of a grain of mustard seed. I agreed with everything the preacher said except one sentence; from that one sentence I surmised that the message was sent from charismatics. The next tape was about an elderly English man named Smith Wigglesworth, a faith-healer that had spread his type of Pentecostalism all over Europe. He was in South Africa in 1936 at the request of a Pentecostal leader named David du Plessis. Wigglesworth prophesied about du Plessis becoming the main person in a great outpouring of the Holy Spirit that would take du Plessis all over the world and that he would help awaken all of the old, dead churches of all denominations. The next tape was about this prophecy being fulfilled through David du Plessis after World War II. I could never get these tapes out of my mind. I had an idea that this prophesy would have something to do with ecumenicalism. Where would I get the information that I needed?

While I was on furlough in 1988, I found five different books on Smith Wigglesworth. I found the first one in Casper, WY. Our son, Carl, was in the Air Force and was stationed at Fairford, England, about 30 miles from Oxford. I wanted to know whether Wigglesworth was who he and others claimed him to be in his native land of England. Leona and I went into Oxford a few days before we left England to visit at least one of the bookstores that furnished books for university students of the many colleges located there. In one of the large bookstores we were sent to the third floor, which was stocked with only religious books. I asked the manager whether he had anything new on Smith Wigglesworth; he replied: "No! But I think I have a book that will interest you." The book was *Streams of Renewal* by British Roman Catholic priest Peter Hocken, who resided in Washington, D.C. I bought the book. On the first page of the book I found the account and importance of the prophecy by Smith Wigglesworth to David du Plessis in 1936. In the book Wigglesworth is mentioned many times. This book confirmed that my hunch was true, for Hocken clearly indicates that Roman Catholicism relies greatly on the second blessing of the Holy Spirit and speaking in tongues to be the major thing that will eventually unite "misguided Protestant brothers to return to Roman Catholicism".

As I returned to the U.S., I also found a large book on David du Plessis. Now with many other books on Pentecostal and charismatic doctrine and practices, I had the material for writing the book about the 20th-century Pentecostal Revival. Again I am amazed how God worked out His way for me to get what I needed for the fifth book, especially the opportunity to go to England. Carl's being stationed 30 miles from Oxford was something that I never would have dreamed of happening. This gave me a chance several times to be in Oxford; this was a special experience. Writing this book caused us mysterious troubles.

We had evidences that Satan was not happy with my writing on the subject 20th-century Pentecostal and charismatic revival that I had decided was not a biblical revival. Once the computer went strangely wild; the mysterious actions confused and worried us. *What if we were losing everything? Would the computer correct itself?* Well, the computer did return to normal, but the weird behavior was scary. Occasionally I sensed a strange feeling while I wrote, but the study of God's Word overpowered the efforts of the evil one to discourage me.

However, good things happened also! I was impressed with how God was working. Several times when I was writing, I received in the mail printed material about the subject exactly on the day I could use it. The material was not from a friend nor anyone that knew about my writings.

The sixth book was entitled *The Stupidity of Struggling with God*. The key verse is *But the vessel that he was making of clay was spoiled in the hand of the potter; so he remade it into another vessel, as it pleased the potter to make. Then the word of the Lord came to me saying, "Can I not, O house of Israel, deal with you as this potter does?" declares the Lord, "Behold, like the clay in the potter's hand, so are you in My hand, O house of Israel"* (Jer. 18:4-6).

The key verse for the seventh book in the Revival Series is *"Come to Me, all who are weary and heavy laden, and I will give you rest. Take My yoke upon you, and learn from Me, for I am gentle and humble in heart; and you shall find rest for your souls. For My yoke is easy, and My load is light"* (Mt. 11:28-30). The title is *Take My Yoke upon You*.

The title for the eighth book is *Your Treasure and Your Heart*. The key verse: *"No one can serve two masters; for either he will hate the one and love the other, or he will hold to one and despise the other. You cannot serve God and mammon"* (Mt. 6:24). The title of the ninth book is *In the World but Not of the World*. The Scripture text is *"I have given them Thy word; and the world has hated them because they are not of the world, even as I am not of the world. I do not ask Thee to take them out of the world, but to keep them from the evil one. They are not of the world, even as I am not of the word"* (John 17:14-16).

A Beer-Truck Driver

In the later years I noticed that our car problems while we traveled had not been as frequent as in the past. Although I have not mentioned all of them in this book, in our later years we did not have as many problems clustered together. I often wondered whether God was not teaching us to pray and rely on Him to resolve our breakdowns while we traveled. Just to prove that God provides, I'll share about two more incidents.

My practice always was to look at the gas gauge when I got into the car. But my gas gauge had stopped working. I knew about how many miles I could travel on a full tank of gas. We had arrived from a trip in the western part of Minas; I filled the tank. I took the car to our mechanic to check out a problem so we could leave the next morning. We got the car and started on a trip toward Valadares. We

491

were climbing a steep hill about 50 miles out of Belo when the motor gasped a few times and stopped. I could not believe it! I rocked the back of the car but heard no gasoline sloshing back and forth. Someone at the mechanic's shop must have almost drained the tank. I trusted the mechanic, but apparently some worker took advantage of the opportunity. We should have been able to make the trip to Valadares without buying more gas. A station was at the foot of the mountain a few miles behind us. I figured that if I could turn around, I could coast all the way down the mountain to the station. I put the car in neutral and let it coast backward until it gained enough speed so I could back across the descending lane and turn around. I pushed the car and got it started down the mountain, but I misjudged the speed. When I turned the car to turn around, it stopped in the middle of the two lanes of traffic. Descending, a semi-truck appeared. The driver stopped the truck, put on the emergency lights, and offered to help me push the car to get it started down the mountain with Leona at the wheel. I was concerned because without the motor, we also didn't have the power brakes. I didn't want to allow the car to gain too much speed as we traveled going down the mountain.

The truck was a 16-wheeler laden with beer. The driver offered to follow us to make sure we reached the bottom of the mountain to the station. Twice the road was level enough that the car stopped; the trucker had to help me push the car until we were on our way down the hill again. Eventually we reached the service station. Leona called him our "angel"; I didn't give him that much credit, even if he was a nice guy, but God did use him to help us.

A Piece of Wire

One night I left Mantena about 9 p.m. with Helio Swartz Lima, pastor of First Baptist Church of Mantena. He was going with me to Governador Valadares. As we were approaching the village of Central de Minas, suddenly from the motor we heard a sound so loud that I thought the motor had blown up. The clanking and clanging noise wasn't like the sound of pistons, but I knew something terrible had happened. I stopped the car and lifted the hood.

With my flashlight I discovered that the screw holding the metal container of the air filter had worked lose. The air-filter container had bounced off the top of the motor and onto the fan. That was making the terrible noise. I had no proper screw in my tool box, but if I had a wire long enough, I could make it do until we reached Governador Valadares. On the dirt road what would be the chance of finding wire long enough to fasten the air filter container in place? Driving without the air filter wouldn't be wise, because dust would get into the carburetor and gasoline.

We had no choice but to trust God to provide. With the flashlight I began looking on the road for a wire. I didn't have to look long before I found the exact piece of wire I needed. Does God provide for all things? Yes! Praise God, exactly when I needed it on a dark night, He provided a piece of wire for me.

Chapter 24

A Missionary Wife's Stories

Death of a Colleague

The Akins family moved into the house in which we had lived on Ponte Nova, across the street from the Baptist school. Wade was an evangelist and did a lot of street preaching. Sherry described herself as the one that stayed with the baggage and prayed (1 Sam. 25:13). She was always the one to help plan our Christmas parties and sometimes a retreat. She had a good rapport with young people and led Bible studies with various groups of youth.

Sherry was having health problems; after she underwent many doctor exams, a doctor in the States confirmed that Sherry was sick with a fatal disease. She refused to give up and stayed as active as her condition permitted. One very busy Saturday we had an associational WMU meeting at the Baptist school and I also had a children's home board meeting. Missionary Barbara Hawthorne called to tell me she would be unable to go to the board meeting because Sherry had asked her to stay with her since Wade was in a conference in a town about four hours out of Belo. I went to see Sherry before I went to the WMU meeting. She wasn't feeling well, but with the help of Barbara, she was trying to prepare refreshments for a youth Bible-study group to be held later that day. Their son, Tim, was the only one of their three children who still lived in Brazil.

When I arrived home later that afternoon from the board meeting, I found on the table a note from Joe; the note said that Sherry had died and he had gone to their house. The Lord had led Wade to return home sooner than he had planned. He obeyed this inclination; when he arrived, Sherry's body still was in the house. Shocked? Yes, but yet we knew she was sick and had limited time. She believed that their time could be spent better with them in Brazil working for the Lord than in the States with the Akinses waiting for her to die.

494

Those were difficult days for our church and especially for our Minas mission. Joe helped with necessities and the death papers.

Work in Juiz de Fora

From Thursday night through Sunday night at least twice a month Joe had a conference; when possible I traveled with him with my boxes of materials for training teachers to teach little children. We were invited by Pastor Mario and Maria Rosa to their church at the edge of Juiz de Fora. Pastor Rosa said they would have a place for us to stay.

Later Maria told us how nervous she was to host Americans. A couple of years earlier another missionary had invited an American team to work in the churches in Juiz de Fora; this team had been very difficult to please. The people were very picky about what they ate. For us to sleep she prepared a classroom next to the bathrooms of the church, since their house was too small. She had prepared the room with the best she had, including satin sheets. She put a rug on the floor and a small table beside the bed. Before we went to bed the first night, she explained that she had cotton sheets, if we preferred to change. Because of the heat we told her we would like the cotton sheets since they are cooler. That arrangement was fine, because we had freedom to study, sleep, or rest without being disturbed. The roof of the class-room was low and without a ceiling. It was made of metal—high in the front and sloped to the back. The sun beating down on the metal made the room scorching hot in the afternoon.

When I plopped down on the bed, I was shocked. That was the same as plopping down on a wooden bench. To remove fitted sheets off a mattress that has no give is very difficult. I lifted up the board mattress to remove the sheet and discovered the other side had thin foam about an inch thick. I said: "Joe, let's turn the mattress over." Once it was turned, we realized why the hard side was up—the thin cloth covering the board was still intact, but on the foam side a hole was worn in the center of the thin covering; even so, the foam side was softer. We opted for the foam side and made up the bed. The bed still was hard. This precious couple tried to do the best for us.

Before we left Belo, Joe was suffering from a cold, but with medication he thought he would get better. On Friday Joe felt so bad that he thought I was going to have to lead the Bible study. I walked to a pharmacy and bought more medicine; by night he was well enough to preach. I've heard his study enough times that I could probably have done the job, but I wasn't eager to try. I prayed for him to feel better. On Saturday afternoon I had a study for all the children's teachers and mothers that wanted to attend. I showed the materials that Baptists published for teaching and explained how to use the teaching centers. Many teachers still held the idea of only telling a Bible story and singing some songs. One big problem was lack of space. The children had to stay together in a small space without making noise that would bother the other classes. We were amazed at how the children did learn even without all the extra activities. God blessed the efforts of the dedicated teachers.

The Rosa couple lived in a house at the back of the church. Because the house was on the church property, many church members believed they had the freedom to enter their home to borrow whatever was needed. One day Maria Rosa said she saw a woman with a dress that looked like hers. She commented to the woman that she had a dress like that. The woman replied, "Yes, it is yours; I borrowed it."

On Sunday afternoon Maria, Joe, and I sat around their little table and shared. She told about her frustration with people walking in without even knocking. I suggested she lock the door, but she said that wouldn't be accepted. She didn't have even enough silverware to set the table for the four of us. She mentioned that on Friday a WMU team from Belo would be there to direct a conference. I told her I wouldn't return since someone else was going to teach in my place.

On Monday morning Joe and I removed the sheets, folded them, turned the mattress back over, and put the folded sheets at the foot of the bed (which is their custom). We said our goodbyes and left. When we arrived in Belo, I discovered that a member of the WMU team wasn't able to go, so I was to return to Juiz de Fora. Our team of four went by bus and got off about a block from the Rosa's church. We carried our materials to the church; Maria greeted us warmly and showed us our "room". This was the same place Joe and I had just left on Monday—same bed. Maria had added two mats; we were to decide which two would sleep on the bed or on the mats. One of the women sat down on the bed and exclaimed, "Oh, my; this is hard!" I had to laugh. Then I shared our secret and made them promise not to tell, because we didn't want to hurt Rosa's feelings. We turned the mattress over and made our bed. The other two insisted that Clelia and I could sleep on the bed; after all, I was an American. Sometimes being spoiled and treated special was nice; however, I doubt the bed was softer than the mats. (The next year we visited retired missionaries Kent and Sarah Faris in Albuquerque and told them our story. Sarah gave us a set of silverware to take to Maria Rosa.)

Birth of Twins–Charlotte's Difficult Pregnancy

Jim was pastor of a small rural church in Burneyville, OK. The Lowrie/Jenkins group had invited Jim and Charlotte to work with them, so our daughter and her husband were excited about their second trip to Brazil. Before they left the States, Charlotte had been to the doctor; he already was suspicious she was carrying twins. They arrived earlier to help with Vacation Bible School for the MK's during mission meeting. We were happy about their being able to visit us and work with the teams in Juiz de Fora.

Even though everyone was very busy, we enjoyed having the kids with us. They like to tease us about taking the best bed in the hotel in Juiz de Fora. But we knew they enjoyed staying up later than we did, so we gave them the bed in the first room; this bed turned out to be a hard mattress. We learned that before we accept a hotel room, we need always to check to see how hard the mattress was. Many Brazilians believe the hard mattresses are much better for the back, so many hotels offer both kinds—hard and a little softer. Jim thought he was sleeping on a board covered with a sheet.

Soon after they returned to the States, Charlotte saw her doctor. They *were* expecting twins! We were excited about the news. For the first months Charlotte did well through the pregnancy; then she began to have some difficulty and had to have bed rest. She went to the hospital in Ardmore but finally on Nov. 1, the doctor ordered an ambulance to take her to Oklahoma City because the smaller hospital didn't have equipment for preemies. On Nov. 2, 1994 the girls were born at 32 weeks by cesarean section. The first 24 hours Charis was on a respirator. Janis stayed in the hospital three weeks and Charis four. Since they had to stay in the hospital for some weeks, I had time to make arrangements to be with Charlotte when the girls were released.

Charlotte was able to breastfeed the twins along with giving them a supplement bottle. I would get up each time they had to nurse in the night to change their diapers and talk with Charlotte so she could stay awake. Because they were so tiny, they nursed very slowly; each took at least 45 minutes.

By Christmastime Charlotte began to feel better. She was able to get the Christmas decorations out for Jim and me to decorate. Kathy (Carl's wife), Michelle, and Andrew spent two nights with us, so I was able to visit with them. They were on their way to visit her folks. The day before Christmas I drove to get Mother at a care center at Keene, TX. Jonathan drove from Dallas to spend Christmas with us and also to see the girls. Mother was so proud of the girls and of course happy to be with us for Christmas.

I was able to stay a month with Charlotte. I was glad that by the time I had to leave, Charlotte was feeling better. After Christmas Mother and I went back to Texas with Jonathan.

Jonathan took us to the home of my brother Alton and his wife Cindy. Our siblings had planned a Christmas get-together to be held before I was to return to Brazil. Doris and Pat, Wayne and Evelyn, and Connie were there. Kathy, Michelle, and Andrew arrived from Kathy's folks' home. We had a great time. When anyone asked about the twins, Mother became emotional.

Joe and I planned to be back in July to stay in Dallas for six months. I kissed mother goodbye and on December 30 left for Brazil. Mother died 10 days later. I was thankful God allowed me the short time to be with her while she was alive and that she was able to see all my family except Carl and Joe. We were thankful God allowed Mother to be as active as she was with Parkinson's disease. We knew she didn't feel well most of the time, but she loved to go. She told Doris, "If I went only when I felt well, I wouldn't go any place. I might as well go and hurt as stay at home and hurt."

Furlough in Dallas

In 1995 Casa View Baptist Church graciously allowed us to use its mission house. This had been Jonathan's church since he moved to Dallas after he finished college. That was very good for us to be close to Jonathan. However, our first plan was to be close to Mother, but God saw best to take her to a better place in which she would be without pain. My brother Wayne and his wife, Evelyn, also lived near Casa View Baptist Church, so we visited them often.

With various churches in the area we had several speaking engagements. We had time to visit with Carl, Kathy, Michelle, and Andrew in Illinois. We decided to take Carl the Toyota that needed a new home; Charlotte had used it. He could certainly use it to get to work. For several years Carl continued to use the Toyota. He said that even in the coldest weather his car always started when other cars had trouble. After he moved to Colorado Springs, he finally gave the car to a neighbor that was without a car.

Jonathan and Kellie's Wedding

In May 1996 we returned to the States for Jonathan's wedding. He met his bride in his church, Casa View Baptist, and they started dating. Mary Evelyn and Benny Hopper both sang in the choir with Jonathan, but he didn't meet their daughter, Kellie, until 1994. The wedding was beautiful and everything seemed to be perfect. When their new pastor started to present the "new" couple he said: "I now present to you Mr. and Mrs . . . Uh, Mr. and Mrs . . . uh, help me, I'm sorry; I forgot your name." Everyone had a good laugh; the tense moment passed. However, the deacons never let the pastor live that down. He said regardless how well he knew them, he learned to always write in the palm of his hand the name of the couple.

After the wedding we stayed a month in the States and visited family. Kellie has a B.A. degree in psychology and a master's in occupational therapy. These two fields have blended very well. She has worked in the school system but now works in a hospital. Jonathan works in the Southwestern Airlines office.

Carl's Family

Carl had been transferred to Colorado Springs. In September 1996 Jennifer was born in Colorado Springs to Kathy and Carl. For their family September is a very important month: it is the birth month of all three of their kids as well as the month of their wedding anniversary. Kathy got her teacher's degree and has taught school. Carl served in Operation Desert Storm and for two months was deployed in support of Operation Enduring Freedom. He was a noncommissioned officer in charge of the command post. Carl now is in the Air Force Reserves.

We didn't see Jennifer until she was little over a year old and just getting use to the idea of traveling upright on her two feet. While Kathy and I shopped, Joe and Jennifer practiced walking. Jennifer was running more than walking, so Granddad got his exercise that day.

Carl taught Andrew a little about chess, so Andrew and I have played chess together since he was small. His attention span was short, but we enjoyed those times together. Each time we were together, we played chess. Now as a young man he doesn't have as much time to spend at home with us, but we try to get in at least one game of chess. When he is careful, he can finish off the game pretty quickly.

Michelle is a pretty young woman and is active in her church. She has participated on mission trips.

Baptist Children's Home

Soon after we moved to Belo Horizonte, I was elected to the Baptist Children's Home board. The board mostly was made up of businesspeople, but they believed a missionary with interest in children would be an asset. Missionary Debbie Richardson, wife of Ken (our state music man), also was elected to the board. The property had a chapel for the children to attend on campus, since transportation into town was a problem. But the chapel was not in use because of the bad condition of the roof. During the rainy season Brazil can receive torrents of rain—I mean *lots* of rain. The roof leaked so bad that the hardwood floor was damaged and the walls were streaked. Missionary Ken Richardson knew of a person that offered help for special cases, so Ken contacted him. Praise the Lord! The person wanted to pay for a new roof.

The home was on a farm about 45 miles west of Belo. The first child to live in the home was Elon Braga, the man who became president of the board of directors. This man was a dedicated Christian and was highly respected in Belo.

Debbie and I believed the children needed to have some professional training so when they had to leave the home when they reached 15, they would have some way to make legal money. Street children have been a big problem for Brazil (and other countries); many of the children at the home had been street children. We didn't want them to go back to that way of life.

The property had a large shed with a cement floor. Debbie and I decided that the area would be excellent for closing in to become a professional training center. We studied how much the cost would be and presented our idea to the directors. They thought the idea was good enough to proceed. I wrote up the plans and made a request to the IMB for funds for the project. Our project was accepted; we received money and work began. We didn't take into account the fact that the shed didn't have a foundation to support cement block walls. In our presence the men didn't say much about the fact that we made a big mistake in our calculations. They forgave us, took up a collection, and continued the work.

The building finally was finished; we had the ribbon-cutting celebration. A large bronze plaque was placed on the front; this gave Debbie and me credit for the building. The building was divided into five classrooms; the largest room was for a carpenter shop. One of the directors worked in the city office of Betim; the mayor took an interest in our project. Because the professional training would help that area, the county paid for carpentry tools and machines for a bakery. A baker was to visit once a week to teach the boys how to make bread, but that plan never worked. so one of the houseparents made bread for the children. Once a week a group of Baptist Women helped with painting on cloth and made cup towels. For two hours each way this group of people traveled by city bus to get from their home to the children's home; this involved their having to take three different buses. For two years they were faithful to give of their time and effort. We were able to buy a few electric sewing machines; the women also taught sewing, embroidery, and crochet. The cuptowels were sold at the Children's Day Fair each year on October 12.

We acquired some typewriters and later a computer. We also set up a manicure shop—giving manicures was the most popular vocation for young girls. The beauty shops are filled more with women to have manicures than for women to have their hair fixed.

I presented an idea that during vacation time would allow the children to get away from the home. This served well. The plan was to get the churches to "adopt" a child. The idea was for a Christian family of the churches during vacation to take the child home in which to stay for a short period of time. This also would give some personal attention the child needed but also give the child an experience of what a Christian home was like. This also gave the houseparents a relief. We had about 85 children; some of the larger churches wanted more than one child. Throughout the year on birthdays and on other special days the church members would remember their "adopted child". The plan worked really well; the kids loved the added attention they received.

One summer vacation I picked up four kids at the Baptist children's home to take to homes in Belo. I was headed back to Belo on the busy Belo-São Paulo highway when I noticed the car wasn't running properly. The night before, Joe and I had gone to a church about two hours out of Belo. At one point Joe mentioned that the car seemed to have less power, but we arrived home and forgot about it. The São Paulo highway was always heavily traveled by trucks; they have no mercy on a car in their way. Going downhill the car ran well, so I would get in the fast lane and pass the trucks chugging along. But when I started up the next hill, the car motor kept cutting out and the trucks passed me. I had to travel about 30 minutes in this terrible traffic before I got to the street on which I was to take three of the kids. The motor situation continued to get worse. Finally we arrived about three blocks from the home at which I was to leave three of the children; at that point I decided the mission car was not going to make it up the next hill, so I pulled into a mechanic's garage. The kids gathered their things; we walked to Clelia's house. I called Joe to let him know I was in town and about the mission car. He arrived in our car and stopped by the mechanic's shop to talk about the car. The mechanic thought he knew the problem and said the car would be ready the next day. The next day we picked up the car; supposedly it was fixed, but Joe hadn't driven but a few blocks until he realized it wasn't. We decided to take it to the Ford garage to be checked out. I followed him to make sure he would get there. The Ford garage mechanic knew very quickly what the problem was—the catalytic converter had gone out. The strange thing about the catalytic converter was it required unleaded gasoline—Brazil didn't even sell unleaded gasoline. Our car was bought new with the catalytic converter.

The children's home had dorms for sleeping—the best the leadership could offer but far from satisfactory. When you take kids that have lived on the streets and put them in a home situation, you could expect problems. And problems we had! The very small children had their room in the girls' half of the building. The girls had two large rooms—one for younger and one for older girls. The younger boys had a room for about 15, but the larger boys (those that gave more problems) were all in the same long dorm-like room. When I saw them, the rooms were always clean and beds well-made, but I could imagine the noise at night with that many boys together. My dream was to have houses of 10 to 12 kids along with a houseparent.

In one of our mission-station meetings I shared my dream. Wade Akins liked our idea and believed he might be able to get funds to finance the building of six homes. Sure enough, he found a man interested in helping. Gary Taylor, an architect, drew the plans for a four-bedroom house. Everyone was excited as the groundwork was prepared. Two teams from the States spent a week each; they worked along with a team of Brazilians. Of course the older children were involved with carrying the cement blocks and other materials. Wade and Barbara Akins made arrangements for the American team to stay nearby for the week. The situation was rustic but was much better than driving back and forth from Belo. (After Sherry's death, Wade married missionary Barbara Hawthorne).

When the houses were completed, we had a big celebration. The children were excited about moving into their new home. Siblings couldn't be separated, so we had boys and girls mixed in the homes. I was concerned about how that would work. The central kitchen continued to prepare and serve the meals in the main dining hall. The homes had a kitchen in which the "mom" could prepare food for special occasions. I can't say the problems ceased, but with fewer kids together the problems certainly were fewer.

Committee Meeting

At various times I served on committees for the association or state, so at our last convention I was named to serve on the committee to examine the Book of Reports. Each messenger received a messenger's book which contained reports from organizations of the various activities of the state. Our committee's responsibility was to study all the reports and to compare them with the decisions made in the last convention. This was a form of accountability to the convention. The committee could make further suggestions that would be presented for a vote at the proper time. This particular year the Minas state convention was held in a large gymnasium; the only problem was the lack of rooms for committee meetings. One of the men's restrooms was converted into a meeting room for our committee. A few eyebrows were raised when people saw me entering or exiting the "meeting" room; I received a lot of teasing.

Young Married Couples

I knew of several young married couples that had dropped out of church. I prayed that God would help us reach out to them. I talked with the leaders of Santa Cruz Baptist Church to get ideas of what we could do. They helped me collect names and addresses of 26 couples; some were the leaders' own children. I planned a monthly meeting of fellowship, spiritual, and informative time. Our deacon had two married sons; both were away from the church. One son was a children's optometrist, so I invited him to speak on how parents could care for their children's eyes. Each couple received in the mail a monthly, printed invitation; these invitations gave the date and location of the meeting. Children's activities also were provided. Each month the program varied so we could meet their needs but also keep their interest. I believe everyone enjoyed the fellowship; only God knows how effective the meetings were spiritually. We saw some results although not as many as we had hoped. One couple was saved; Joe and I were their witnesses at their civil wedding. Joe and I had Bible studies at the home of another couple. We made some lasting friendships with several of these couples and trust their friendship with God will grow.

After 15 Years of Prayer

For 15 years Santa Cruz Baptist Church had prayed to find a better location. In 1998 a group of nine adults started (eight finished) the study *Experiencing God* by Henry Blackaby. I can't say I taught the book, because we all shared in the study; I merely led out. For six months we met each Monday night for two hours. The study is planned to complete in three months, but because of the group members' work schedules I knew they couldn't do all the required daily study, so I divided a week study into two weeks' study. We met and shared the experiences since the last meeting, discussed the lesson of the week, and finished with prayer. One main prayer request was for a better location for the church. During those six months of study we saw many prayers answered, but the biggest one was a lot for our church. Our only deacon, Elmo, for many years on his way to work walked past a vacant lot on his street; he had inquired about buying it. The owner lived in North Brazil but planned to move back to Belo, so she wasn't interested in selling. The lot was one of very few level ones in the neighborhood. The owner had the old construction removed, so the lot was clean. A concrete fence was around all but the front. One day as Elmo was walking to work, a neighbor told him that he heard the lot was for sale but that it hadn't been listed yet. Elmo called Joe, who immediately made contact with the owner and told him our interest in buying it. The only problem was that the price was $35,000. We knew it would be expensive because recently a wide, six-lane avenue had been constructed near the Santa Cruz neighborhood; that avenue went all the way to the new airport. A big shopping mall was on that avenue across from Santa Cruz neighborhood. But God had opened the door for us to buy the property, so we knew He would provide the money.

As soon as we bought the lot, we celebrated our victory by having the whole church meet on the new property for a thanksgiving service. During the service I found the figure of a saint about four-inches tall; it partially was buried in the ground, but it didn't have a head. I guess the owner had thrown it away, since it was broken. When it had been whole, someone had prayed to it with faith that his or her prayer would be answered. Now that it was broken, the saint had lost its power. The wonderful power of Jesus was working for

505

Baptists to have that property for a genuine church so we could worship Jesus Christ without depending on a saint.

Whitley Family

In 1998 the SBC International Mission Board appointed Jim and Charlotte to go to Romania. Charlotte was expecting their third child in September. I planned my arrival in the States to be there before the baby arrived so I could keep the twins, then almost 4-years old. The latest date that James Sherman Whitley could arrive so Jim and Charlotte could attend the fall orientation at Missionary Learning Center was exactly the day he was born—September 16. God really was testing our faith. The MLC policy was that to attend orientation babies needed to be at least 4-weeks old. Charlotte had a difficult delivery, but James was healthy and strong (7 pounds, 10 ounces)—larger than the sonogram indicated and too large for her. Charlotte is petite—barely five-feet tall. She had a slow recovery.

Joe arrived in time to help Jim pack. Jim had marked the date for the moving truck to pick up the things they planned to take to Romania. Joe and I worked with Jim as Charlotte gave instructions for what to pack. Movers can pack up everything, but when one is packing for overseas shipping, you want to take advantage of every square inch. Many movers aren't concerned about conserving space but just to get things packed up. We left the dishes and glassware for the movers to pack, but we boxed up everything else.

After their container was packed, we all headed for Colorado Springs to visit with Carl and Kathy and family. Charlotte's doctor wasn't too happy about her taking that trip, but Charlotte wanted to see her brother before she went to Romania; this seemed to be the only time.

After new-missionary orientation Jim and Charlotte and kids were off to Romania. They served as missionaries to the Roma (Gypsy) people. In 2005 they received a request to move to Brazil to minister to the Gypsy people. So after Stateside assignment they moved to Campinas, São Paulo, Brazil.

Jonathan and Kellie's Visit

We were so happy that Jonathan was able to bring Kellie to visit in March 1999 before we left Brazil for retirement. We knew this meant a lot to Jonathan for Kellie to see the places in which he grew up and to allow her to get a touch of Brazilian life.

We visited Governador Valadares and showed her the house in which we lived for eight years. She saw the church in which Jonathan was baptized and even met some of his buddies. Since he last was there in 1983, the city had grown. Along the highway we saw "Dallas Motel", except this was a "sleazy" place. This was impressive to Kellie because Dallas is her hometown. In Brazil we do not stay in motels—those are places in which one pays by the hour and the car is parked inside an enclosed area so passersby can't see.

In Belo Horizonte we took Jonathan and Kellie to the EABH–American School. To Jonathan's surprise his nickname "Shish" still was written in chalk on a brick near the ceiling in the library. The Brazilian couple that lived on the campus as well as a few teachers he knew still worked for the school.

Of course we had to show the churches that we had started and with which we had worked. Planalto Baptist Church finally was in its new building. Kellie also had the experience of going to a home service for a birthday of an elderly woman. Kellie didn't think any other people possibly could crowd in—but they did. She had the experience of eating at a real *Churrascaria*– a restaurant that serves meat cooked on spits over charcoals. Throughout the meal the servers bring various cuts of meat and serve all you can eat.

My Calling

To end my part of these memoirs I believe I need to tell about how I arrived at this point. My parents were Christians, so I don't recall a time in which we didn't go to church—church was a part of our lives.

In 1943 Daddy bought a farm on the east edge of Portales; that winter we moved from Deming. We were involved in all areas of First Baptist Church. Since an early age when I was a Sunbeam, I can remember studying about missionaries and having missionaries talk to us. Then as a G.A I was able to go to Inlow Camp in the mountains south of Albuquerque. I have fond memories of these times and enjoyed hearing the experiences of missionaries. I completed the G.A. steps up through Queen with Scepter.

At age 9 I was saved and baptized in First Baptist Church. When I was 12, I began believing God called me to serve in foreign missions. My pastor, L.A. Doyle, strongly encouraged young people to obey God. The church had a Christian Service Band for the group that had felt God's call for Christian service. I went with the group to Grady, NM, and was asked to give my personal testimony. That was scary, but God used that experience plus Training Union to prepare me for talking before a group.

When I was in high school, I was leader of the Sunbeams. One summer in a Vacation Bible School in Clovis, NM, our associational missionary needed help, so my parents allowed me, along with a friend, to help for a week.

Ray Buster was a missionary to Brazil, but her hometown was Clovis. When Ray was on furlough, Mother would take me with her to visit. I didn't dream that someday I would be working in the same place in which Ray had worked—Belo Horizonte. I knew of two other people—Gene Wise and Lonnie Doyle, Jr.—that were missionaries in Brazil. These missionaries probably played a part in our choice, several years later, to go to Brazil.

During my junior year of high school I began to bargain with God. Our youth director, Rena Taylor, was my ideal person. I told God I could stay in the States and work with the youth as Rena was doing. I had a miserable time as I sought to do MY will and not God's. Finally I re-surrendered to do God's will. Soon after this Joe appeared on the scene.

Joe had felt the call to preach and to missions. God had our lives planned to meet at just the right time. As you have already read, the rest is history. I never doubted my call, though at times the work was discouraging. After a difficult time God always seemed to send a blessing to brighten our way.

One furlough I was invited to speak to the Mission Friends at University Baptist Church in Portales. I don't know what the teacher had told the children, but when I entered the meeting room, one of the little ones turned to her mother and said: "Mother, she is just a woman." Yes, I am just a woman that God called to do a job. I'm nothing special; nothing Joe and I did is so special; we only were doing what God asked of us. All the praise goes to Him. Looking back I stand amazed how God has worked to change lives, including mine. For my experience in going from being very timid farm girl to the wonderful life of a missionary wife, I give God thanks. I shudder to think what would be my life today had I insisted on going MY way. In no way can I name all the many people that played a part in molding my life, but special thanks go to my parents that gave me a Christian home.

Chapter 25

Finishing the Race
1997-1999

*Do you not know that those who run in a race all run, but only one
receives the prize? Run in such a way that you may win . . ..
Therefore I run in such a way, as not without aim; I box in such a
way, as not beating the air; but I buffet my body and make it my
slave, lest possibly, after I have preached to others, I myself should
be disqualified* (1 Cor. 9:24, 26-27).

Our call and therefore our goal was to be career missionaries. We
enjoyed our work, although we had many trials, disappointments,
challenges, and a constant battle against Satan. For Jesus' sake we had
to stay on course and win the race! God our Father, Savior, and Holy
Spirit were for us all the way!

Visit to the Equatorial Baptist Seminary
For the spring of 1997 I was invited to be the guest speaker at the
Equatorial Baptist Seminary. I was thankful to God for this wonderful
opportunity. I sent about 700 books early so they would be at the seminary by the time I arrived. Throughout the week I had an hour in the
morning and an hour at night to speak. I hung around at break time to
chat with students that wanted to discuss certain subjects. I also had
the opportunity to preach in three churches. I sold the books at cost so
those with little money could buy at least one.

A Frightening Experience
One of the major fears for missionaries is that of an automobile

accident or in some way hitting a pedestrian. We know of some incidents in which a pedestrian ran across a highway or street into a missionary car. Even though the accident clearly was the pedestrian's fault, missionaries go through a very difficult time, because most Brazilians scrutinize the incident as being the driver's fault. The majority is inclined to cast the blame on the driver.

One day in 1997 I left the house before 7 a.m. to take some mail to Wade Akins' home. Someone visiting the Akinses was returning to the United States and had agreed to take our mail to the States (saving about 50 cents per letter). I was driving down the busy street in front of the huge complex of hospitals. I was slowing down for an intersection. I noticed a man on the sidewalk looking straight at me as I was stopping. Suddenly the man purposely threw his legs under the car. I had no way to stop before the left front wheel passed over his feet and ankles. I stopped immediately and jumped out of the car! I said: "*Senhor*, why did you throw yourself under my car?" The man was moaning and writhing in pain. Whether he was really hurt, I don't know, but I was very frustrated because I knew that all that day I would be tied up in paperwork at a police station. Everyone knows the driver is not to leave a scene of an accident. However, another pedestrian saw the accident and stepped up to my aid. He said the man probably did this thing purposely because he was sick and couldn't get into a hospital without doing something such as he did. This man told me to leave the man with him and that he would get the man into one of the hospitals; he said to go on and not worry!

I was nervous with anxiety about the busy day I had planned, so I accepted his offer. We helped the unapologetic man onto the sidewalk; I drove away. Before I arrived at the Akins' residence, I began thinking the worst. *What if the plan was a set-up? What if that Good Samaritan man took my license number and planned to help the victim sue me later? The police would be involved. I would be charged for hit-and-run; the courts would not be kind to me. If I hadn't been in such a hurry with a busy schedule ahead, I would have been a good witness and would have taken the man to the emergency room and witnessing to him.* I told Leona about the incident. We had to leave the case in God's hands; the "Good Samaritan" turned out to be real. After two or three months I could relax!

Eyes on Pedro Leopoldo

Araci Maria de Jesus had been given a lot in Pedro Leopoldo, a small town on the way to Prudente de Morais, in which Laisete and Genilda were working. Those that signed up and voted for a specific political candidate were promised a lot in a new area to be developed. The joke became, "oh yeah, only on the moon." The man did win and did give half a lot to those that had applied. The new neighborhood was called *Lua* (Moon), because the politician fulfilled his promise. Pedro Leopoldo was the birthplace of Chico Xavier, the most famous spiritist leader in Brazil. Although Chico Xavier had moved to Uberaba, Minas Gerais, Pedro Leopoldo was greatly influenced by him and was a difficult place to witness; most of the people were both Roman Catholic and spiritist. In 1993 little by little Araci started building her dream house. As she saved up money, she would buy materials; then when she had enough, she would have a little more built. Many Brazilians took years building their house. Her heart was set on starting a mission in her house when she finally moved to Pedro Leopoldo. When the half lot next to her was put up for sale, I encouraged her to buy it, because that would give her a full lot, even though the purchase would slow down the construction of her house. She did buy it. We kept praying for Pedro Leopoldo, this strategic place, with great anticipation for the day when Araci "finally" would move into her house.

"Finally" in 1997 the house was finished enough that she, her mother, and her niece could move in. The house wasn't finished, the walls weren't plastered, and the floor was rough concrete. The house had a living room, three bedrooms, a kitchen and dining room, and two bathrooms. She had built a large room in the back for the beginning of a mission. By the time we left in October of 1999, her house almost was finished; it was the nicest house in the neighborhood. The neighbors thought she was rich.

Araci became known in the whole neighborhood. She didn't have a car, so she walked over the area and invited people to worship. She rounded up the children that wanted to learn about Jesus. This was the beginning of the work in Pedro Leopoldo. Once or twice a month Leona and I visited the work. Sometimes other members of Santa Cruz Church visited also. Araci taught literacy, because many of the adults couldn't read or write. She was an amazingly good counselor for young people and adults alike. In July 1998 a group of six seminary students from Southeastern Baptist Seminary spent a week with us doing house-to-house witnessing. They worked in two neighborhoods near Araci.

The Brazilian Home Mission Board had a missionary couple living and working in the center of Pedro Leopoldo, but that work wasn't going well. In these two new neighborhoods among the poorer people the possibilities were far more promising. Several people made decisions. Our experience in all of our years in Brazil was that the Lord's work grows faster in new neighborhoods. The people had pulled up roots and lived among people they hadn't known, so they can change their religious beliefs more easily.

By the time we left Brazil in October 1999, the mission was running more than 30 people regularly. In 2001 (we were retired and in the U.S.) the group had grown so much that the space at Araci's house no longer could accommodate the people. Araci was trying to buy property in the area for a church. Occasionally we would call her to see how things were in Brazil. Then one day we received a telephone call from Brazil saying that Araci was in ICU with acute leukemia. A few days later she died. We were told that a very large crowd was at her funeral; the crowd included people from various churches in Belo Horizonte and many from Pedro Leopoldo. Everyone loved Araci. We don't understand God's timing, but Araci was a person that was 100 percent for Jesus. Her name was "Araci of Jesus"; she certainly was of Jesus. Her work in Pedro Leopoldo has continued through Santa Cruz Baptist Church. We miss her; Leona does especially. She cleaned house for us once a week and did Leona's fingernails for 10 years. The best part was that we were able to help her become what Jesus had in mind for her.

1998

I realized that during our last year in Brazil I would have to put Santa Cruz Church in first place. As a church Santa Cruz had had two pastors besides me, but neither stayed more than two years. In our many years of ministry God answered prayer sometimes "immediately", other times "later", sometimes "finally", and sometimes "no". For

15 years we prayed to find property to which we could relocate because the building flooded every year and sometimes two or three times. We have mentioned the difficulty with the spiritist family above us and the problematic family by the side of the church. We finally were able to visit and talk with the family by the side of us; the last two years we were in that location, some of this family's grandchildren attended our VBS. We located two or three lots for sale in the area but never were able to make a deal. Now, with only two years before we were to retire, we were praying fervently. Santa Cruz was an old neighborhood, so very few vacant lots existed. At the end of chapter 24 Leona tells about the study of *Experiencing God* and how God "finally" answered our prayers for finding and buying a strategic lot for Santa Cruz Church.

We hadn't begun construction, because the man that bought our property hadn't paid us. I decided that in my last year of ministry in Brazil, God would have me put Santa Cruz first. I would work to strengthen the church and direct the construction on our new property. We had already cleaned the lot, put a nice, tall, metal fence in front, and built a small house with two bathrooms on one side near the front of the property. This was built to store materials and tools and later would be used for a kitchen until an educational building could be built.

I found a Baptist architect to draw up a plan, which was a dream of a building but impractical for us at the time. His plan was a three-story building, but just the foundation for that building would take all the money we would get from the sale of our property. So another architect drew up a plan that would allow us to build an auditorium at the back of the lot; the auditorium would hold about 200 people. The educational building later would be built in front and would reach the street. I know this sounds impractical, but to take advantage of every inch we had to build the auditorium on the property lines on each side, which meant we could have no windows, but we would have three feet more on both sides of building space. If we had built on the property lines at the front, we would have had to carry building materials through the building to build at the back later. We needed another miracle of God—for us to finish the building enough for us to move in before we left. At the end of October we would be leaving for retirement. We needed a pastor for this Santa Cruz Baptist Church.

1999—Finishing the Last Book and Finding a New Publisher

I had skipped the fourth book in the Revival Series, because that book would take much research. That book covered the period of the Reformation through the 19th century. *Destroying Faith in the Bible,* the fourth book, was the only book I wrote that wasn't published by the Evangelical Press in Belo Horizonte. In 1998 I had been looking for a publisher or editorial company that would continue printing the books and distribute them. One day I received a phone call from a Baptist man that worked for a large Evangelical publication company in São Paulo. He wanted to start his own Christian publishing company, Editora Hosana, and wanted to publish my books. I believed this was an answer to prayer, so we made a contract. In 1999 he began with the publication of *Destroying Faith in the Bible* and then volumes one, two, three, and five. For four years the economy in Brazil was pretty good; other Evangelical groups started publishing Christian books and literature. Suddenly in 2005 after publishing five of the Revival Series, the publishing business had serious financial troubles; Editora Hosana went broke. Today the books are not being published in Portuguese, but our prayer is that God will open a door for publishing this series again.

In a room in the Minas Baptist state office building I had a stock of about 4,000 books. Since I was leaving, the executive secretary asked me to remove the books because he had another purpose for the storage room. I believed the best way to dispense the books was to give half of them to the Brazilian foreign missionaries and the other half to the Brazilian home missionaries. Both of these mission entities had headquarters in Rio de Janeiro, so the books were taken to Rio. I have the pleasure of knowing that 35,000 books are in the hands of Portuguese-speaking people.

God Continued to Answer Prayer

Pastor Ader Alves de Assis was a highly educated and prominent pastor before he was selected as director of the Baptist school in Belo for several years. Pastor Ader retired in November 1998. One day Pastor Bittencourt suggested that I ask Pastor Ader whether he would consider being pastor of Santa Cruz Baptist Church. I talked with the church about the possibility; it voted to invite him. I thought to myself: *Santa Cruz Baptist Church is small; he has been pastor of large churches. Why would he be a possible pastor?* I asked him; a few days later he accepted. God works in unimaginable ways! Ader had bought an apartment in a large apartment complex near the shopping center in the Santa Cruz neighborhood and was interested in Santa Cruz Baptist Church. Even better, he could start in the month of May. This was a wonderful answer to prayer and a relief, because he would be involved with me in helping during the construction phase. I never would have imagined that Pastor Ader could be interested in such a small church that couldn't pay him even one-tenth of what he had been receiving. He was retired, but retirement didn't pay much. He had plans, however, to start a counseling service on the side. His willingness to assume the pastorate of the church in May thrilled my heart. His son could play the keyboard, so that was an added blessing. The next big concern was having something built so the church could move before we left. Surely this also would happen.

Brazilian Baptist Convention

In January 1999 we traveled by bus with our Baptist group from Minas Gerais to the national convention in Serra Negra, São Paulo. The Brazilians seemed to appreciate Leona and me going in the bus with them. We had a good time singing, visiting, and joking. This was the second time the Minas group and we had traveled together to a convention.

The day after we arrived for the convention I had a bad rash under one arm and down my side. Leona looked at my problem and suggested I see Dr. Manuel Romano; he had been on our bus. Leona called him in the hotel and asked him to take a look. He confirmed what Leona had thought: shingles. One of our missionary colleagues, a doctor, also was at the convention; Leona called him. He also confirmed I had shingles. I was uncomfortable but didn't miss any of the convention.

An appreciation service for all the Southern Baptist missionaries retiring was held at the Brazilian Baptist Convention. We were honored with nice plaques that bore the Brazilian and American flags and that were engraved with the number of years we had spent in Brazil . We received the genuine thanks of the Brazilian Baptist Convention. The National WMU recognized Leona along with other missionary women that were retiring.

Visiting Churches in Which We Had Worked

Later in May I was relieved from much of my responsibilities at Santa Cruz Church. The last six months of the year we began visiting most of the churches to which we had ministered or had started as missions. These visits were a blessing but also very emotional for them and for us. We suddenly were aware that our lives had whizzed by very fast and that signs in our bodies convinced us we were aging. For most of the visits we just popped in without the people expecting us. We did not want the churches to feel obligated to do something special for us.   .

In July Leona was honored by the state Women's Missionary Union and I was honored by the Baptist State Men's organization. We were given special gifts. Later the Central Baptist of the Sweet River Valley Association had a special recognition for us. The Central Association in Belo Horizonte presented a special program for us and presented the "story of our lives"; this included a video from our daughter, Charlotte, and her family in Romania. We were overwhelmed that 18 organizations, churches, and entities held a special recognition service for us. The state convention also gave us a beautiful engraved plaque and clock. After so many "going-away" celebrations and so many gifts, we could not change our minds; we had to leave Brazil!

Our last Sunday was very special, because the new worship area of Santa Cruz Church was dedicated. The building was packed; to my surprise Joao Leite, the former professional soccer player and now a member of the state senate, was the main speaker. When I wrote about Joao Leite earlier, I didn't mention that his parents lived in the Planalto neighborhood. Joao had asked us to visit them and hoped they would accept Jesus. Leona and I visited his parents several times. His dad was more interested in salvation than his mother was, but neither of them trusted Jesus. Joao Leite forever was grateful that we had tried. He preached a wonderful evangelistic message. Pastor Ader had some very warm and kind words to say about us and our ministry. This is not the end of The Marvel of It All. God's grace, mercy, and spiritual experiences continue to amaze us; we know this will continue as long as we live. TO GOD BE THE GLORY UNTIL THE DAY HE TAKES US TO BE WITH HIM!

Recent Mission Endeavors

Since we retired, we have been to Brazil several times—twice with the Lowrie-Jenkins Summer Evangelism teams. Leona and I worked in the state of Maranhao with the New Mexico partnership teams. In 2007 by special invitation of the state evangelism leader, Marcelo de Oliveira, I went to Maranhao twice. I helped Marcelo in four of his interior seminary clinics while Leona taught a class on teacher training for preschool. To my surprise I was invited to be the major speaker at the Maranhao state pastors' meeting and also brought the last message of the Maranhao state convention. In 2008 we worked with an Artesia, NM, team in a revival at a church in Bacabal; during the day we did home visitation and at night had children's worship. I led a breakout session at the state convention. The Maranhao Baptist Convention gave special recognition to the group from New Mexico for the closing of the Maranhao/New Mexico Partnership. I praise God for these opportunities in my retirement.

Leona and I also had the wonderful experience of going to Romania twice to visit our daughter, son-in-law, and kids, especially the grandkids—Janis, Charis, and James. I had a few opportunities to preach. Charlotte planned a trip for us all to go into Greece to follow the path of Paul; we started with Philippi. We walked the streets of Athens, Corinth, and other places. What a blessing! Earlier in the year Jim and a Romanian group had gone into Greece to help a Greek pastor begin work with some Roma. We visited that work; I was able to preach in that church.

Jim and Charlotte worked among the Roma people (Gypsy) in Romania until they transferred to Brazil. They are the only IMB missionaries working with Gypsies in South America. In 2008 we visited them in Campinas, São Paulo.

We also went to Bangkok, Thailand, on a two-week mission trip with New Mexico Baptists. This was a very rewarding mission experience. But our major project in our retirement is writing some of the books in English that the Lord led me to write in Portuguese.

The Mescalero Apache reservation begins just outside the city limits of Ruidoso. Over the years after we moved to Ruidoso I was invited occasionally to preach at the Mescalero Apache Baptist Mission; Leona played the piano for the worship services. Later, First Baptist Church in Ruidoso was requested to be the mother church of the mission; Leona and I were asked to be representatives, since Leona was serving on the missions committee. We served for four years, with Leona as pianist and a Sunday-school teacher. For three years I was music director and then for a year was pastor and music director. We marvel about this opportunity to serve another group of God's wonderful people, the Mescalero Apache!

Final Word

We have shared our hearts and minds with you and thank you for going on this journey with us. All Christians have a story of God's work in their lives. Leona and I enjoy hearing how God is working in other people's lives, because human-life stories represent the greatest testimonies on earth. The Bible is made up of "life stories"—some good and some bad.

We give thanks that we had as our examples and leaders such great mission-minded men as Dr. Baker James Cauthen and Dr. Frank Means. We are thankful that these two men believe that the Holy Spirit leads missionaries on the field and that missionaries are to have the freedom to follow the Holy Spirit's guidance.

(In chapter 21 I reported that after a time of spiritual dryness, I learned to follow this outline as I began my day in prayer to God. Doing this has made a major impact on my spiritual life.)

Daily Preparation
for Walking with God

I. Praising Jesus

Beloved, Amazing, Wonderful, Marvelous, Precious, Jesus Christ, my Savior, Lord, Master, Friend closer than a brother, and One and Only Great High Priest, I worship You, Jesus, adore You, honor You, thank You, and praise You because You are everything to me. You are bread and water for my spiritual life. You are resurrection and life. The day I accepted You as my Lord and Savior when I was 8 years of age, I began to really live. On that day I felt as though I was taken into God's presence. You are the narrow door that I entered 65 years ago to begin my journey to heaven on the straight and narrow road. You are the Light of the World and the Vine from which I get my daily strength. You are the Truth and the Lamb of God that takes away my sins. You are the Living Word that in every way shows us how God is. You were involved in the creation of the universe also.

As the ancient Hebrews and Israelites said, you are the Lily of the Valley, the Bright and Morning Star, the Rose of Sharon, the Prince of Peace, Counselor, Almighty God, the King of Kings, Lord of Lords, the Good Shepherd, and the Solid Rock on which I stand. These are some of the expressions that tell me Who You really are.

I thank You, Jesus, because You paid the price for my sins and for the sins of every person in the world in the past and future. I thank You because Your blood is sufficient to save me and to take me back into fellowship with Triune God. I ask You, as the Head of Your churches and my Great High Priest, to purify me now so that I can enter into the presence of Holy Father. If I in any way have grieved the Holy Spirit, forgive me. Since You are my Savior and High Priest, I admit that I have not and will not be able to reach perfection. My imperfection makes me very ashamed. Forgive me now and take me to my place at the foot of Holy Father's throne of grace.

II. Praising Holy Father

Beloved Heavenly Father, I thank You for this special place before You. Although thousands of people are praying at the same time, I feel You are giving me personal attention. Thank You! I kneel to worship and adore You as well as when I worship and pray before Jesus. I am grateful that You, Father, as well as Jesus and the Holy Spirit, are pure in Your virtues. I understand that these four principal virtues—Holiness, Love Truth, and Justice—make up Your spiritual personality. I understand that these are reciprocal, for you want us to be Holy as You are Holy, Love You with all of our hearts, spirits, and bodies, practice truth as you are The Truth, and be just as You are Just. I understand that all other virtues are connected to these four. I am so thankful, Father, that Triune God is perfect in the holy attributes. The attributes, I know, are not reciprocal, for only You as eternal Father, Jesus as Savior-Son, and the Holy Spirit are One in Omniscience, Omnipotence, and Omnipresence. These make You, God, totally different from Your human creatures.

I offer myself as a living sacrifice. I want to be a person after Your own heart, as David was during most of his life. I want to be someone like Joseph of Egypt, who did not want to do anything that would bring shame on Your Holy Name. Therefore I pray to You in praise, Heavenly Father, for the plan You have for my life today. Help me to be aware of You as Heavenly Father, the commission Jesus has given me, and the presence and power of Your Holy Spirit within me all day. In Your presence I put on the spiritual armor about which Paul spoke. I understand that salvation is eternal; therefore, I sleep with the helmet of salvation on my head. I now take the breastplate of righteousness and fasten it over my chest. I put the belt of truth around my waist. Now I put on my battle boots so everywhere I go, I will be prepared to spread the gospel of peace. Now I take the shield of faith to keep Satan at a distance. Increase my faith, dear Father. Now with my right hand I take the sword of the Spirit. May the words of my mouth and the meditation of my heart be only in praise to You all day long. Finally, I intend with the help of You, Father, Savior, and Holy Spirit, to walk all day long in the spirit of prayer.

III. After I praise Jesus and Holy Father,

I am ready to make my requests to my Heavenly Father. Most of these are made throughout the day as someone or some situation enters my mind. As you can see, I take about 30 minutes to prepare myself to have a really good day. Sometimes I begin this preparation at night if I wake up and cannot immediately go back to sleep. My goal is to walk in the Spirit; I confess this often does get sidetracked. Traveling usually interferes with preparing for my days in the best way. I find having more time now than I did when the children were at home to be easier. Work hours for most people, because of secular professions, are more difficult than for a preacher, although you would not believe how many things happen to deter a preacher from preparing well for each day. The key is to return our thoughts to God at any moment of the day that our minds do not have to be absorbed in doing something that is not spiritual. If you can become so disciplined as to think on spiritual matters every time you have even a small break in your daily routine, you can learn to walk in the Spirit.

Joe E. Tarry

Photo Album

Photo Album

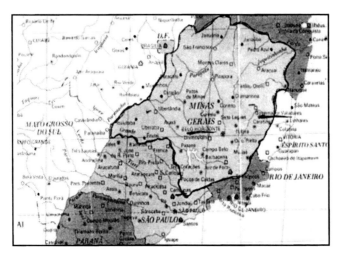

Map of Minas Gerais and bordering states

Leona with Carl, Jonathan, and Charlotte as the
Tarry family boards the ship for Brazil

Leona buys vegetables at a street market in Governador Valadares.

Joe buys milk from a horse-drawn wagon in Governador Valadares.

Carl on wooden bridge

527

The Tarry family in 1975:
from left, Jonathan, Carl, Charlotte, Leona, and Joe

Joe baptizes Carl in the Rio Doce River.

First building of Fifth Baptist Church
in Governador Valadares, 1966

Fifth Baptist Church
in Governador Valadares today

Our blue Veraneio on barge. Rural Willys in front is like our first car.

First building of Island Baptist Church in Governador Valadares in 1972

Island Baptist Church in Governador Valadares in 2005

Gonzaga Baptist Mission
with evangelism team

Present Gonzaga
Baptist Church

Altinopolis
mission in
Governador
Valadares—
open-air service.
Leona plays the
accordion; her
parents and aunt
are present.

Altinopolis mission in Governador Valadares, first building

Altinopolis
Baptist Church
present building

Palmeiras Baptist
Mission in
Governador
Valadares, 2004

Organization of Baptist church in Virginiopolis with help of military band

Esperanca Baptist Church in Governador Valadares

Joe playing trumpet at church

Joe with puppet Joaozinho

Planalto Baptist Church in Belo Horizonte in 2005

Joe baptizing in swimming pool at Araujo home in Planalto

First location of São Bernardo mission in Belo Horizonte along river

Construction of São Bernardo mission; notice curved windows.

535

Prudente de Morais Baptist Church, built by Brazilian team

Men mixing cement in street with hoes for construction

Santa Cruz Baptist Church in Belo Horizonte in old location; notice embankment.

Santa Cruz Baptist Church in Belo Horizonte in new location

Pedro Leopoldo Mission

Order more copies of

The Marvel
of It All

Call toll free: 1-800-747-0738
Visit: www.hannibalbooks.com
Email: hannibalbooks@earthlink.net
FAX: 1-888-252-3022
Mail copy of form below to:
Hannibal Books
P.O. Box 461592
Garland, TX 75046

Number of copies desired _____

Multiply number of copies by $29.95 _____

Please add $4 for postage and handling for first book and add 50-cents for each additional book in the order.

Shipping and handling $_____

Texas residents add 8.25% ($1.23) sales tax $_____

Total order $_____

Mark method of payment:

check enclosed _____

Credit card# _____

exp. date_____ (Visa, MasterCard, Discover, American Express accepted)

Name _____

Address _____

City, State, Zip _____

Phone _____ FAX _____

Email _____

Other Titles from Hannibal Books

Jesus Restores True Spirituality by Joe E. Tarry. Walking the reader through key New Testament events from the Messiah's birth through Revelation, the author shows how the enemy uses strategies to try to darken Christ's brilliance as the Light of the World. The book challenges us to exalt Christ over Satan and to make Jesus' lifestyle our goal.
_____**Copies at $19.95=**_____

Created to Be Spiritual by Joe E. Tarry. Why do we constantly struggle against Satan's cruel attacks? This previous volume to *Jesus Restores True Spirituality* walks readers through critical moments in the Old Testament.
_____**Copies at $19.95=**_____

Did Paul Approve of the Tongues Spoken in Corinth? by Joe Tarry. How does the Apostle Paul resolve the "tongues" debate? The author steps up to the daunting challenge of clarifying what Paul attempts to convey to the Corinthian church, which was seriously impacted by the tongues practice.
_____**Copies at $14.95=**_____

Be a 24/7 Christian by Wade Akins. Want to make Jesus truly the Lord your life but don't know how? This renowned missionary evangelist/strategist tells how to live the adventure of being totally sold out to the Lord every moment of every day, every day of every year.
_____**Copies at $12.95=**_____

Add $4 shipping for first book, plus $1 for each additional book.

Shipping & Handling _____

Texas residents add 8.25% sales tax _____

TOTAL ENCLOSED_____

check _____ or credit card # _____ exp. date_____

(Visa, MasterCard, Discover, American Express accepted)

Name _____

Address _____ Phone _____

City _____ State _____ Zip _____

See page 539 for address, phone number, email address, and website.

LaVergne, TN USA
03 September 2010
195837LV00001B/9/P